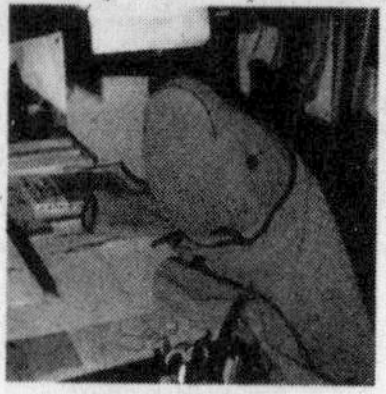

樋口大輔

Finally! We're on volume 9! When this manga first got serialized, my goal was to make it past ten installments. But before I knew it, almost two years have passed already. It fills me with deep emotion. This is thanks to you. I truly appreciate your support. I've been thinking recently that "continuation is power." Whether it's a manga series or whatever else it might be, I think continuing to do one thing is really hard and requires a lot of energy. But I also think one can gain a lot by continuing to do one thing. In my case, I gained confidence. Although my confidence may be broken easily, it is my asset nonetheless.

- Daisuke Higuchi

...began in 1992 when the ... in the 43rd Osamu ... guchi debuted as ... titled ***Itaru***. In 1998, ... lizing ***Whistle!*** ... came an instant hit with readers and eventually inspired an anime series, debuting on Japanese TV in May of 2002.

WHISTLE!
VOL. 9: NOBODY IS PERFECT

The SHONEN JUMP Graphic Novel Edition

STORY AND ART BY
DAISUKE HIGUCHI

English Adaptation/Drew Williams
Translation/Naomi Kokubo
Touch-up Art & Lettering/Jim Keefe
Cover, Graphics & Layout/Sean Lee
Editor/Andy Nakatani

Managing Editor/Elizabeth Kawasaki
Director of Production/Noboru Watanabe
Vice President of Publishing/Alvin Lu
Vice President & Editor in Chief/ Yumi Hoashi
Sr. Director of Acquisitions/Rika Inouye
Vice President of Sales & Marketing/Liza Coppola
Publisher/Hyoe Narita

Printed in the U.S.A.

Published by VIZ Media, LLC
P.O. Box 77010
San Francisco, CA 94107

SHONEN JUMP Graphic Novel Edition
10 9 8 7 6 5 4 3 2 1
First printing, December 2005

PARENTAL ADVISORY
WHISTLE! is rated A and is
suitable for readers of all ages.

THE WORLD'S
MOST POPULAR MANGA

SHONEN JUMP
GRAPHIC NOVEL

www.viz.com

www.shonenjump.com

WHISTLE!™

Vol. 9

NOBODY IS PERFECT

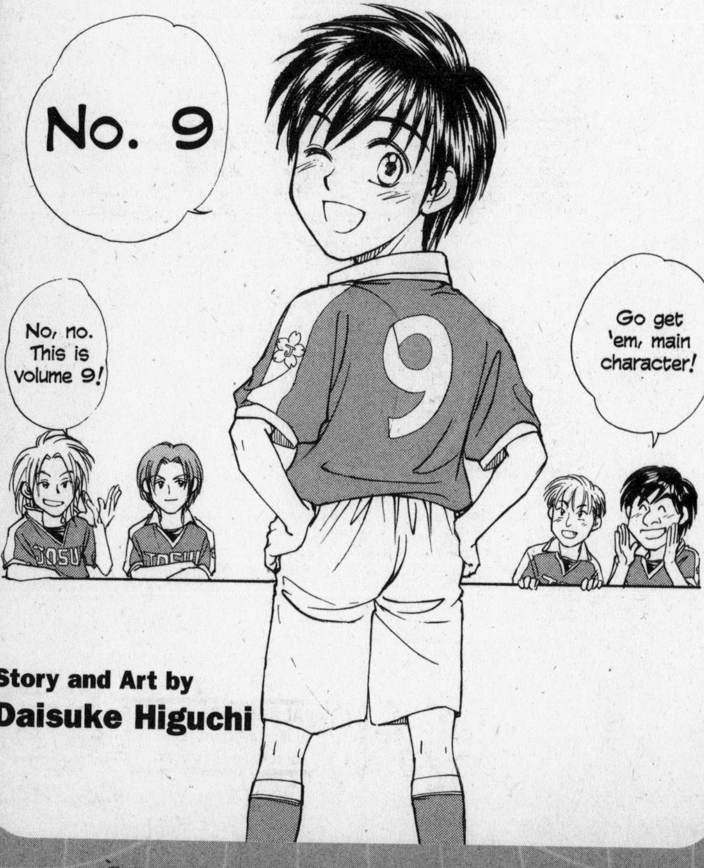
No. 9
Go get 'em, main character!
No, no. This is volume 9!

Story and Art by
Daisuke Higuchi

CHARACTERS

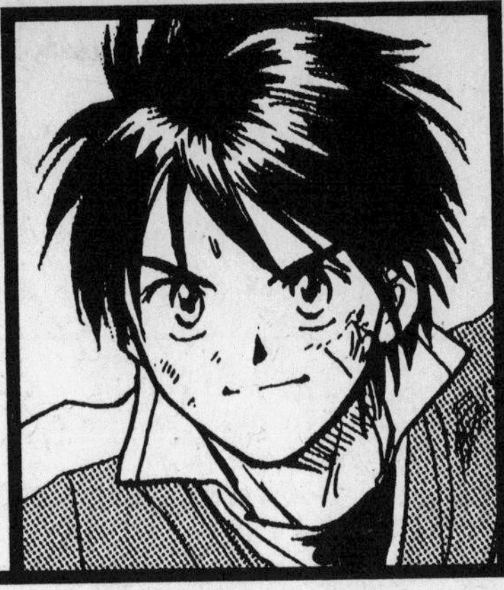

SHŌ
KAZAMATSURI

- JOSUI JUNIOR HIGH SOCCER TEAM FORWARD

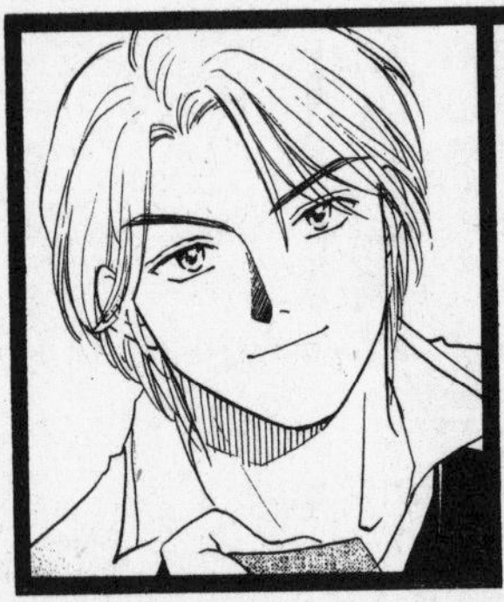

KŌ
KAZAMATSURI

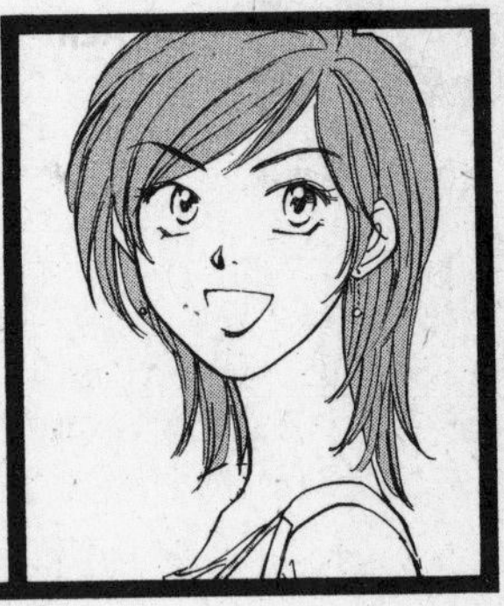

YŪKO
KATORI

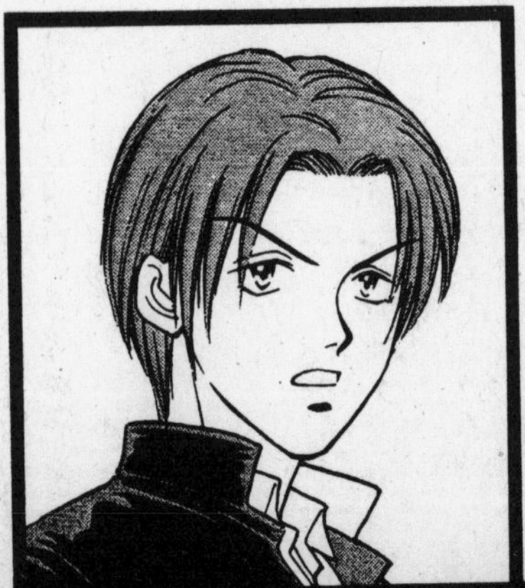

TATSUYA
MIZUNO

- JOSUI JUNIOR HIGH SOCCER TEAM MIDFIELDER

SOUJŪ MATSUSHITA

FORMER JAPAN LEAGUE PLAYER

JOSUI JUNIOR HIGH COACH

SHIGEKI SATŌ

JOSUI JUNIOR HIGH SOCCER TEAM

FORWARD

SOUICHIRO KIRIHARA

MUSASHINOMORI PRIVATE SCHOOL SOCCER TEAM

COACH

To REALIZE HIS DREAM, SHO KAZAMATSURI, A BENCH-WARMER AT SOCCER POWERHOUSE MUSASHINOMORI, TRANSFERRED TO JOSUI JUNIOR HIGH SO HE COULD PLAY THE GAME HE LOVES.

SOON AFTER SHŌ'S ARRIVAL, SOUJŪ MATSUSHITA, A FORMER JAPAN LEAGUE PLAYER, BECAME JOSUI'S COACH, AND THE TEAM HEADED INTO THE SUMMER CHAMPIONSHIP.

THINGS WERE GOING WELL UNTIL A RUMOR SURFACED THAT TATSUYA MIGHT TRANSFER TO MUSASHINOMORI. IT LED TO AN AWKWARD SITUATION BETWEEN TATSUYA AND SHŌ, AND BEFORE THE ISSUE WAS RESOLVED, COACH MATSUSHITA CALLED FOR THEM TO SWITCH POSITIONS ON THE FIELD. THE THIRD GAME OF THE TOURNAMENT STARTED IN RAIN, AND THE OPPOSING TEAM SCORED FIRST. NOW, TEAM JOSUI IS MIRED IN A RAIN-DRENCHED FIELD, AND STRUGGLING FOR A GOAL!

S T O R Y

WHISTLE!

**Vol. 9
NOBODY IS
PERFECT**

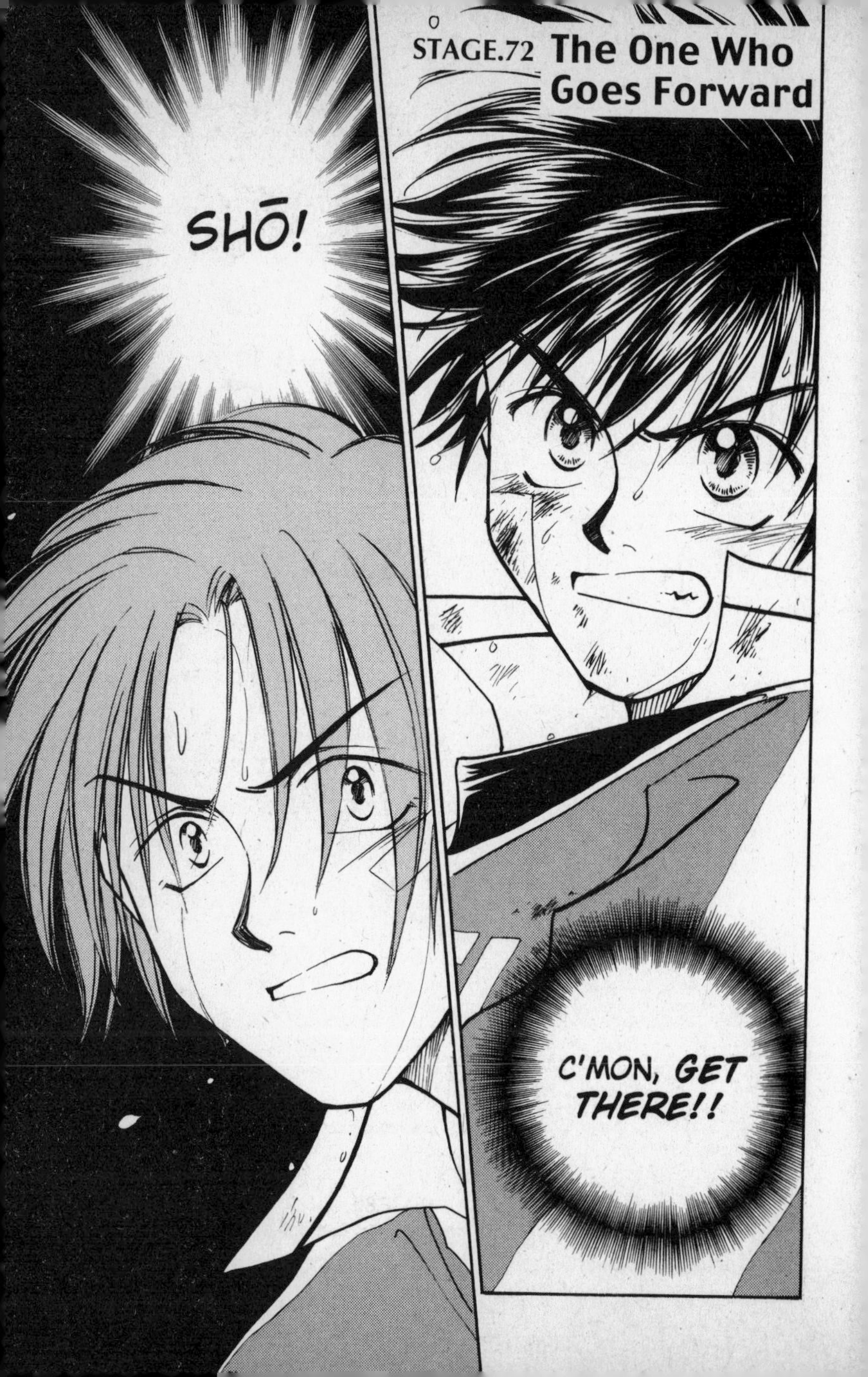
STAGE.72 The One Who Goes Forward
C'MON, GET THERE!!
SHŌ!

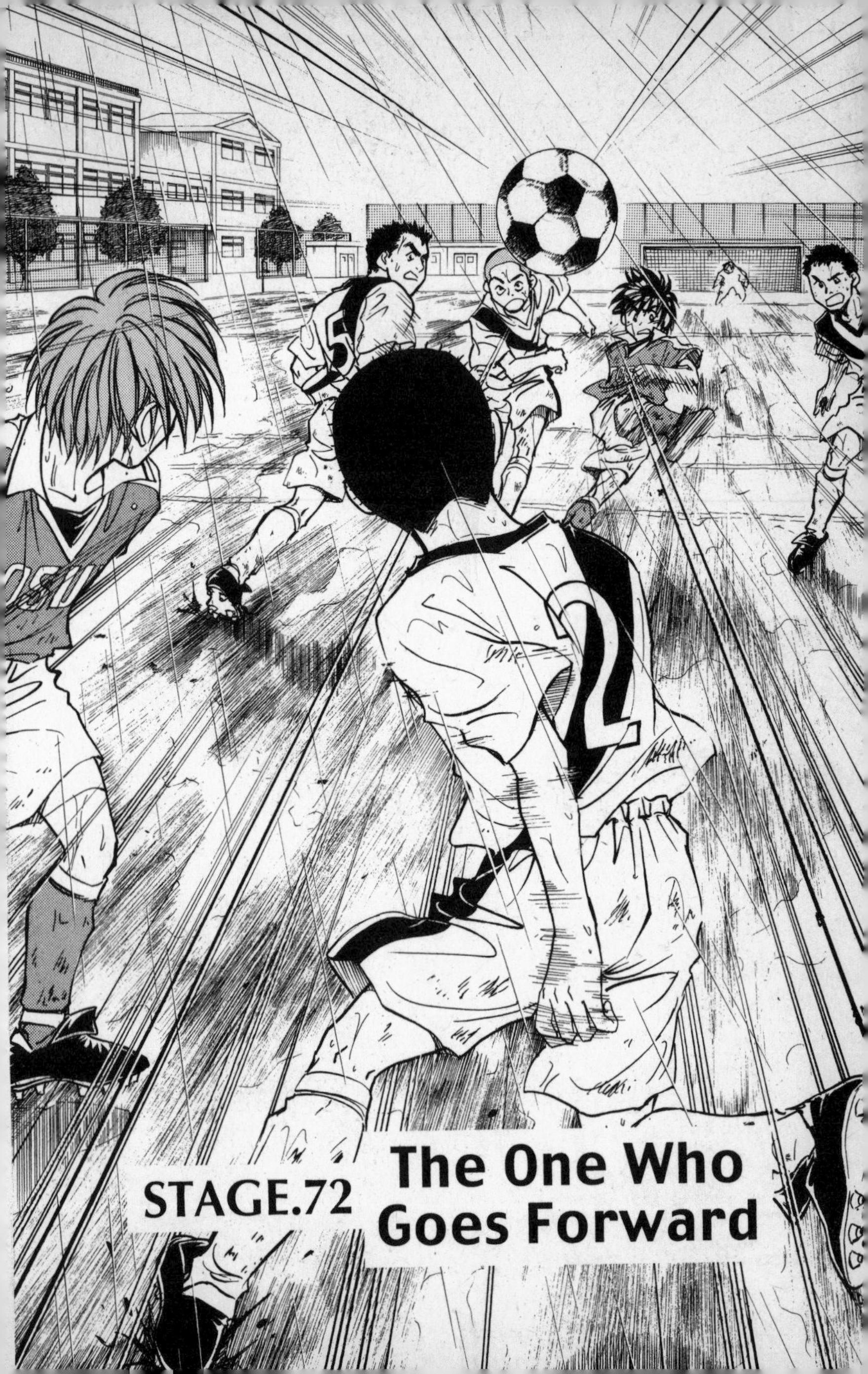
STAGE.72
The One Who Goes Forward

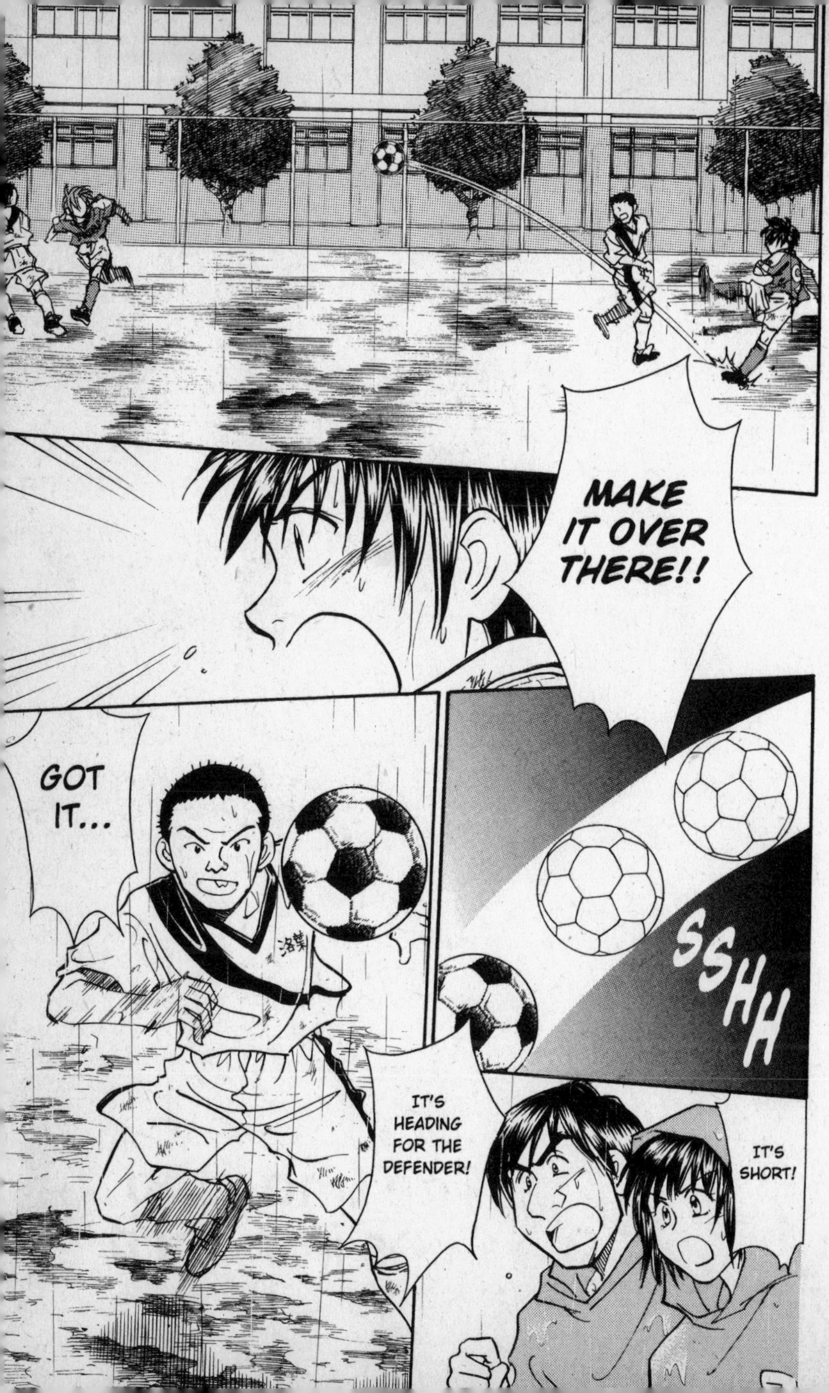
MAKE IT OVER THERE!!
SSHH
IT'S SHORT!
IT'S HEADING FOR THE DEFENDER!
GOT IT...

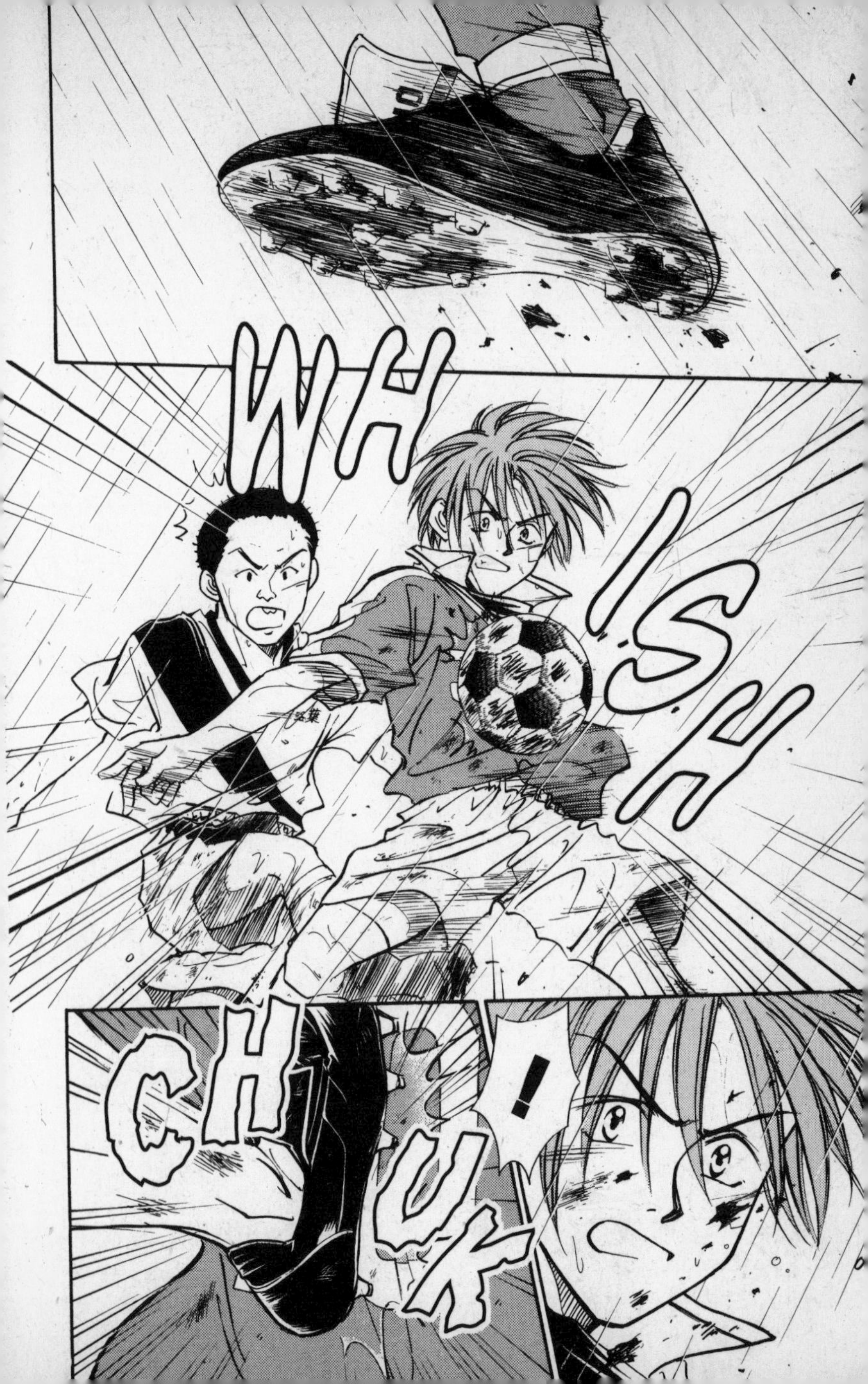
WHISH
CHUK
!

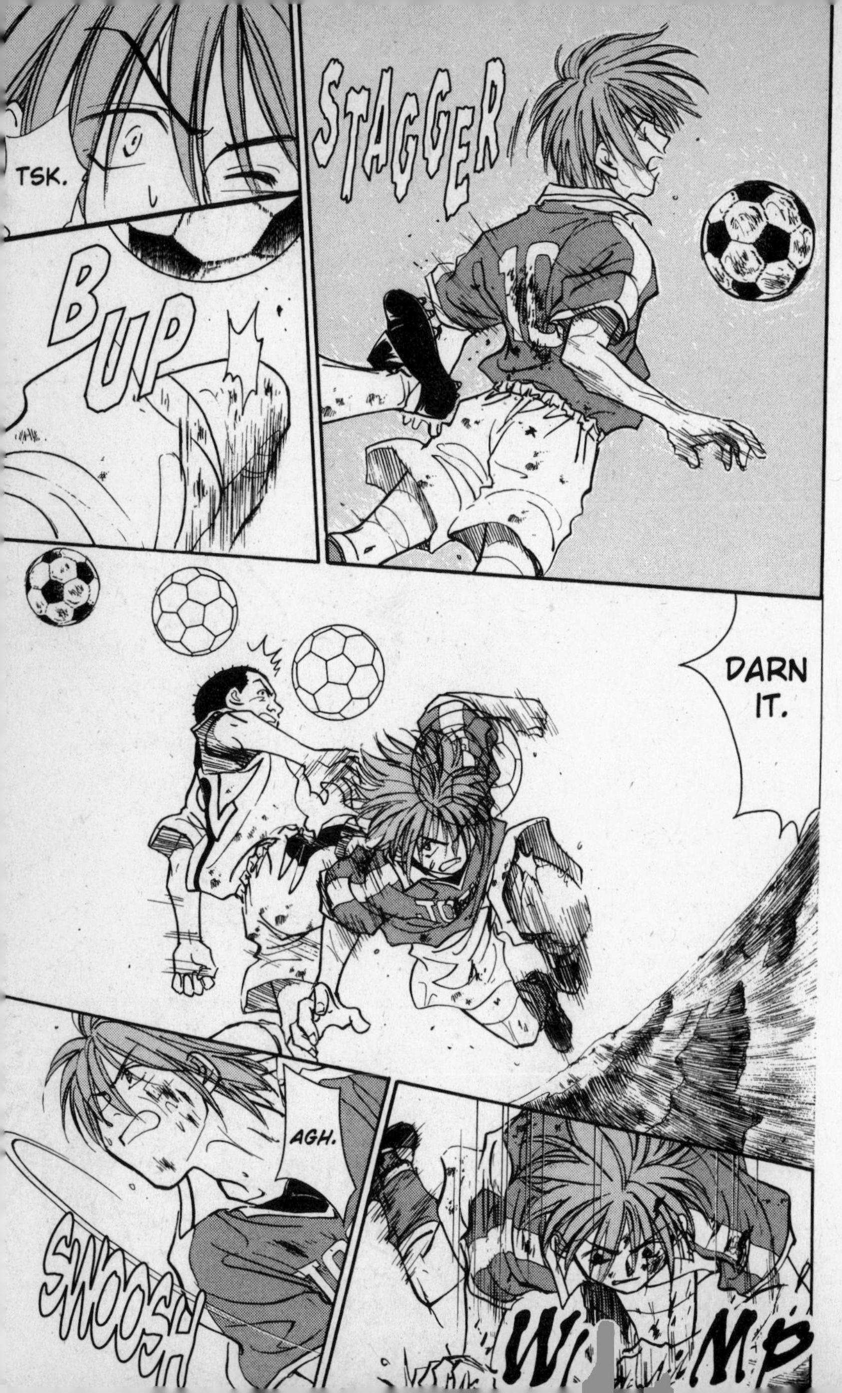
STAGGER
TSK.
BUP
DARN IT.
AGH.
SWOOSH

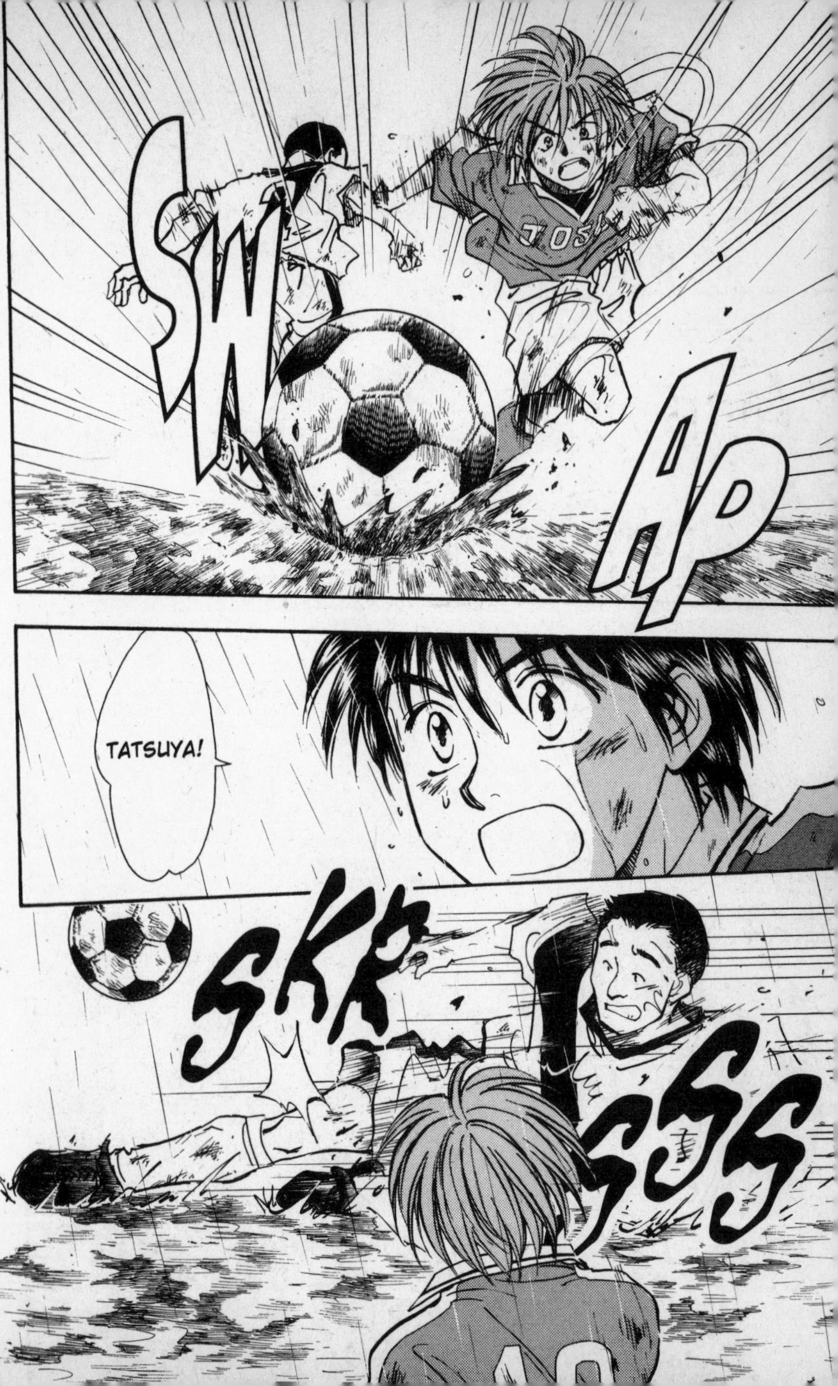
SW
AP
TATSUYA!
SKR
SSS

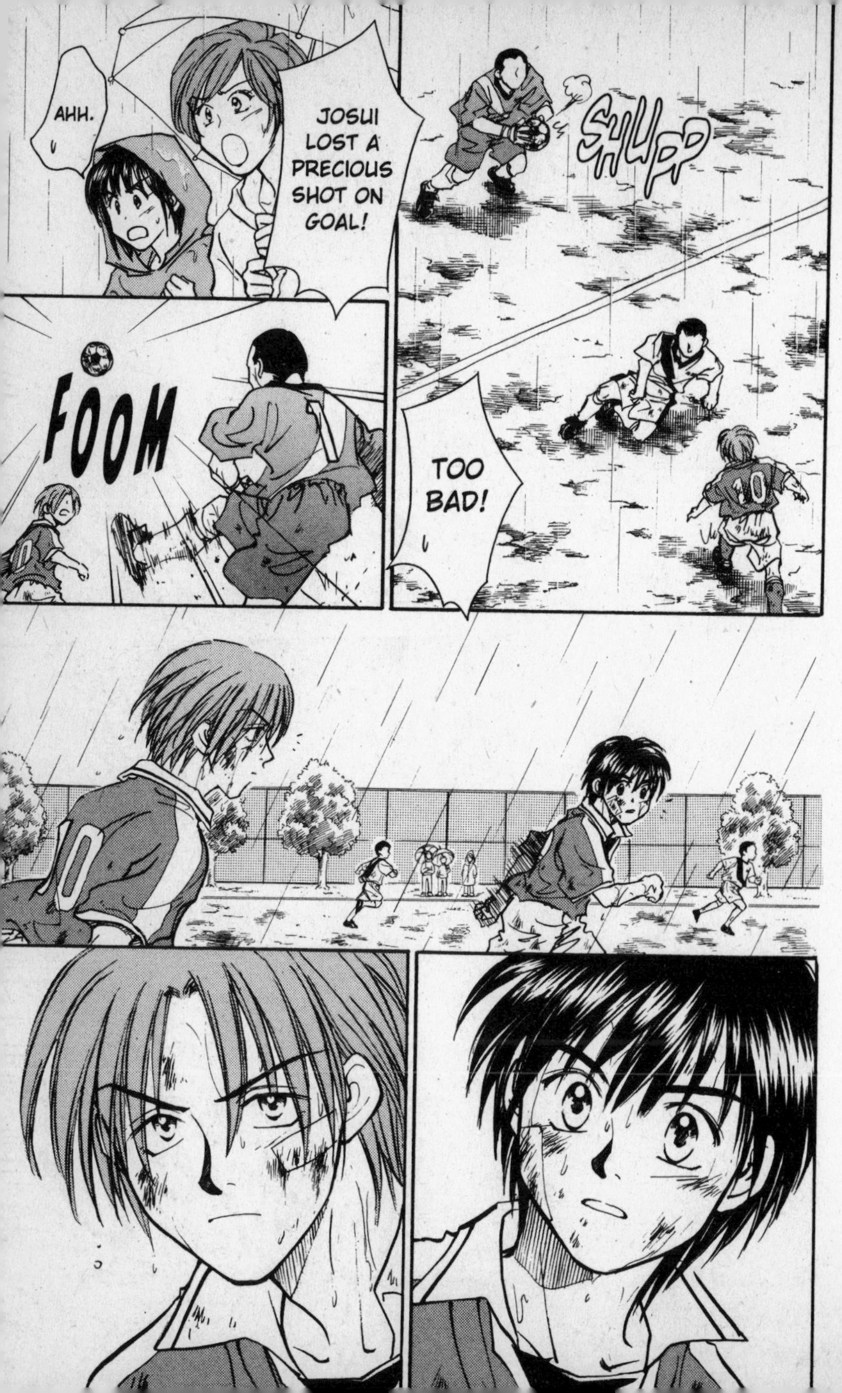
SHUPP
TOO BAD!
JOSUI LOST A PRECIOUS SHOT ON GOAL!
AHH.
FOOM

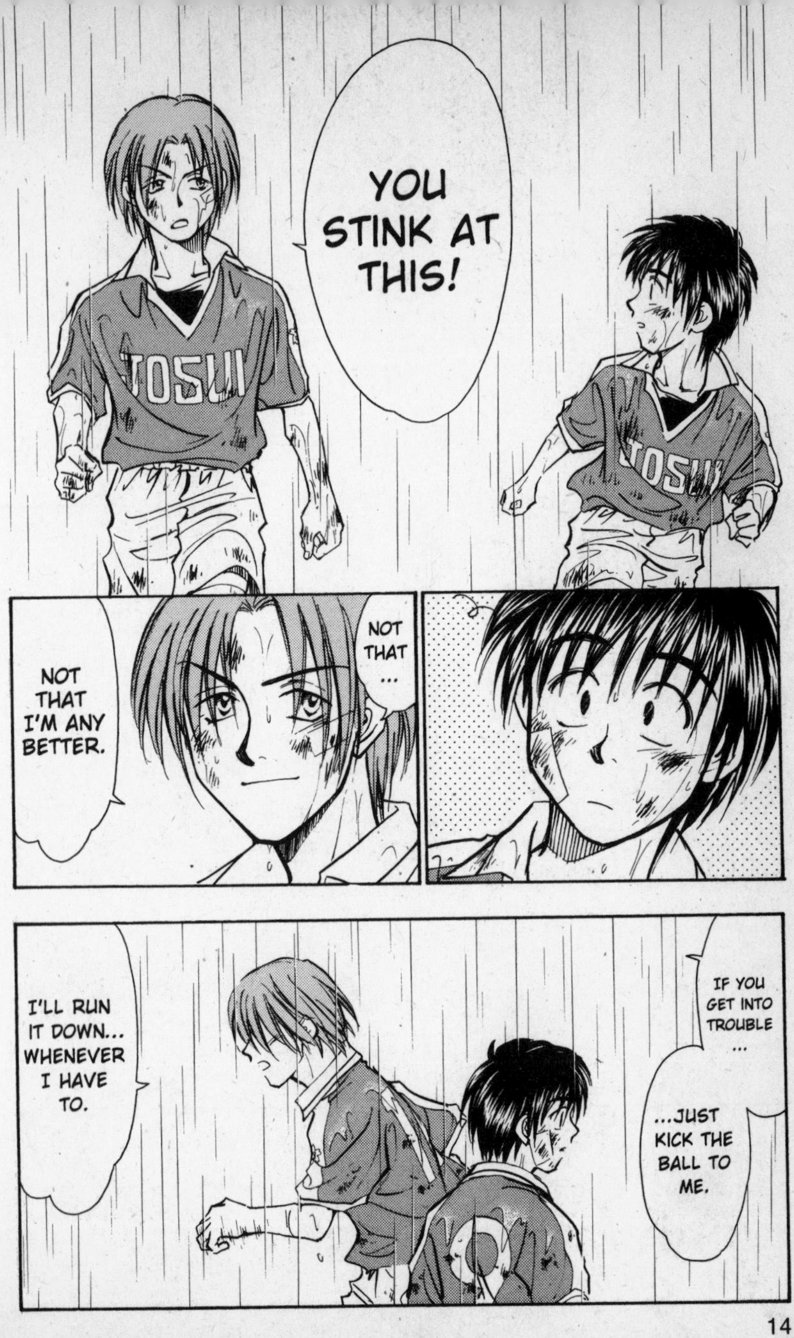
YOU STINK AT THIS!
NOT THAT ...
NOT THAT I'M ANY BETTER.
IF YOU GET INTO TROUBLE ...
...JUST KICK THE BALL TO ME.
I'LL RUN IT DOWN... WHENEVER I HAVE TO.

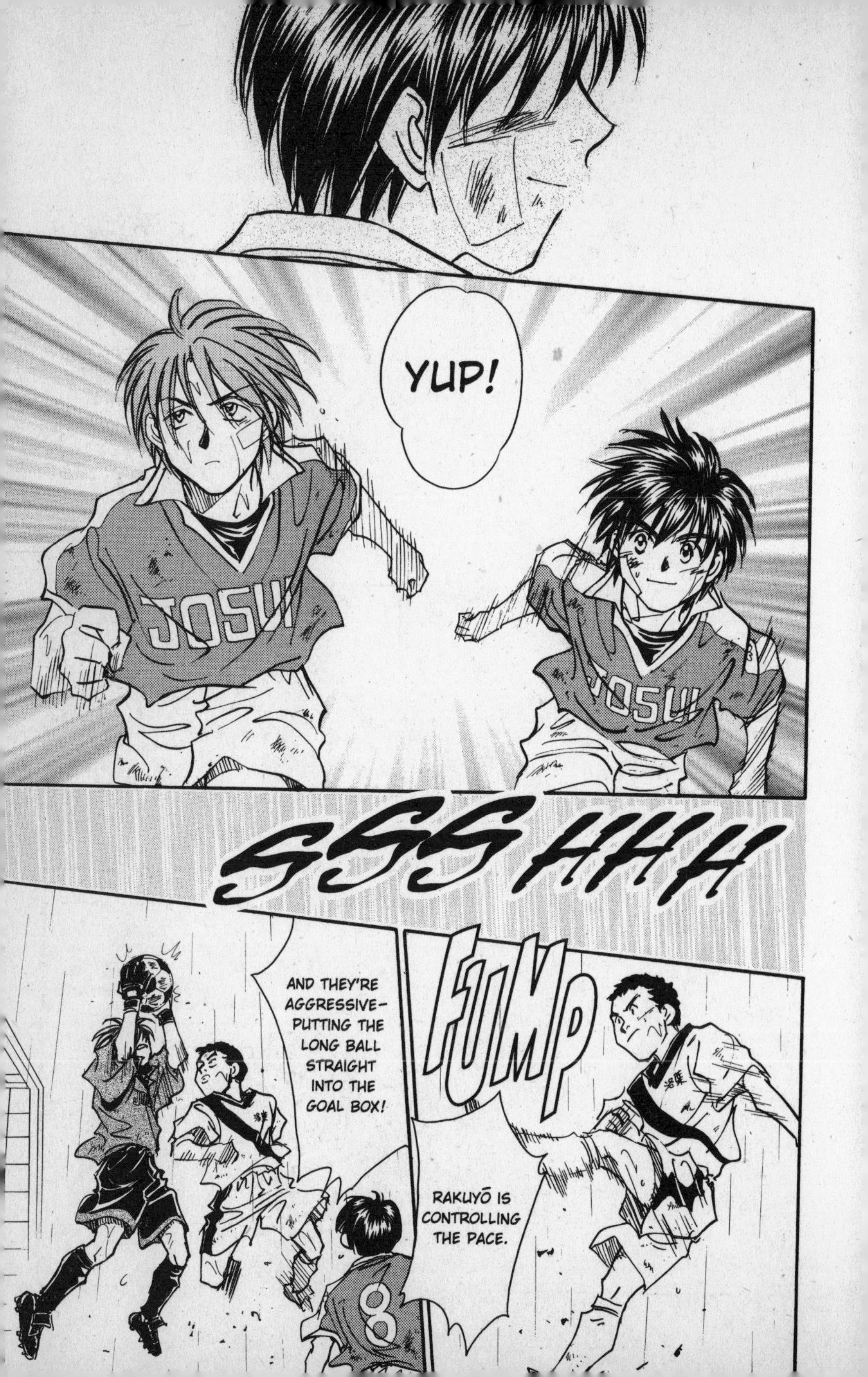
YUP!
JOSUI
JOSUI
SSSHHH
FUMP
RAKUYŌ IS CONTROLLING THE PACE.
AND THEY'RE AGGRESSIVE- PUTTING THE LONG BALL STRAIGHT INTO THE GOAL BOX!

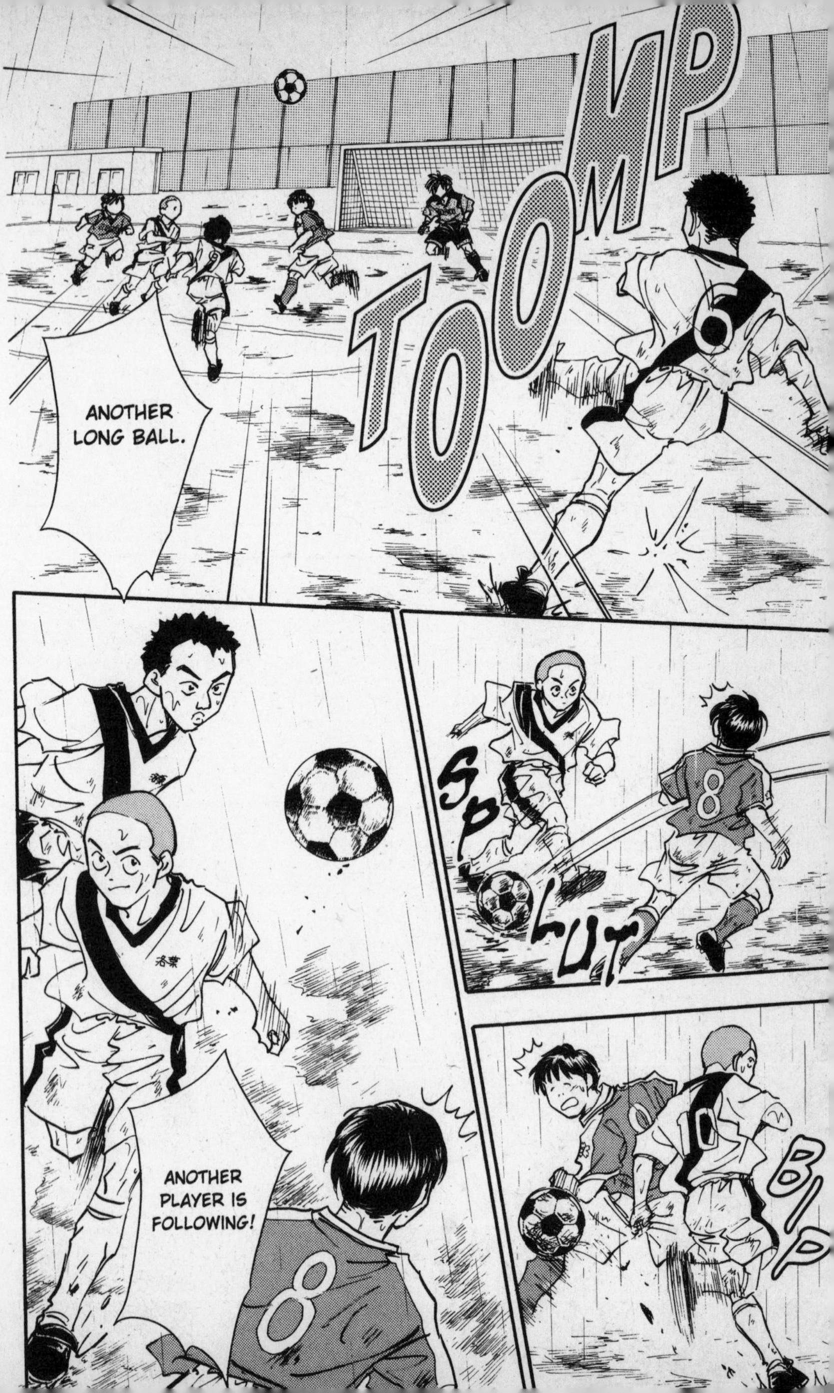
TOOOMP
ANOTHER LONG BALL.
SPLUT
BIP
ANOTHER PLAYER IS FOLLOWING!

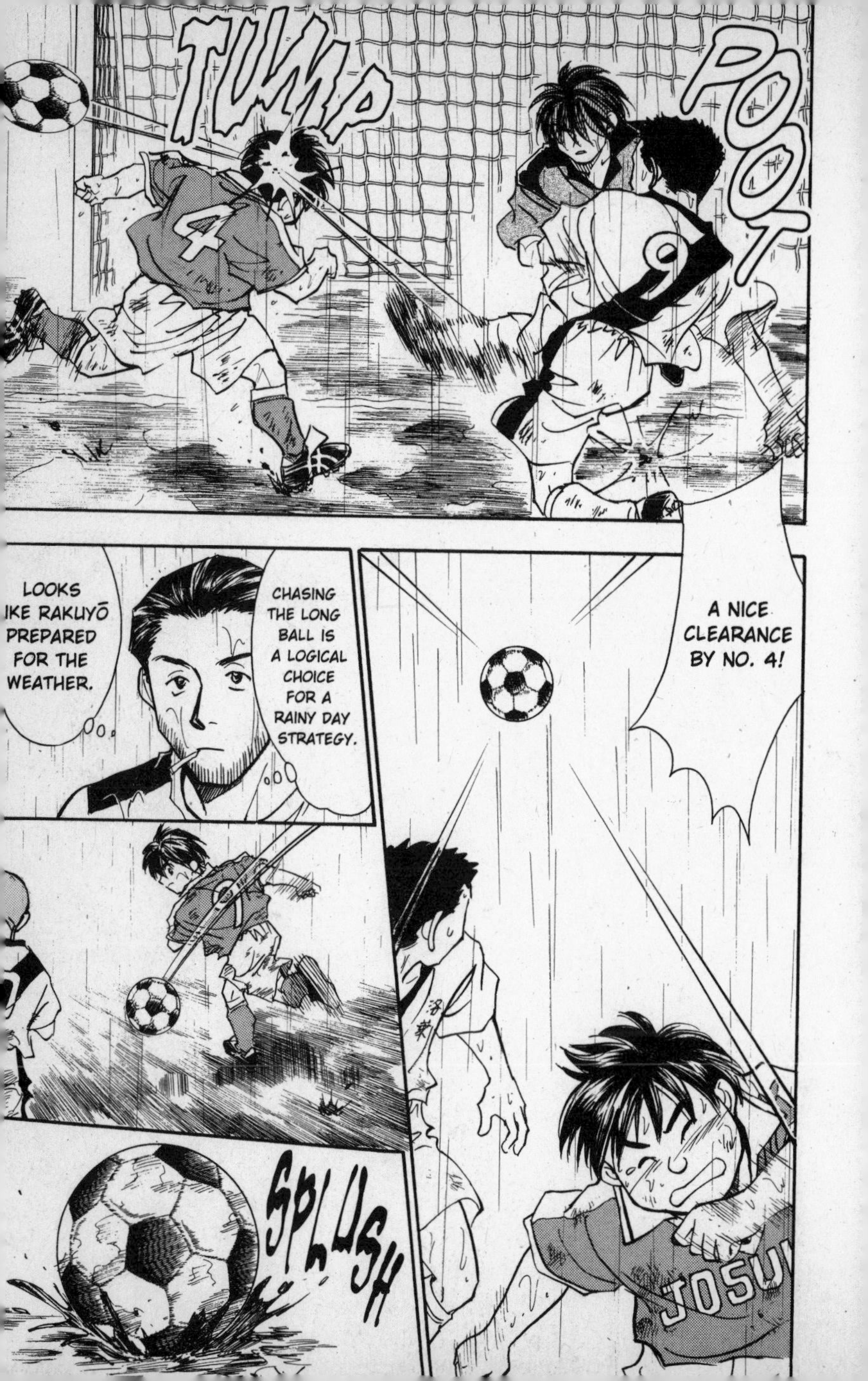
POOOT
TUMP
A NICE CLEARANCE BY NO. 4!
CHASING THE LONG BALL IS A LOGICAL CHOICE FOR A RAINY DAY STRATEGY.
LOOKS IKE RAKUYŌ PREPARED FOR THE WEATHER.
SPLUSH

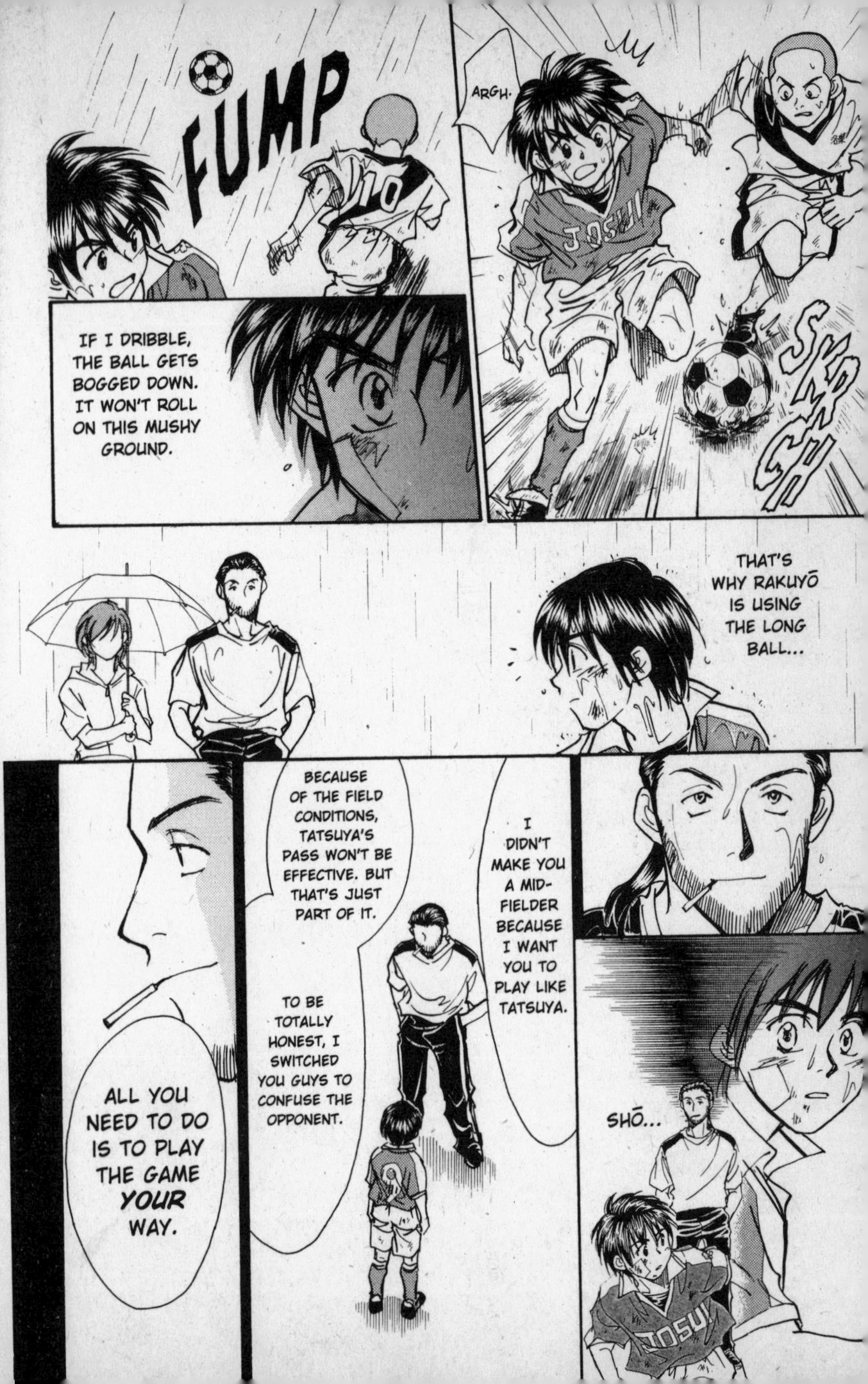
ARGH.
SKRCH
FUMP
IF I DRIBBLE, THE BALL GETS BOGGED DOWN. IT WON'T ROLL ON THIS MUSHY GROUND.
THAT'S WHY RAKUYŌ IS USING THE LONG BALL...
SHŌ...
I DIDN'T MAKE YOU A MID-FIELDER BECAUSE I WANT YOU TO PLAY LIKE TATSUYA.
BECAUSE OF THE FIELD CONDITIONS, TATSUYA'S PASS WON'T BE EFFECTIVE. BUT THAT'S JUST PART OF IT.
TO BE TOTALLY HONEST, I SWITCHED YOU GUYS TO CONFUSE THE OPPONENT.
ALL YOU NEED TO DO IS TO PLAY THE GAME *YOUR* WAY.

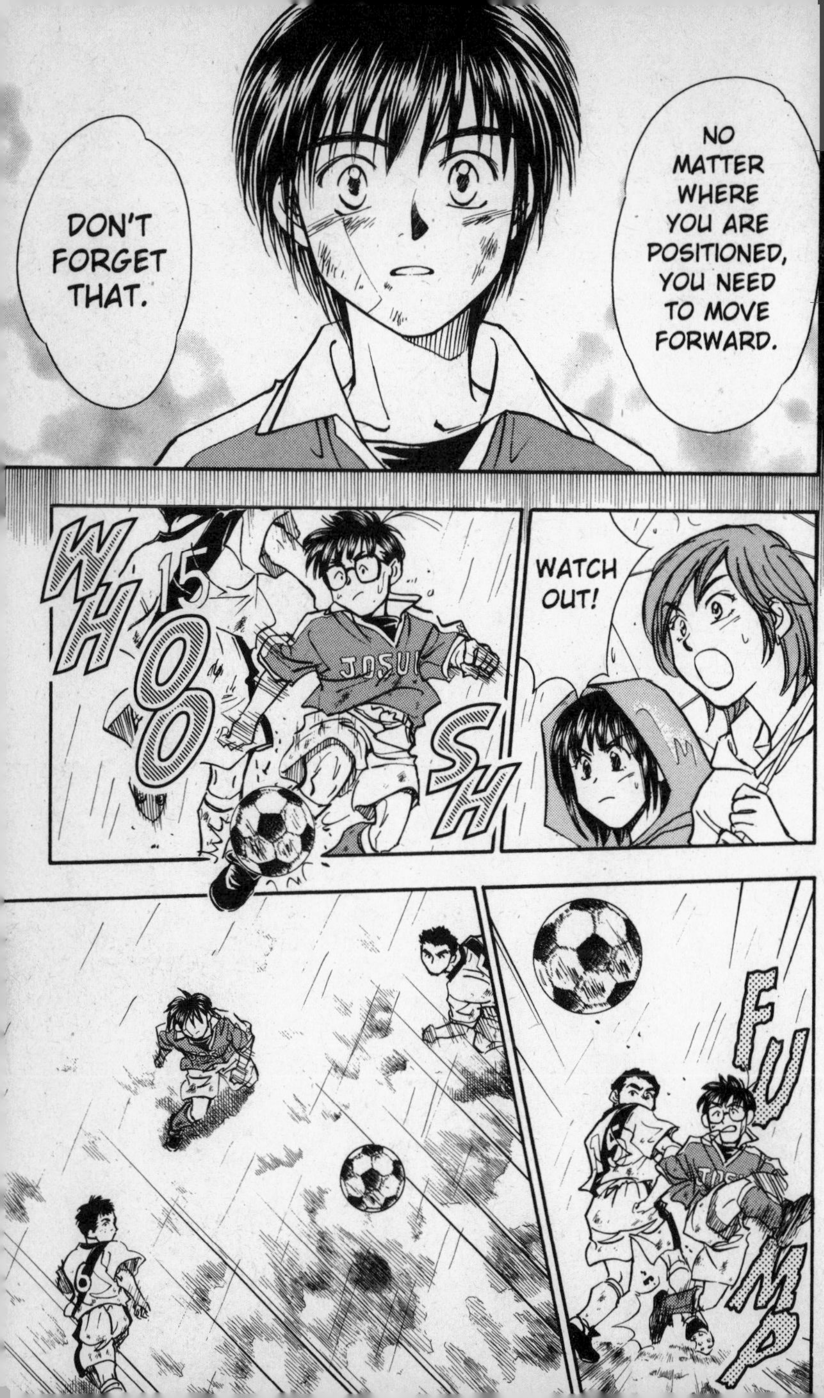
NO MATTER WHERE YOU ARE POSITIONED, YOU NEED TO MOVE FORWARD.
DON'T FORGET THAT.
WATCH OUT!
WHOOSH
FUMP

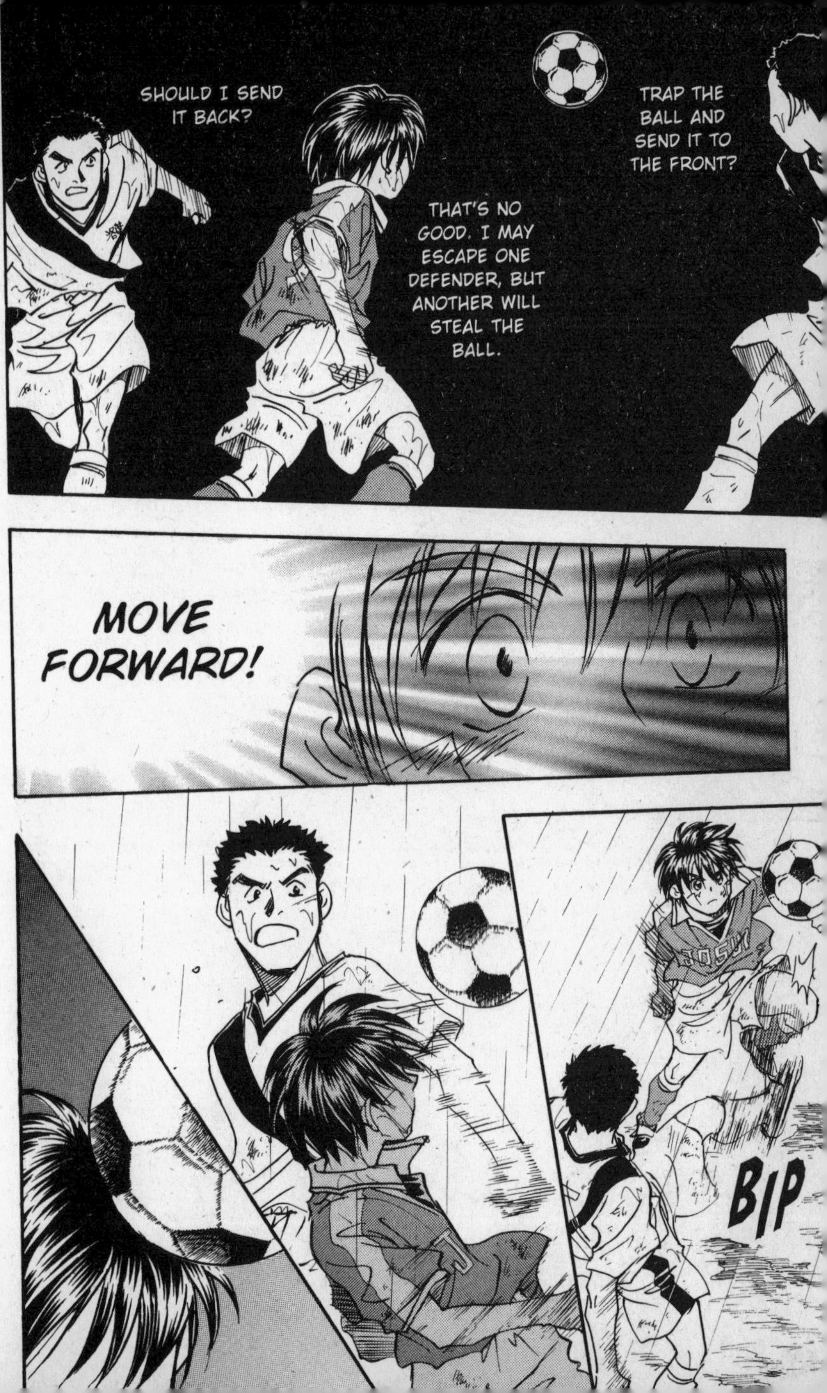
TRAP THE BALL AND SEND IT TO THE FRONT?
THAT'S NO GOOD. I MAY ESCAPE ONE DEFENDER, BUT ANOTHER WILL STEAL THE BALL.
SHOULD I SEND IT BACK?
MOVE FORWARD!
BIP

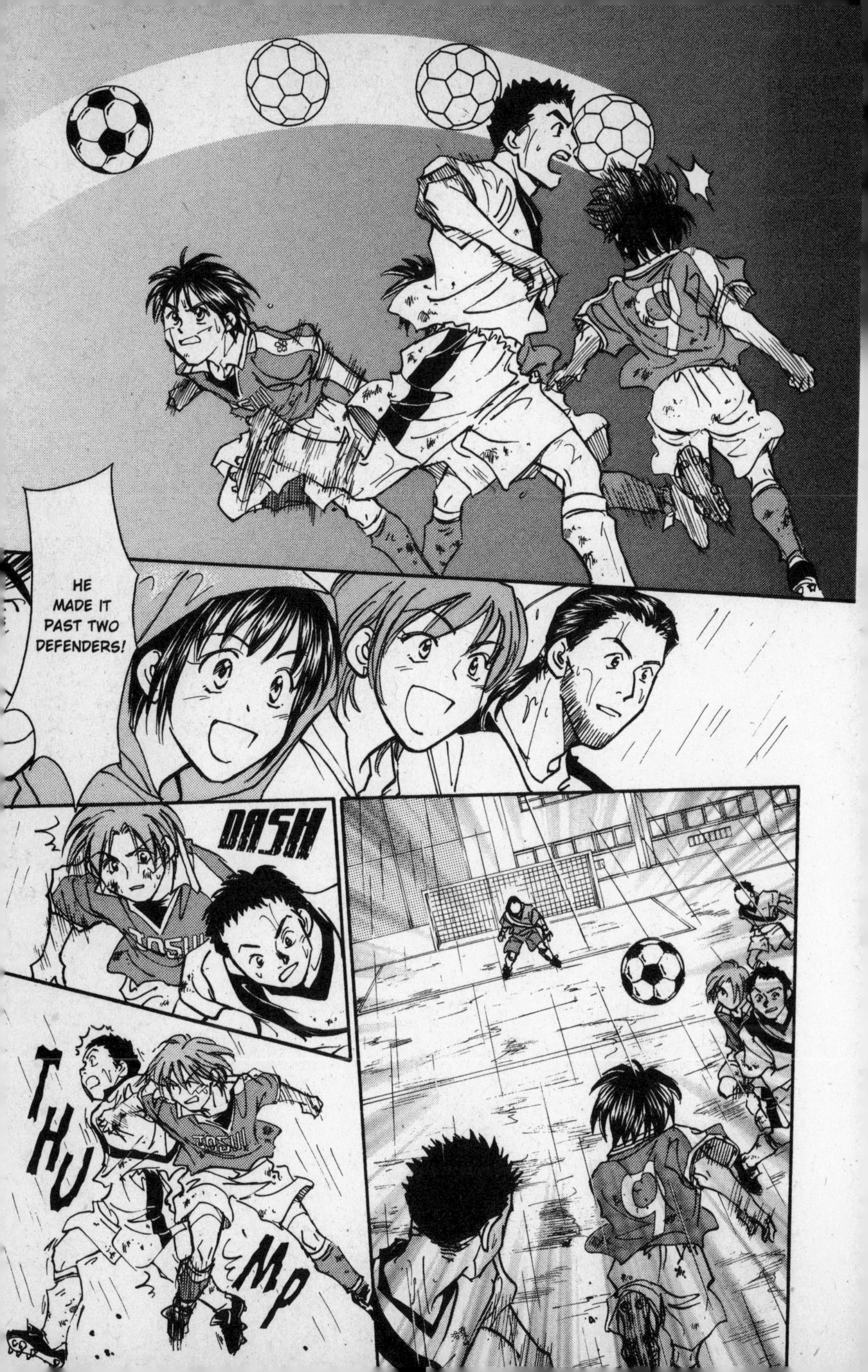
HE MADE IT PAST TWO DEFENDERS!
DASH
THUMP

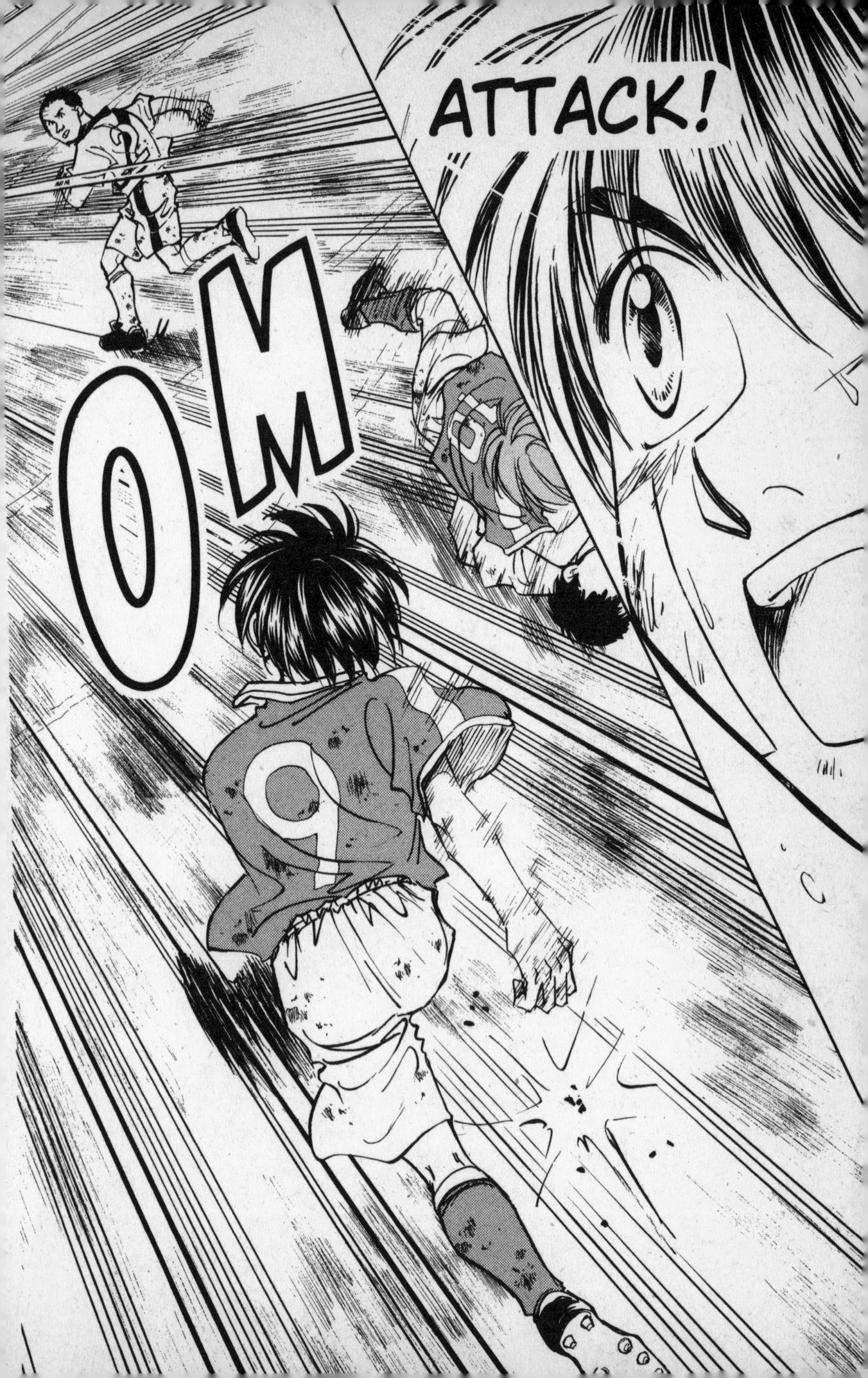
ATTACK!
OM

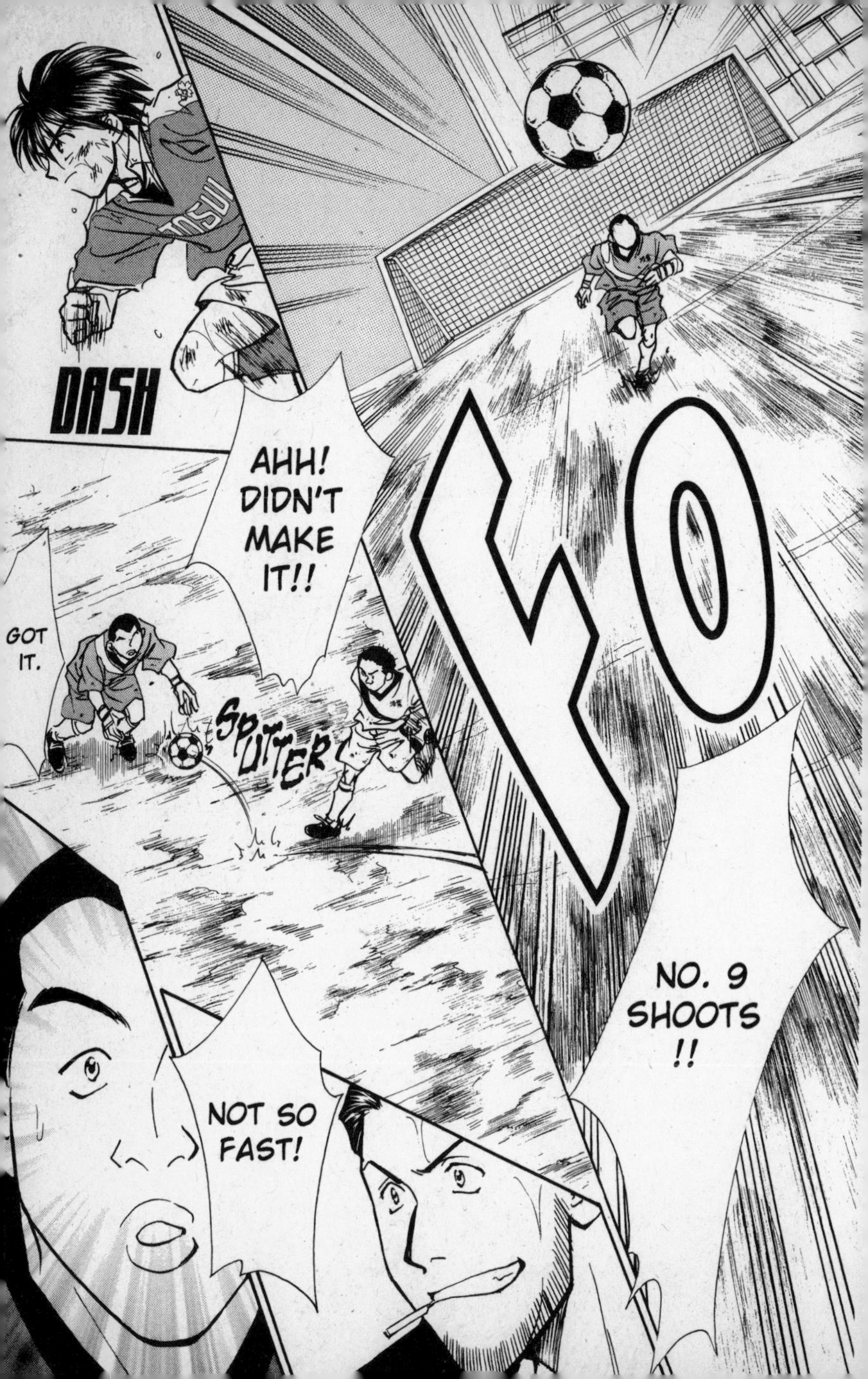
GO
NO. 9 SHOOTS!!
DASH
AHH! DIDN'T MAKE IT!!
GOT IT.
SPUTTER
NOT SO FAST!

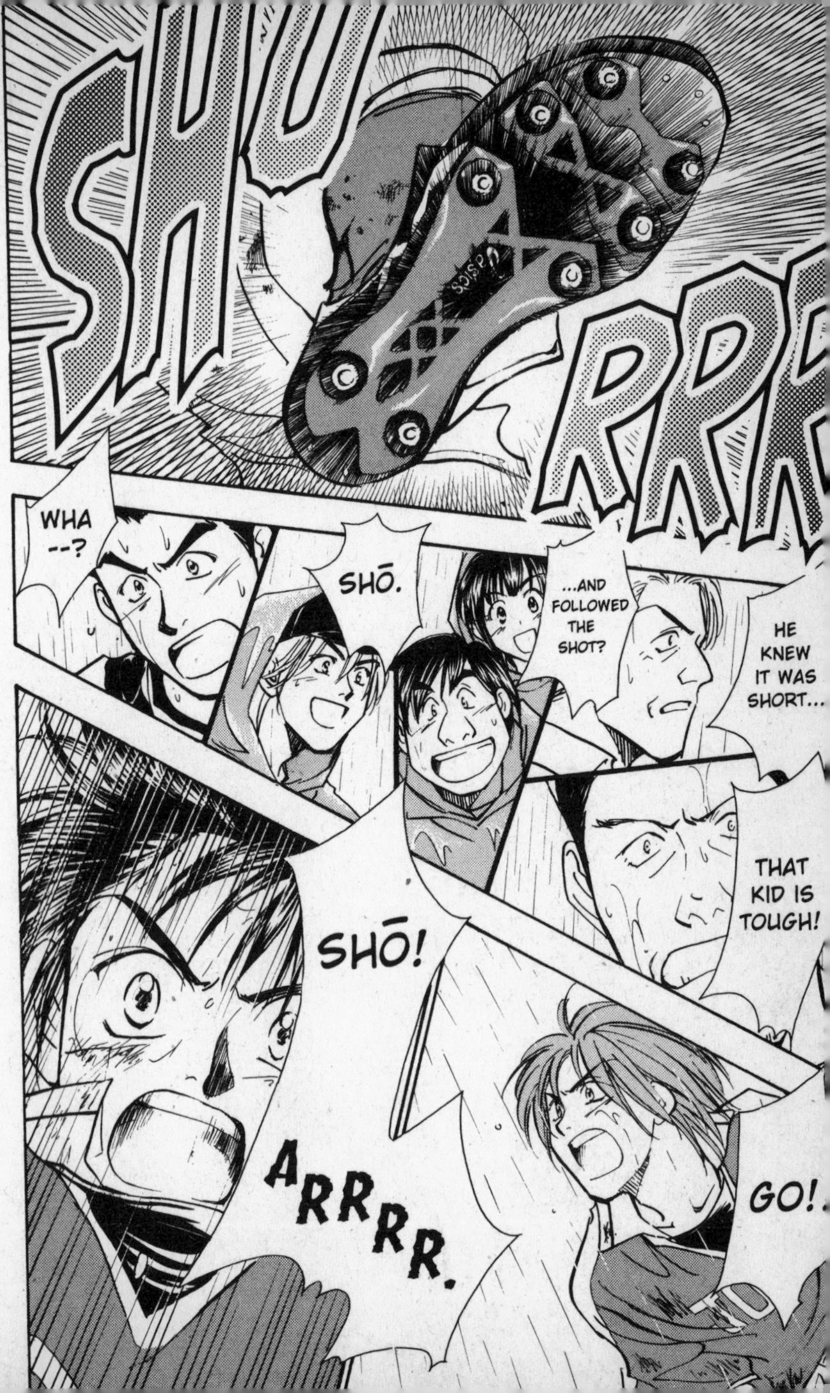
SHURRR
HE KNEW IT WAS SHORT...
...AND FOLLOWED THE SHOT?
SHŌ.
WHA --?
THAT KID IS TOUGH!
GO!
SHŌ!
ARRRRR.

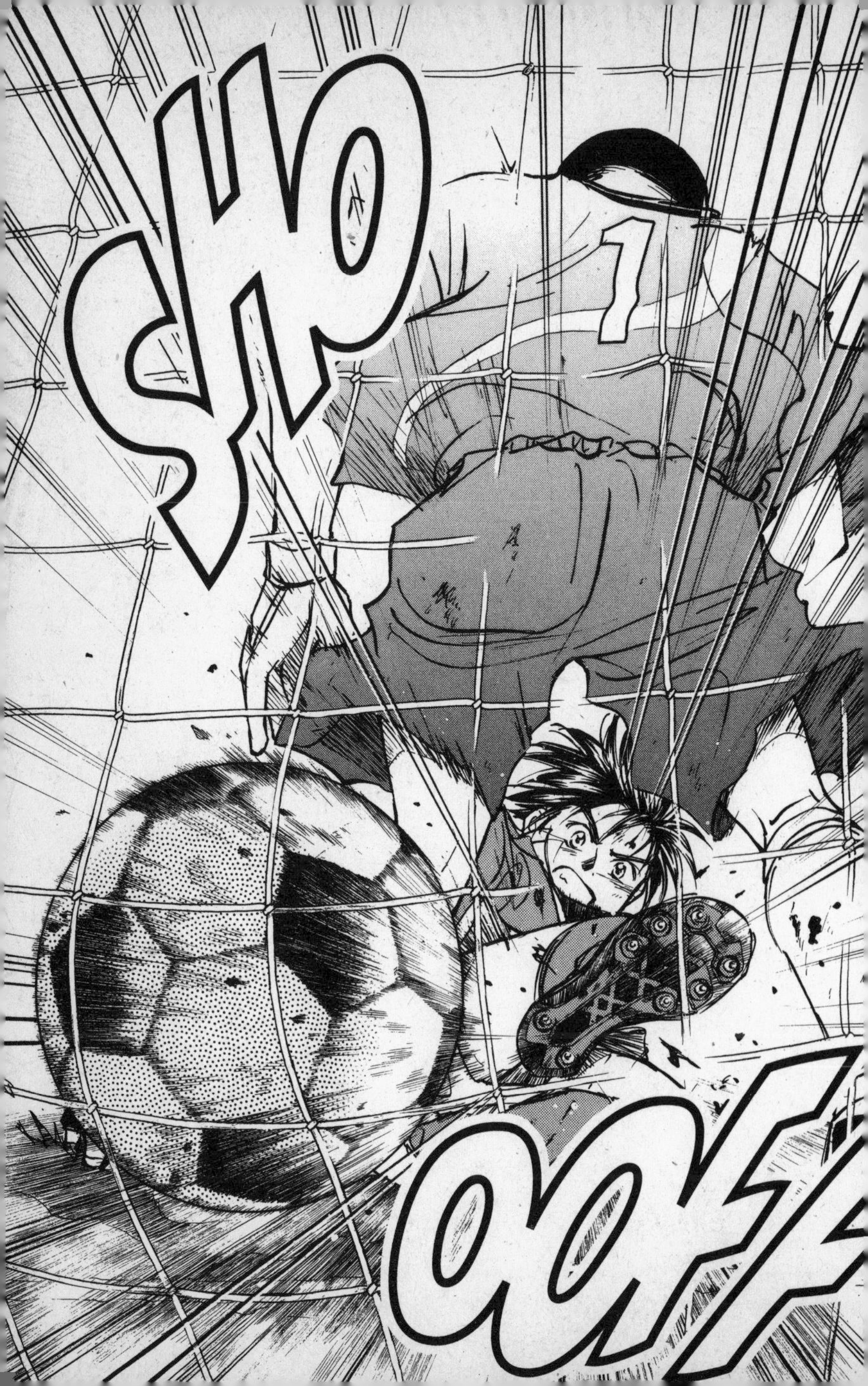
SHO
OOT

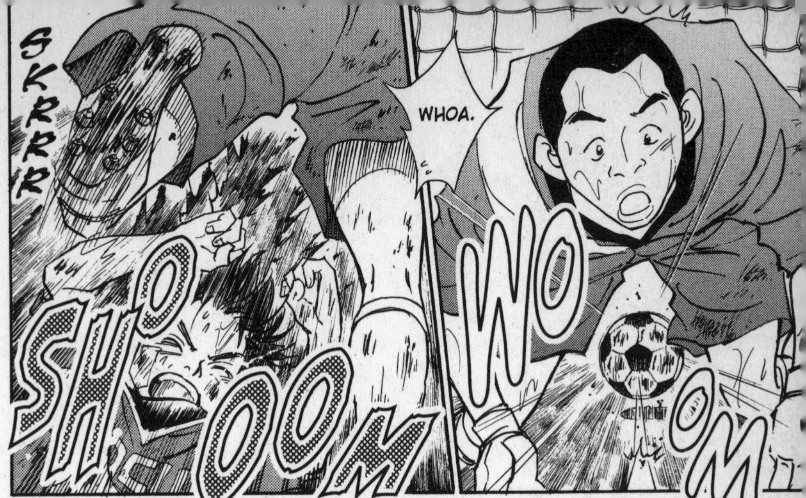
WHOA.
WOOOM
SHOOOM
SKRRRR

STAGE.73
Josui Team, the Ascending Current

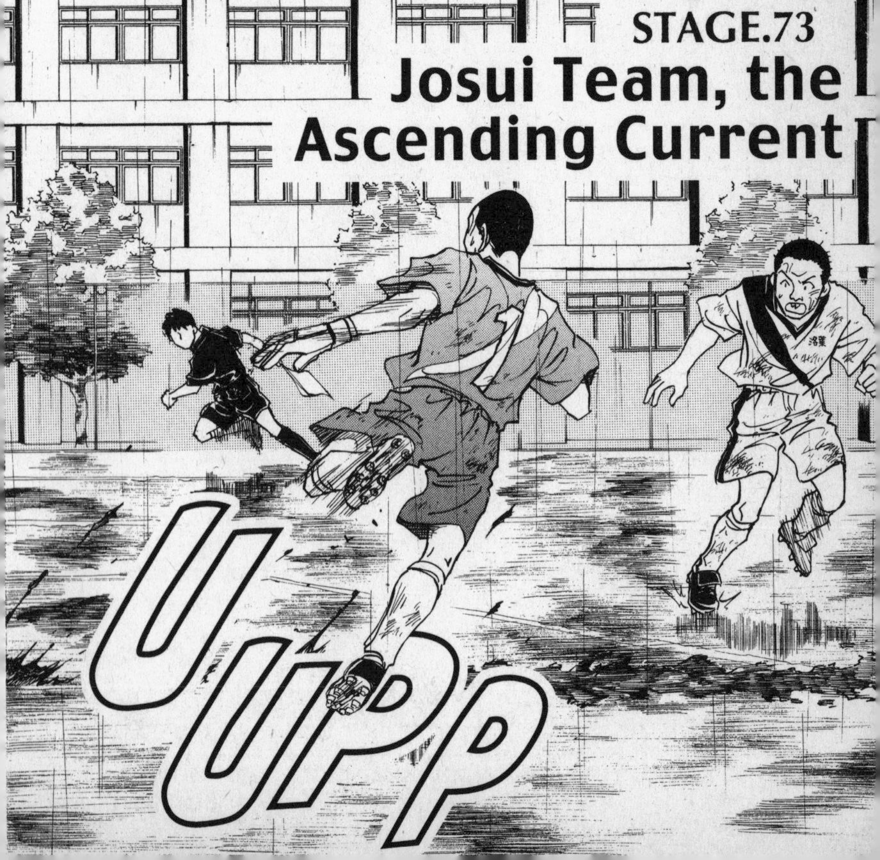
UUPP

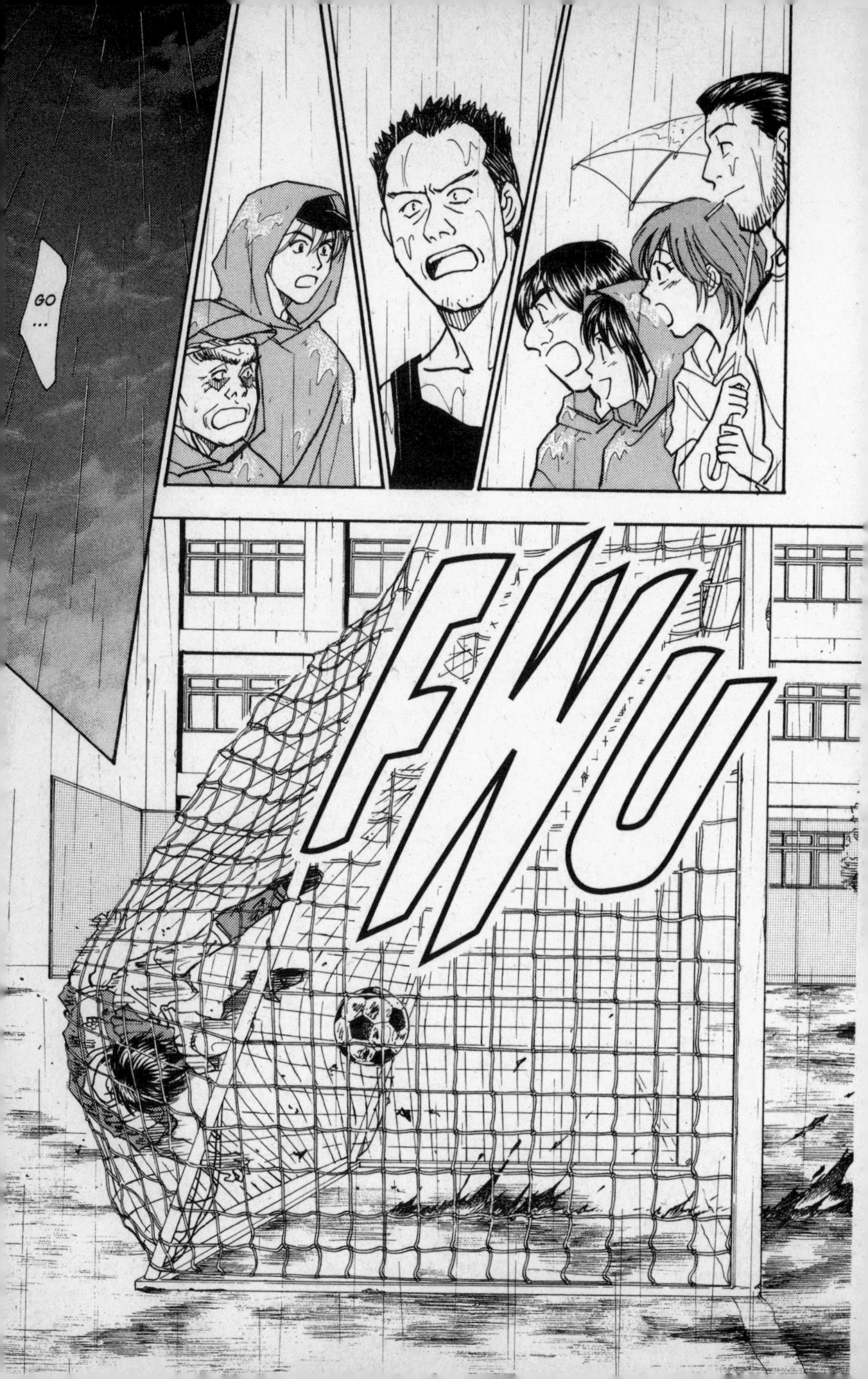
GO ...
FWU

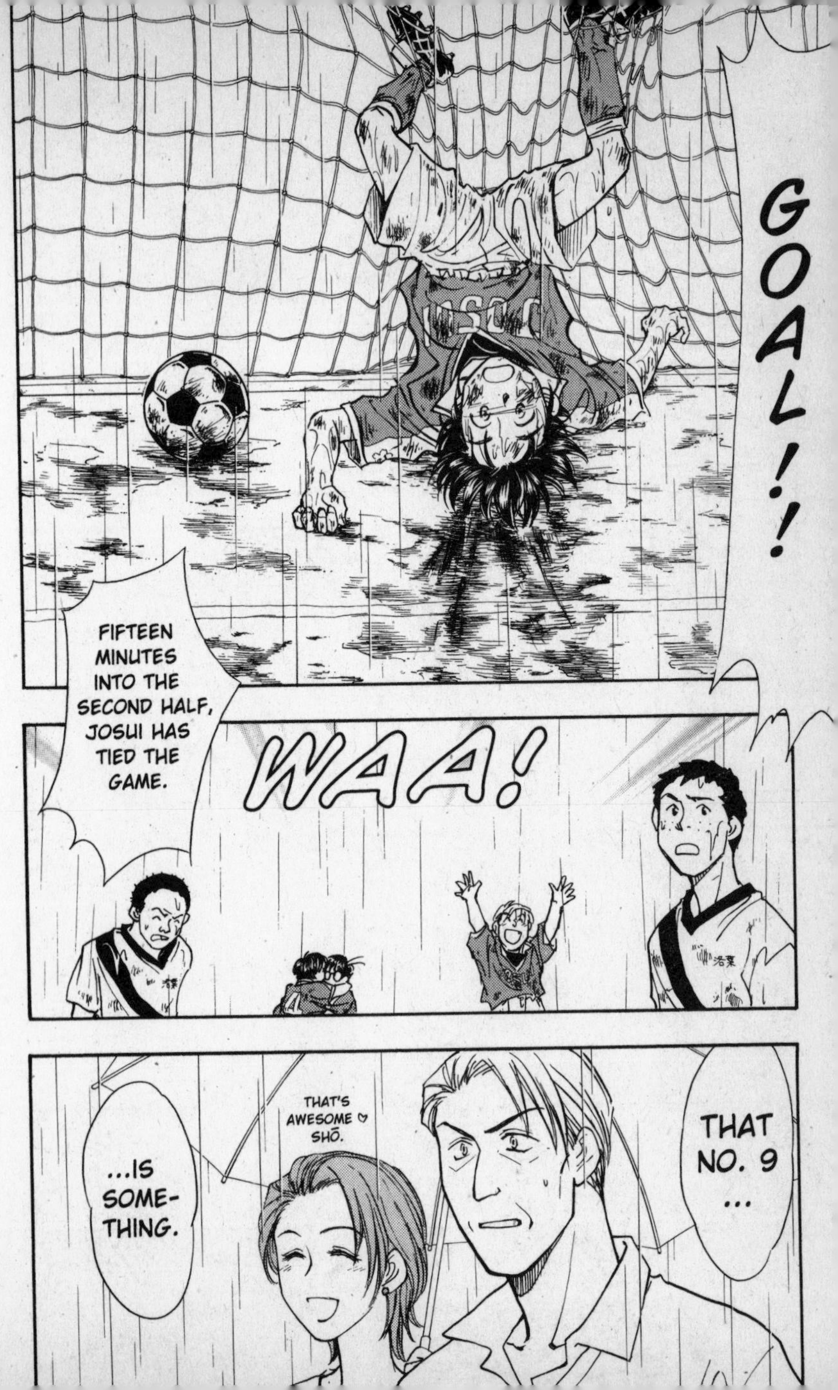
GOAL!!
WAA!
FIFTEEN MINUTES INTO THE SECOND HALF, JOSUI HAS TIED THE GAME.
THAT NO. 9 ...
THAT'S AWESOME ♡ SHŌ.
...IS SOMETHING.

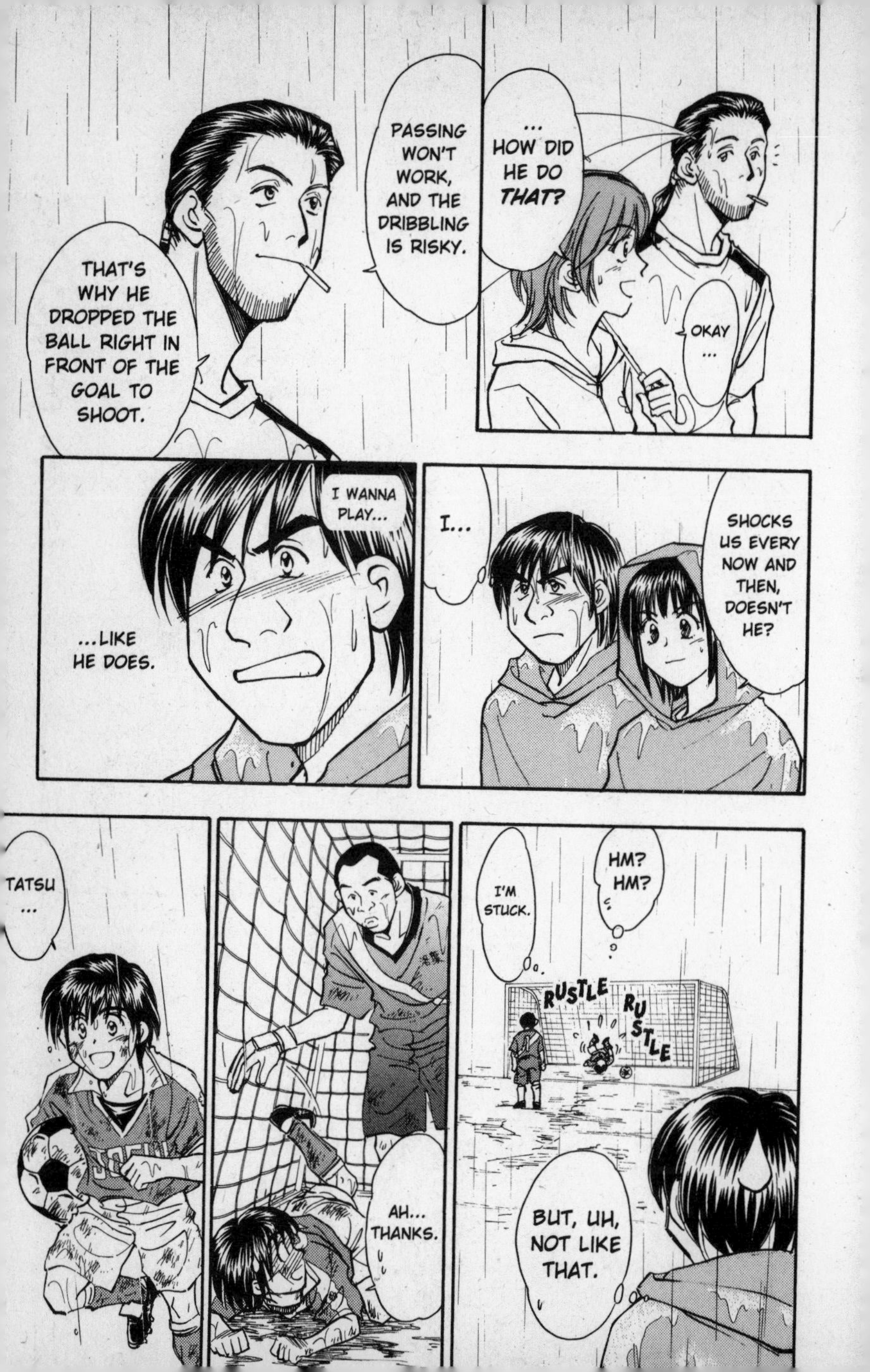
...HOW DID HE DO THAT?
OKAY...
PASSING WON'T WORK, AND THE DRIBBLING IS RISKY.
THAT'S WHY HE DROPPED THE BALL RIGHT IN FRONT OF THE GOAL TO SHOOT.
SHOCKS US EVERY NOW AND THEN, DOESN'T HE?
I...
I WANNA PLAY...
...LIKE HE DOES.
HM? HM?
I'M STUCK.
RUSTLE
RUSTLE
BUT, UH, NOT LIKE THAT.
AH... THANKS.
TATSU...

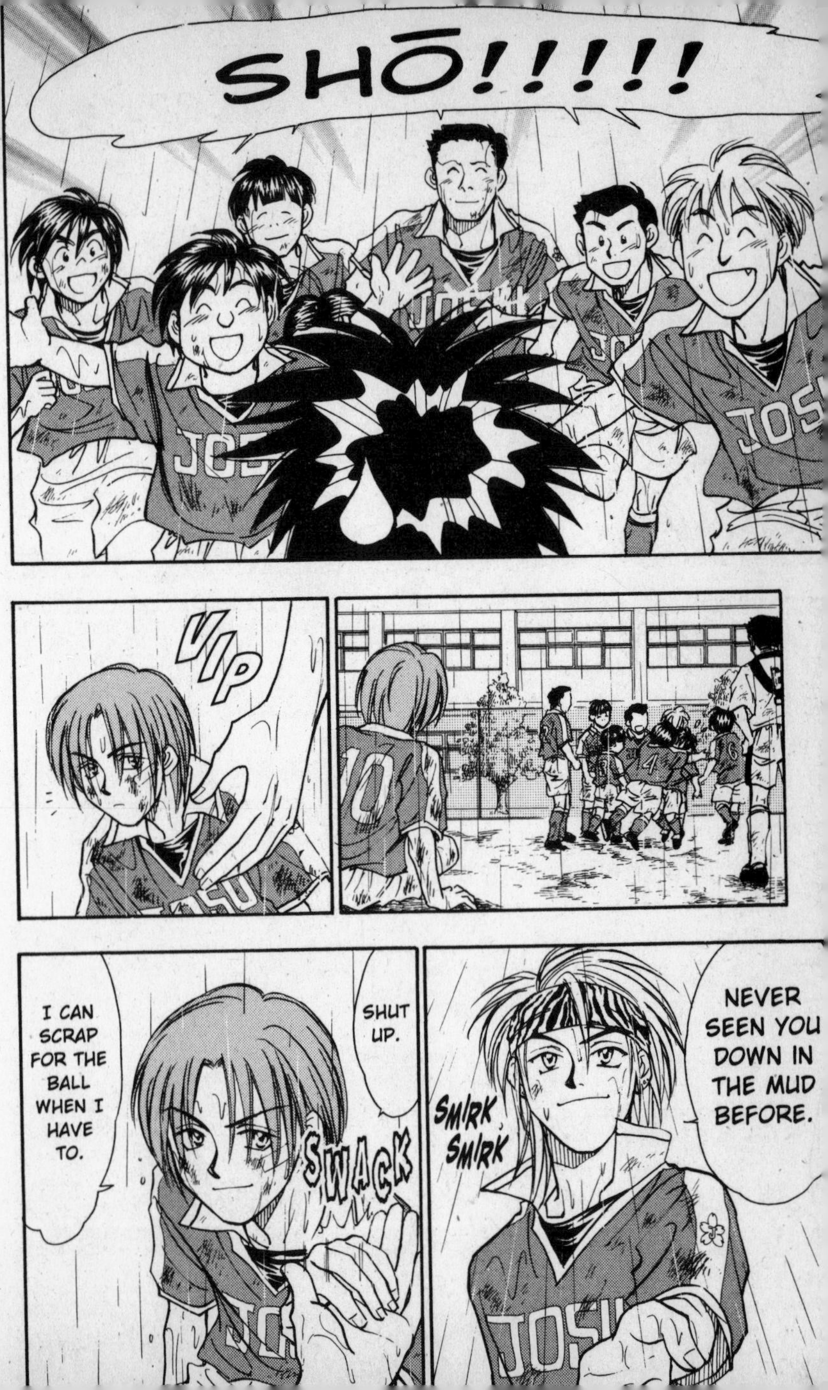
SHŌ!!!!!
VIP
NEVER SEEN YOU DOWN IN THE MUD BEFORE.
SMIRK SMIRK
SHUT UP.
I CAN SCRAP FOR THE BALL WHEN I HAVE TO.
SWACK

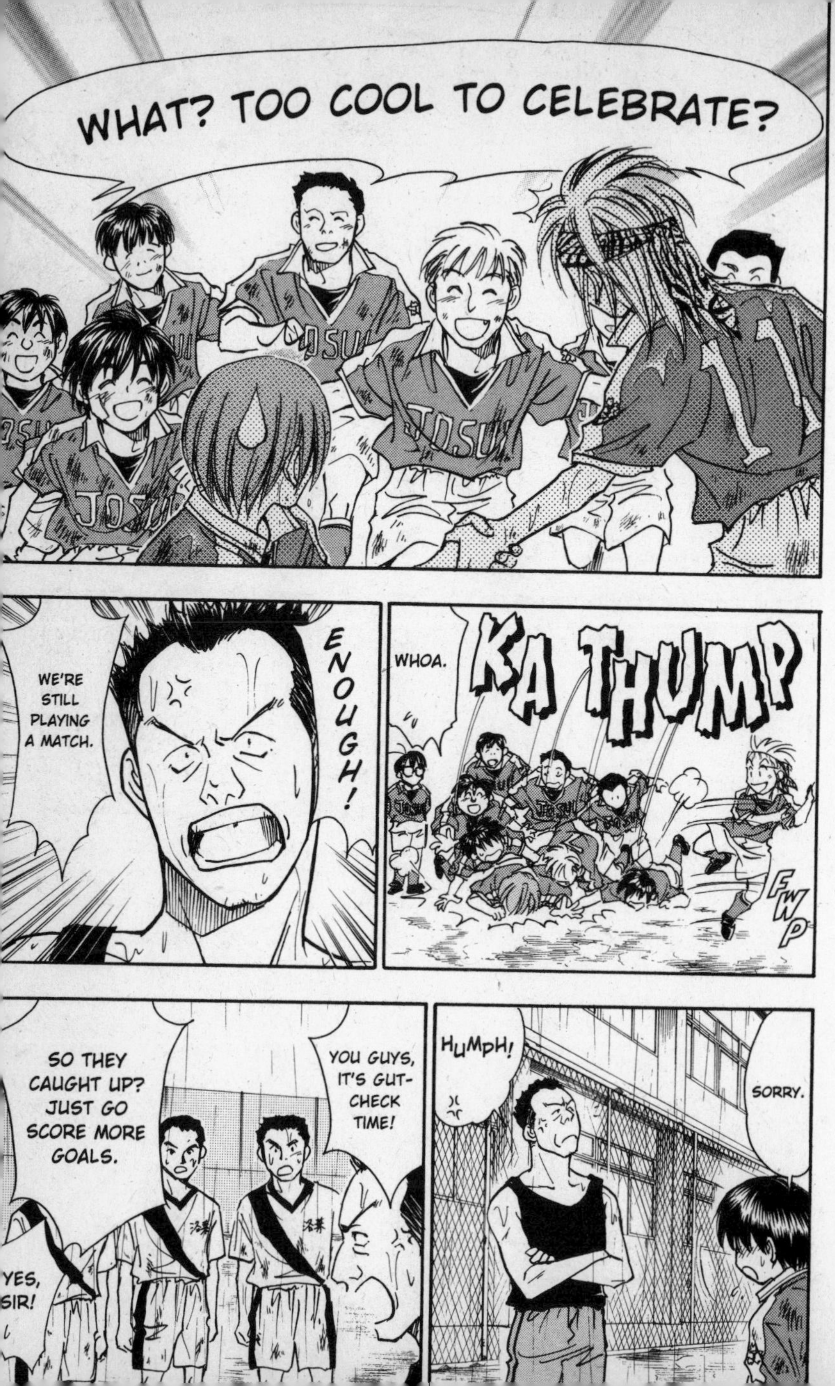
WHAT? TOO COOL TO CELEBRATE?
WHOA.
KA THUMP
FWP
ENOUGH!
WE'RE STILL PLAYING A MATCH.
SORRY.
HUMPH!
YOU GUYS, IT'S GUT-CHECK TIME!
SO THEY CAUGHT UP? JUST GO SCORE MORE GOALS.
YES, SIR!

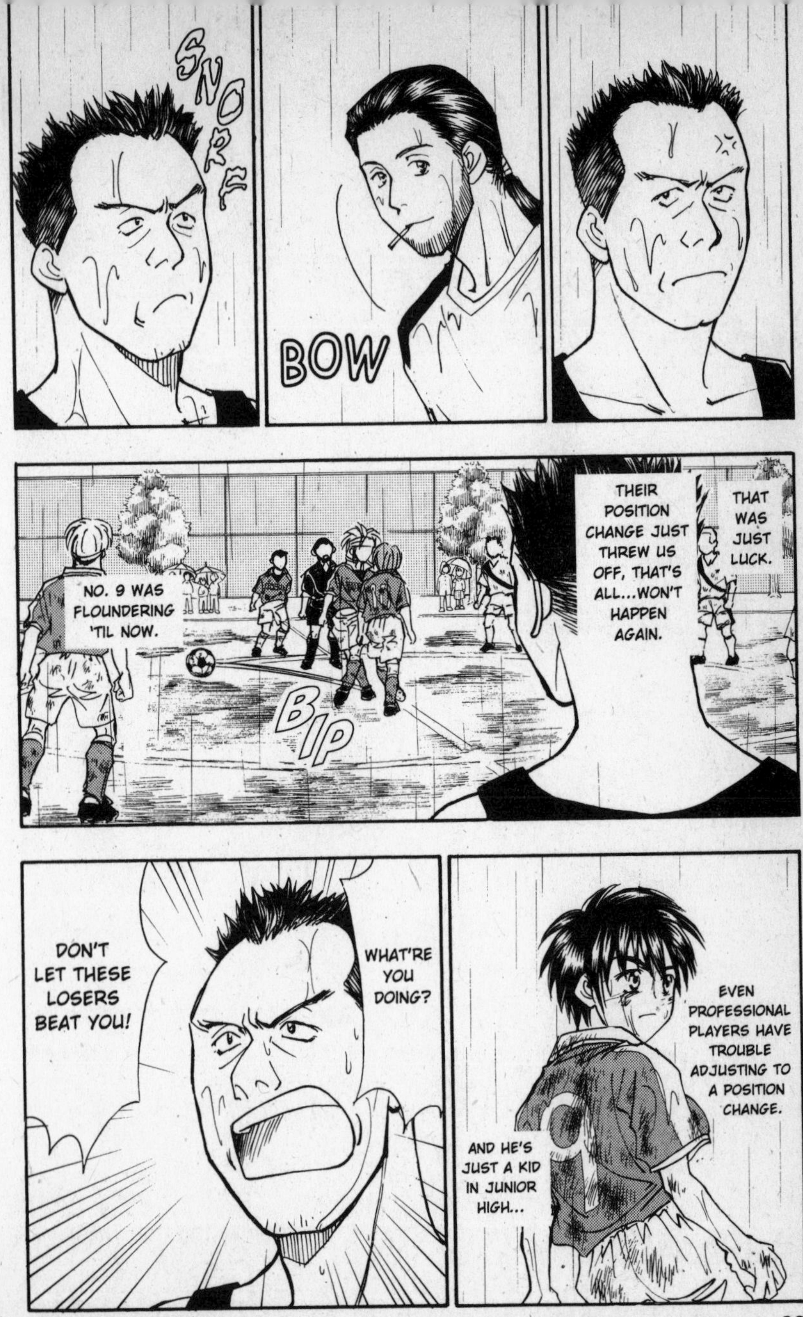
BOW
SNORF
THAT WAS JUST LUCK.
THEIR POSITION CHANGE JUST THREW US OFF, THAT'S ALL...WON'T HAPPEN AGAIN.
NO. 9 WAS FLOUNDERING 'TIL NOW.
BIP
EVEN PROFESSIONAL PLAYERS HAVE TROUBLE ADJUSTING TO A POSITION CHANGE.
AND HE'S JUST A KID IN JUNIOR HIGH...
WHAT'RE YOU DOING?
DON'T LET THESE LOSERS BEAT YOU!

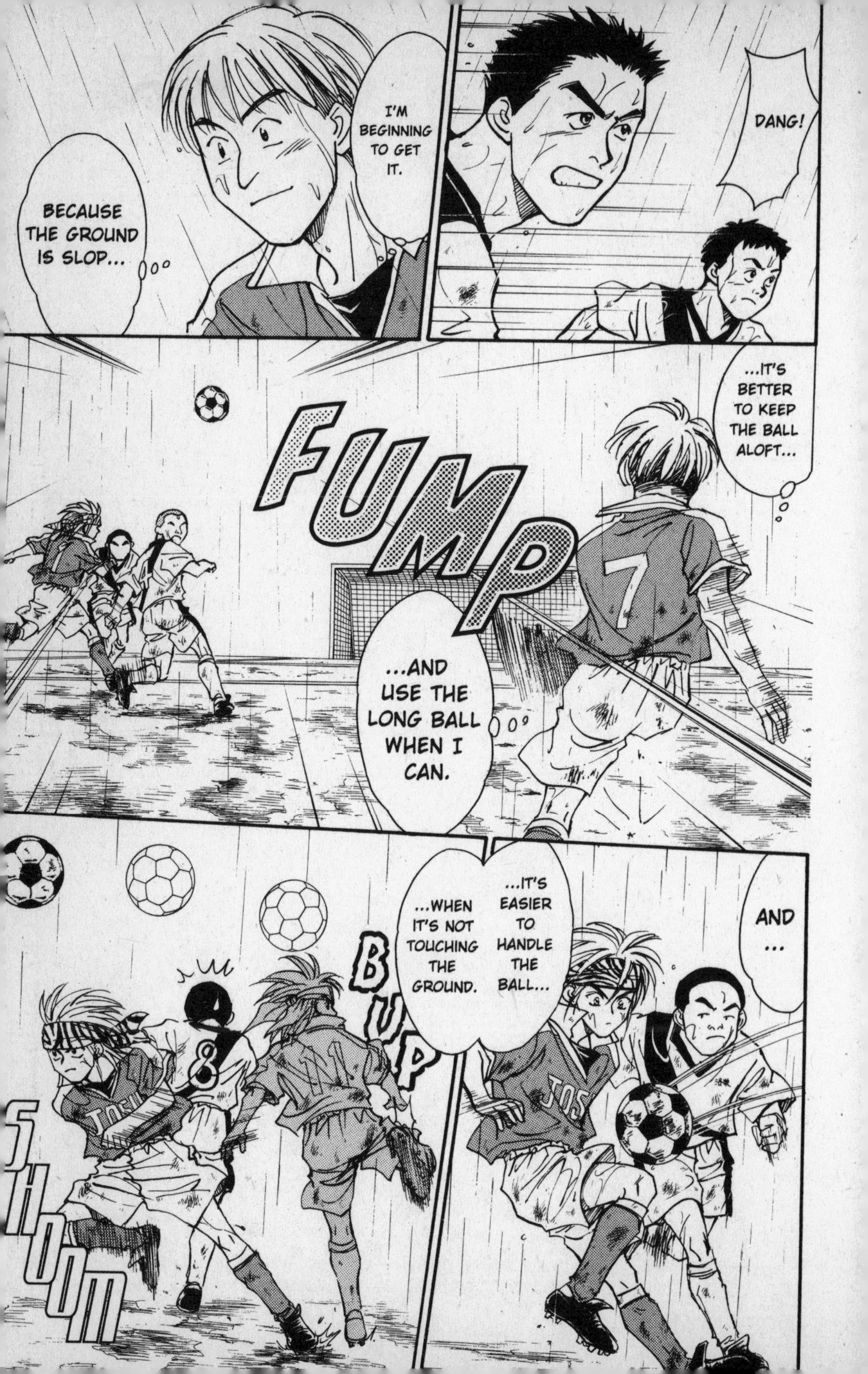
DANG!
I'M BEGINNING TO GET IT.
BECAUSE THE GROUND IS SLOP...
...IT'S BETTER TO KEEP THE BALL ALOFT...
FUMP
...AND USE THE LONG BALL WHEN I CAN.
AND ...
...IT'S EASIER TO HANDLE THE BALL...
...WHEN IT'S NOT TOUCHING THE GROUND.
BUP
SHOOM

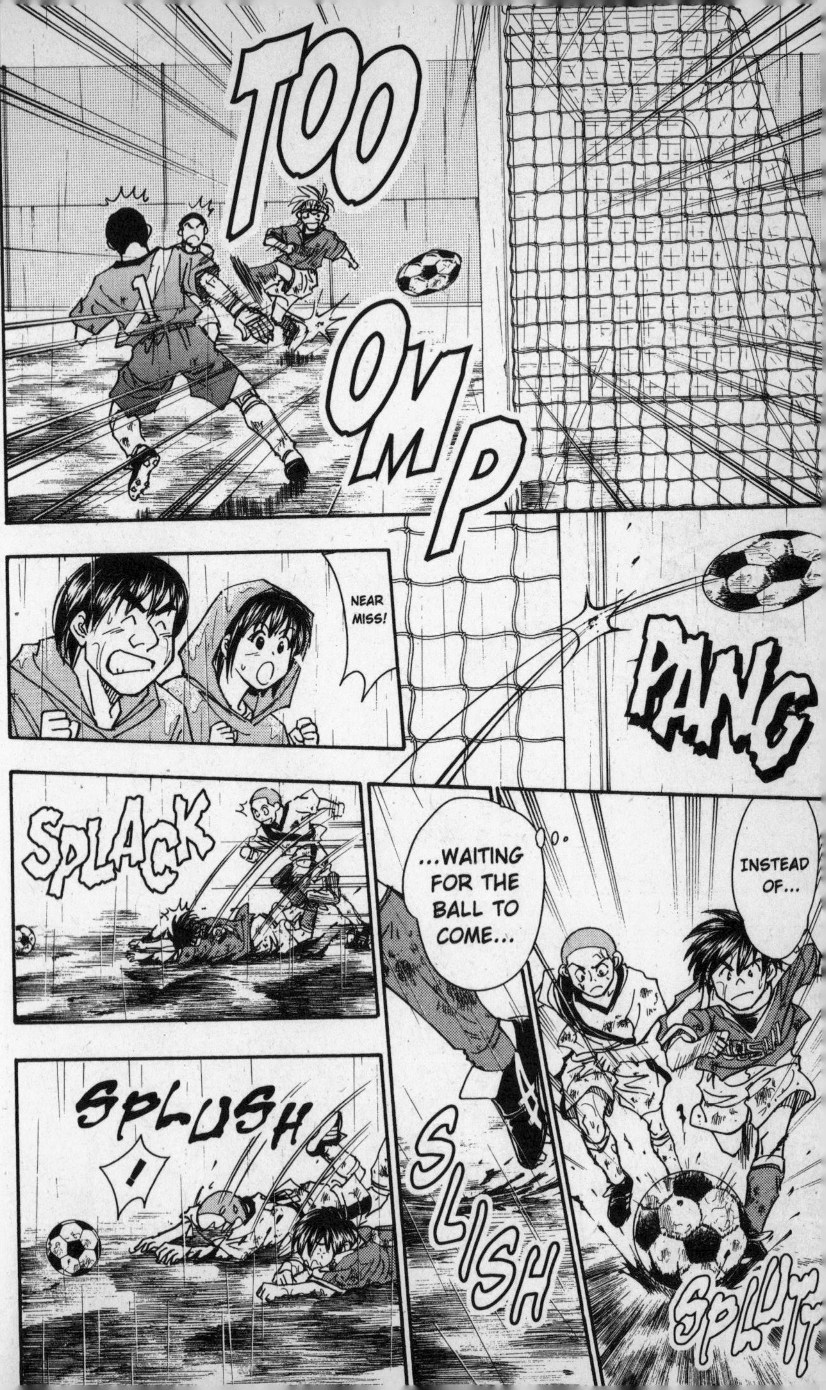
TOOOMP
PANG
NEAR MISS!
INSTEAD OF...
...WAITING FOR THE BALL TO COME...
SLISH
SPLUT
SPLACK
SPLUSH
!

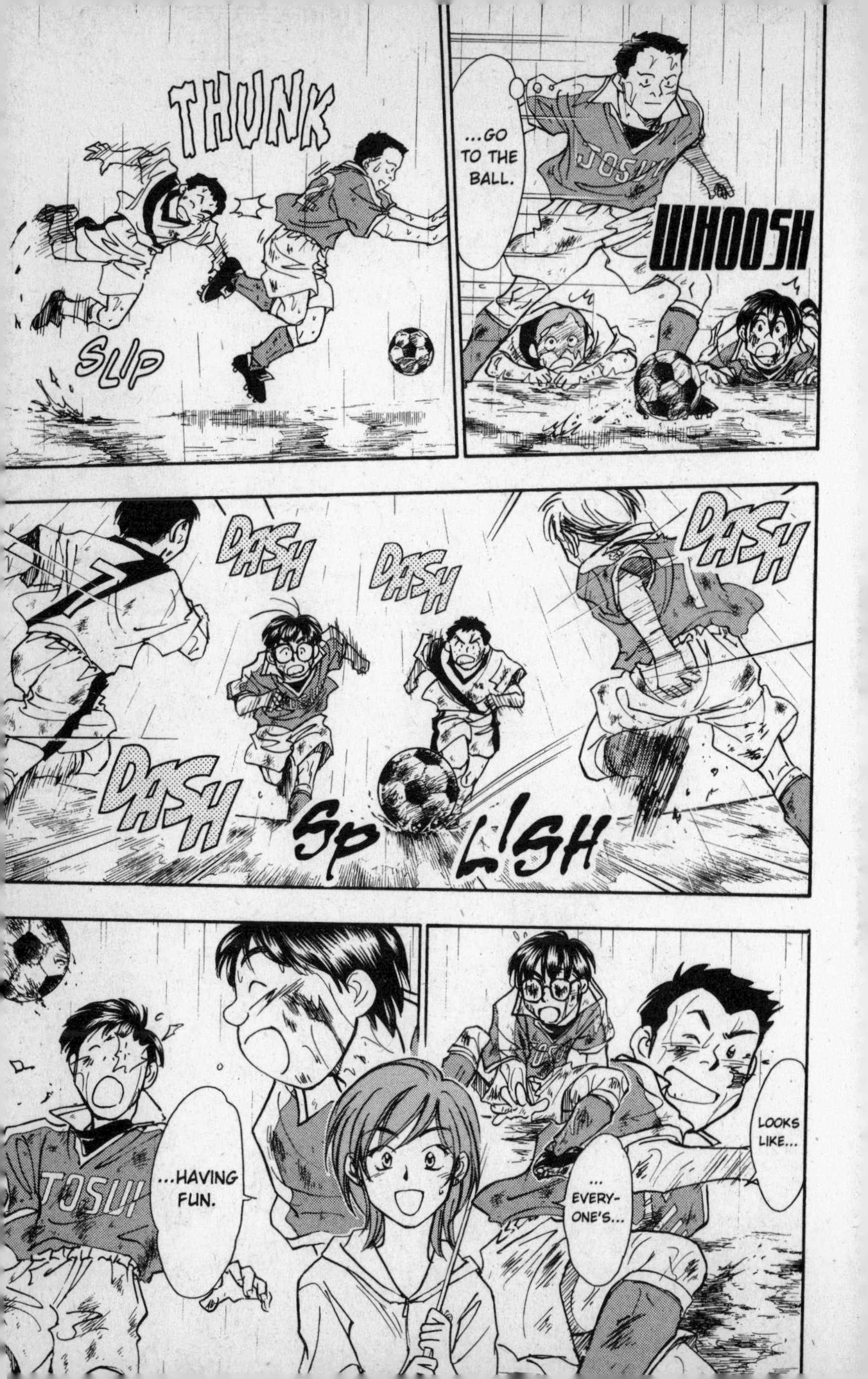
...GO TO THE BALL.
WHOOSH
THUNK
SLIP
DASH
DASH
DASH
SPLISH
DASH
LOOKS LIKE...
...EVERY-ONE'S...
...HAVING FUN.

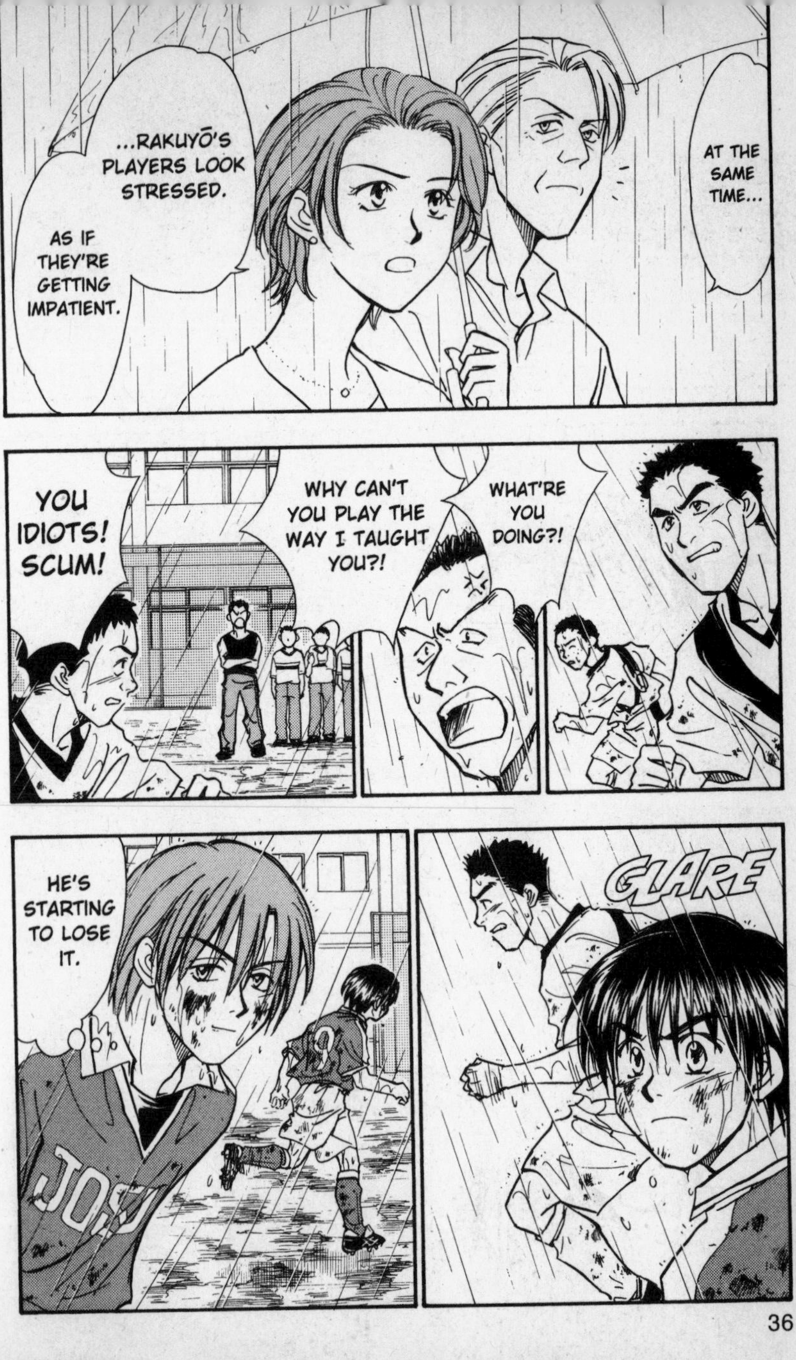
AT THE SAME TIME...
...RAKUYŌ'S PLAYERS LOOK STRESSED.
AS IF THEY'RE GETTING IMPATIENT.
WHAT'RE YOU DOING?!
WHY CAN'T YOU PLAY THE WAY I TAUGHT YOU?!
YOU IDIOTS! SCUM!
GLARE
HE'S STARTING TO LOSE IT.

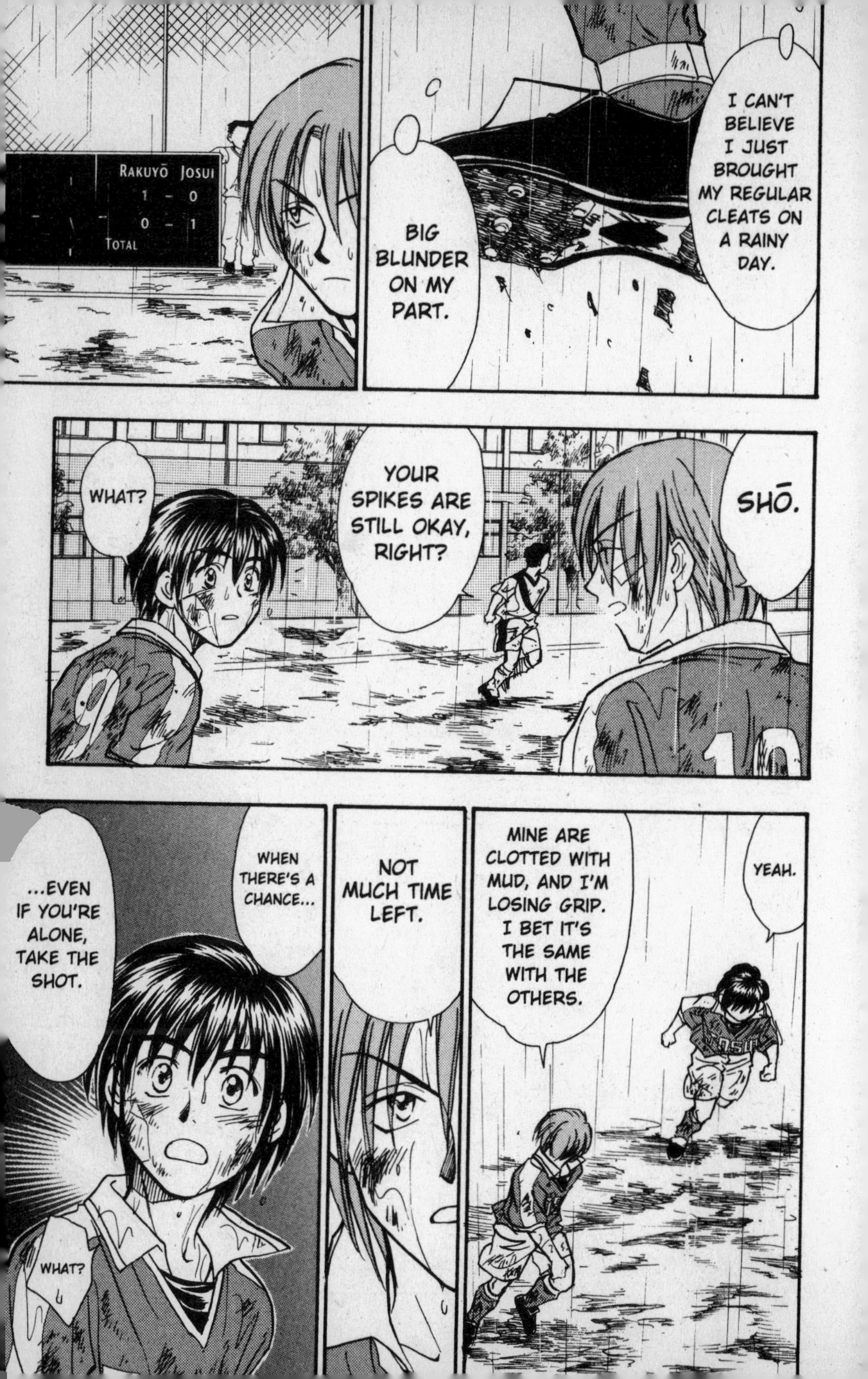
I CAN'T BELIEVE I JUST BROUGHT MY REGULAR CLEATS ON A RAINY DAY.
BIG BLUNDER ON MY PART.
RAKUYŌ JOSUI
1 - 0
0 - 1
TOTAL
SHŌ.
YOUR SPIKES ARE STILL OKAY, RIGHT?
WHAT?
YEAH.
MINE ARE CLOTTED WITH MUD, AND I'M LOSING GRIP. I BET IT'S THE SAME WITH THE OTHERS.
NOT MUCH TIME LEFT.
WHEN THERE'S A CHANCE...
...EVEN IF YOU'RE ALONE, TAKE THE SHOT.
WHAT?

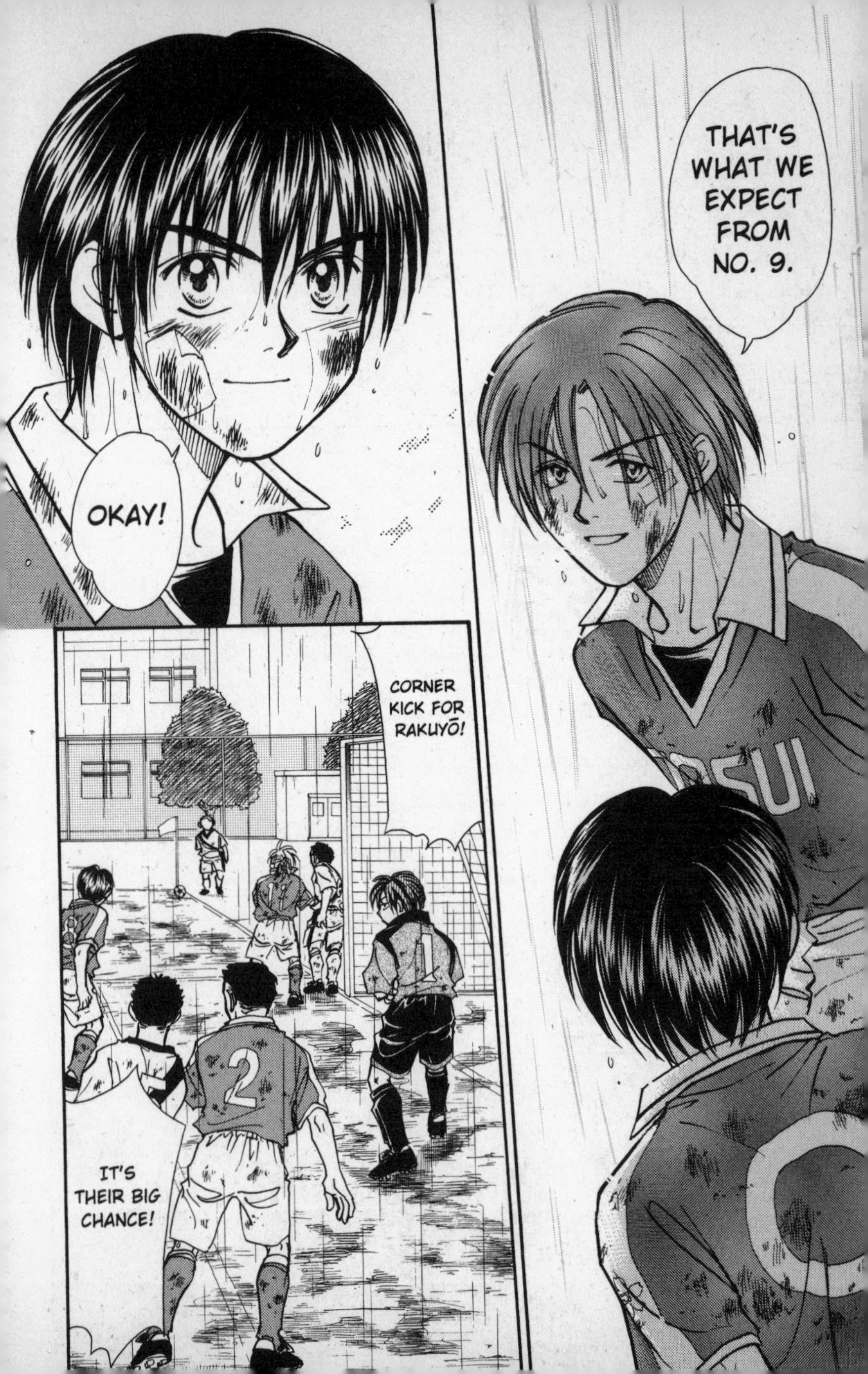
THAT'S WHAT WE EXPECT FROM NO. 9.
OKAY!
CORNER KICK FOR RAKUYŌ!
IT'S THEIR BIG CHANCE!

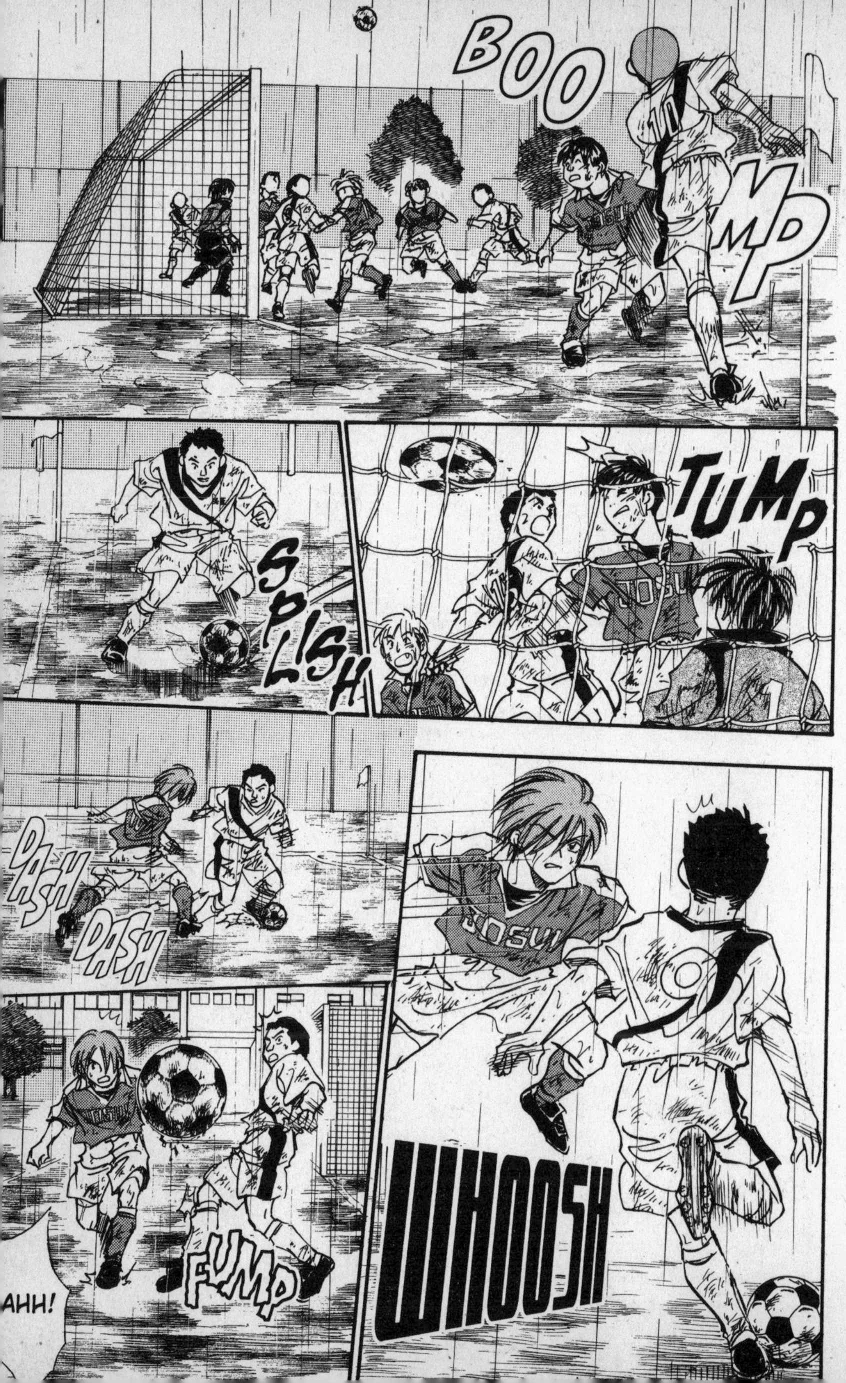
BOOMP
TUMP
SPLISH
WHOOSH
DASH
DASH
FUMP
AHH!

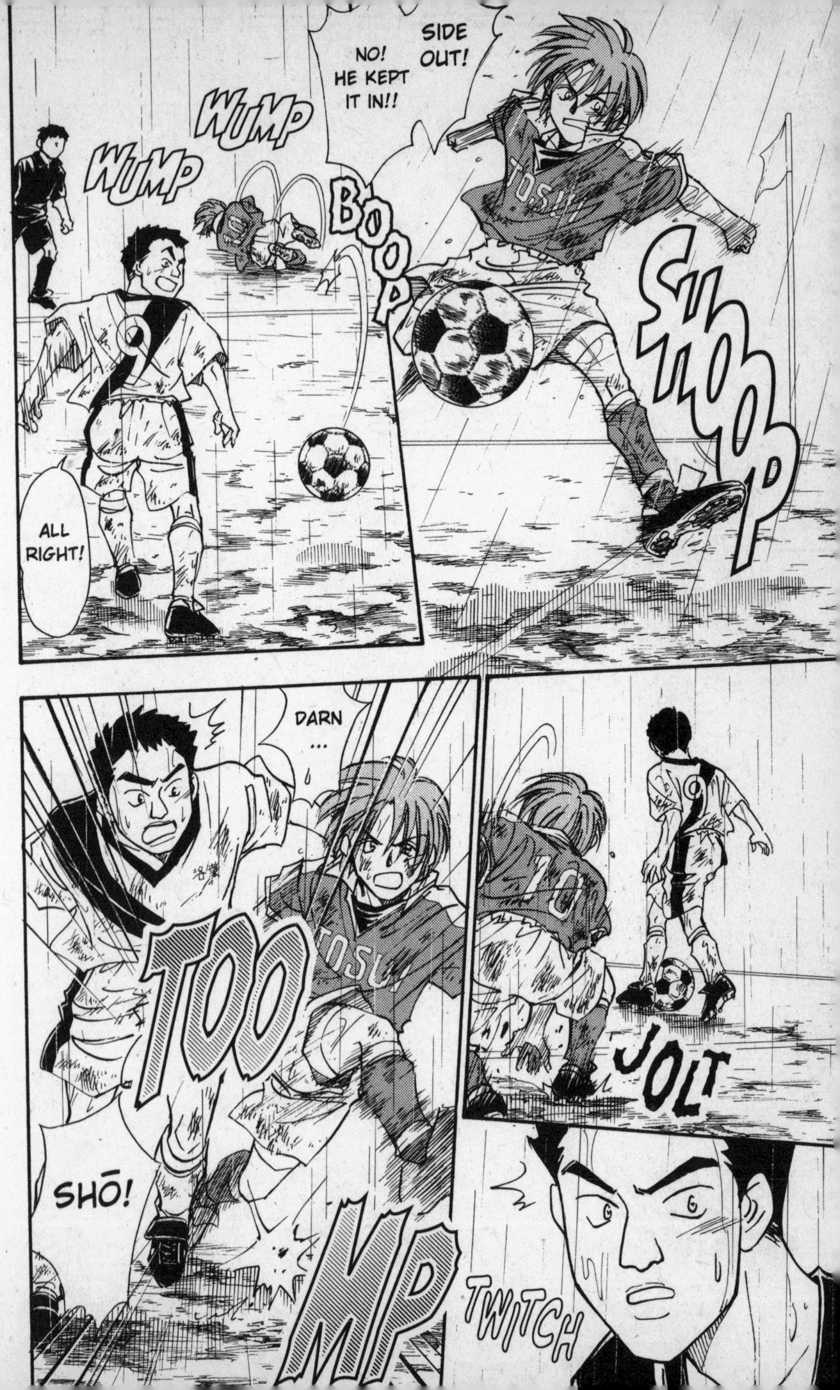
SIDE OUT!
NO! HE KEPT IT IN!!
SHOOP
BOOP
WUMP
WUMP
ALL RIGHT!
JOLT
TWITCH
DARN ...
TOOMP
SHŌ!

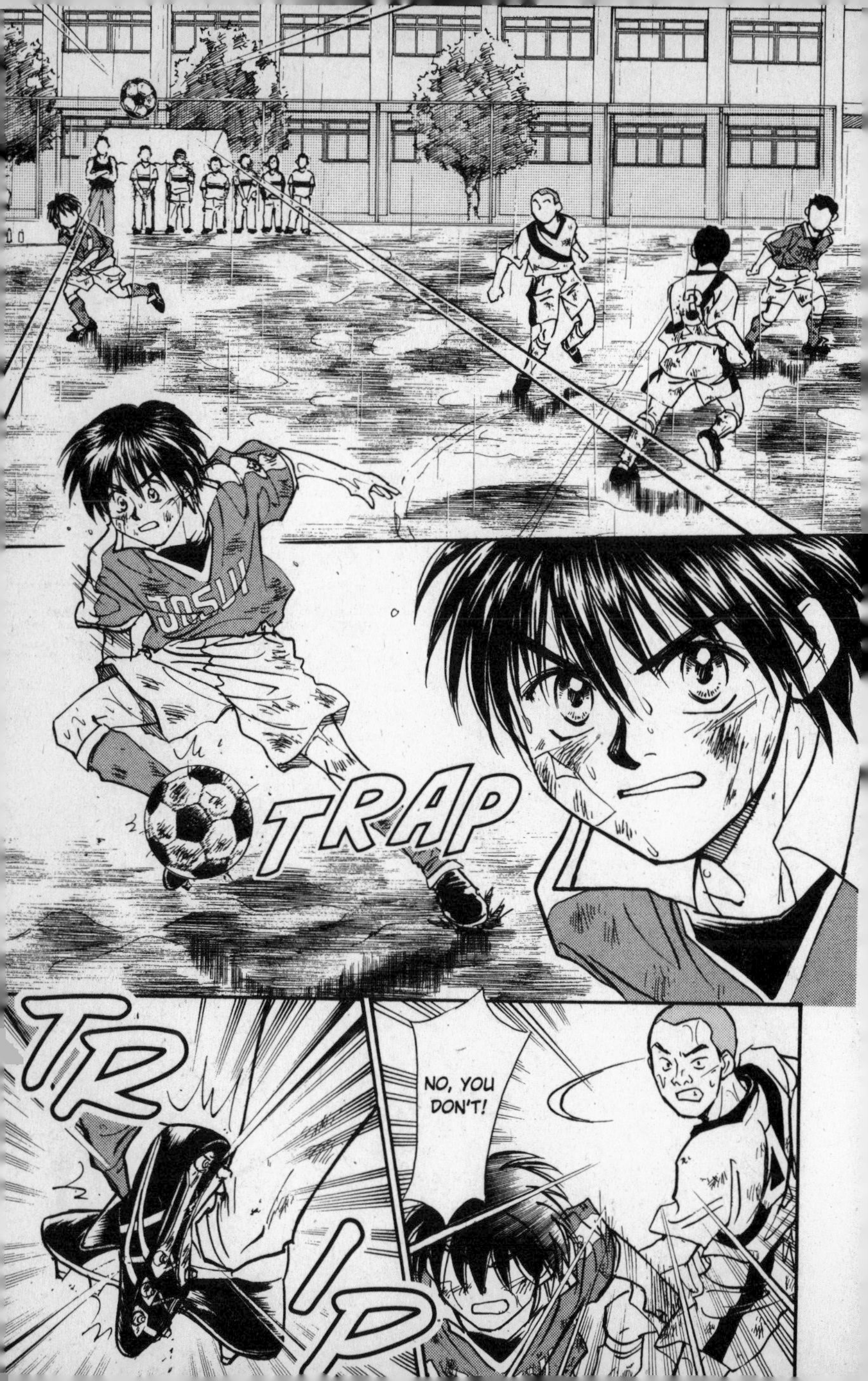
TRAP
NO, YOU DON'T!
TRIP

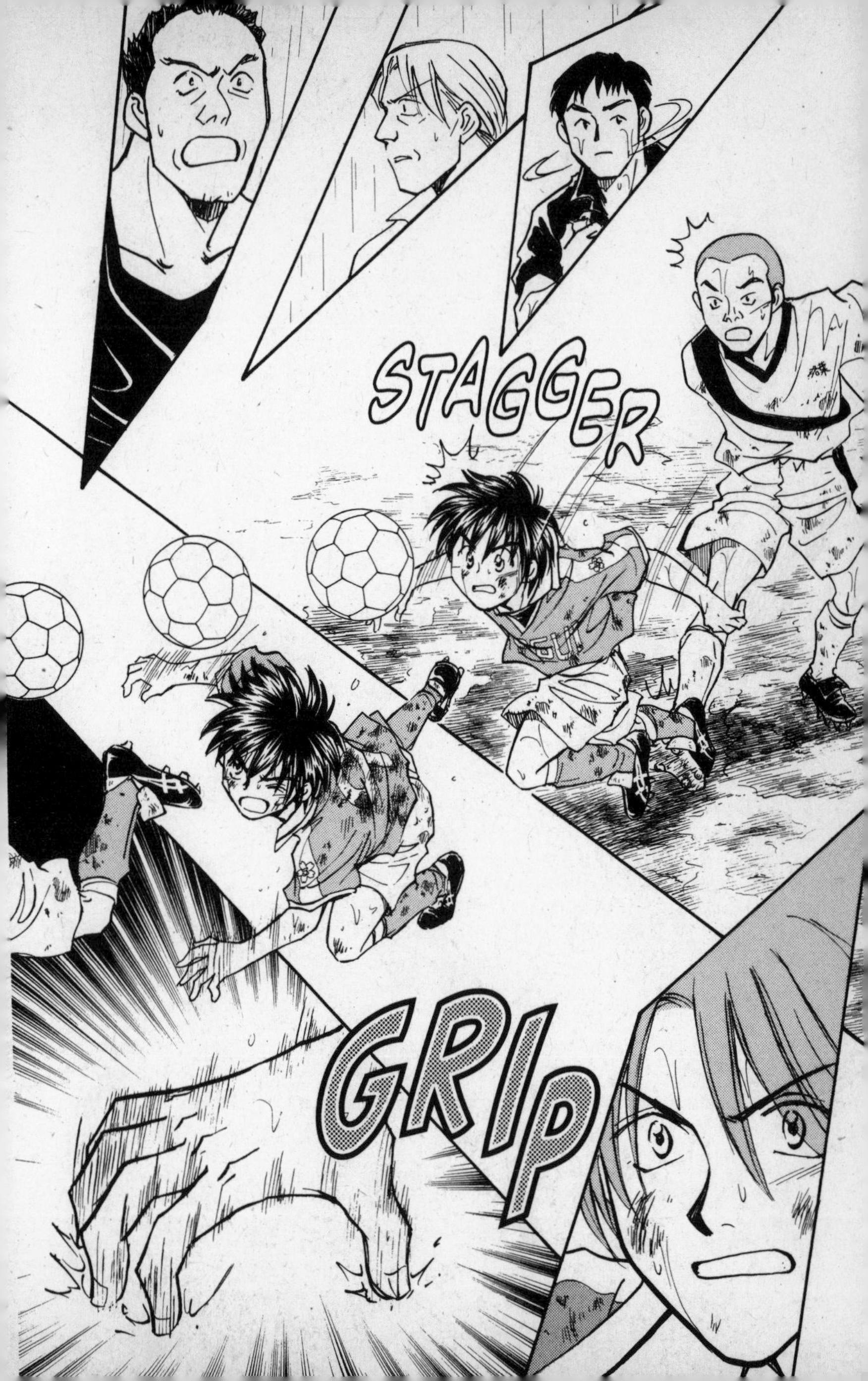
STAGGER
GRIP

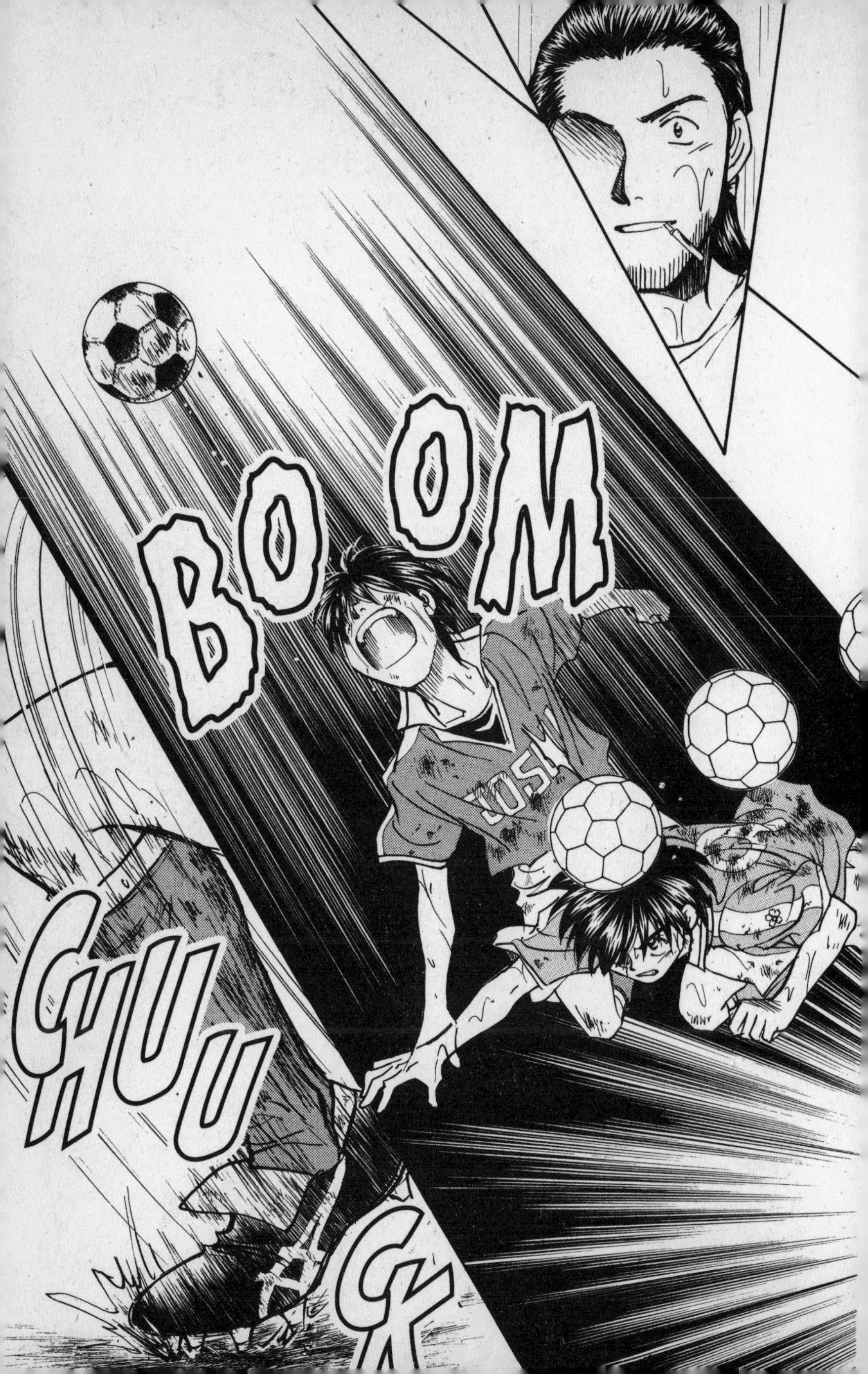
BOOM
CHUU

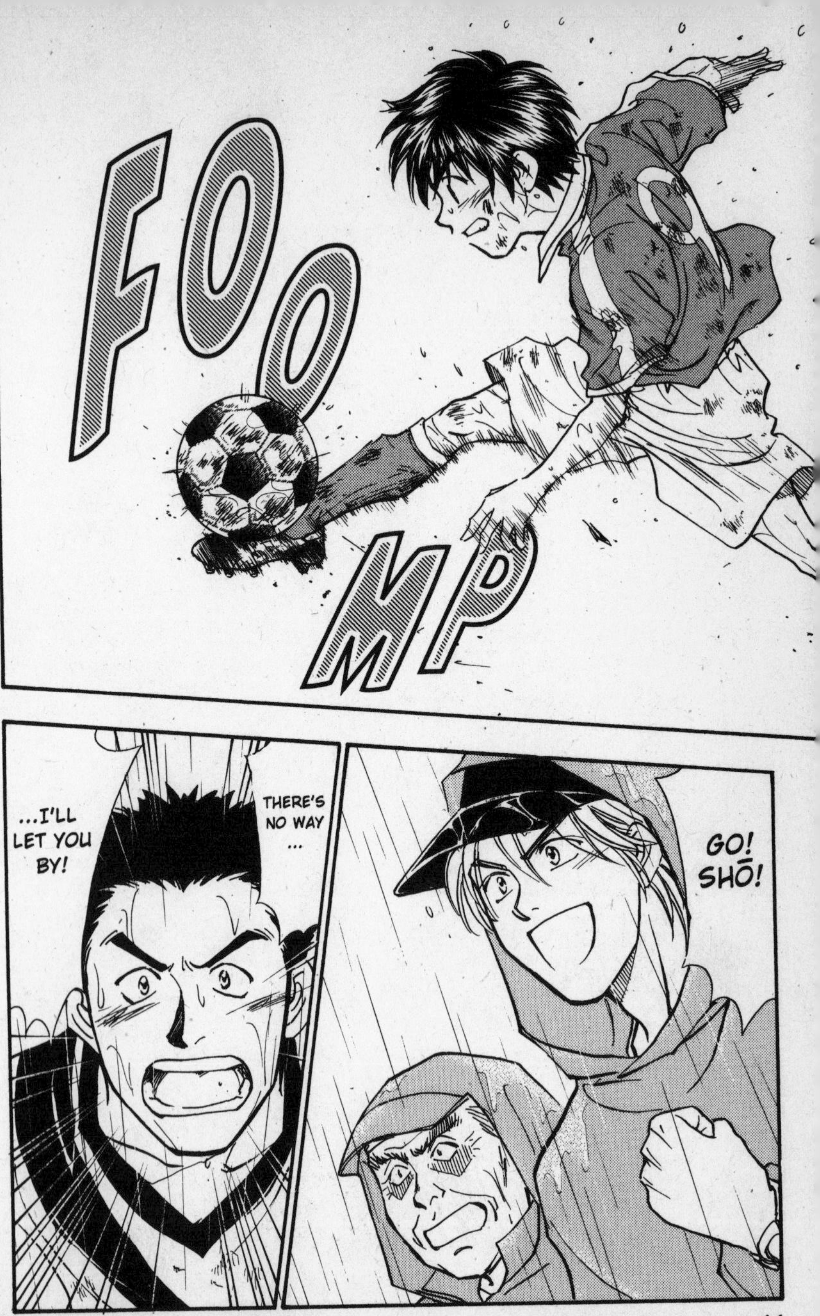
FOOMP
GO! SHŌ!
THERE'S NO WAY ...
...I'LL LET YOU BY!

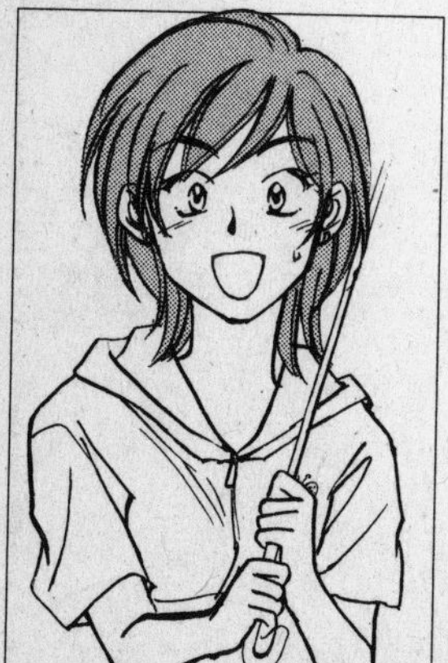

WHISTLE!

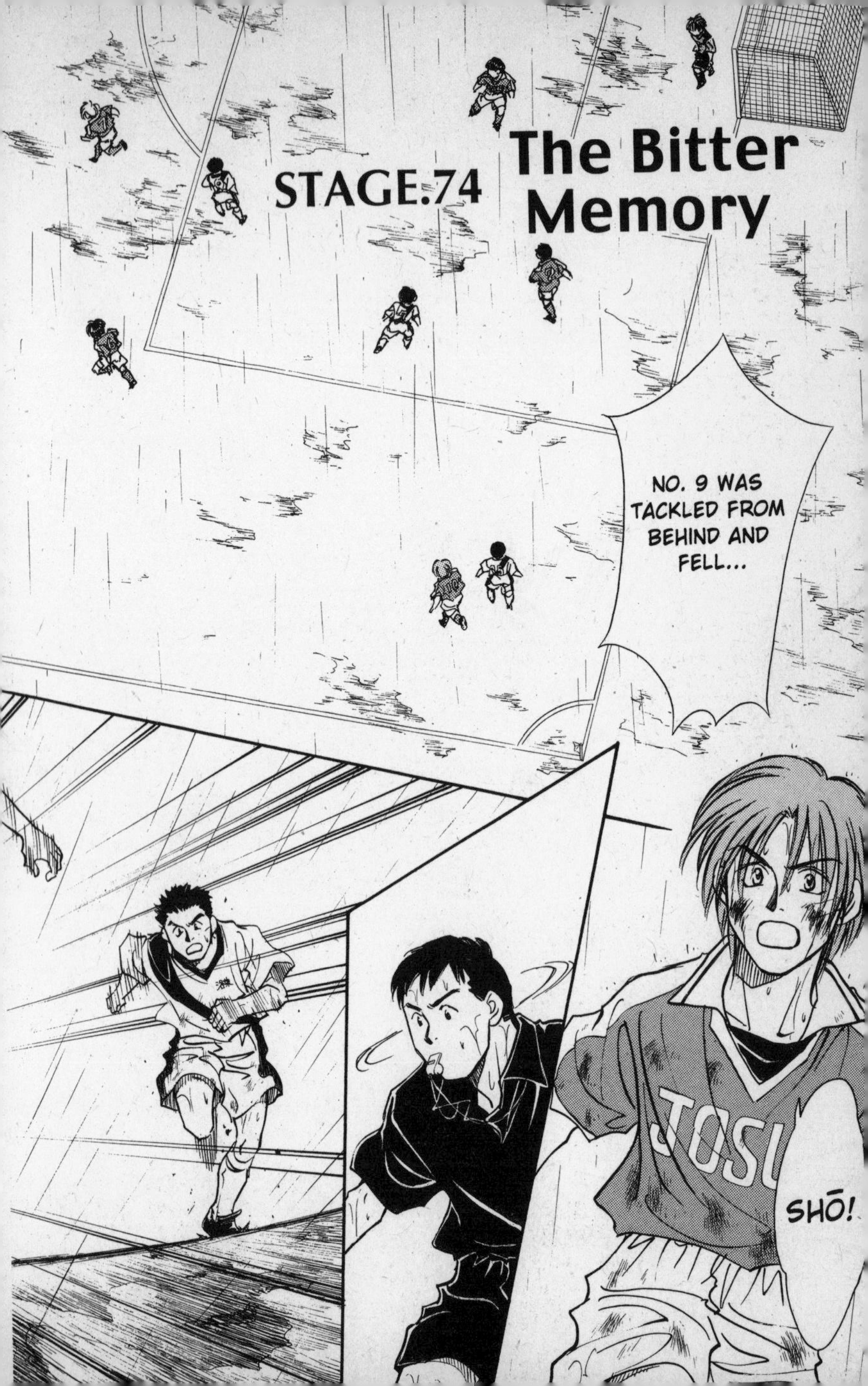
STAGE.74
The Bitter Memory
NO. 9 WAS TACKLED FROM BEHIND AND FELL...
SHŌ!

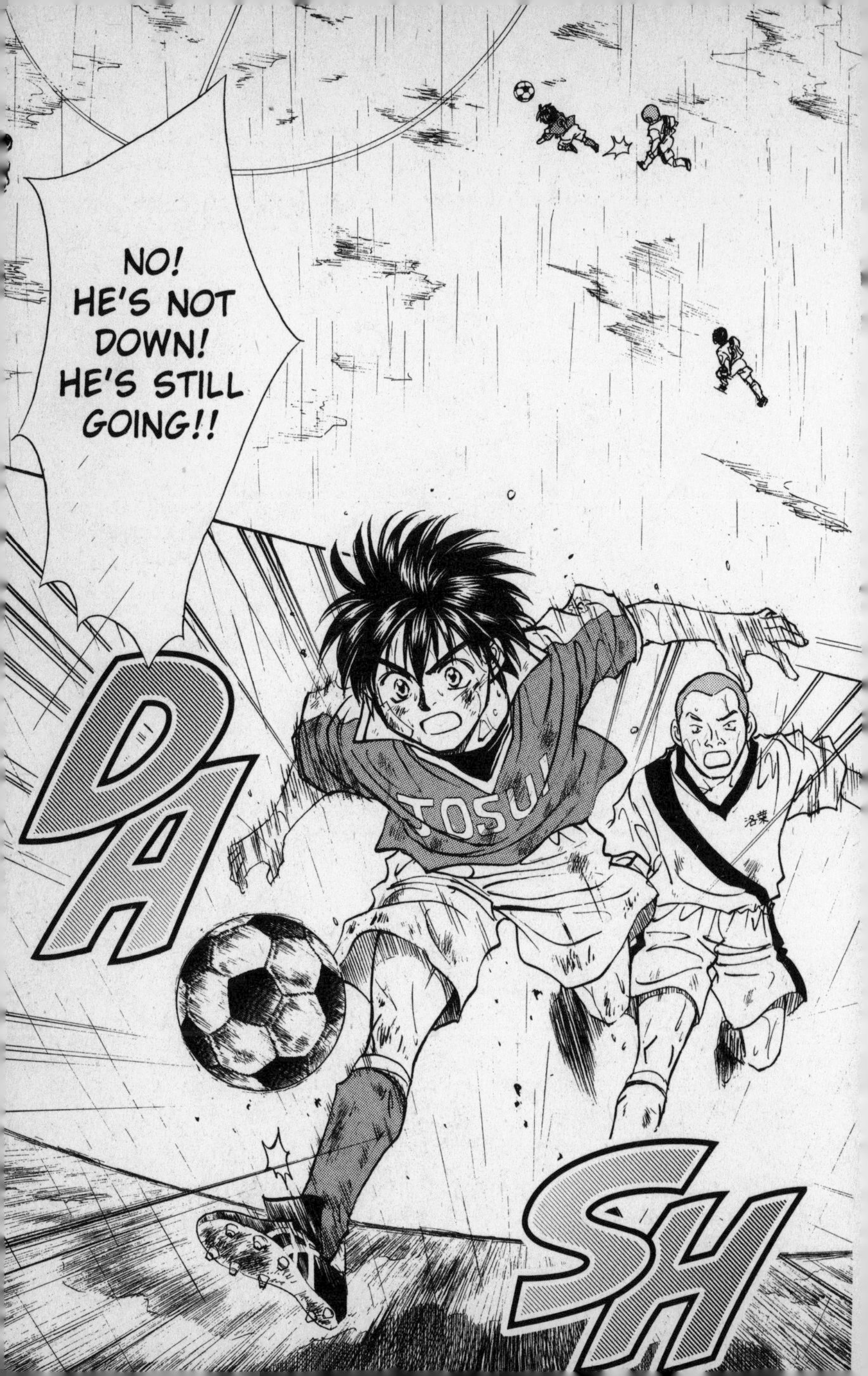
NO! HE'S NOT DOWN! HE'S STILL GOING!!
DA
SH
TOSU

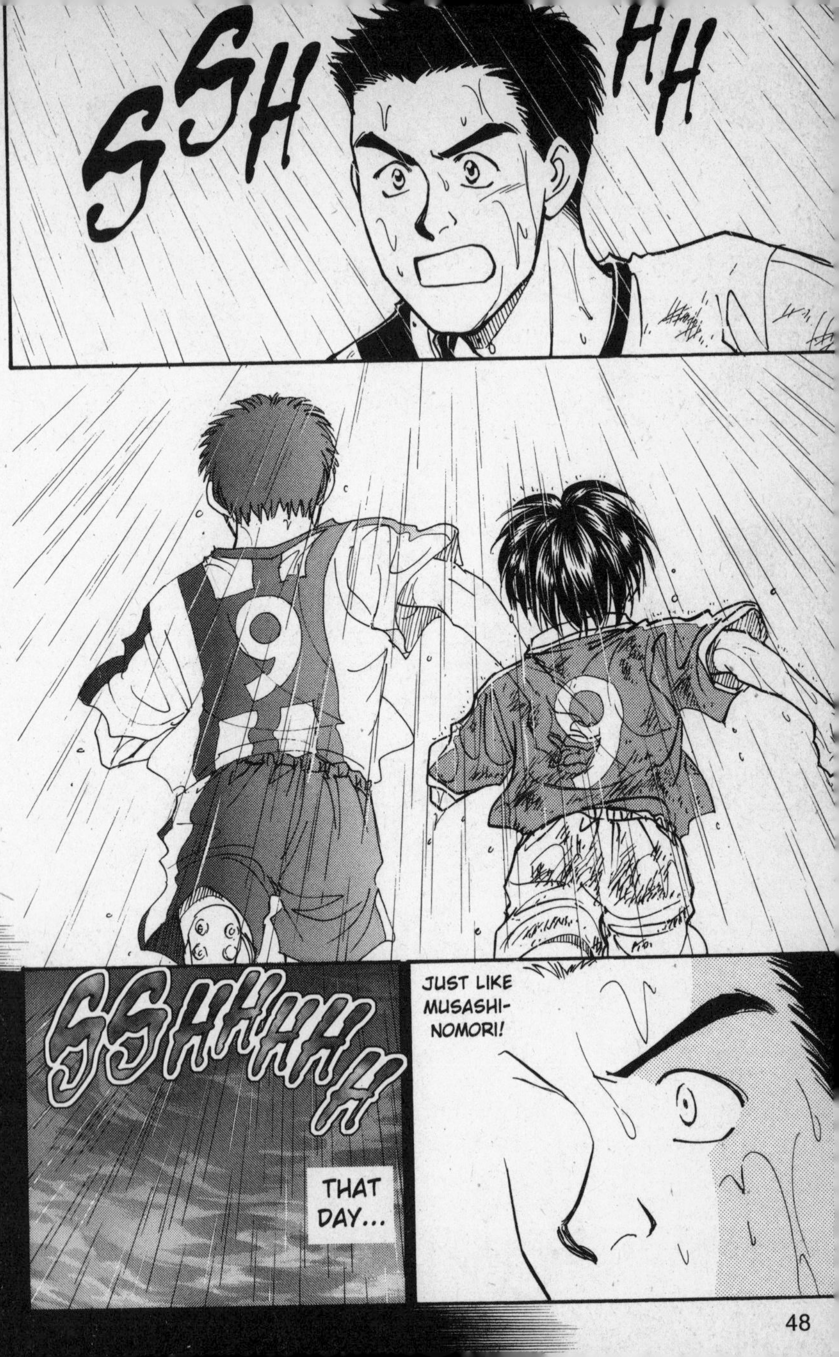
SSH HH
JUST LIKE MUSASHI-NOMORI!
SSHHHHH
THAT DAY...

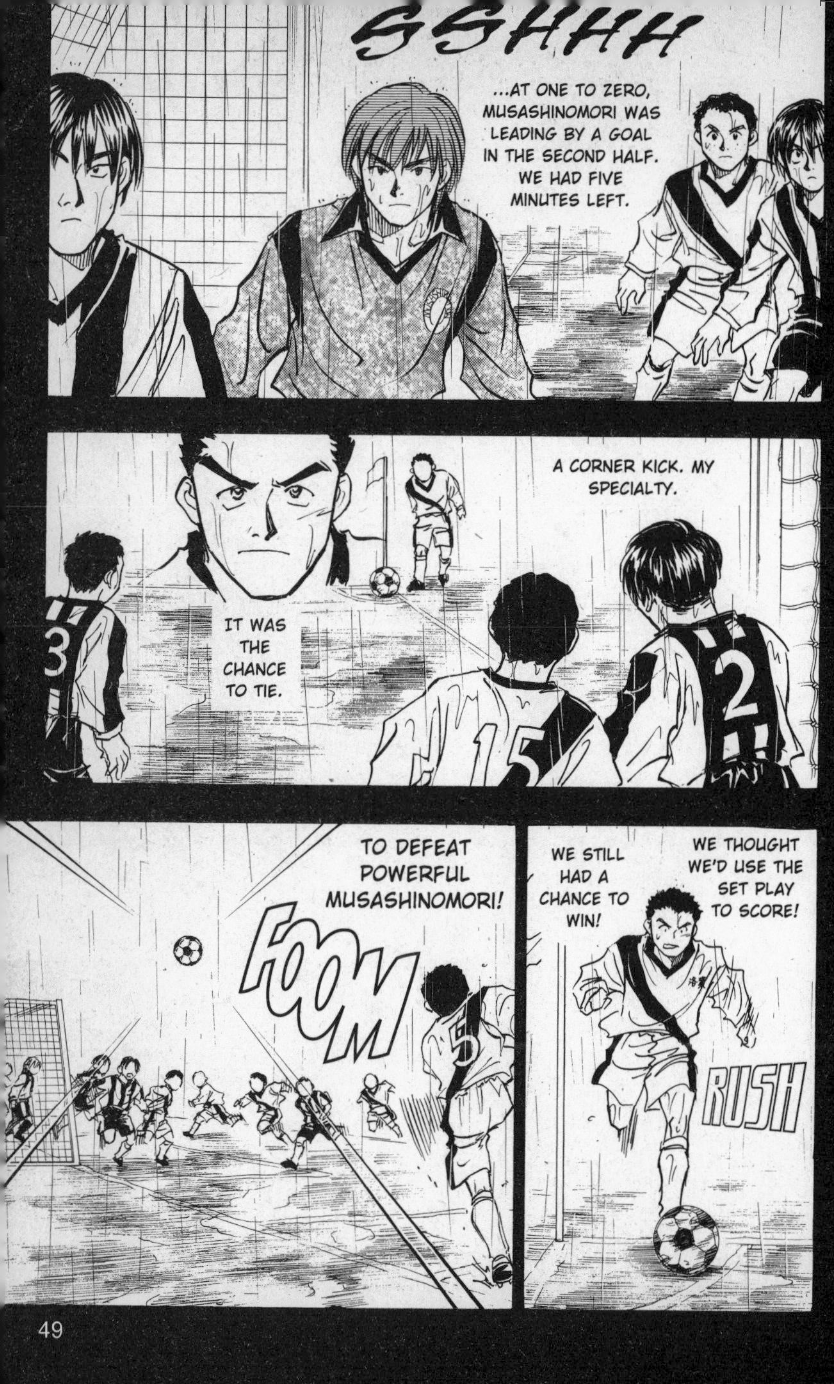
SSHHH
...AT ONE TO ZERO, MUSASHINOMORI WAS LEADING BY A GOAL IN THE SECOND HALF. WE HAD FIVE MINUTES LEFT.
A CORNER KICK. MY SPECIALTY.
IT WAS THE CHANCE TO TIE.
WE THOUGHT WE'D USE THE SET PLAY TO SCORE!
WE STILL HAD A CHANCE TO WIN!
RUSH
TO DEFEAT POWERFUL MUSASHINOMORI!
FOOM

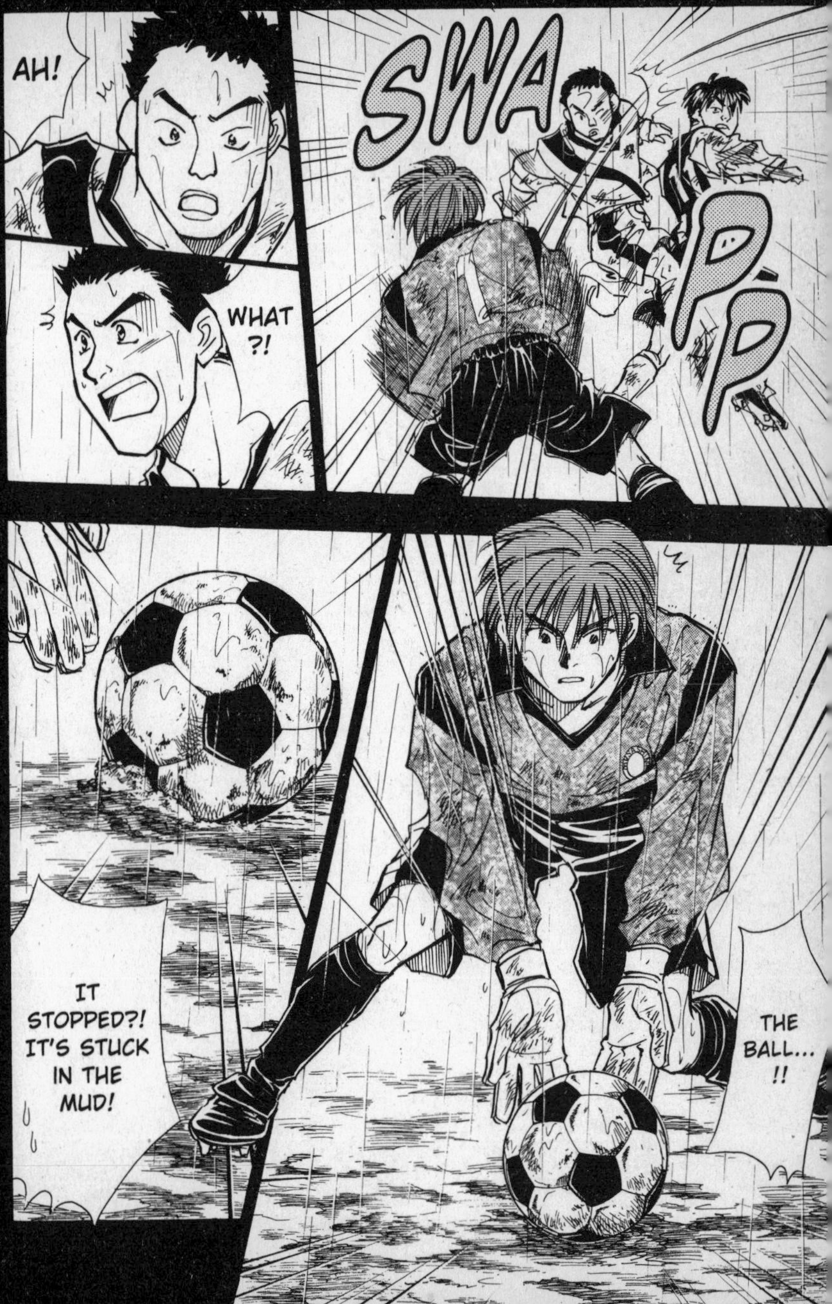
SWA
PP
AH!
WHAT ?!
THE BALL... !!
IT STOPPED?! IT'S STUCK IN THE MUD!

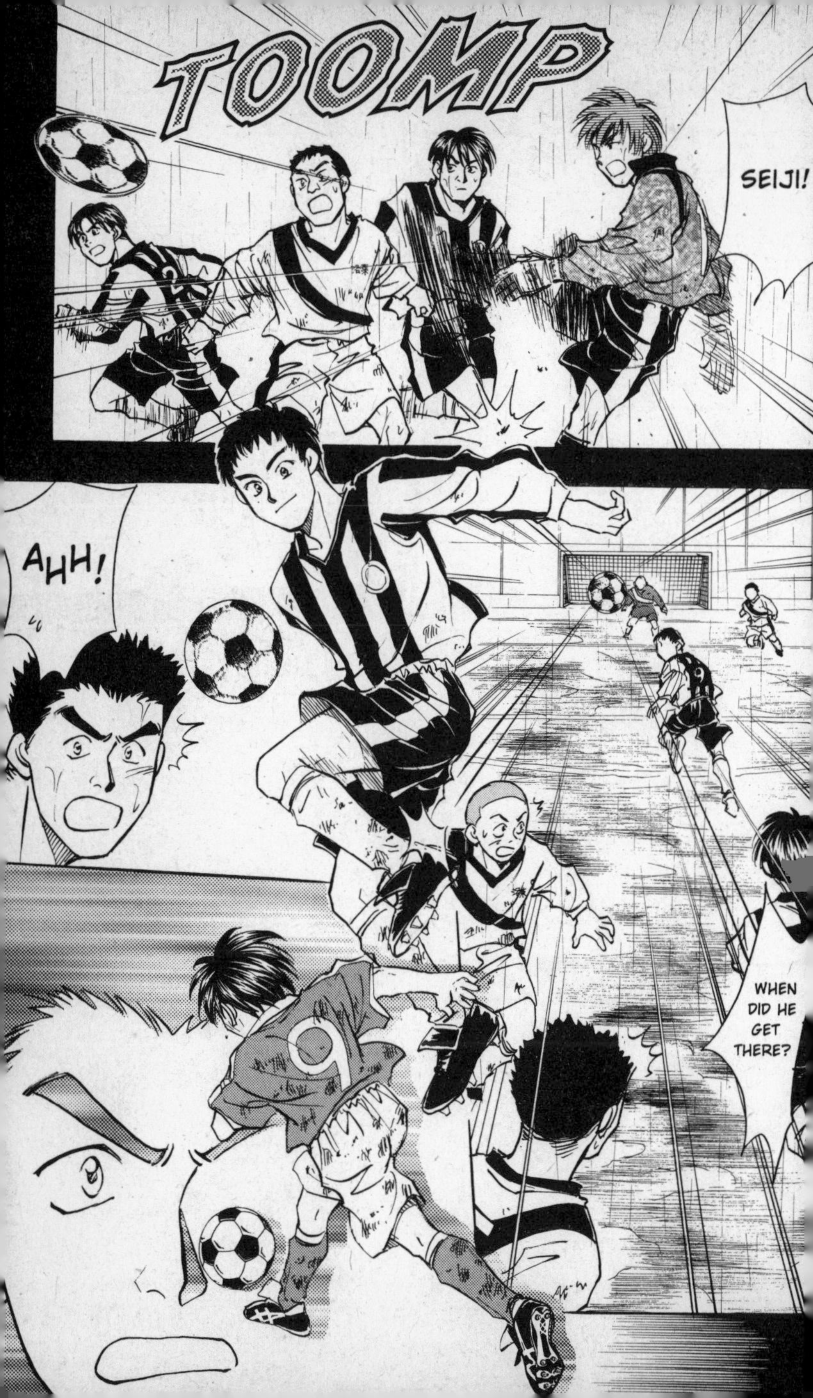
SEIJI!
TOOMP
AHH!
WHEN DID HE GET THERE?

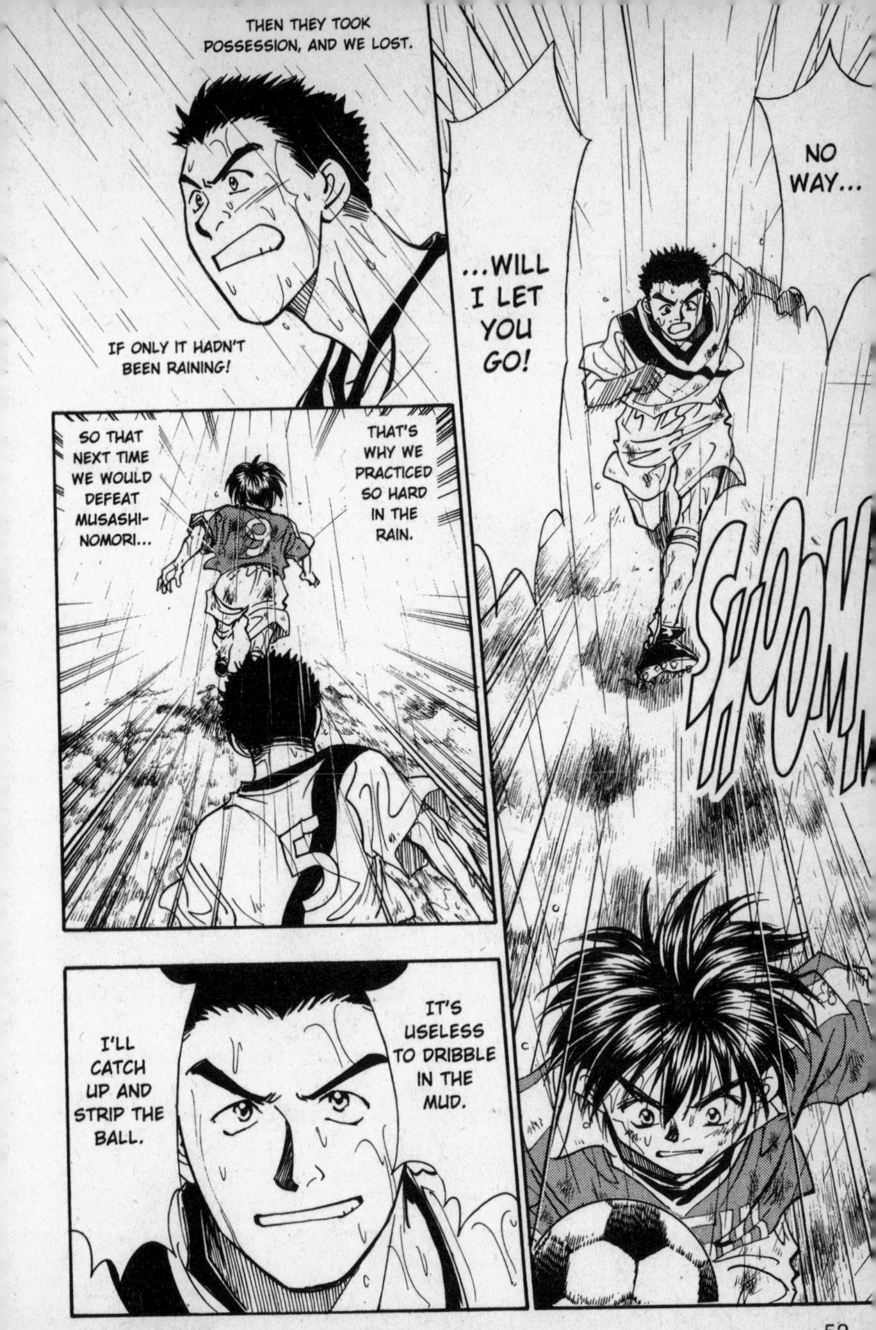
NO WAY...
...WILL I LET YOU GO!
SHOOM
THEN THEY TOOK POSSESSION, AND WE LOST.
IF ONLY IT HADN'T BEEN RAINING!
THAT'S WHY WE PRACTICED SO HARD IN THE RAIN.
SO THAT NEXT TIME WE WOULD DEFEAT MUSASHI-NOMORI...
IT'S USELESS TO DRIBBLE IN THE MUD.
I'LL CATCH UP AND STRIP THE BALL.

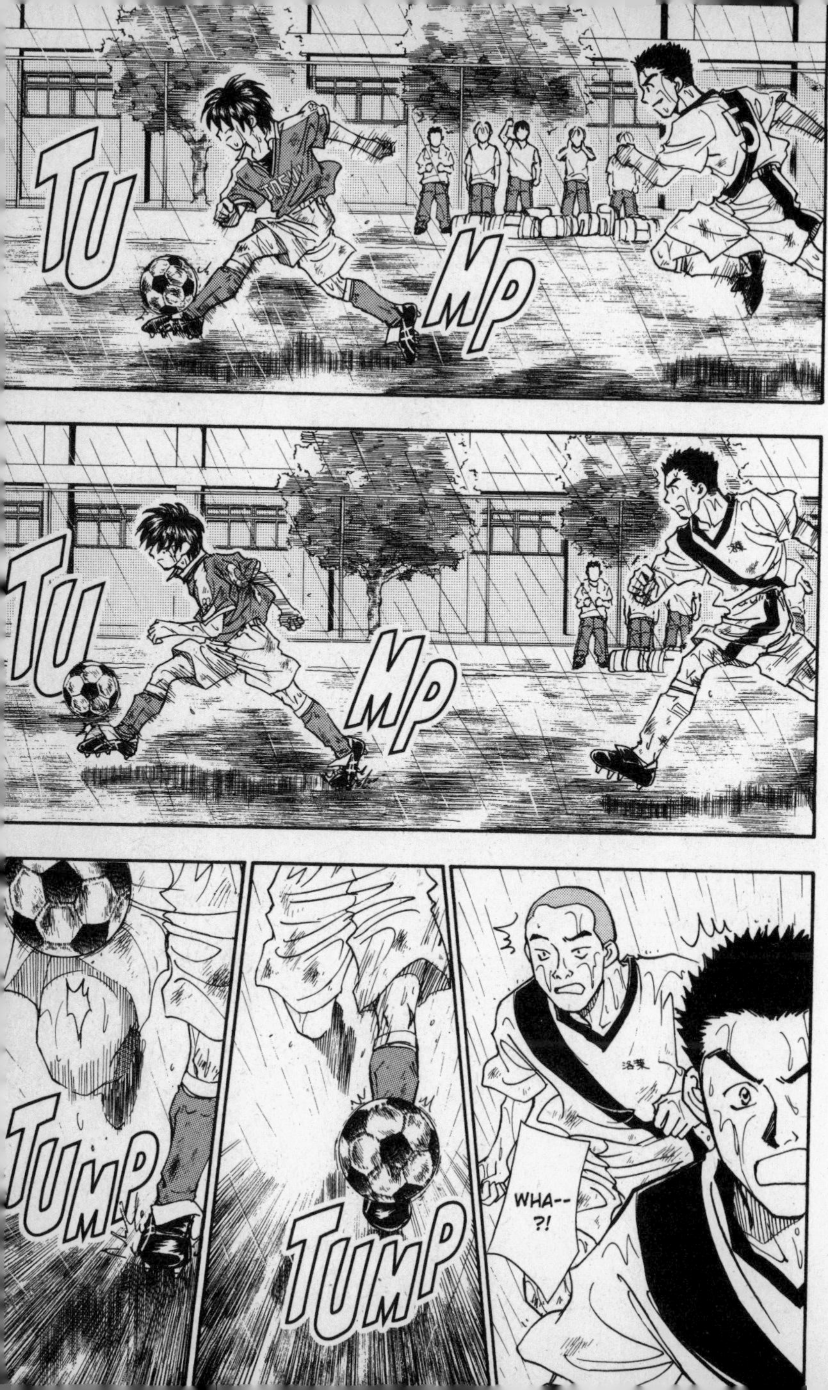
TU
MP
TU
MP
WHA-- ?!
TUMP
TUMP

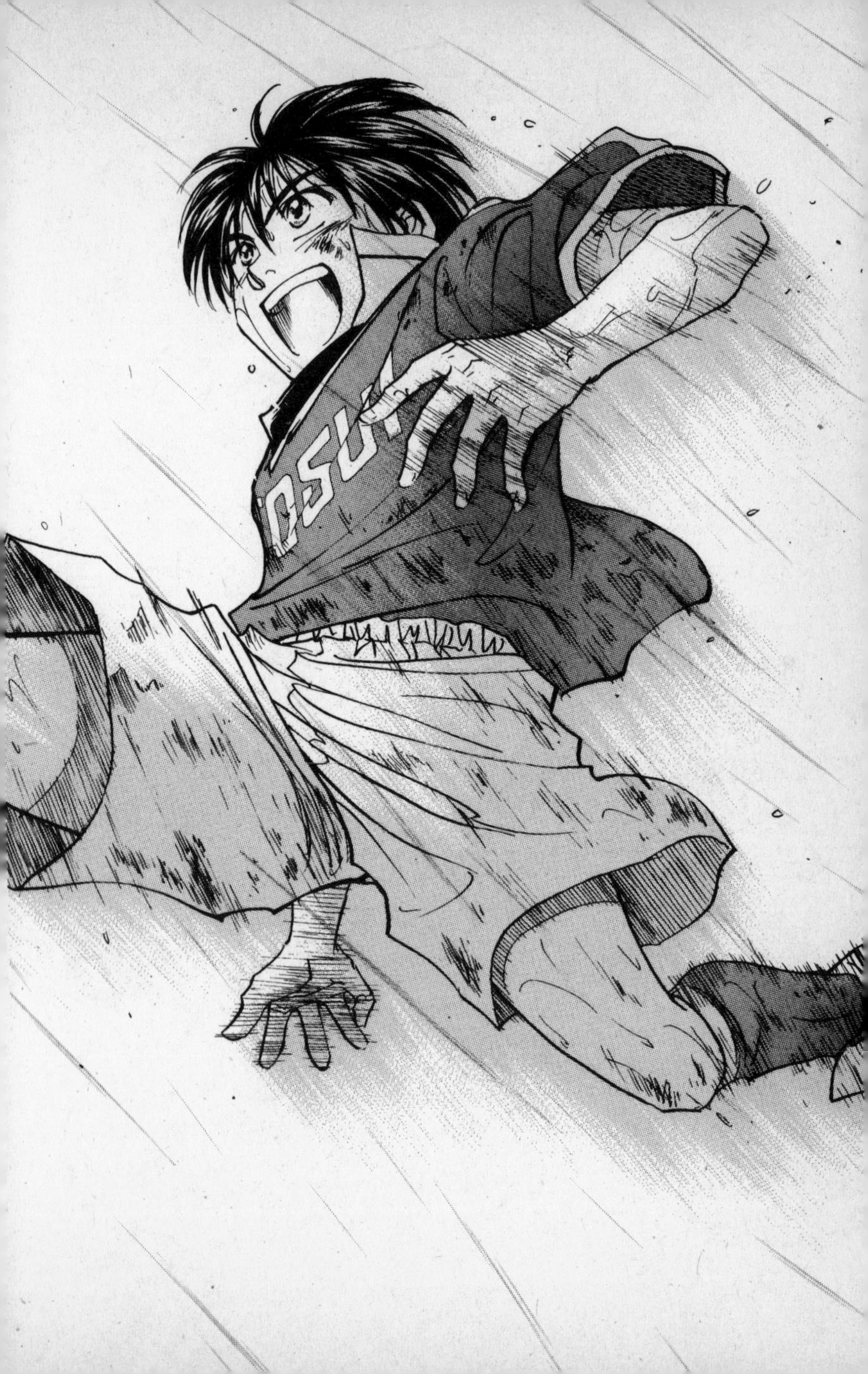

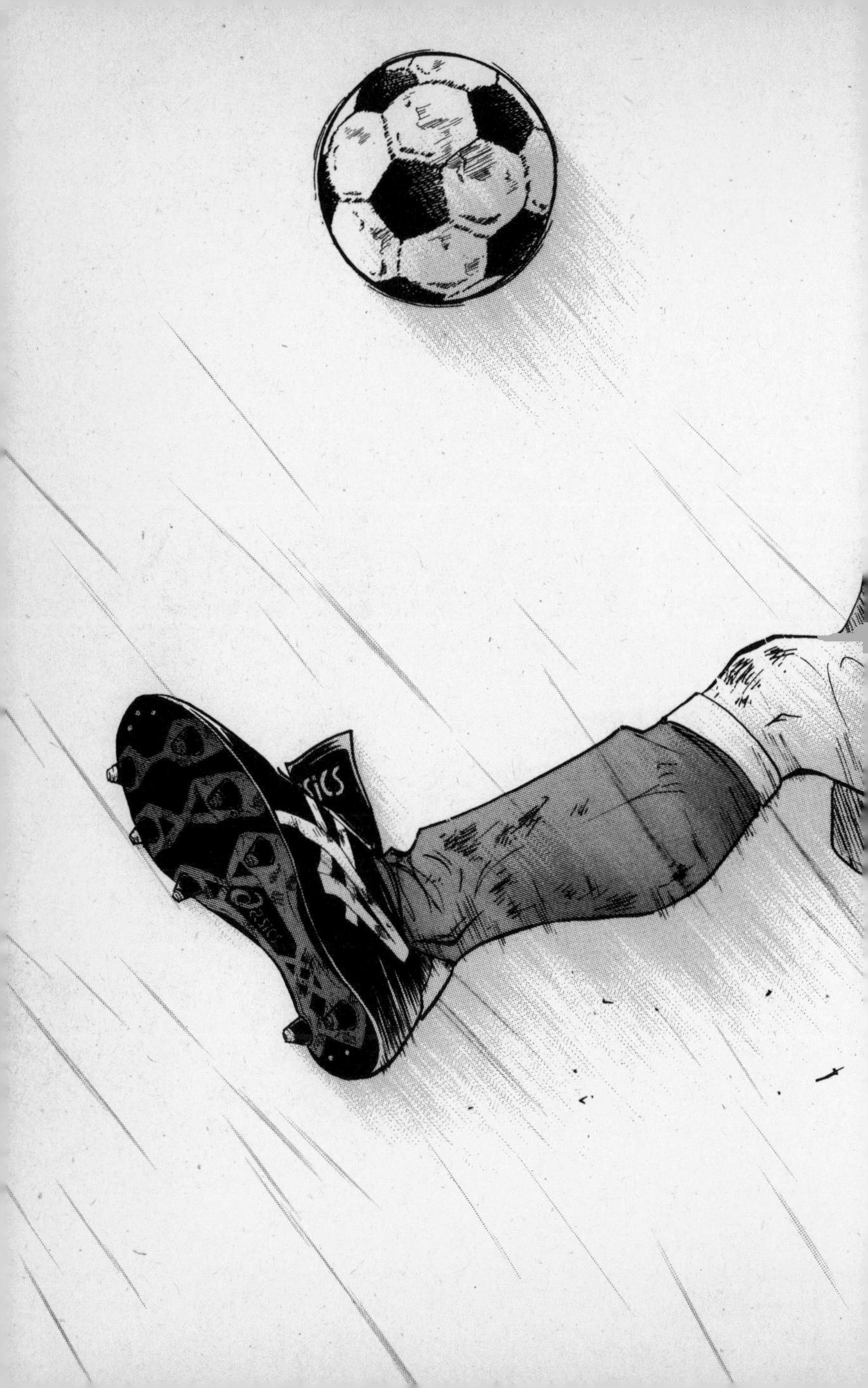

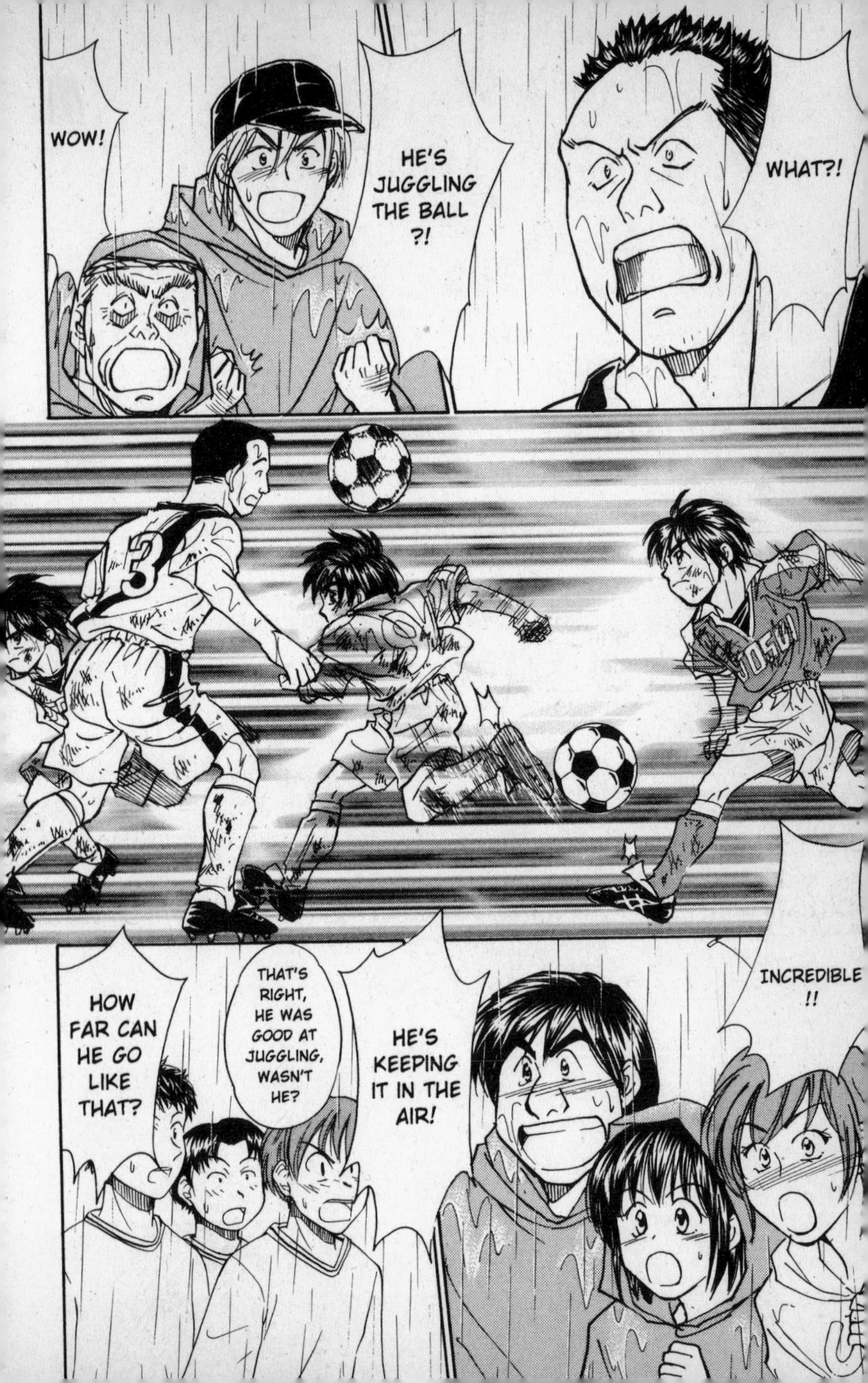
WHAT?!
HE'S JUGGLING THE BALL ?!
WOW!
INCREDIBLE !!
HE'S KEEPING IT IN THE AIR!
THAT'S RIGHT, HE WAS GOOD AT JUGGLING, WASN'T HE?
HOW FAR CAN HE GO LIKE THAT?

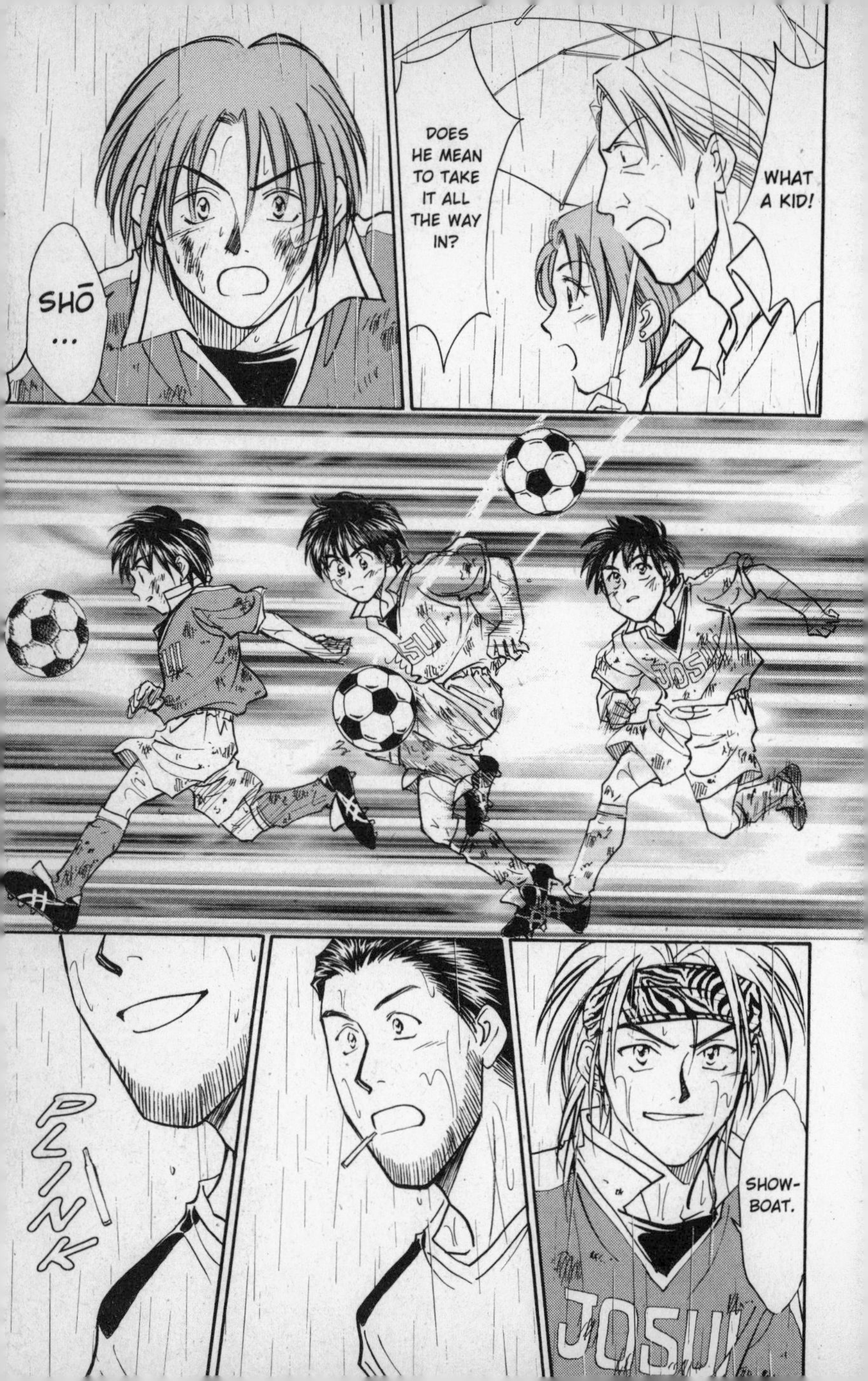
WHAT A KID!
DOES HE MEAN TO TAKE IT ALL THE WAY IN?
SHŌ ...
SHOW-BOAT.
PLINK

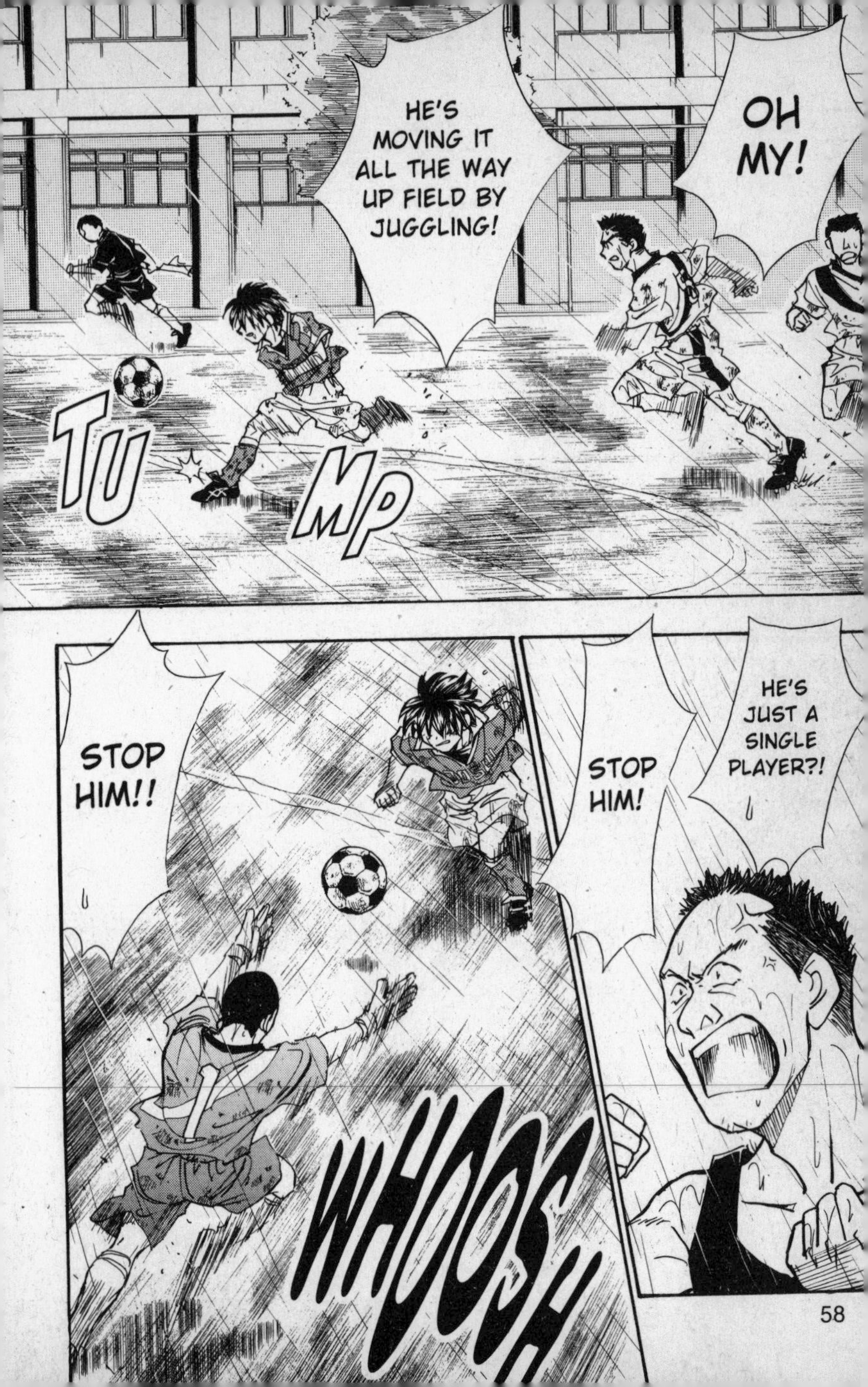
OH MY!
HE'S MOVING IT ALL THE WAY UP FIELD BY JUGGLING!
TUMP
HE'S JUST A SINGLE PLAYER?!
STOP HIM!
STOP HIM!!
WHOOSH

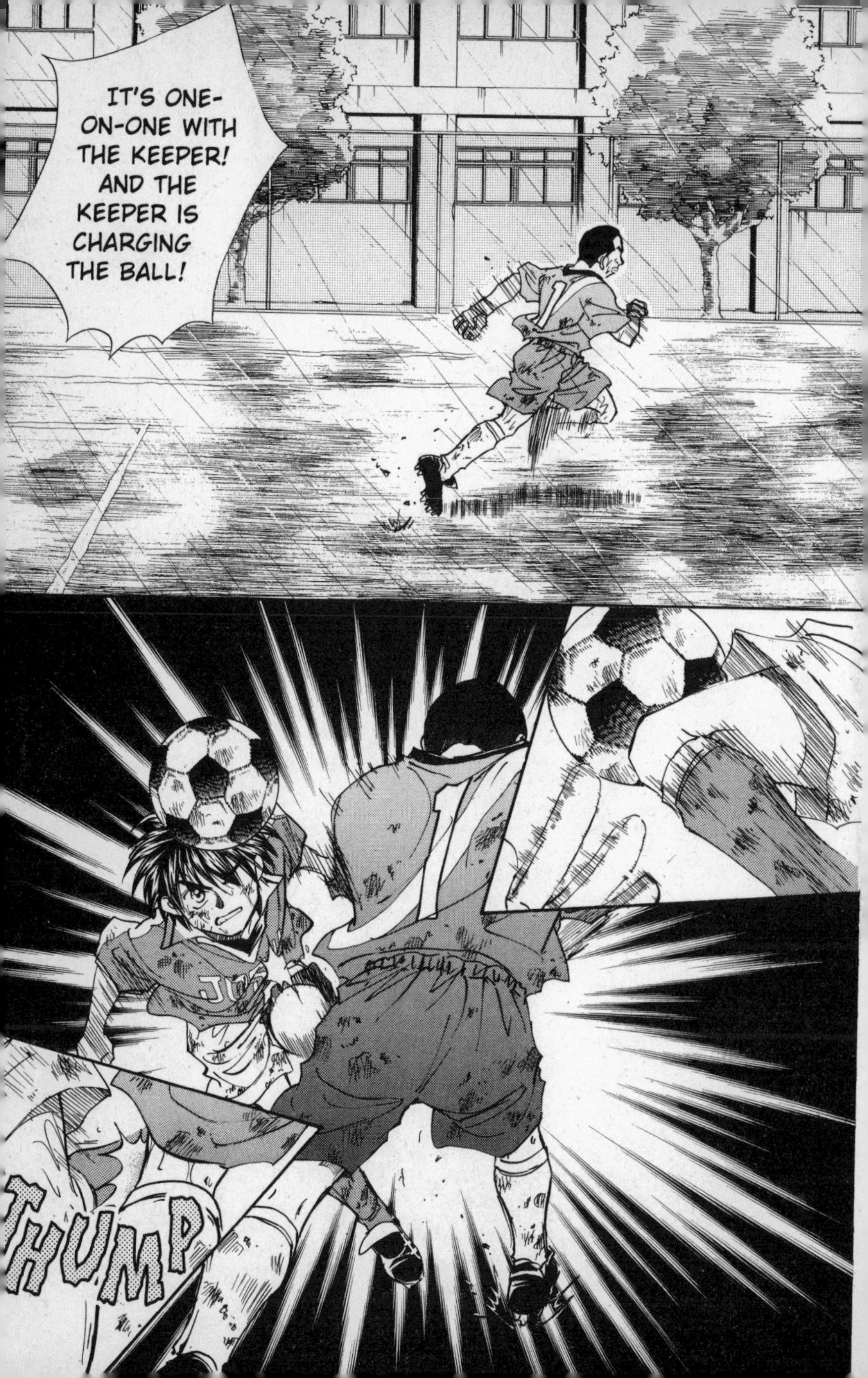
IT'S ONE-ON-ONE WITH THE KEEPER! AND THE KEEPER IS CHARGING THE BALL!
THUMP

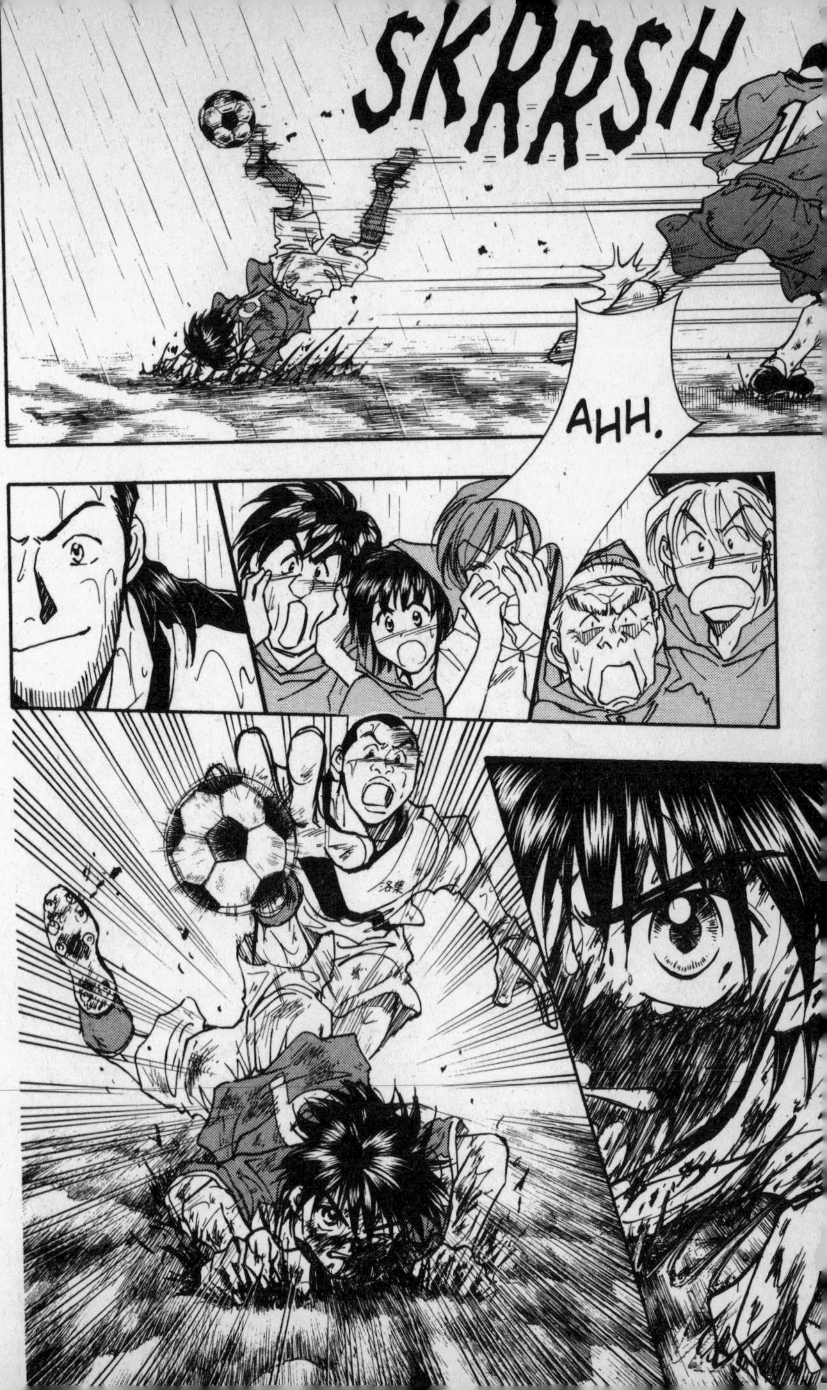
SKRRSH
AHH.

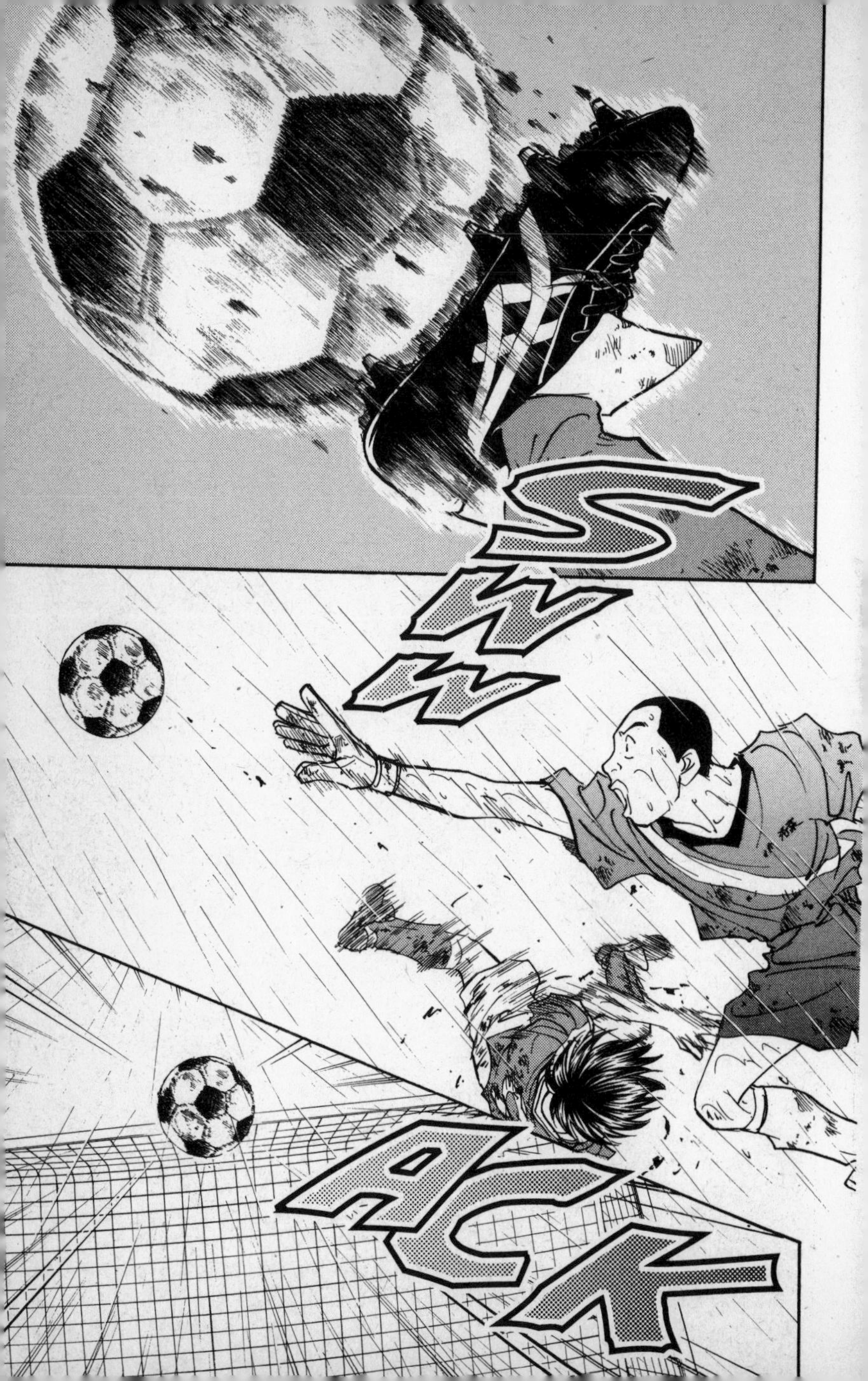
SWWACK

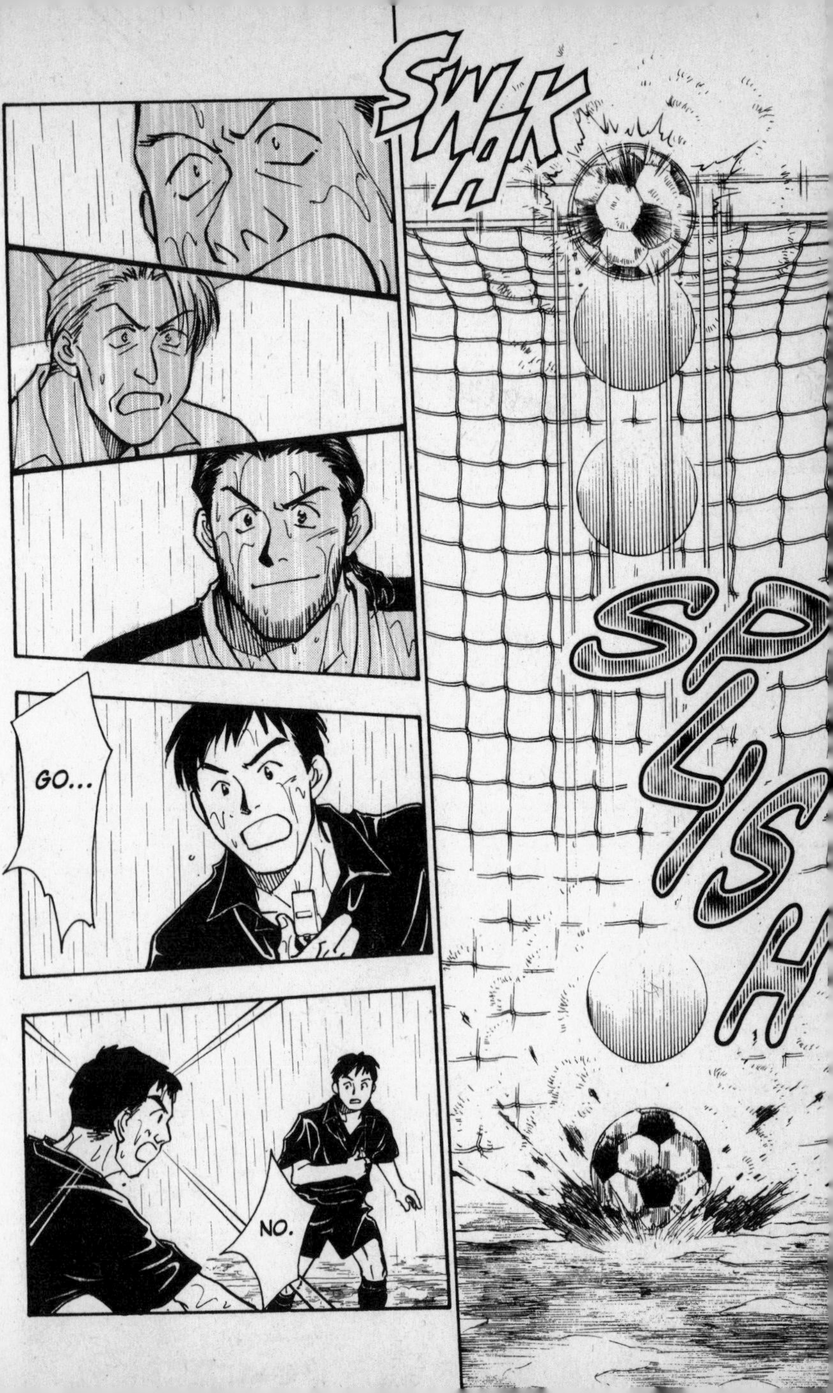
SPLISH
GO...
NO.

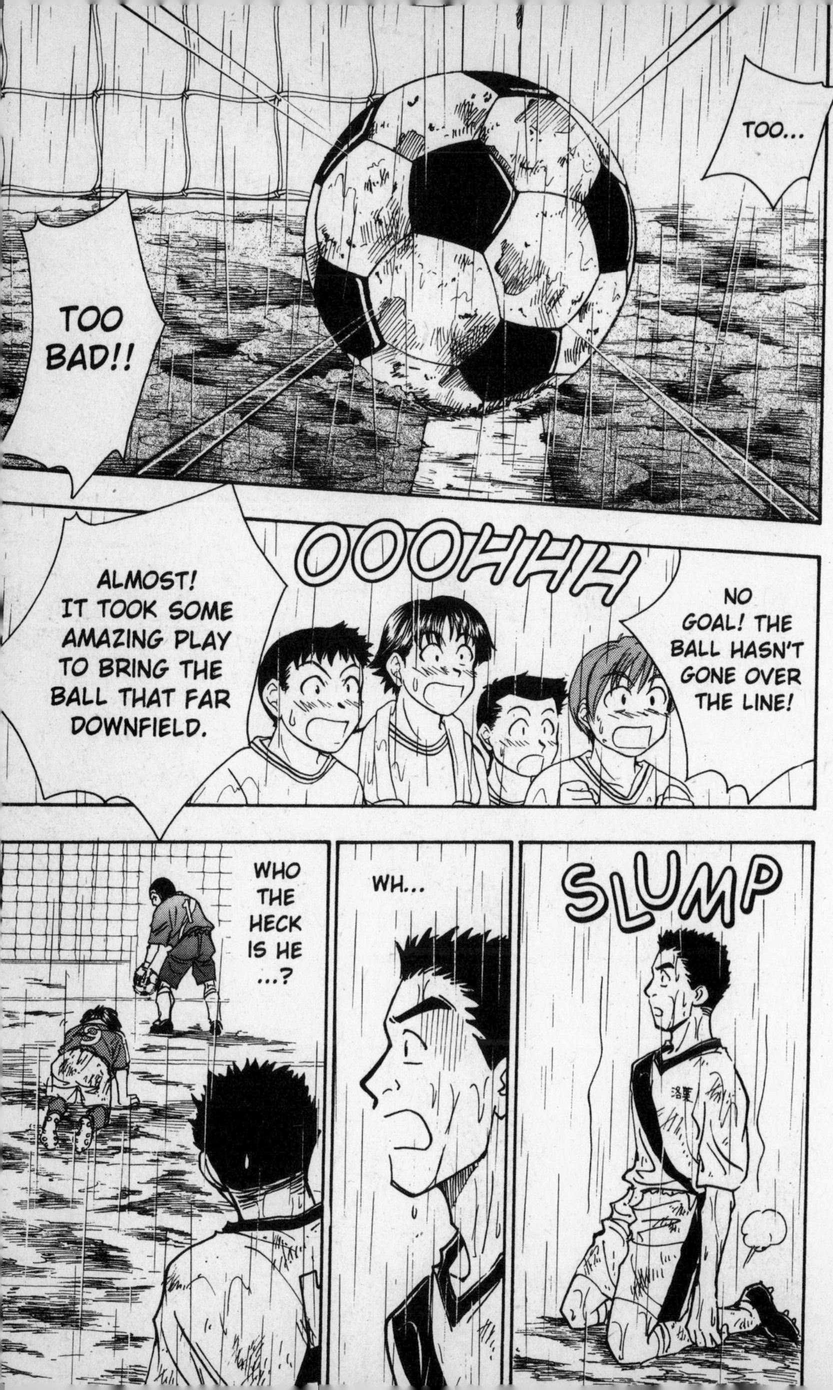
TOO...
TOO BAD!!
OOOHHH
NO GOAL! THE BALL HASN'T GONE OVER THE LINE!
ALMOST! IT TOOK SOME AMAZING PLAY TO BRING THE BALL THAT FAR DOWNFIELD.
SLUMP
WH...
WHO THE HECK IS HE ...?

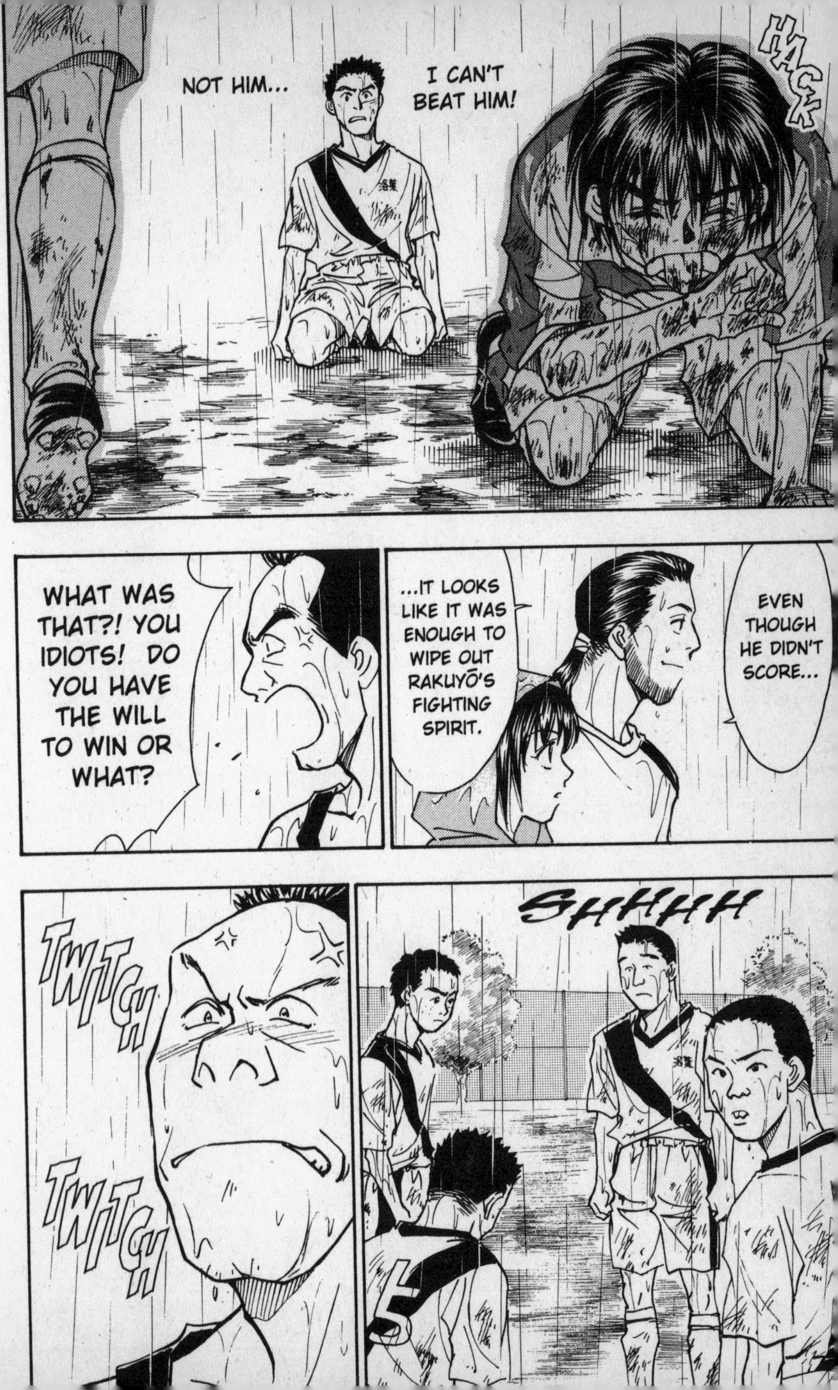
HACK
I CAN'T BEAT HIM!
NOT HIM...
EVEN THOUGH HE DIDN'T SCORE...
...IT LOOKS LIKE IT WAS ENOUGH TO WIPE OUT RAKUYŌ'S FIGHTING SPIRIT.
WHAT WAS THAT?! YOU IDIOTS! DO YOU HAVE THE WILL TO WIN OR WHAT?
SHHHH
TWITCH
TWITCH

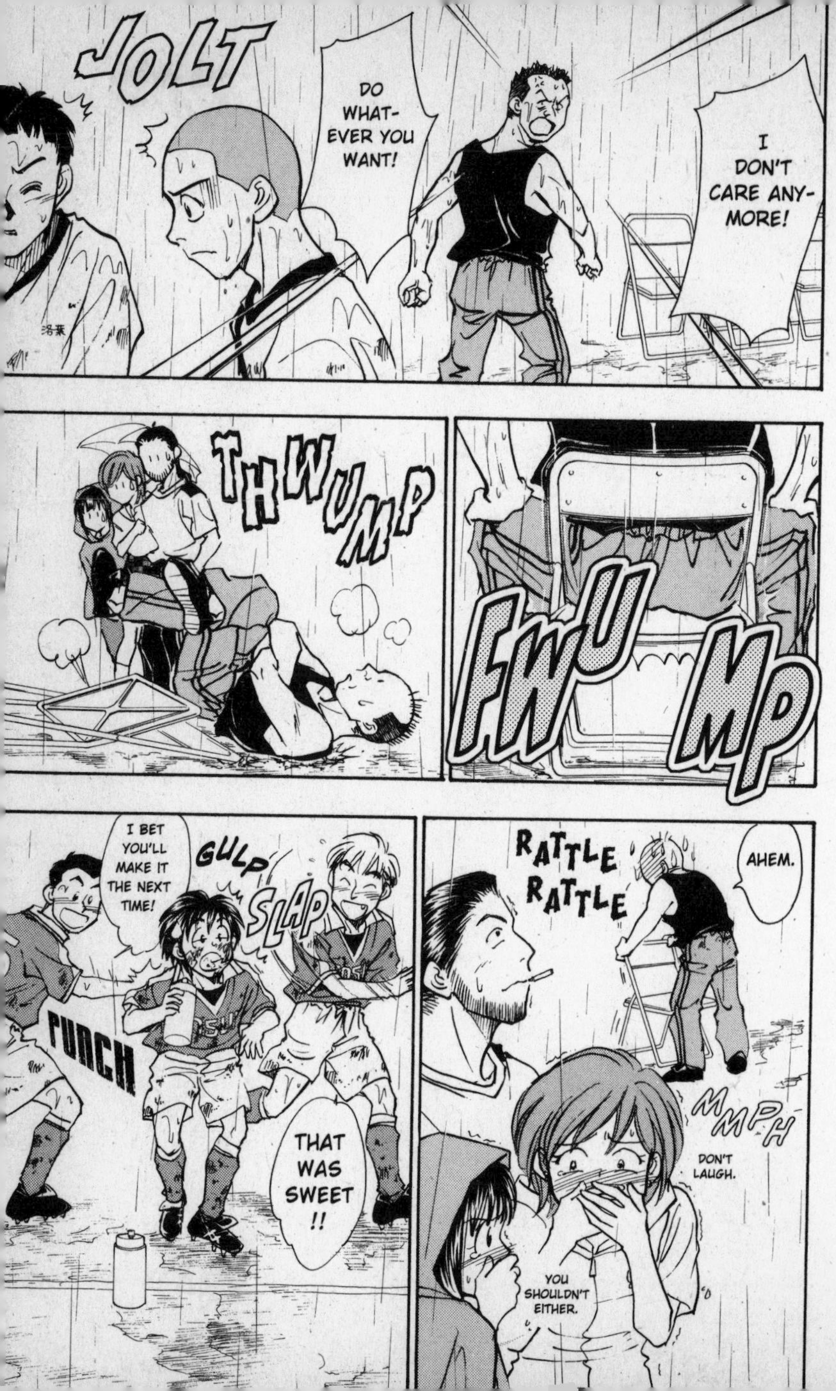

I DON'T CARE ANY-MORE!
DO WHAT-EVER YOU WANT!
JOLT
FWUMP
THWUMP
AHEM.
RATTLE RATTLE
MMPH
DON'T LAUGH.
YOU SHOULDN'T EITHER.
GULP
SLAP
I BET YOU'LL MAKE IT THE NEXT TIME!
PUNCH
THAT WAS SWEET !!

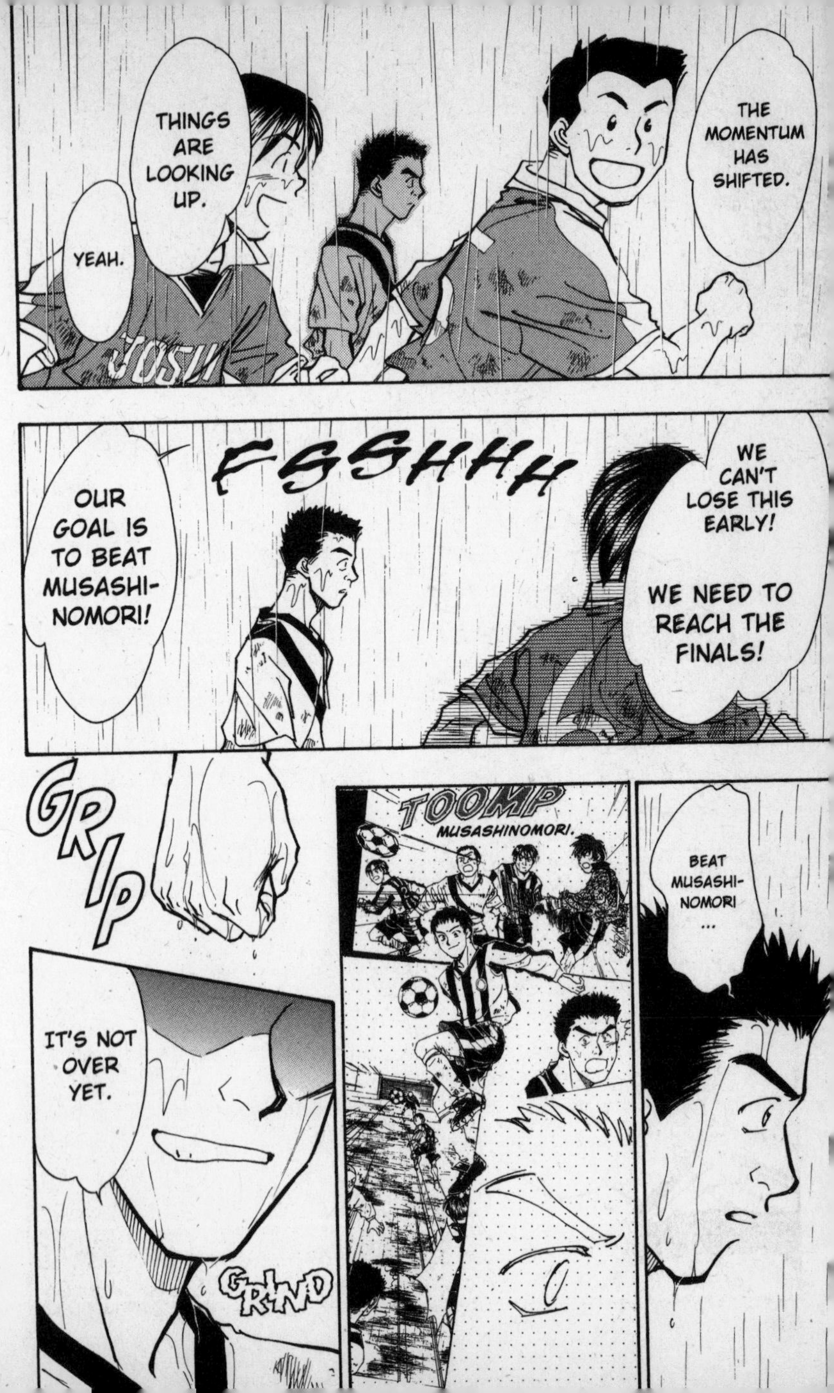
THE MOMENTUM HAS SHIFTED.
THINGS ARE LOOKING UP.
YEAH.
JOSHU
WE CAN'T LOSE THIS EARLY!
WE NEED TO REACH THE FINALS!
FSSHHH
OUR GOAL IS TO BEAT MUSASHI-NOMORI!
BEAT MUSASHI-NOMORI ...
TOOMP
MUSASHINOMORI.
GRIP
IT'S NOT OVER YET.
GRIND

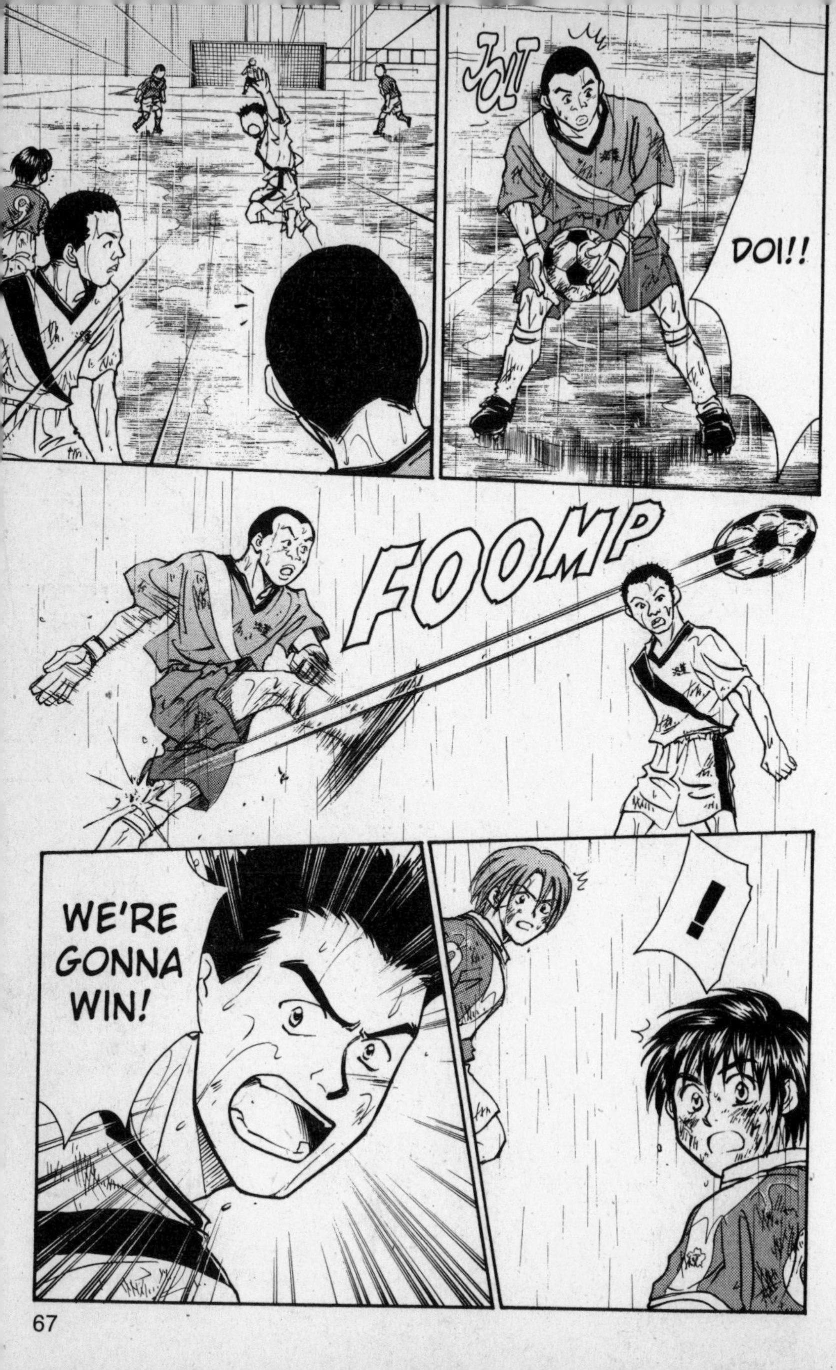
JOLT
DOI!!
FOOMP
!
WE'RE GONNA WIN!

WHISTLE!

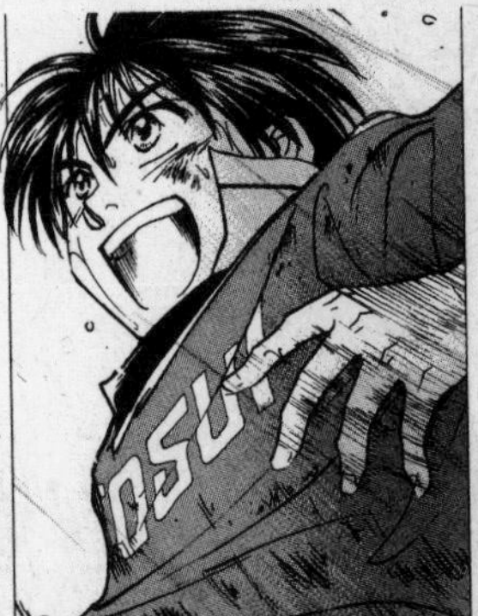

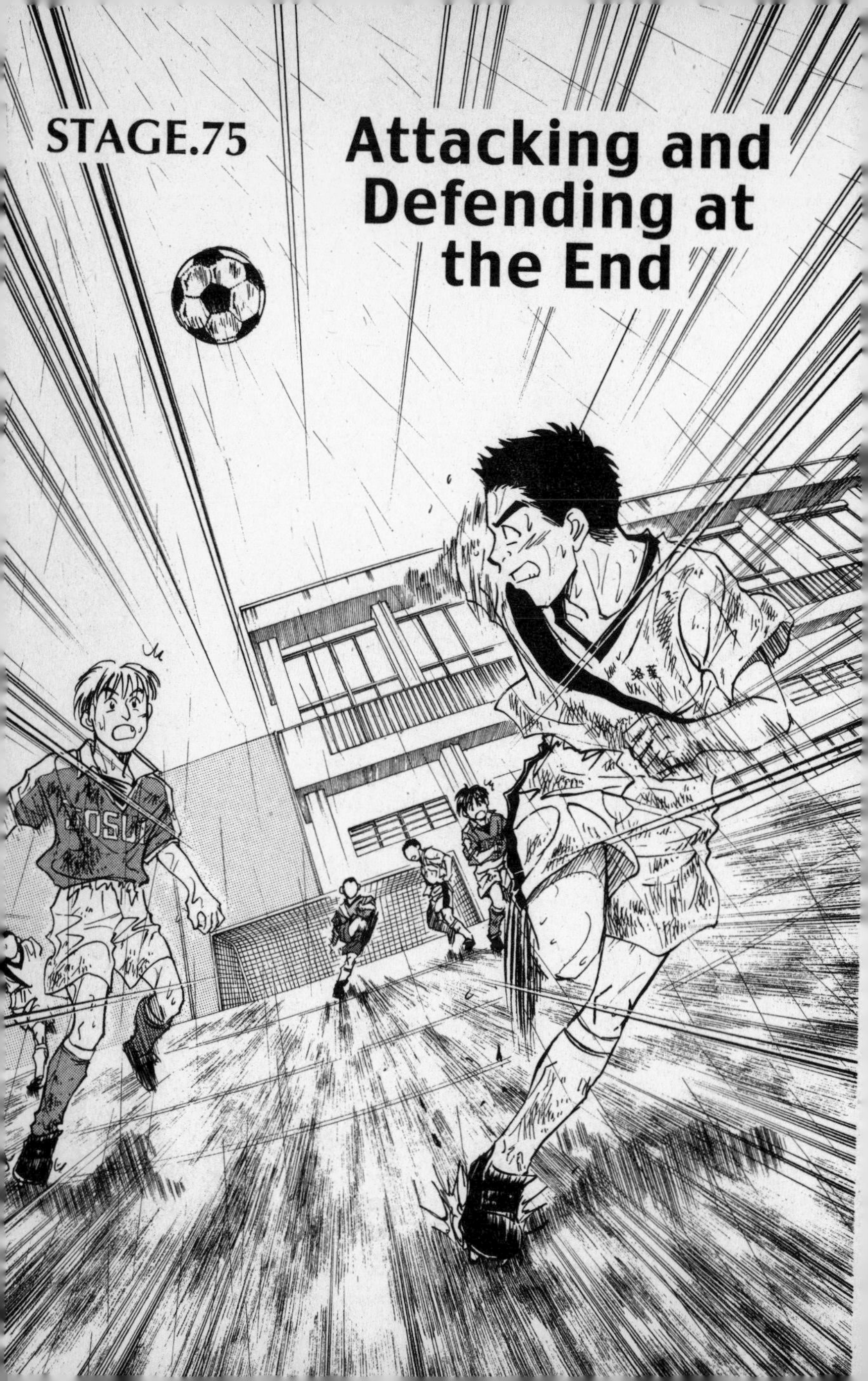
STAGE.75
Attacking and Defending at the End

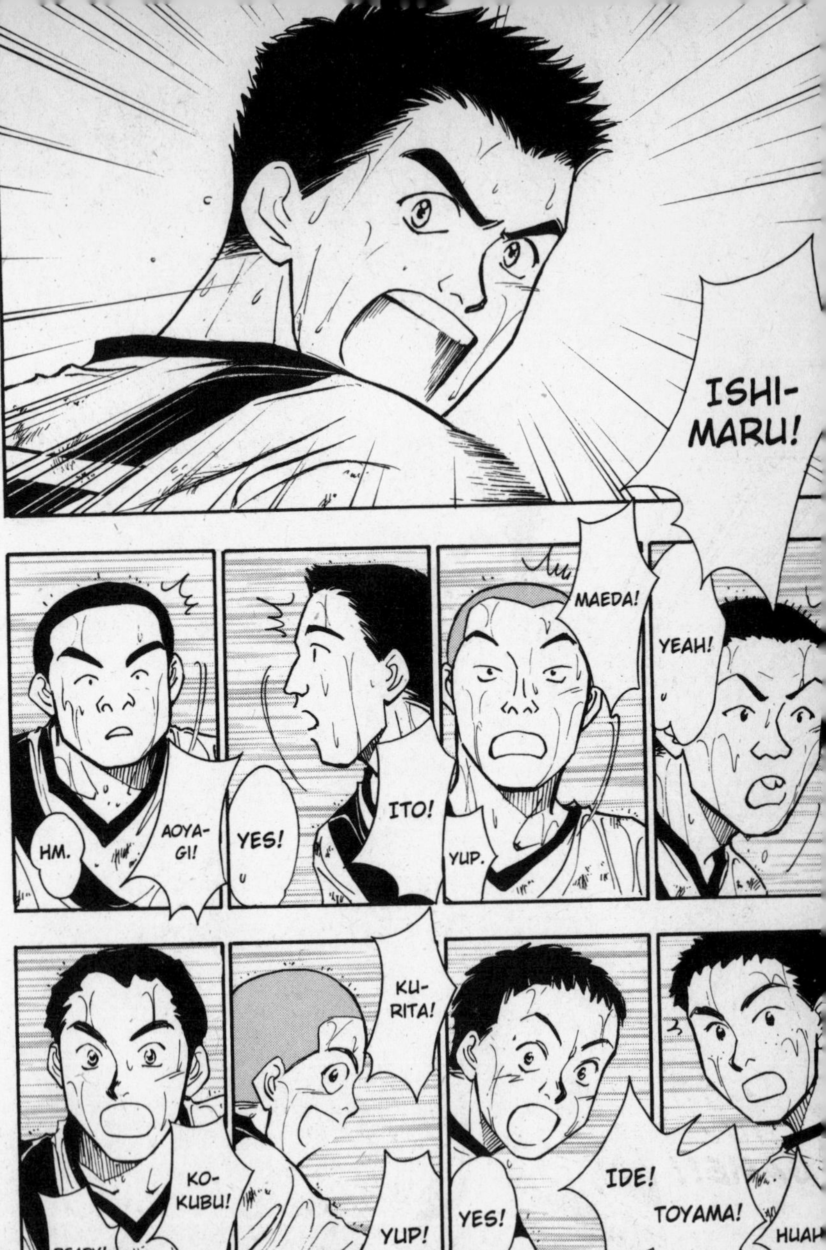
ISHI-MARU!
MAEDA!
YEAH!
ITO!
YUP.
AOYA-GI!
YES!
HM.
IDE!
TOYAMA!
HUAH
YES!
KU-RITA!
YUP!
KO-KUBU!
READY!

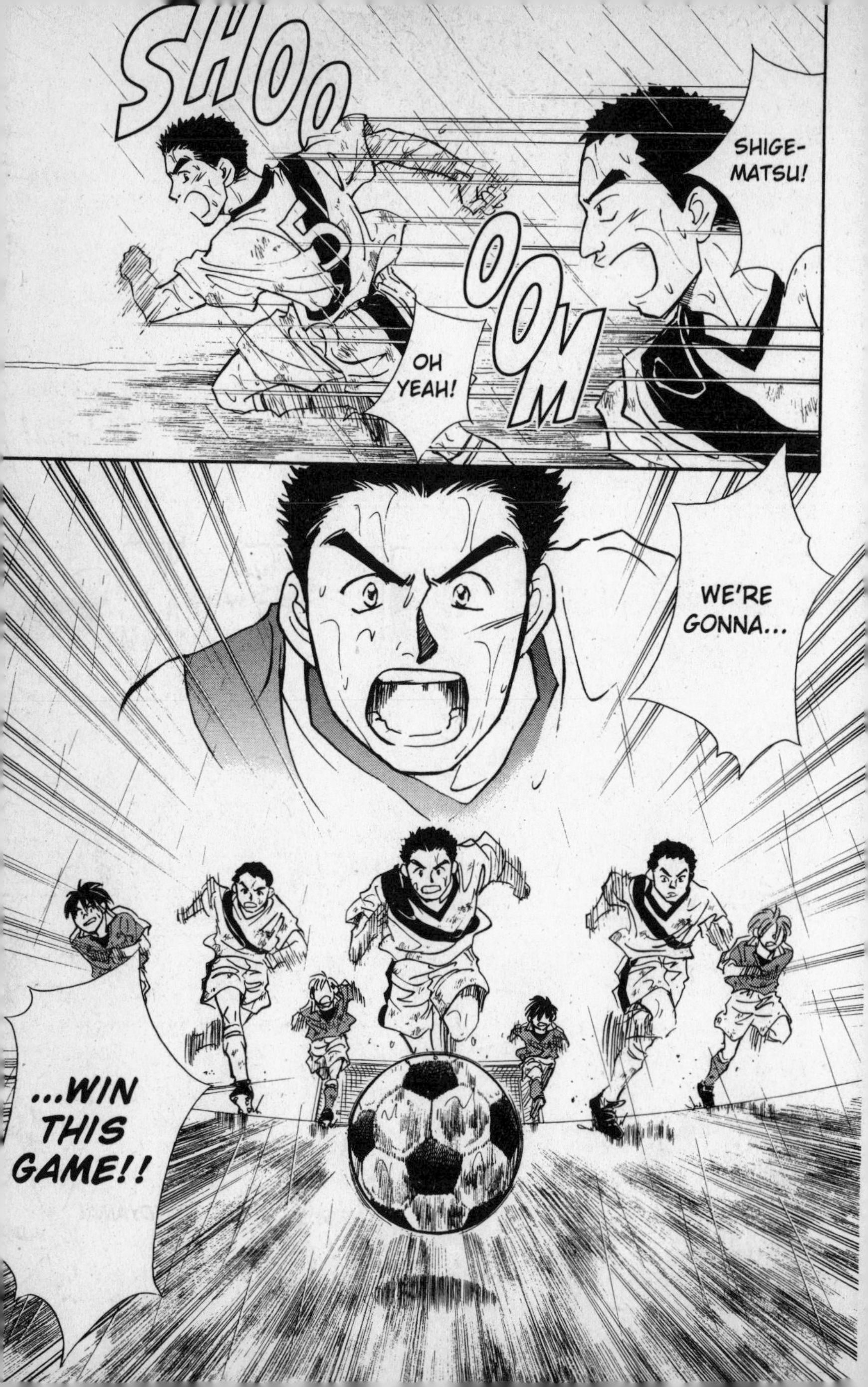
SHIGE-MATSU!
SHOOOOOM
OH YEAH!
WE'RE GONNA...
...WIN THIS GAME!!

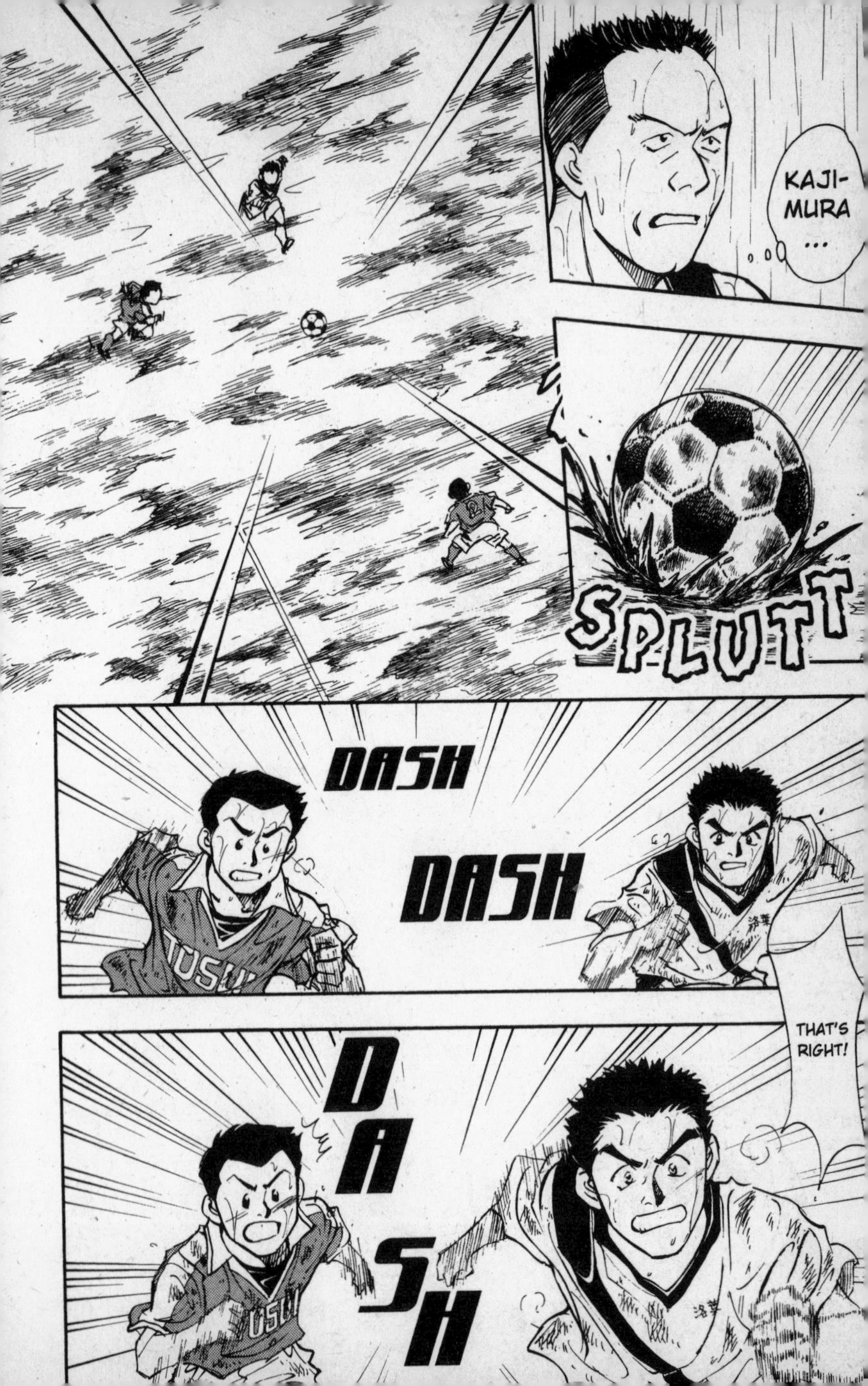
KAJI-MURA ...
SPLUTT
DASH
DASH
THAT'S RIGHT!
DASH

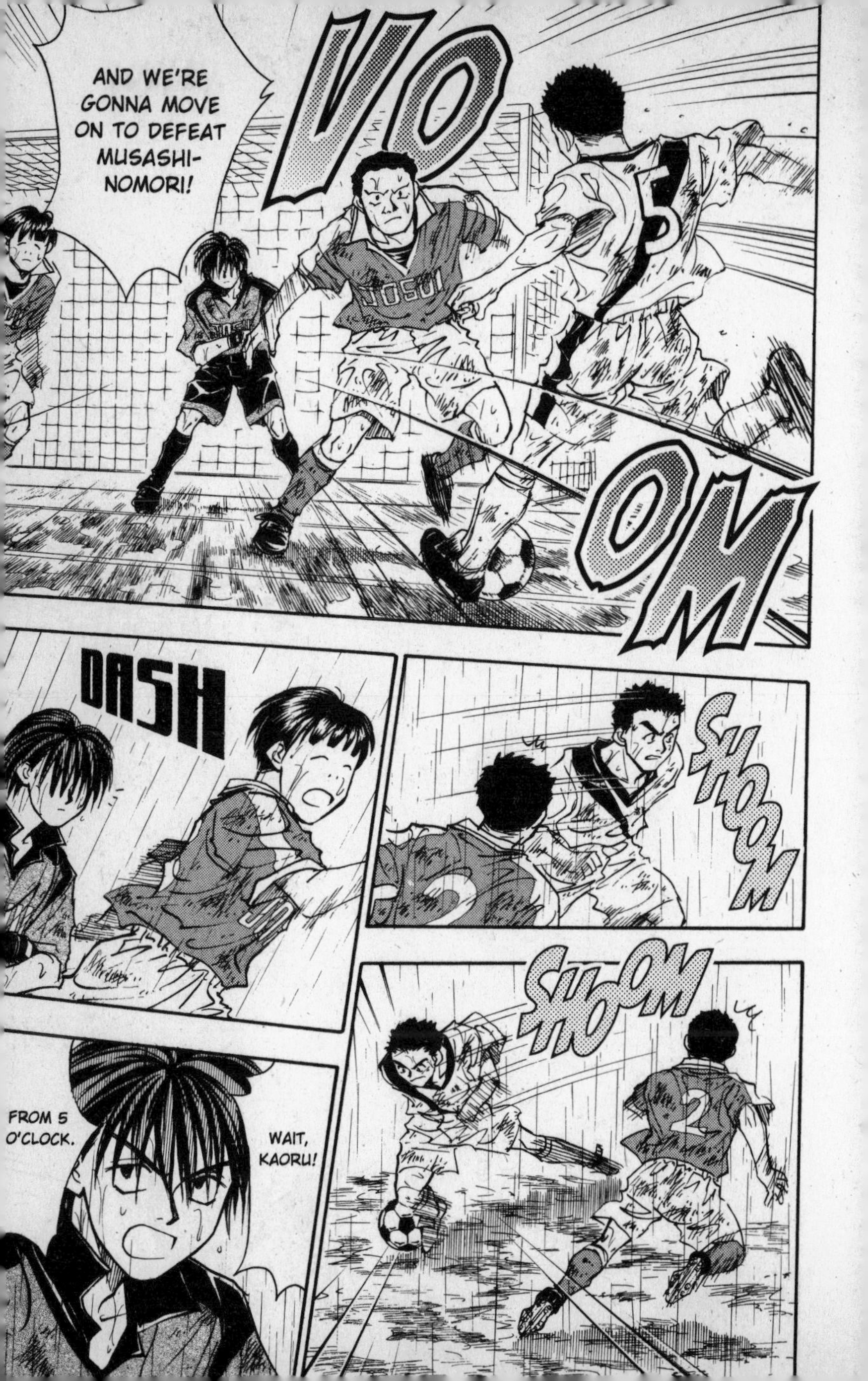
AND WE'RE GONNA MOVE ON TO DEFEAT MUSASHI-NOMORI!
VOOM
SHOOOM
DASH
SHOOM
WAIT, KAORU!
FROM 5 O'CLOCK.

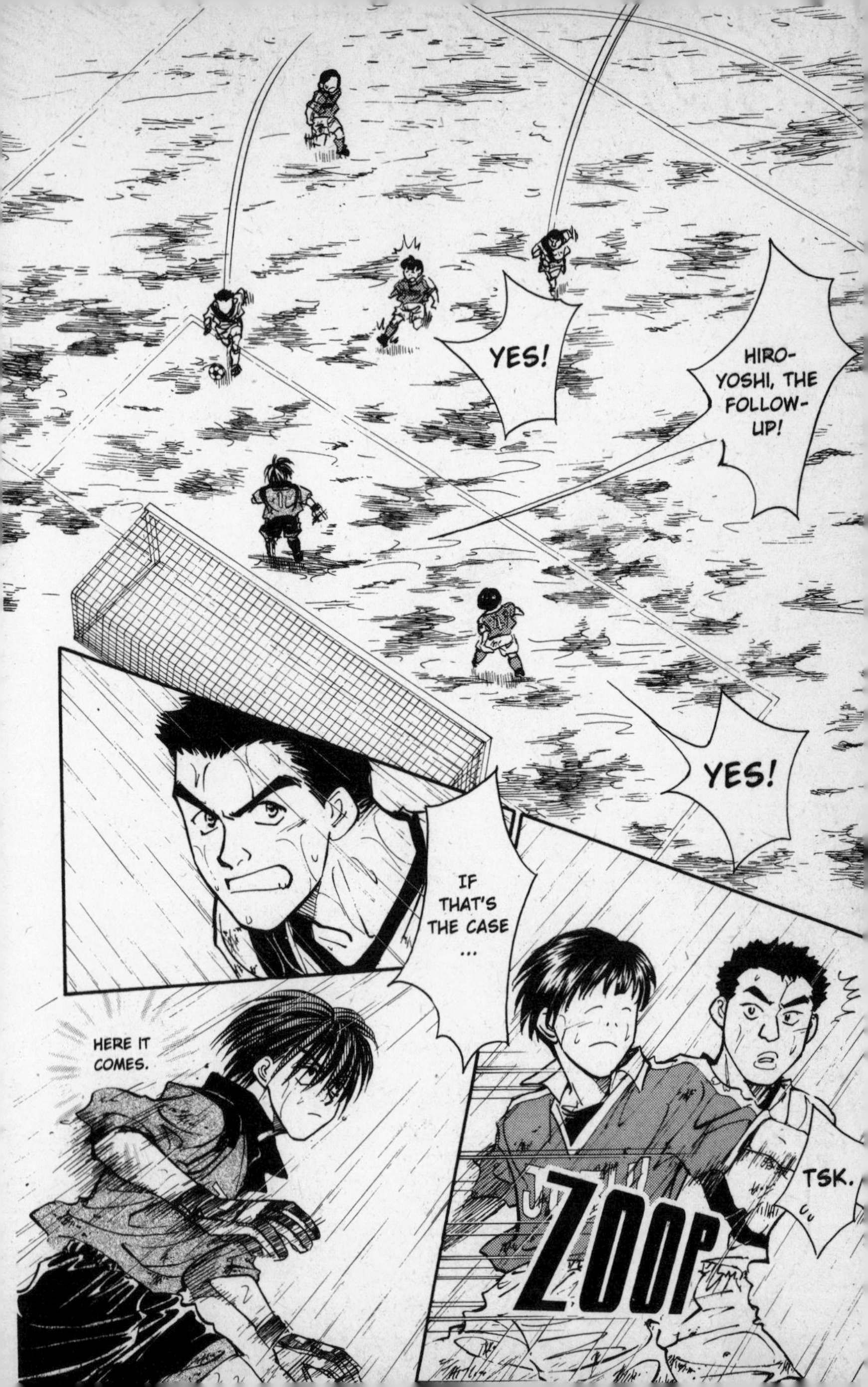
HIRO-YOSHI, THE FOLLOW-UP!
YES!
YES!
IF THAT'S THE CASE ...
TSK.
ZOOP
HERE IT COMES.

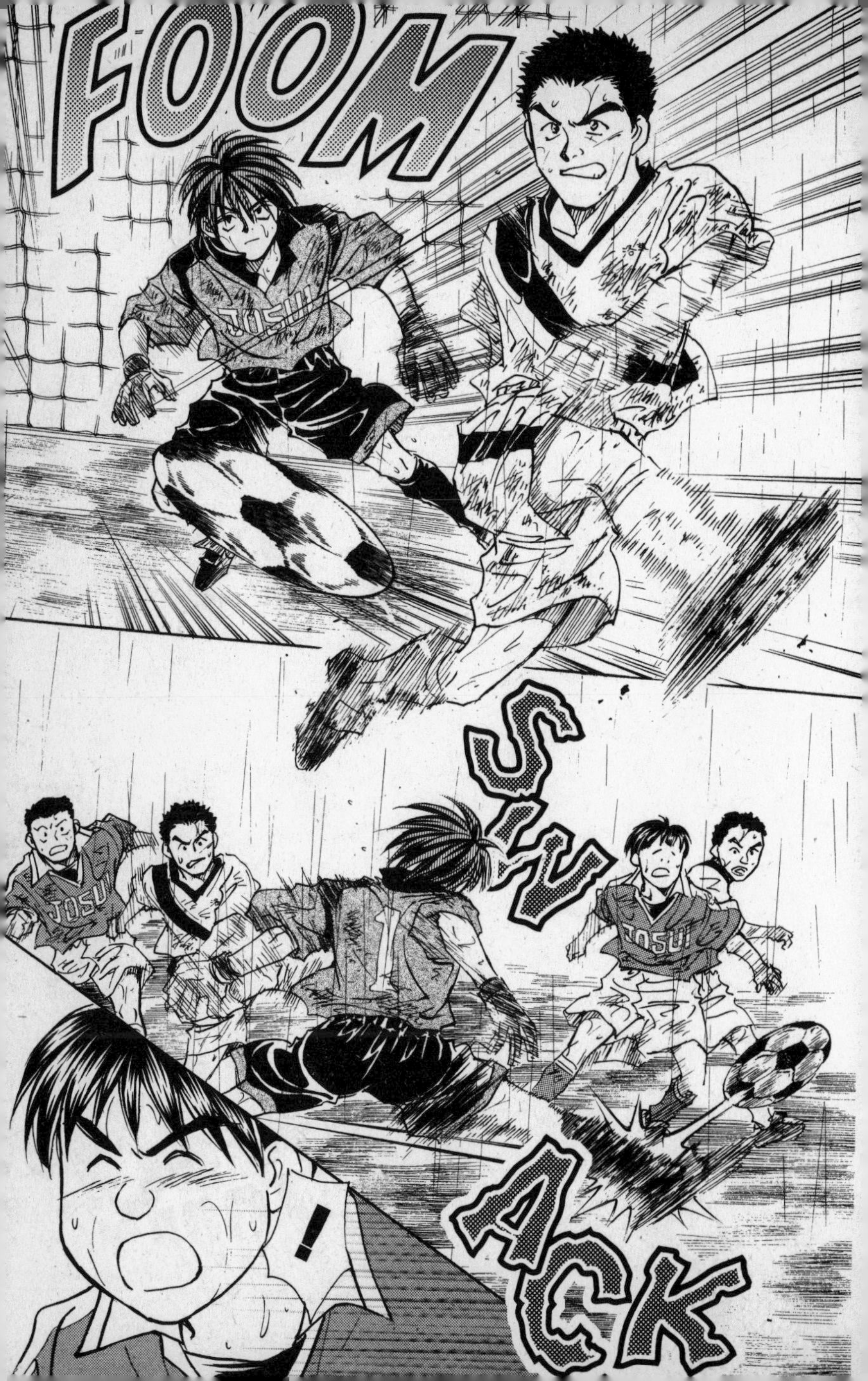
FOOM
SWACK
!

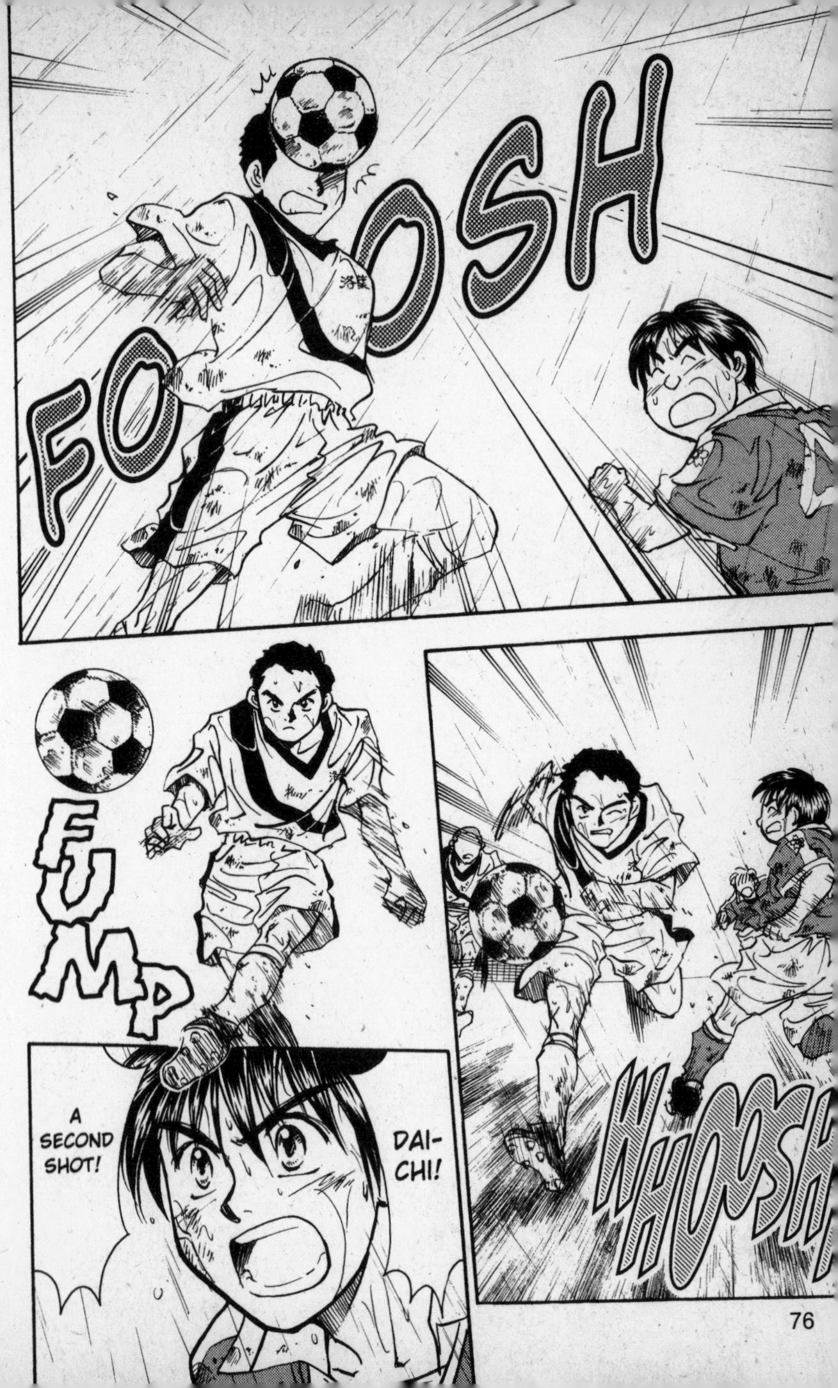
FOOSH
WHOOSH
FUMP
DAI-CHI!
A SECOND SHOT!

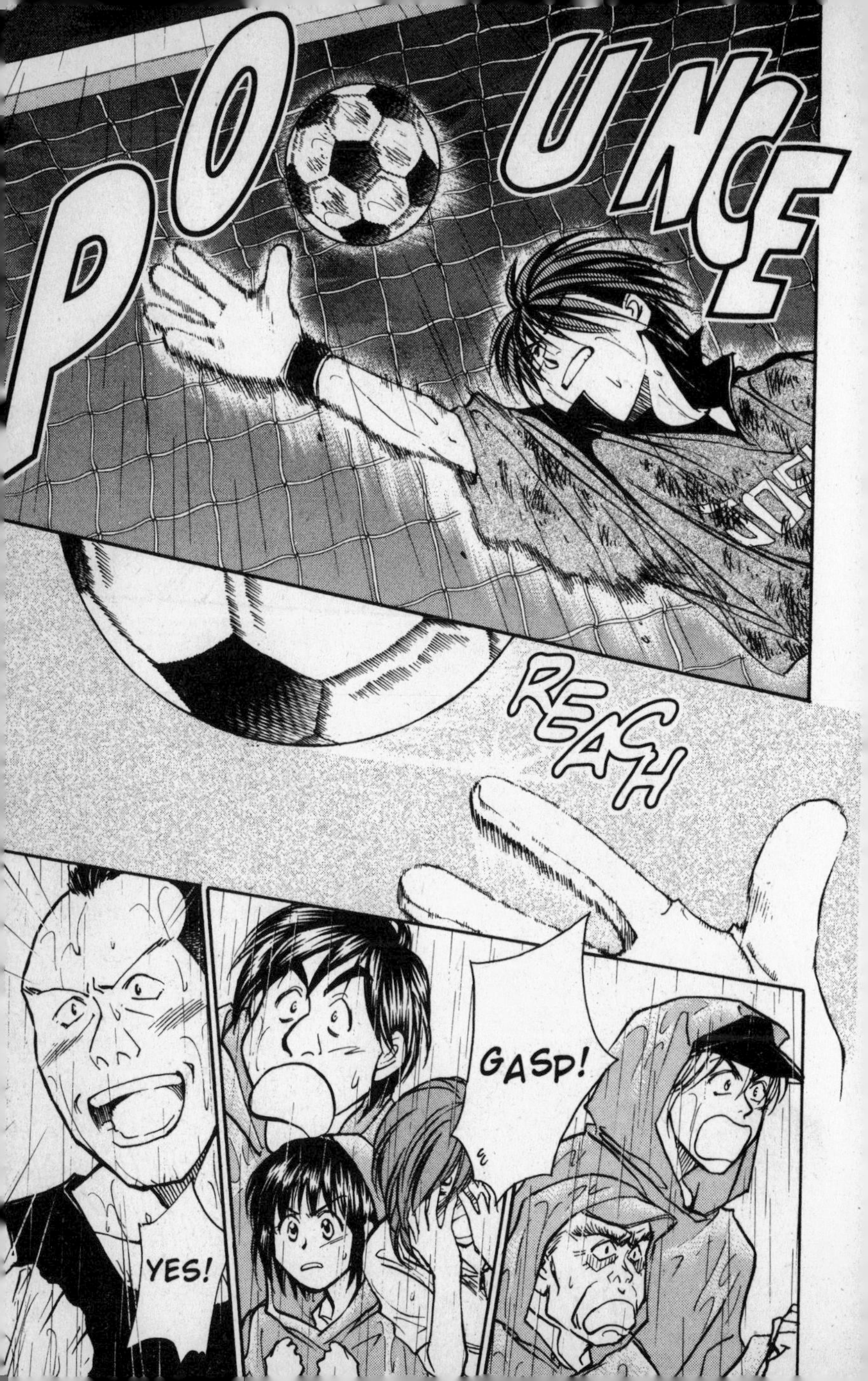
POUNCE
REACH
GASP!
YES!

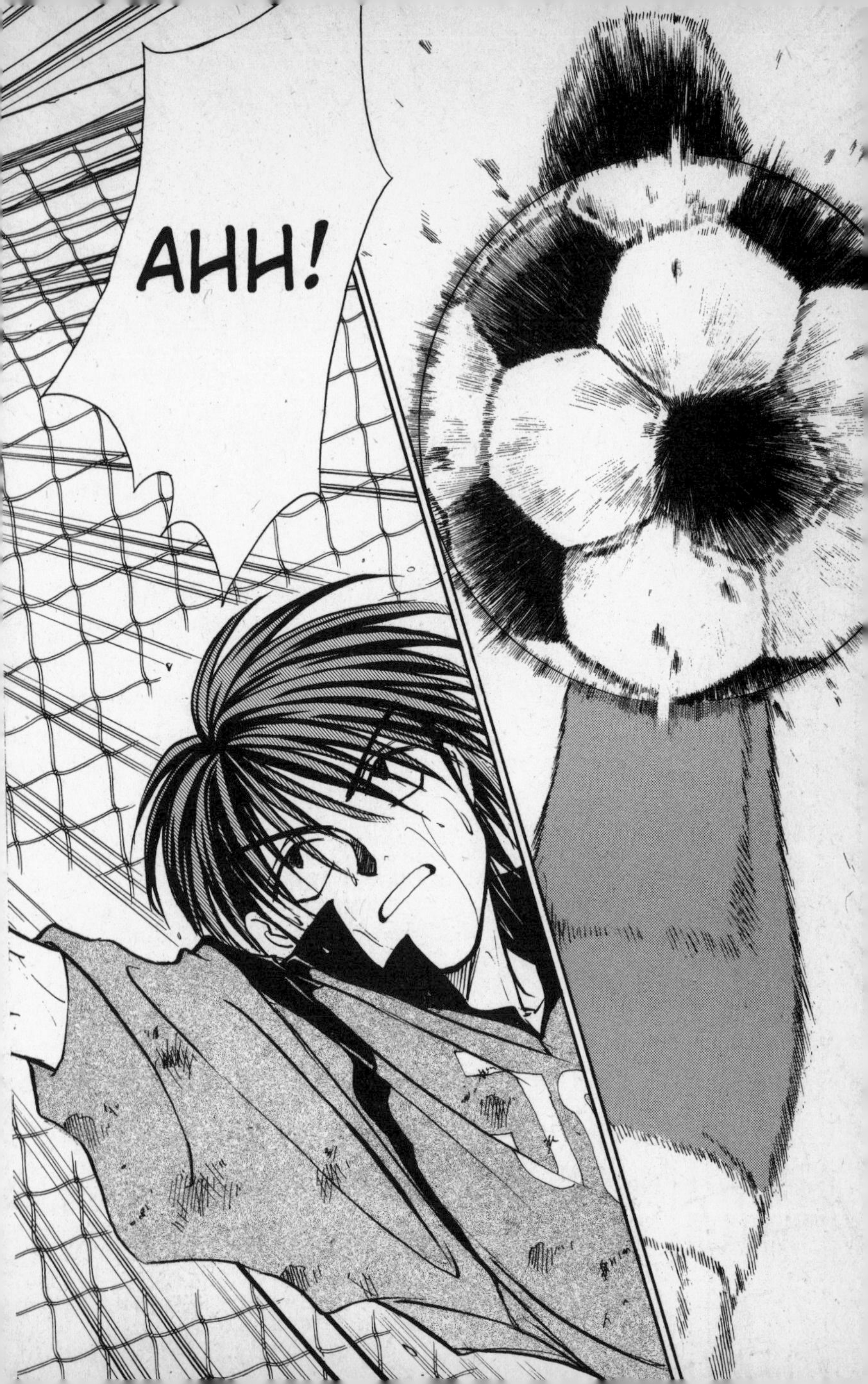
AHH!

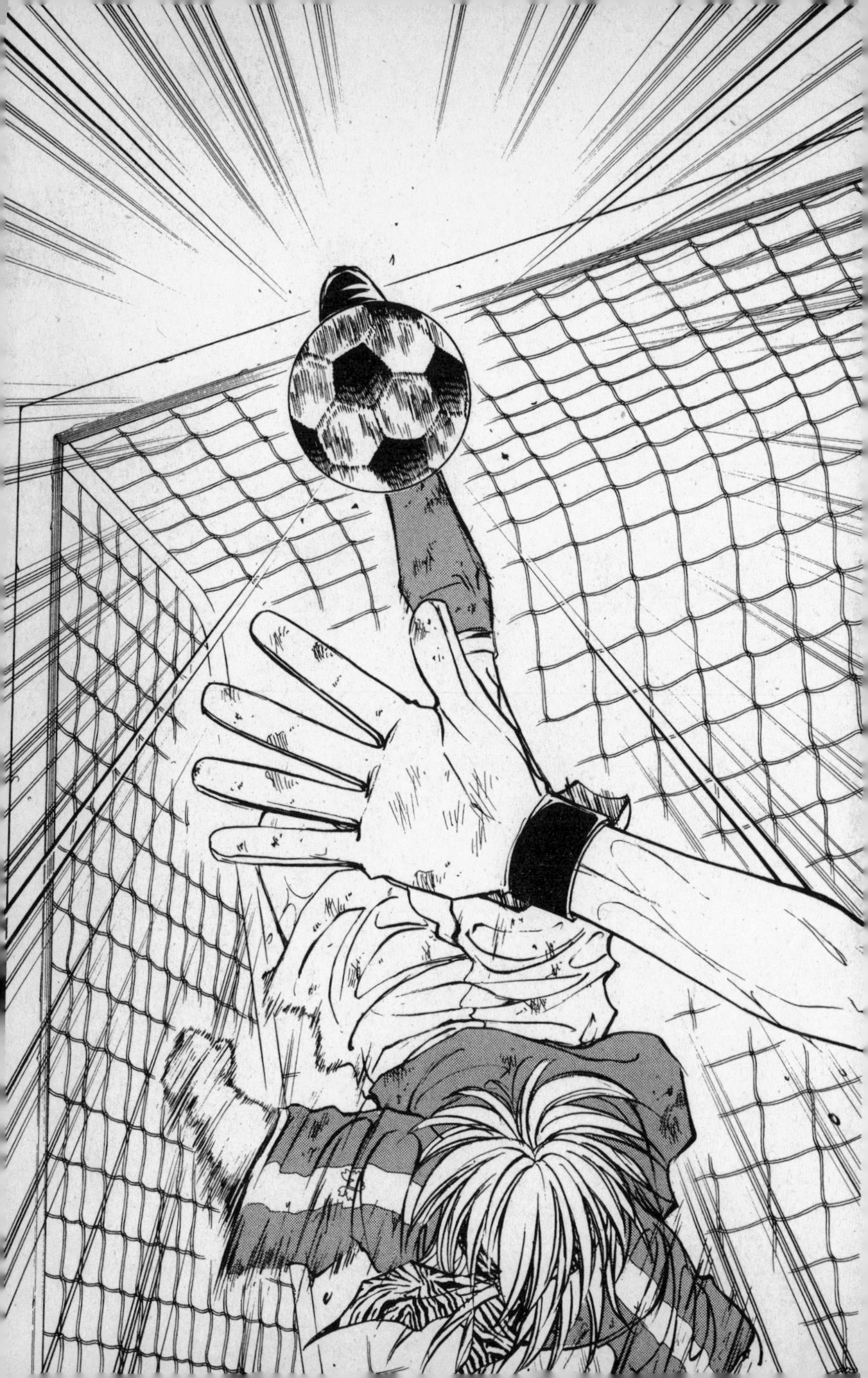

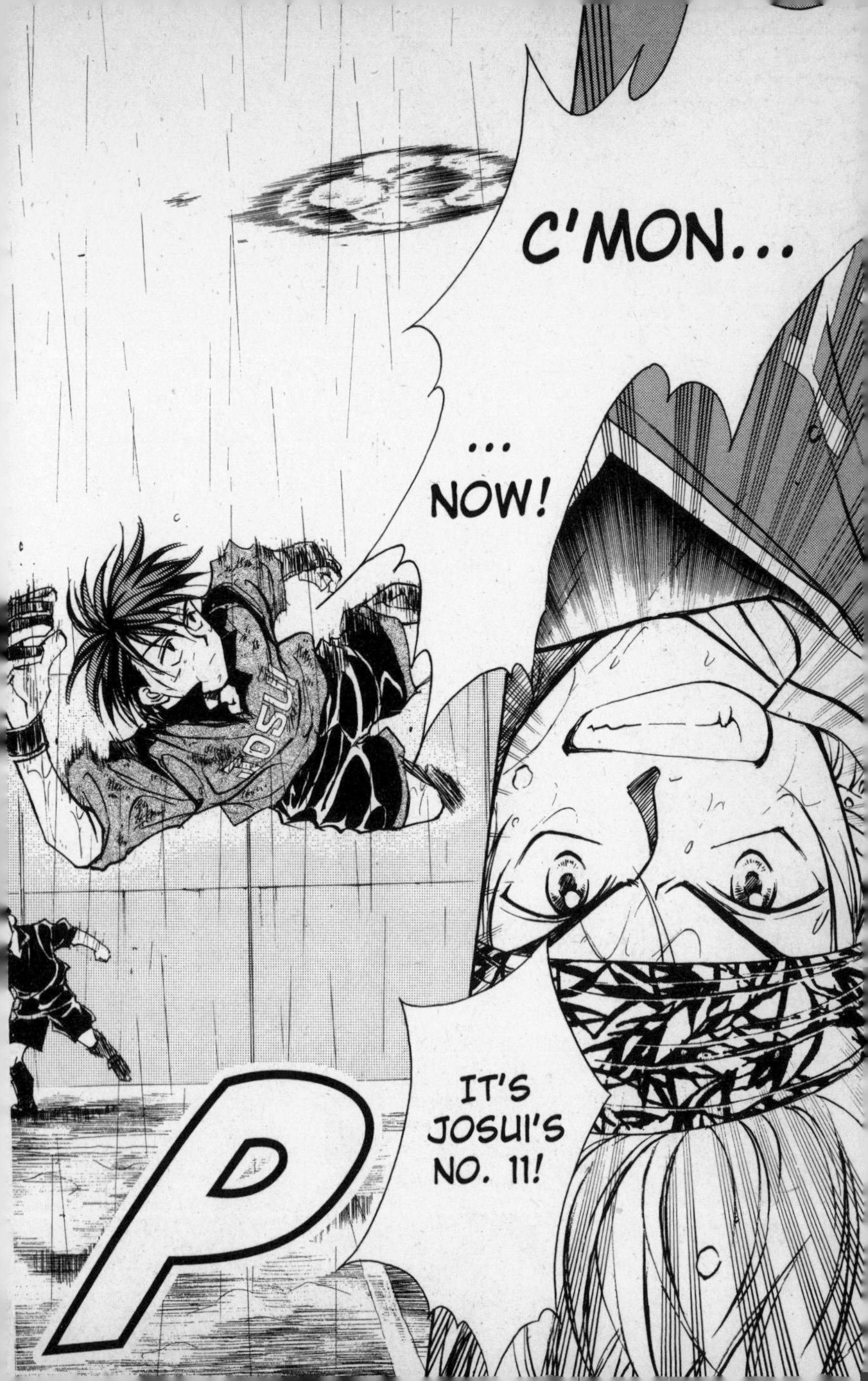
C'MON...
... NOW!
IT'S JOSUI'S NO. 11!
P

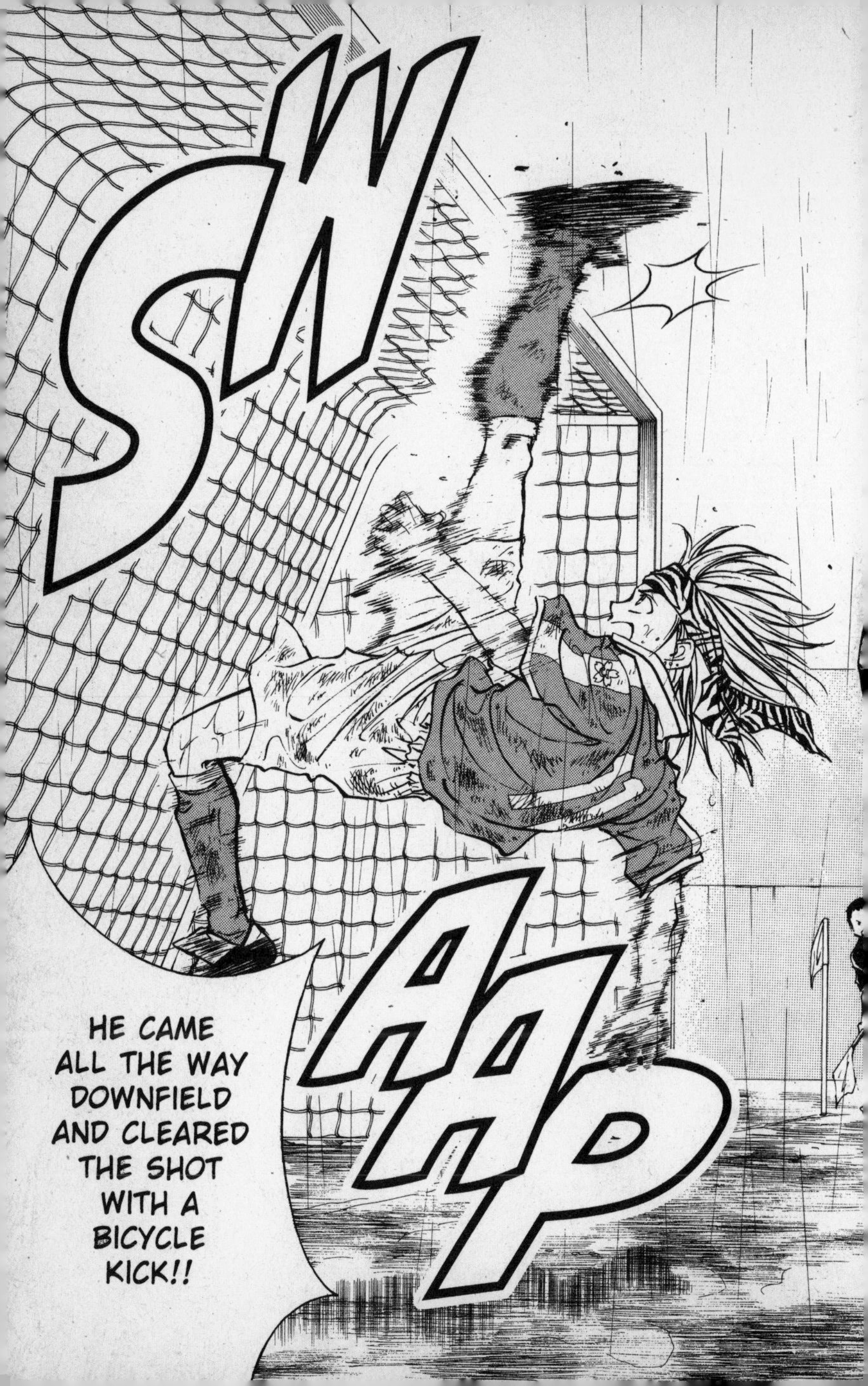
SHWAP
HE CAME ALL THE WAY DOWNFIELD AND CLEARED THE SHOT WITH A BICYCLE KICK!!

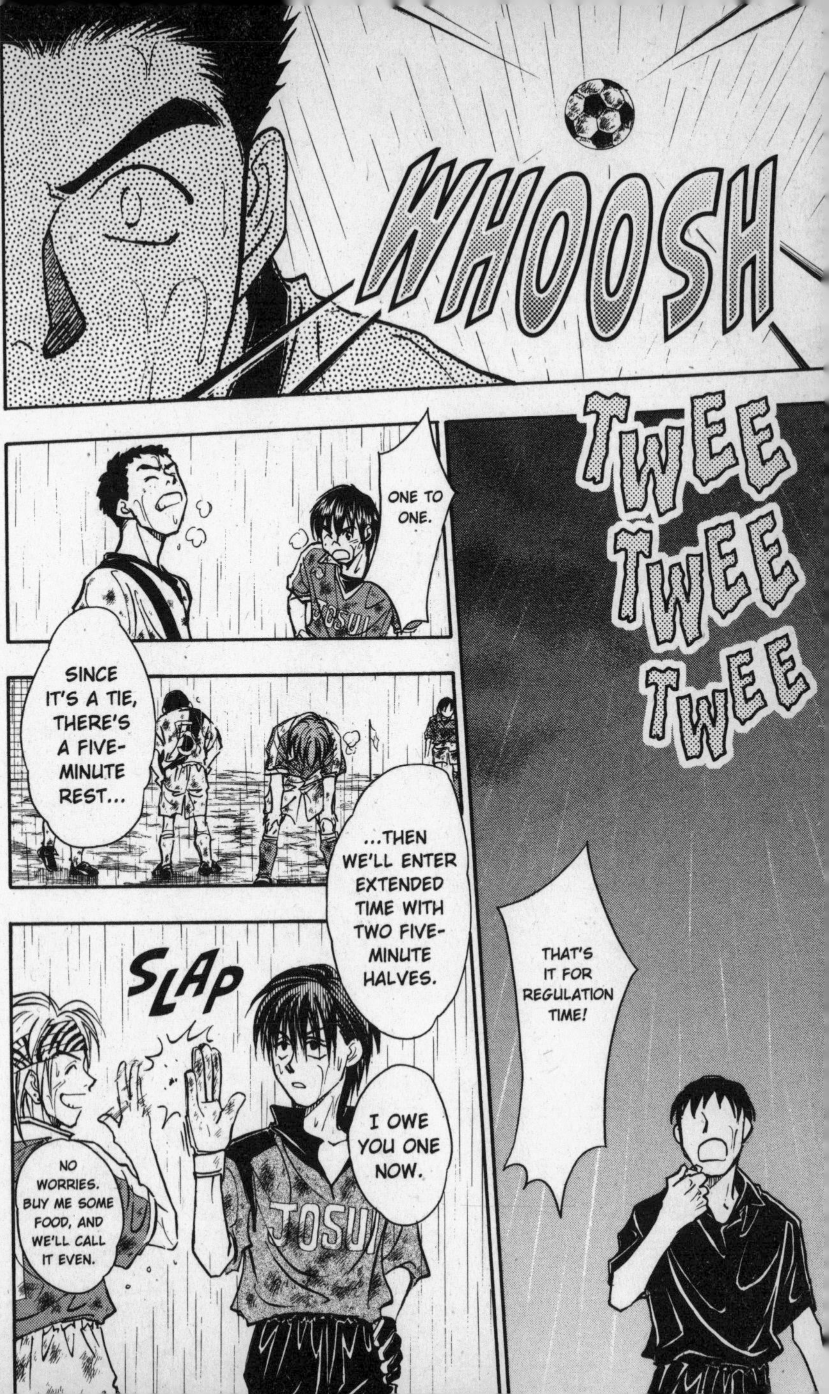
WHOOSH
TWEE TWEE TWEE
THAT'S IT FOR REGULATION TIME!
ONE TO ONE.
SINCE IT'S A TIE, THERE'S A FIVE-MINUTE REST...
...THEN WE'LL ENTER EXTENDED TIME WITH TWO FIVE-MINUTE HALVES.
SLAP
I OWE YOU ONE NOW.
NO WORRIES. BUY ME SOME FOOD, AND WE'LL CALL IT EVEN.

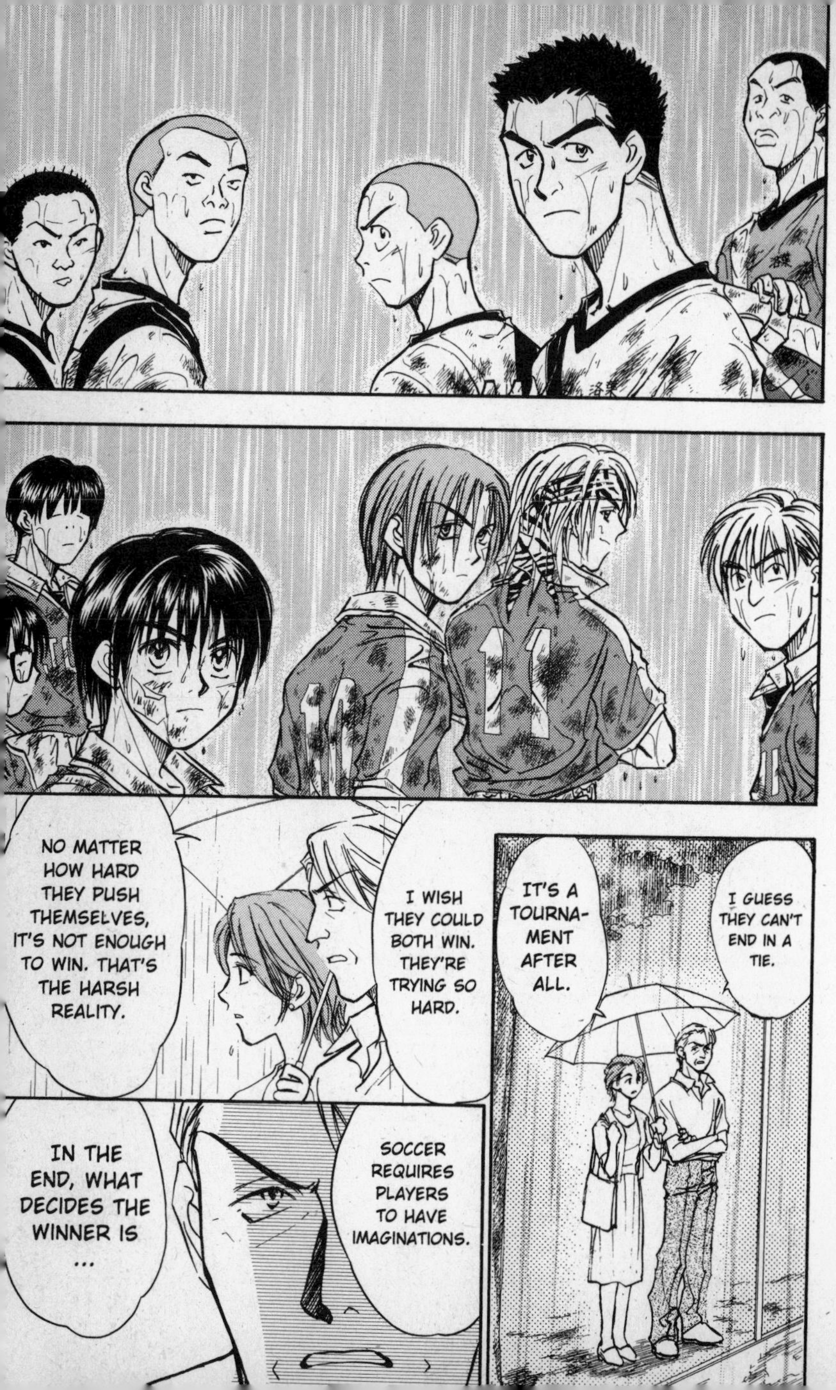
I GUESS THEY CAN'T END IN A TIE.
IT'S A TOURNAMENT AFTER ALL.
I WISH THEY COULD BOTH WIN. THEY'RE TRYING SO HARD.
NO MATTER HOW HARD THEY PUSH THEMSELVES, IT'S NOT ENOUGH TO WIN. THAT'S THE HARSH REALITY.
SOCCER REQUIRES PLAYERS TO HAVE IMAGINATIONS.
IN THE END, WHAT DECIDES THE WINNER IS ...

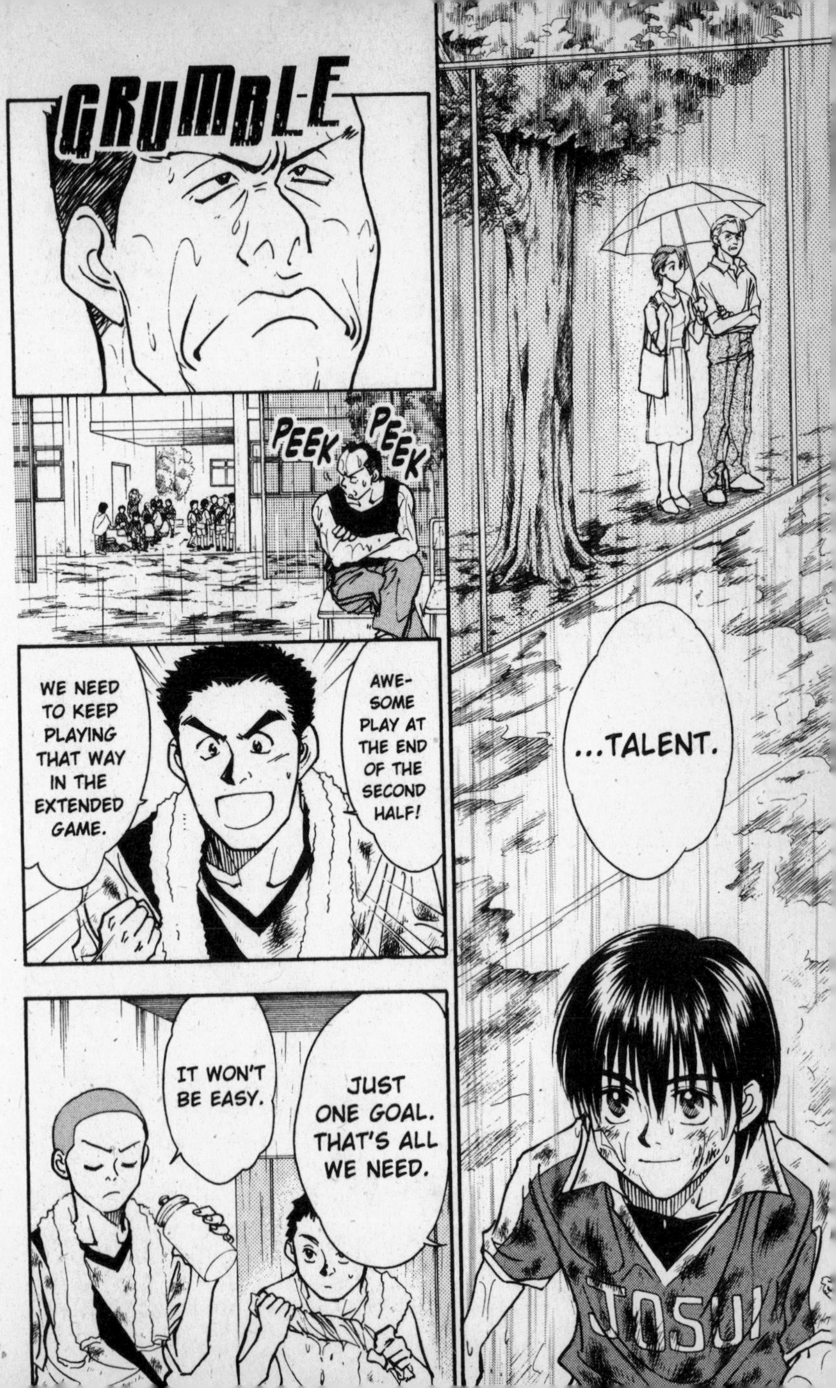
...TALENT.
GRUMBLE
PEEK
PEEK
AWESOME PLAY AT THE END OF THE SECOND HALF!
WE NEED TO KEEP PLAYING THAT WAY IN THE EXTENDED GAME.
JUST ONE GOAL. THAT'S ALL WE NEED.
IT WON'T BE EASY.

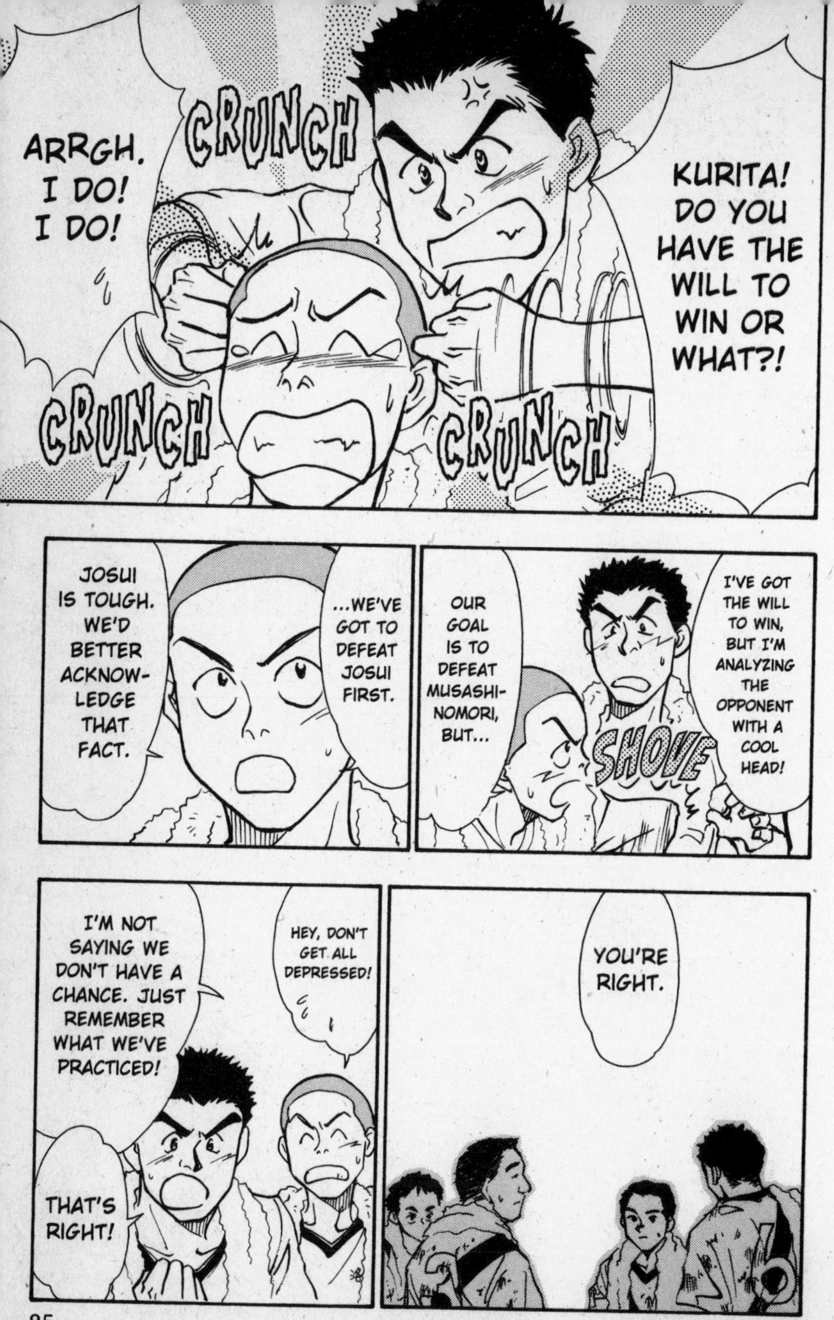
KURITA! DO YOU HAVE THE WILL TO WIN OR WHAT?!
CRUNCH
ARRGH. I DO! I DO!
CRUNCH
CRUNCH
I'VE GOT THE WILL TO WIN, BUT I'M ANALYZING THE OPPONENT WITH A COOL HEAD!
OUR GOAL IS TO DEFEAT MUSASHI-NOMORI, BUT...
SHOVE
...WE'VE GOT TO DEFEAT JOSUI FIRST.
JOSUI IS TOUGH. WE'D BETTER ACKNOW-LEDGE THAT FACT.
YOU'RE RIGHT.
HEY, DON'T GET ALL DEPRESSED!
I'M NOT SAYING WE DON'T HAVE A CHANCE. JUST REMEMBER WHAT WE'VE PRACTICED!
THAT'S RIGHT!

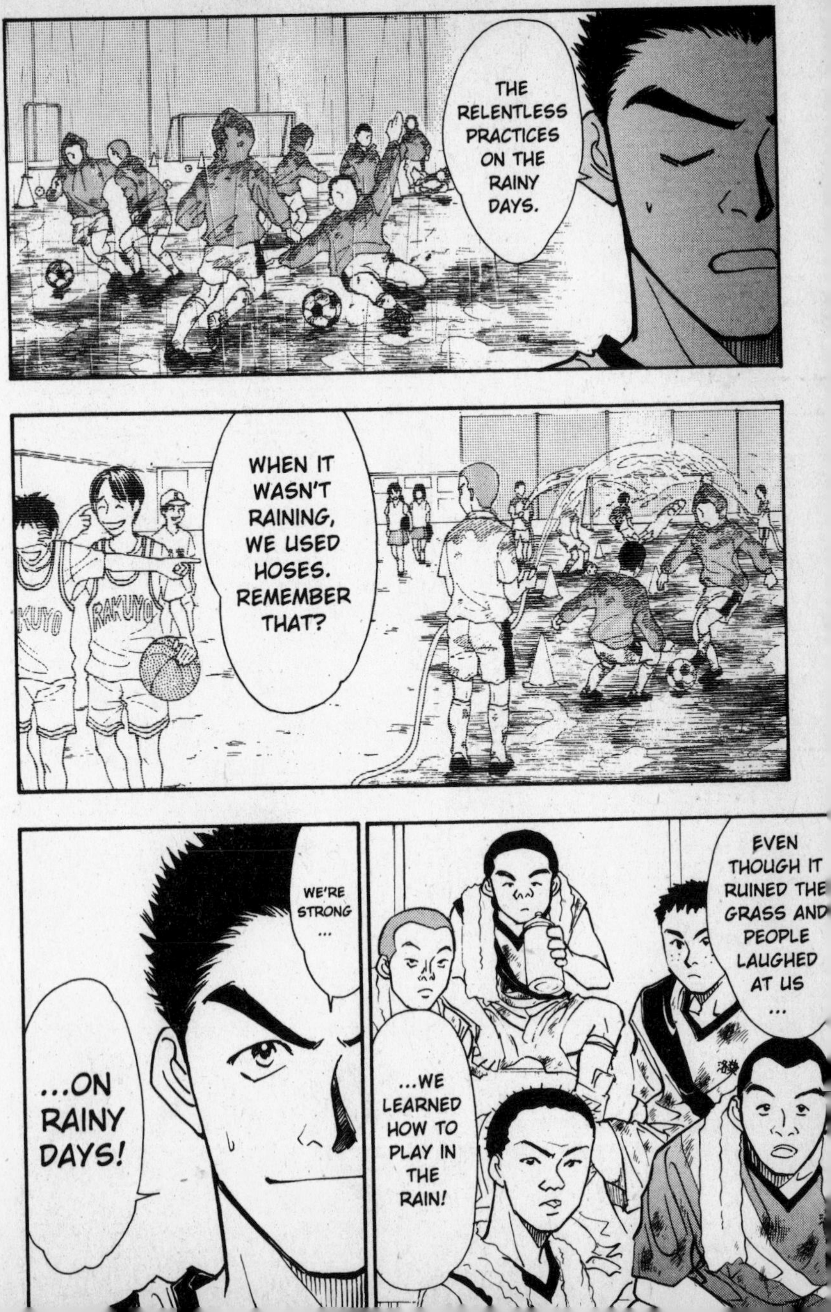
THE RELENTLESS PRACTICES ON THE RAINY DAYS.
WHEN IT WASN'T RAINING, WE USED HOSES. REMEMBER THAT?
RAKUYO
EVEN THOUGH IT RUINED THE GRASS AND PEOPLE LAUGHED AT US ...
...WE LEARNED HOW TO PLAY IN THE RAIN!
WE'RE STRONG ...
...ON RAINY DAYS!

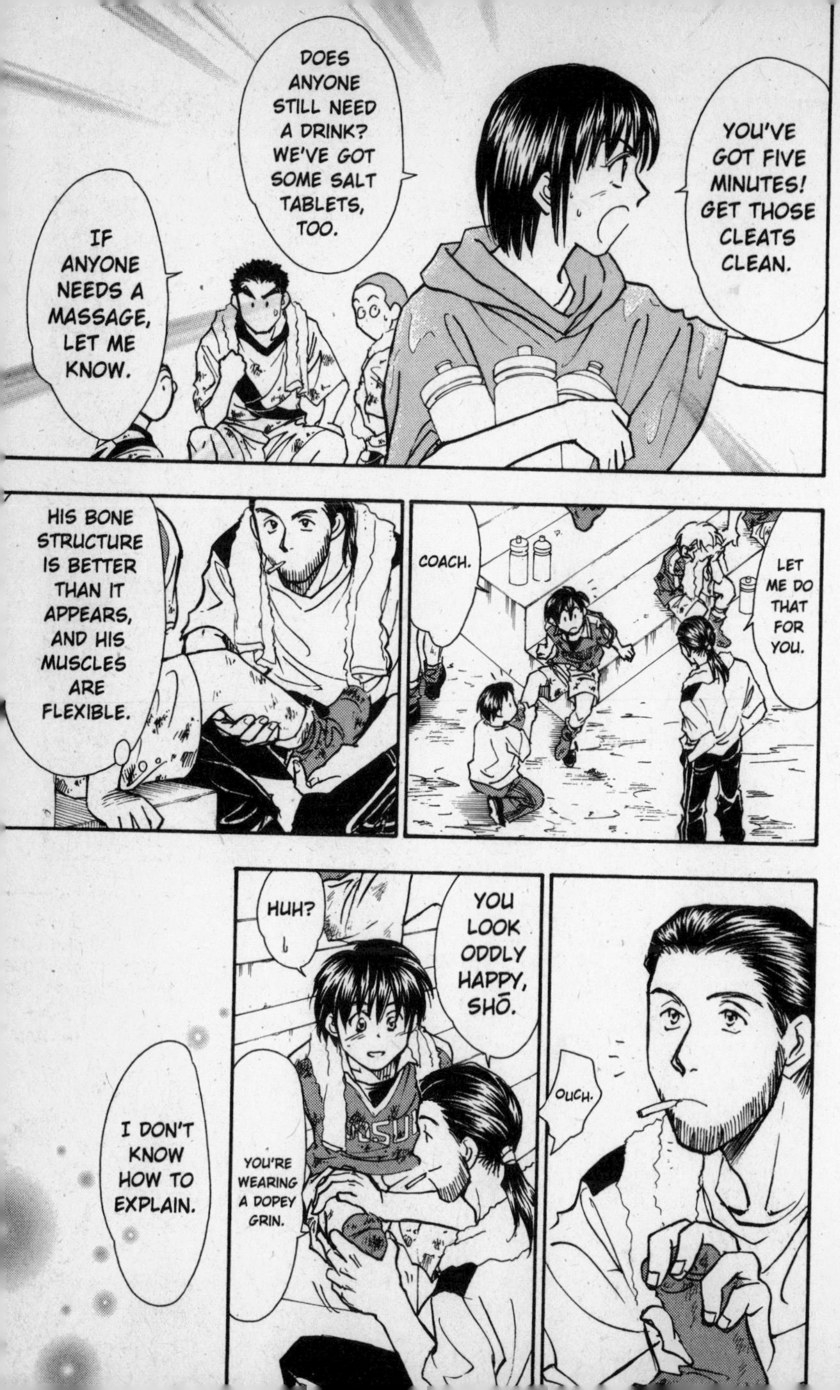
YOU'VE GOT FIVE MINUTES! GET THOSE CLEATS CLEAN.
DOES ANYONE STILL NEED A DRINK? WE'VE GOT SOME SALT TABLETS, TOO.
IF ANYONE NEEDS A MASSAGE, LET ME KNOW.
LET ME DO THAT FOR YOU.
COACH.
HIS BONE STRUCTURE IS BETTER THAN IT APPEARS, AND HIS MUSCLES ARE FLEXIBLE.
OUCH.
YOU LOOK ODDLY HAPPY, SHŌ.
HUH?
YOU'RE WEARING A DOPEY GRIN.
I DON'T KNOW HOW TO EXPLAIN.

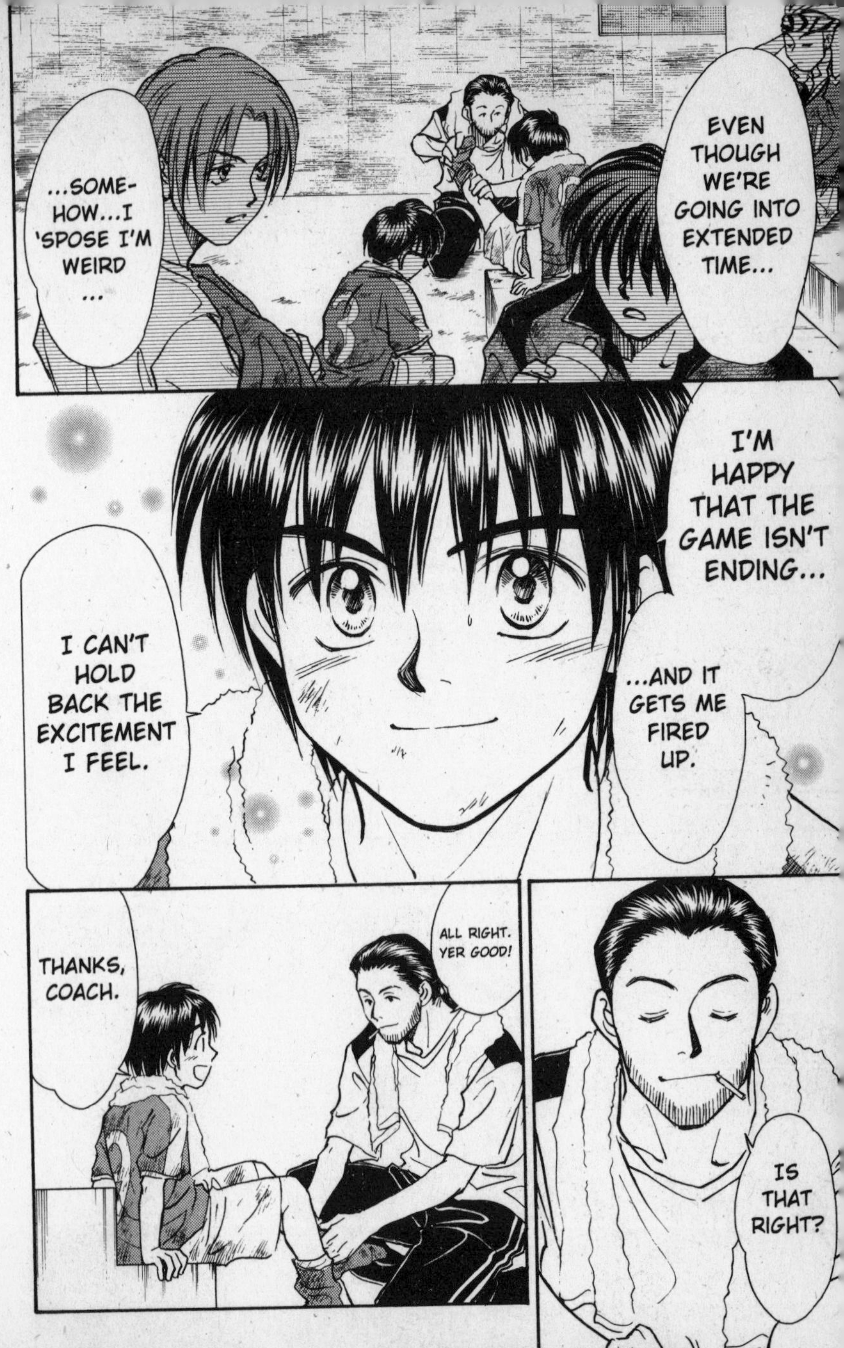
EVEN THOUGH WE'RE GOING INTO EXTENDED TIME...
...SOME-HOW...I 'SPOSE I'M WEIRD ...
I'M HAPPY THAT THE GAME ISN'T ENDING...
...AND IT GETS ME FIRED UP.
I CAN'T HOLD BACK THE EXCITEMENT I FEEL.
IS THAT RIGHT?
ALL RIGHT. YER GOOD!
THANKS, COACH.

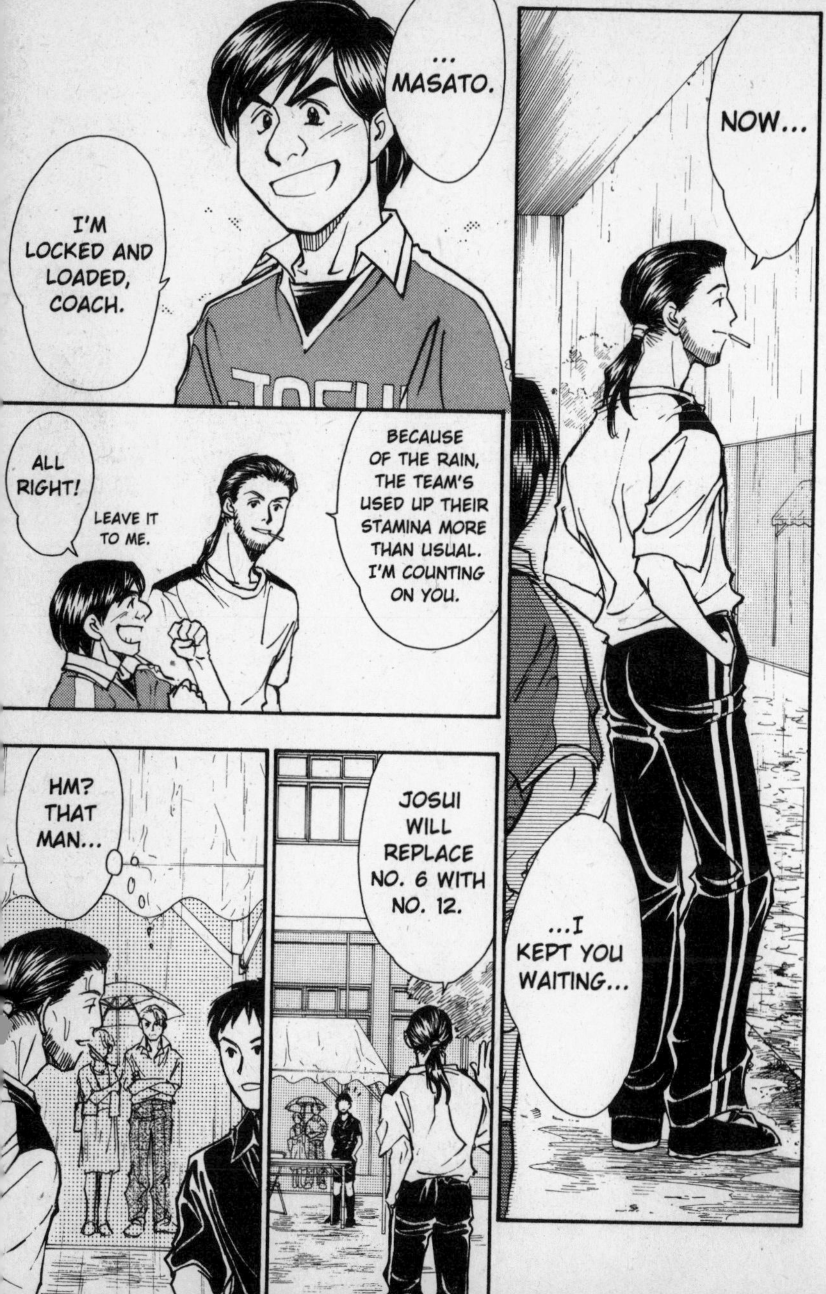
NOW...
...I KEPT YOU WAITING...
...MASATO.
I'M LOCKED AND LOADED, COACH.
BECAUSE OF THE RAIN, THE TEAM'S USED UP THEIR STAMINA MORE THAN USUAL. I'M COUNTING ON YOU.
ALL RIGHT!
LEAVE IT TO ME.
JOSUI WILL REPLACE NO. 6 WITH NO. 12.
HM? THAT MAN...

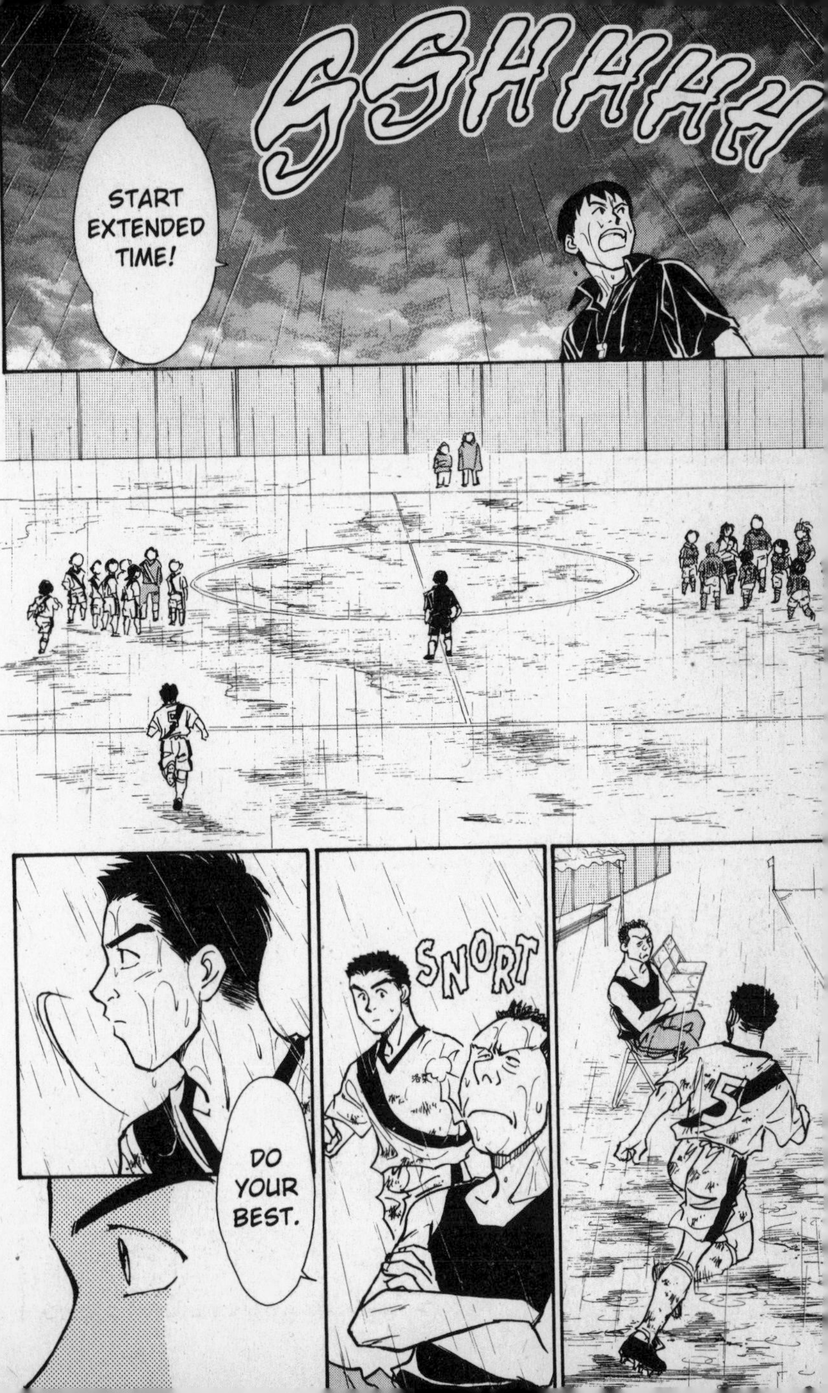
GSHHHH
START EXTENDED TIME!
SNORT
DO YOUR BEST.

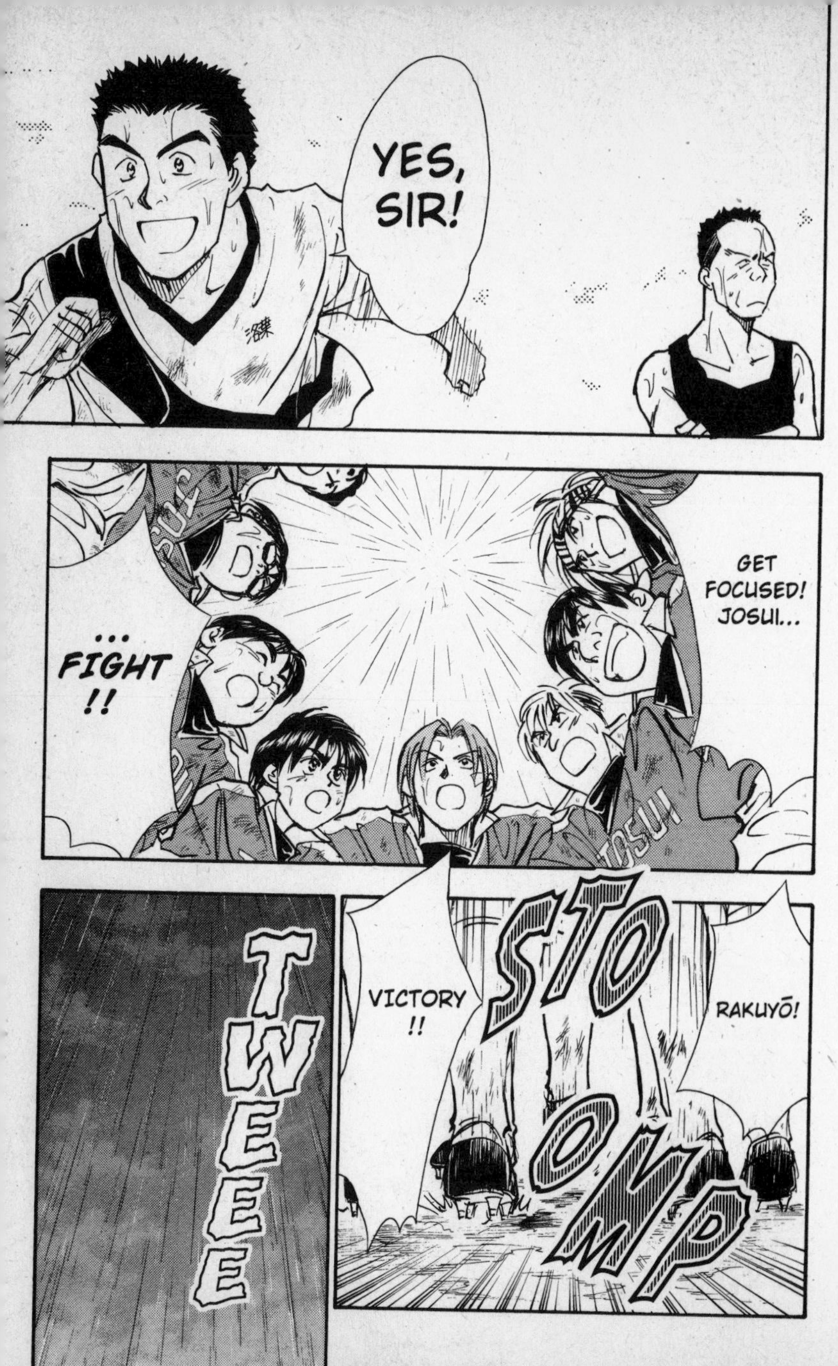
YES, SIR!
GET FOCUSED! JOSUI...
... FIGHT !!
RAKUYŌ!
STOMP
VICTORY !!
TWEEE

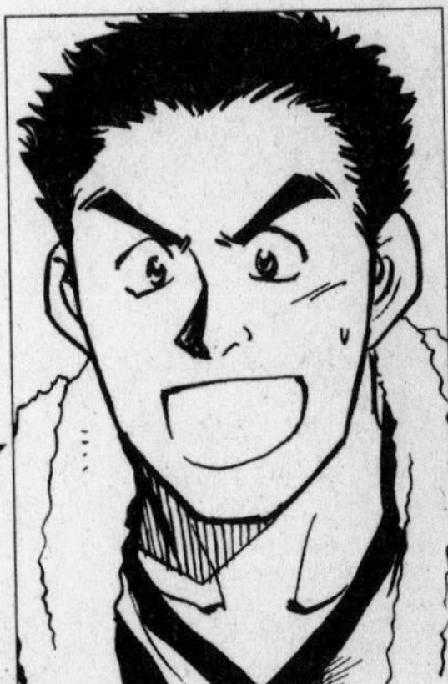

WHISTLE!

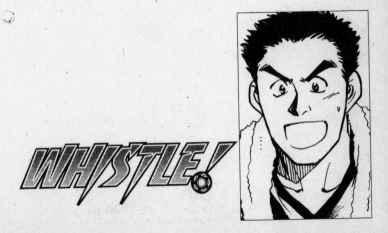

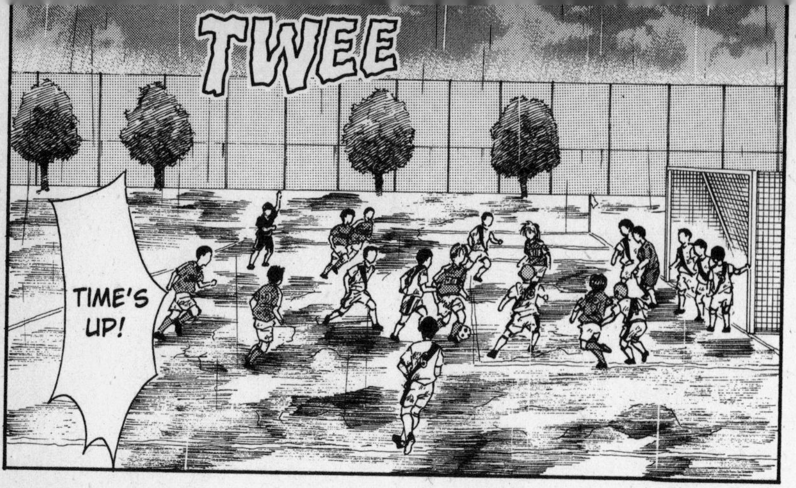
TWEE
TIME'S UP!

STAGE.76 Josui Team Unites (NOBODY IS PERFECT)

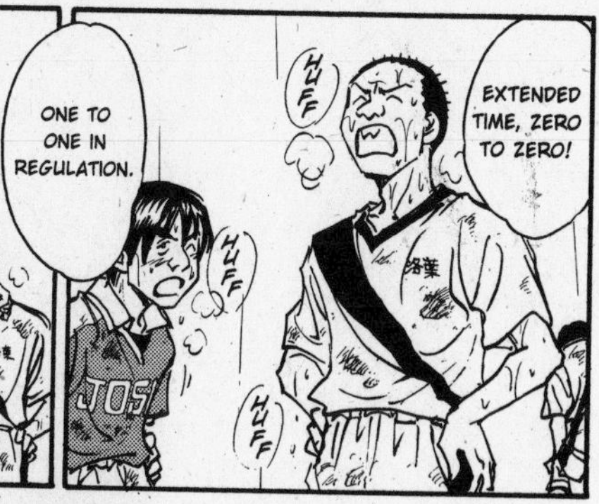
EXTENDED TIME, ZERO TO ZERO!
HUFF
ONE TO ONE IN REGULATION.
HUFF
HUFF

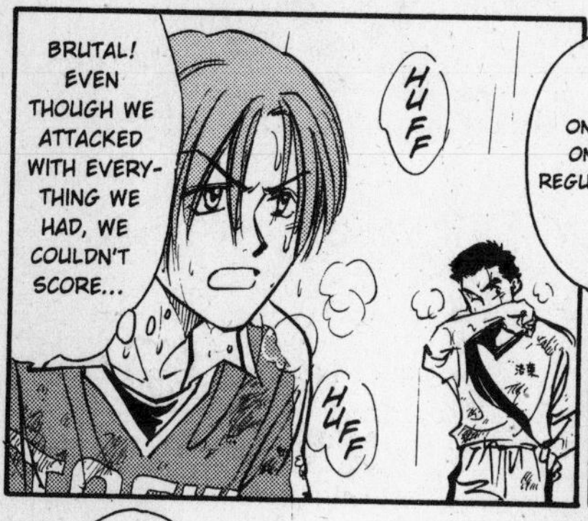
HUFF
BRUTAL! EVEN THOUGH WE ATTACKED WITH EVERY-THING WE HAD, WE COULDN'T SCORE...
HUFF

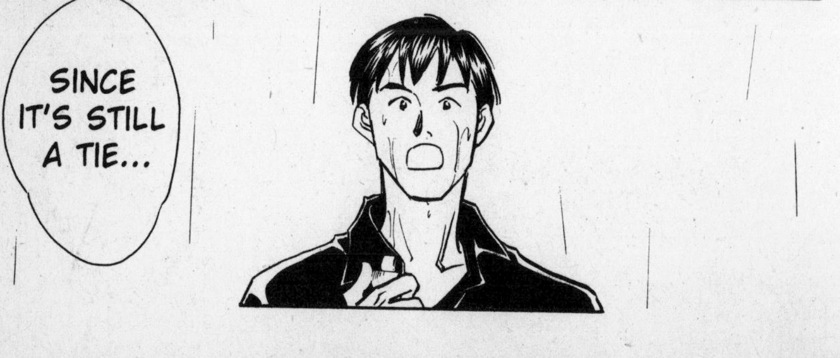
SINCE IT'S STILL A TIE...

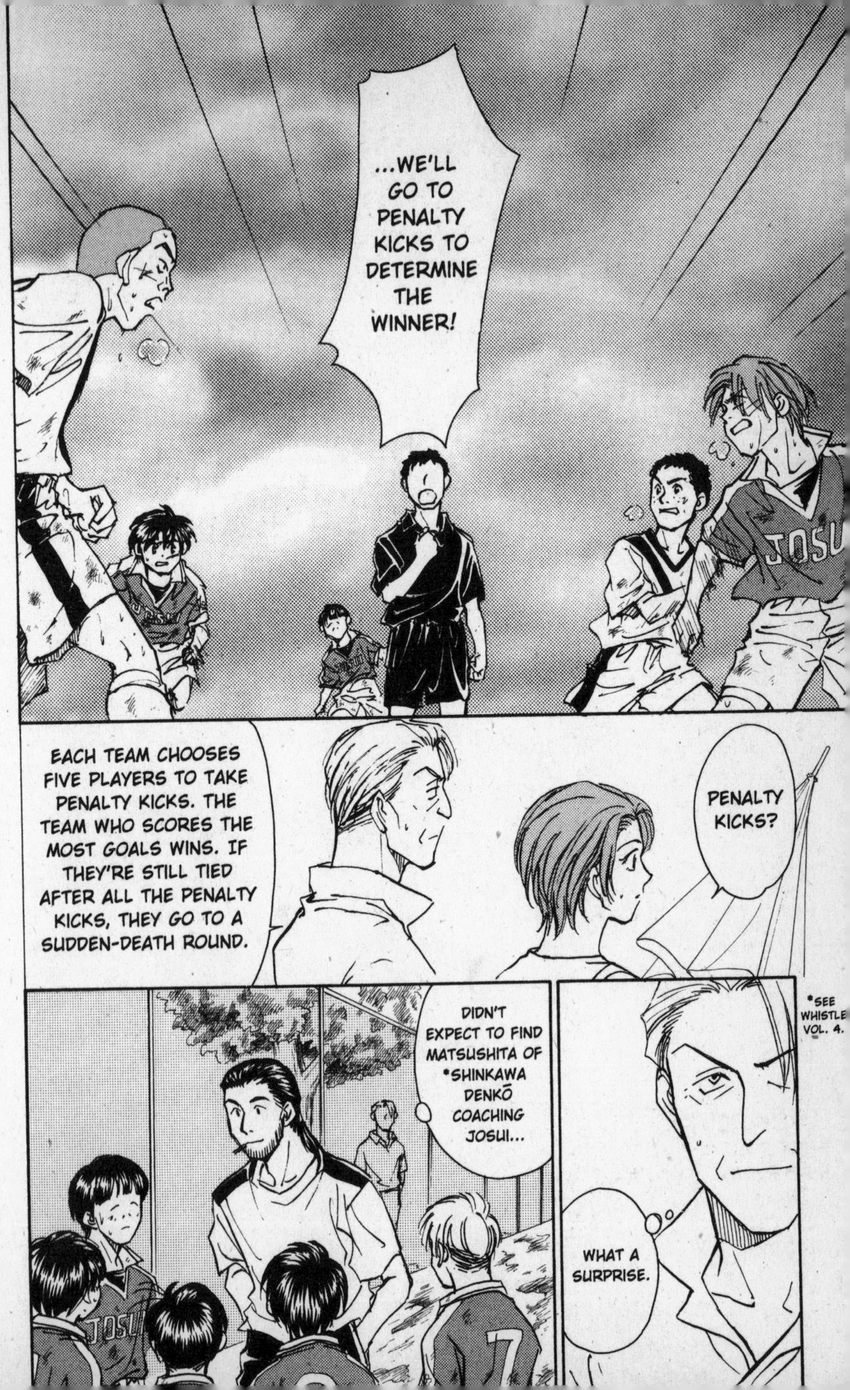
...WE'LL GO TO PENALTY KICKS TO DETERMINE THE WINNER!
JOSUI
PENALTY KICKS?
EACH TEAM CHOOSES FIVE PLAYERS TO TAKE PENALTY KICKS. THE TEAM WHO SCORES THE MOST GOALS WINS. IF THEY'RE STILL TIED AFTER ALL THE PENALTY KICKS, THEY GO TO A SUDDEN-DEATH ROUND.
WHAT A SURPRISE.
DIDN'T EXPECT TO FIND MATSUSHITA OF *SHINKAWA DENKŌ COACHING JOSUI...
JOSUI
7
*SEE WHISTLE VOL. 4.

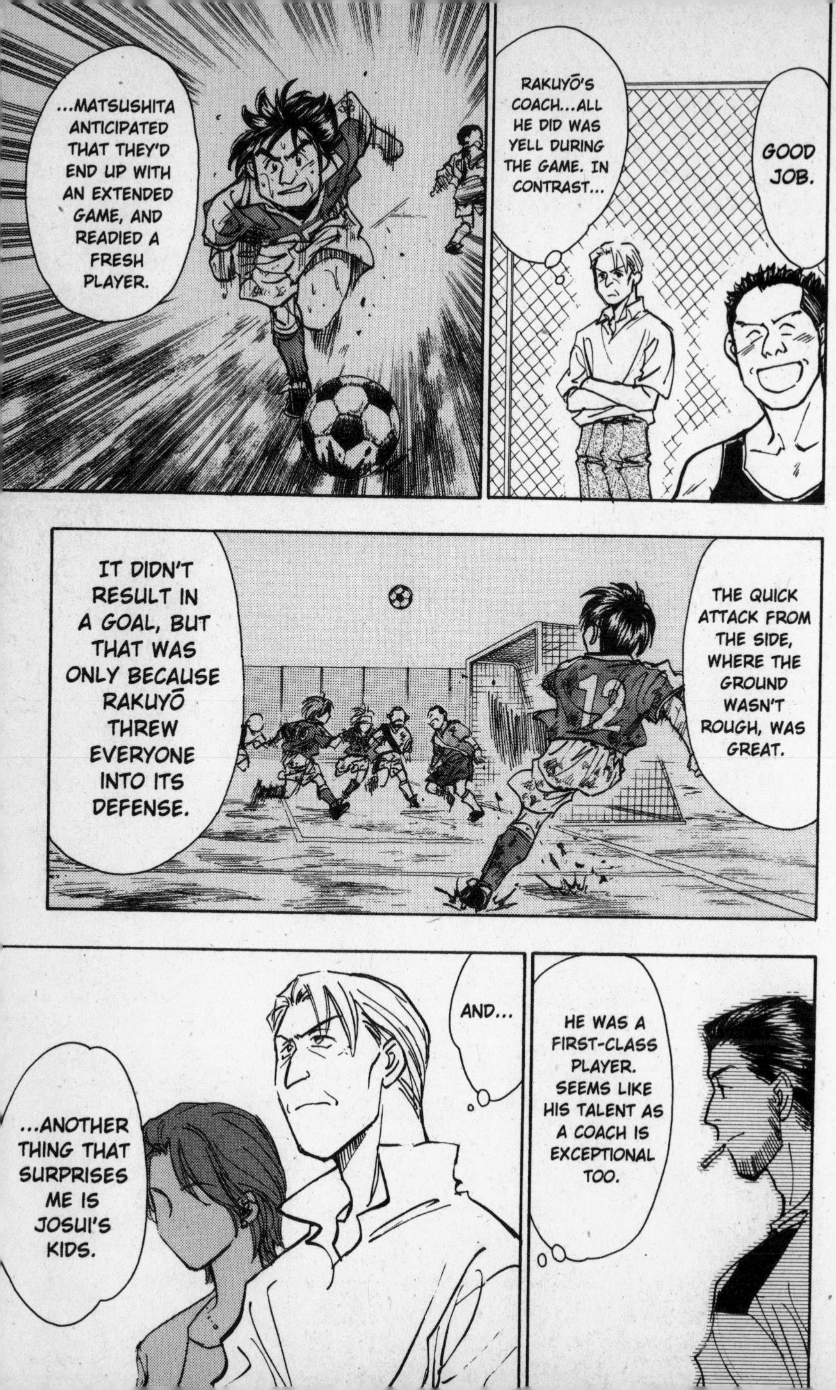
GOOD JOB.
RAKUYŌ'S COACH...ALL HE DID WAS YELL DURING THE GAME. IN CONTRAST...
...MATSUSHITA ANTICIPATED THAT THEY'D END UP WITH AN EXTENDED GAME, AND READIED A FRESH PLAYER.
THE QUICK ATTACK FROM THE SIDE, WHERE THE GROUND WASN'T ROUGH, WAS GREAT.
IT DIDN'T RESULT IN A GOAL, BUT THAT WAS ONLY BECAUSE RAKUYŌ THREW EVERYONE INTO ITS DEFENSE.
HE WAS A FIRST-CLASS PLAYER. SEEMS LIKE HIS TALENT AS A COACH IS EXCEPTIONAL TOO.
AND...
...ANOTHER THING THAT SURPRISES ME IS JOSUI'S KIDS.

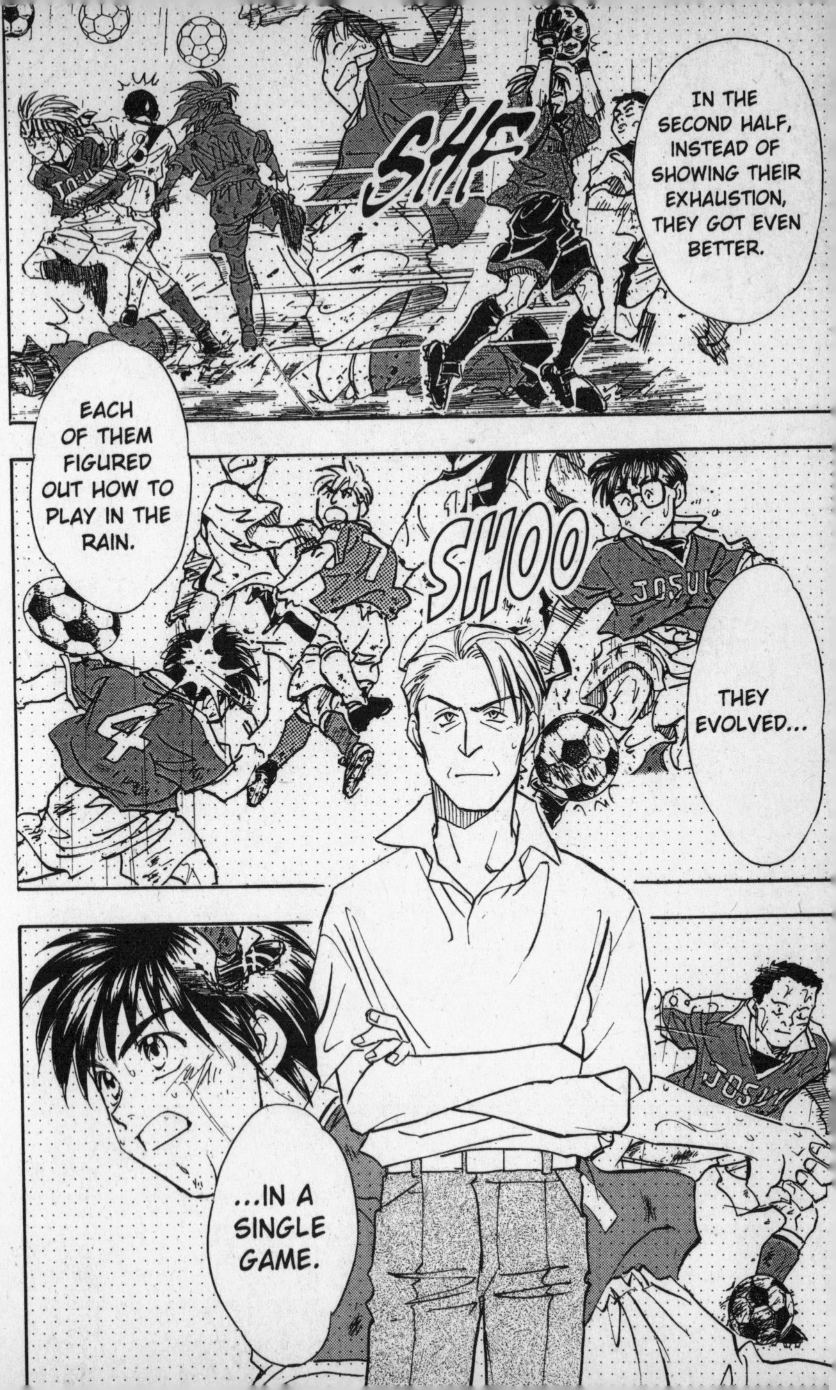
IN THE SECOND HALF, INSTEAD OF SHOWING THEIR EXHAUSTION, THEY GOT EVEN BETTER.
SHF
EACH OF THEM FIGURED OUT HOW TO PLAY IN THE RAIN.
SHOO
THEY EVOLVED...
...IN A SINGLE GAME.

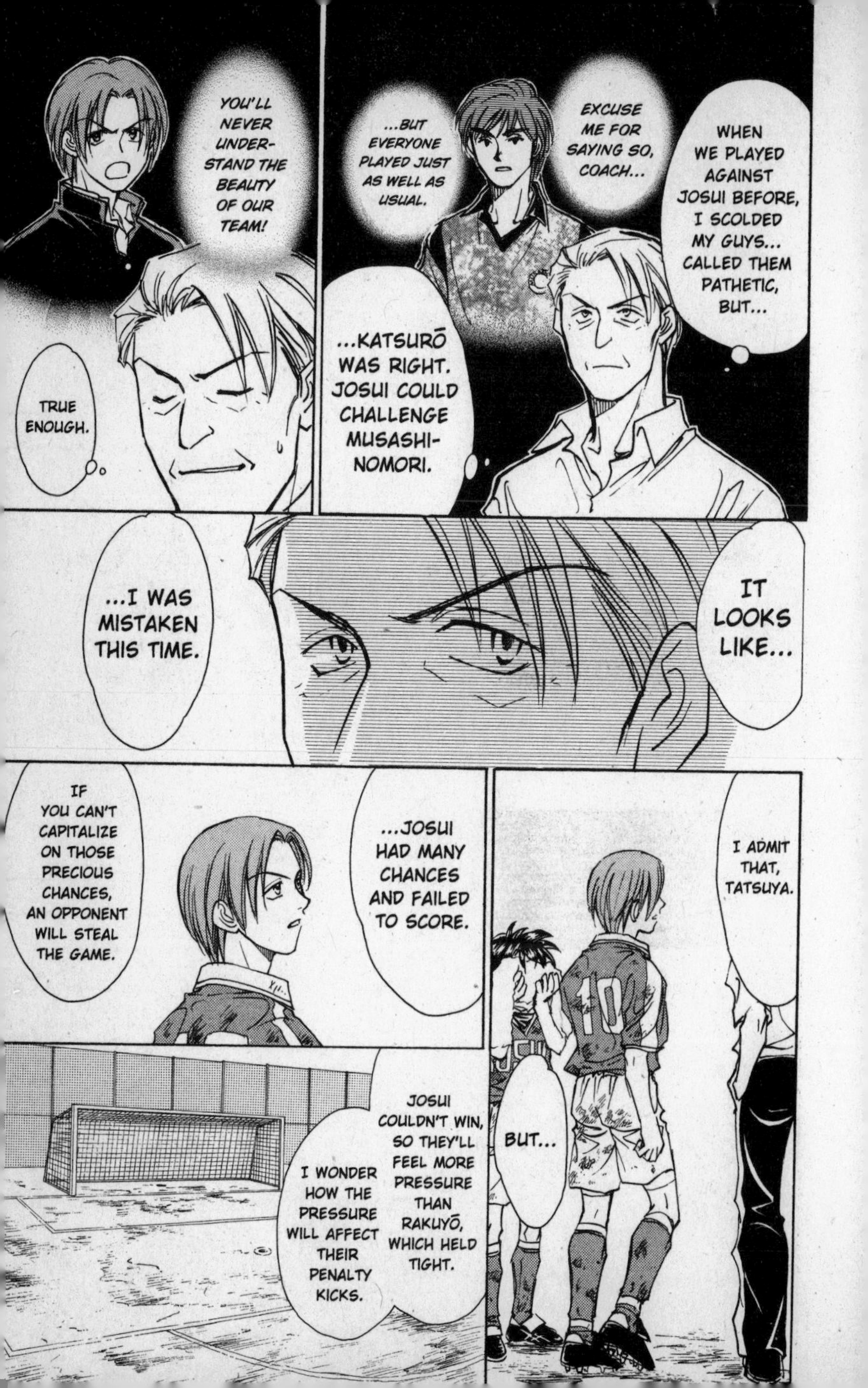
WHEN WE PLAYED AGAINST JOSUI BEFORE, I SCOLDED MY GUYS... CALLED THEM PATHETIC, BUT...
EXCUSE ME FOR SAYING SO, COACH...
...BUT EVERYONE PLAYED JUST AS WELL AS USUAL.
...KATSURŌ WAS RIGHT. JOSUI COULD CHALLENGE MUSASHI-NOMORI.
YOU'LL NEVER UNDER-STAND THE BEAUTY OF OUR TEAM!
TRUE ENOUGH.
IT LOOKS LIKE...
...I WAS MISTAKEN THIS TIME.
I ADMIT THAT, TATSUYA.
BUT...
...JOSUI HAD MANY CHANCES AND FAILED TO SCORE.
IF YOU CAN'T CAPITALIZE ON THOSE PRECIOUS CHANCES, AN OPPONENT WILL STEAL THE GAME.
JOSUI COULDN'T WIN, SO THEY'LL FEEL MORE PRESSURE THAN RAKUYŌ, WHICH HELD TIGHT.
I WONDER HOW THE PRESSURE WILL AFFECT THEIR PENALTY KICKS.

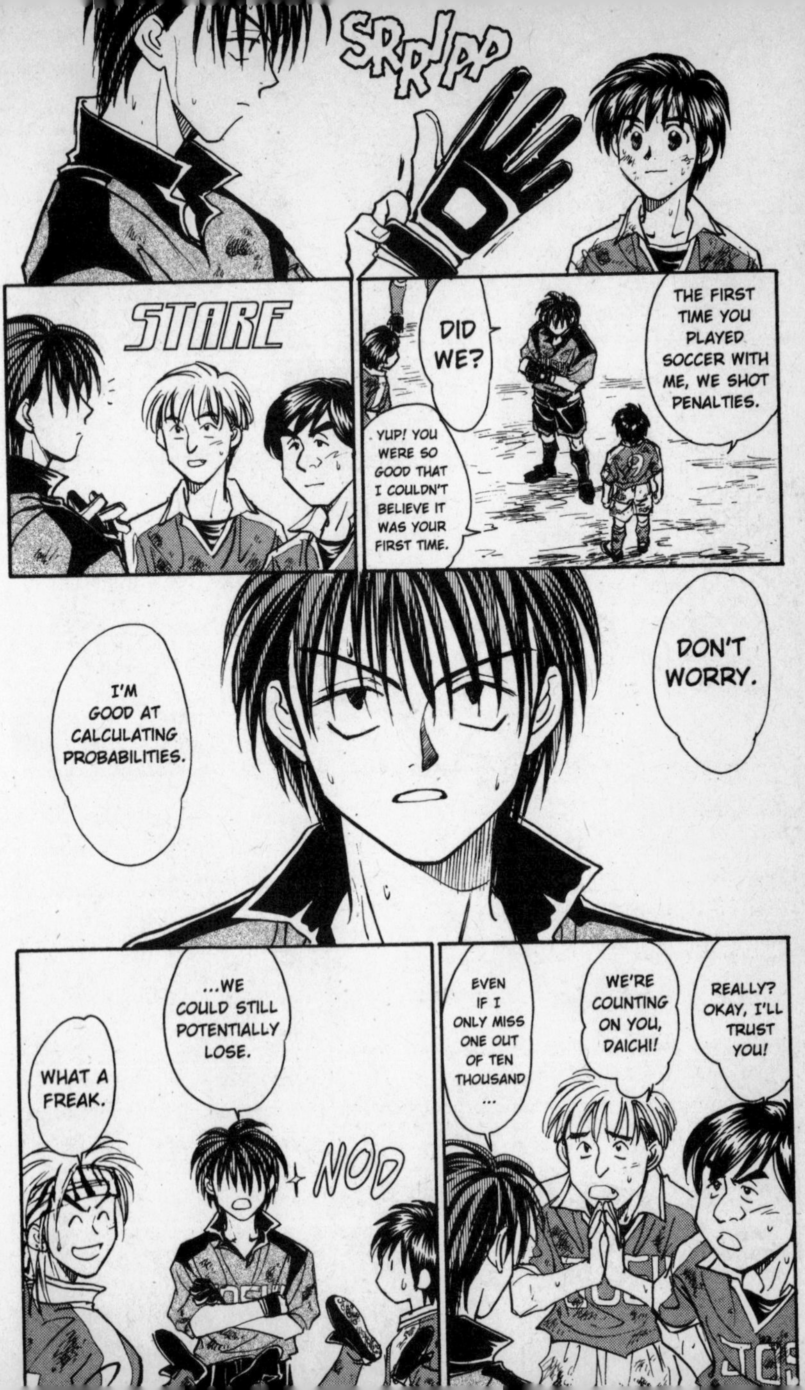
SRRIPP
THE FIRST TIME YOU PLAYED SOCCER WITH ME, WE SHOT PENALTIES.
DID WE?
YUP! YOU WERE SO GOOD THAT I COULDN'T BELIEVE IT WAS YOUR FIRST TIME.
STARE
DON'T WORRY.
I'M GOOD AT CALCULATING PROBABILITIES.
REALLY? OKAY, I'LL TRUST YOU!
WE'RE COUNTING ON YOU, DAICHI!
EVEN IF I ONLY MISS ONE OUT OF TEN THOUSAND ...
...WE COULD STILL POTENTIALLY LOSE.
NOD
WHAT A FREAK.

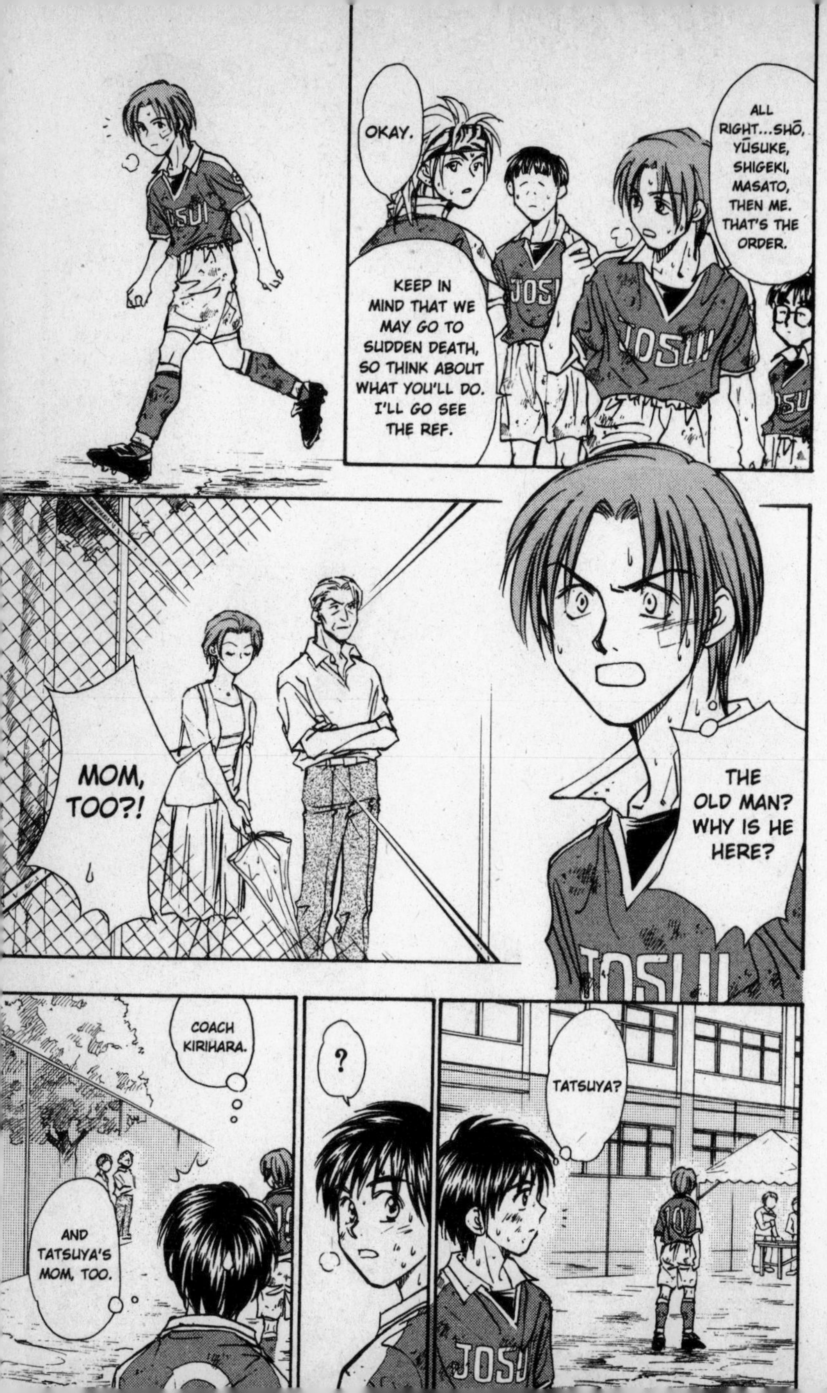
ALL RIGHT...SHŌ, YŪSUKE, SHIGEKI, MASATO, THEN ME. THAT'S THE ORDER.
OKAY.
KEEP IN MIND THAT WE MAY GO TO SUDDEN DEATH, SO THINK ABOUT WHAT YOU'LL DO. I'LL GO SEE THE REF.
THE OLD MAN? WHY IS HE HERE?
MOM, TOO?!
TATSUYA?
?
COACH KIRIHARA.
AND TATSUYA'S MOM, TOO.

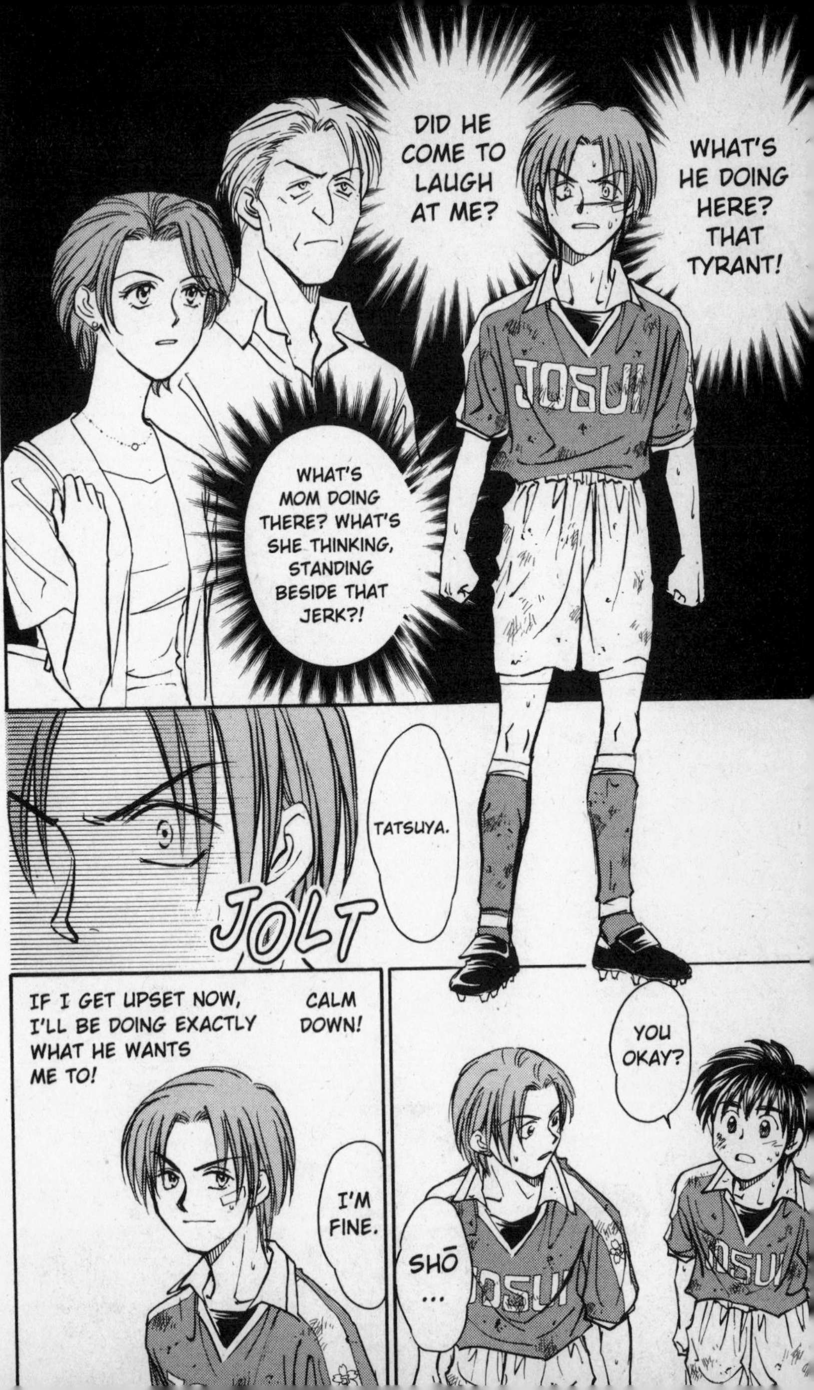
WHAT'S HE DOING HERE? THAT TYRANT!
DID HE COME TO LAUGH AT ME?
WHAT'S MOM DOING THERE? WHAT'S SHE THINKING, STANDING BESIDE THAT JERK?!
TATSUYA.
JOLT
YOU OKAY?
SHŌ ...
CALM DOWN!
IF I GET UPSET NOW, I'LL BE DOING EXACTLY WHAT HE WANTS ME TO!
I'M FINE.

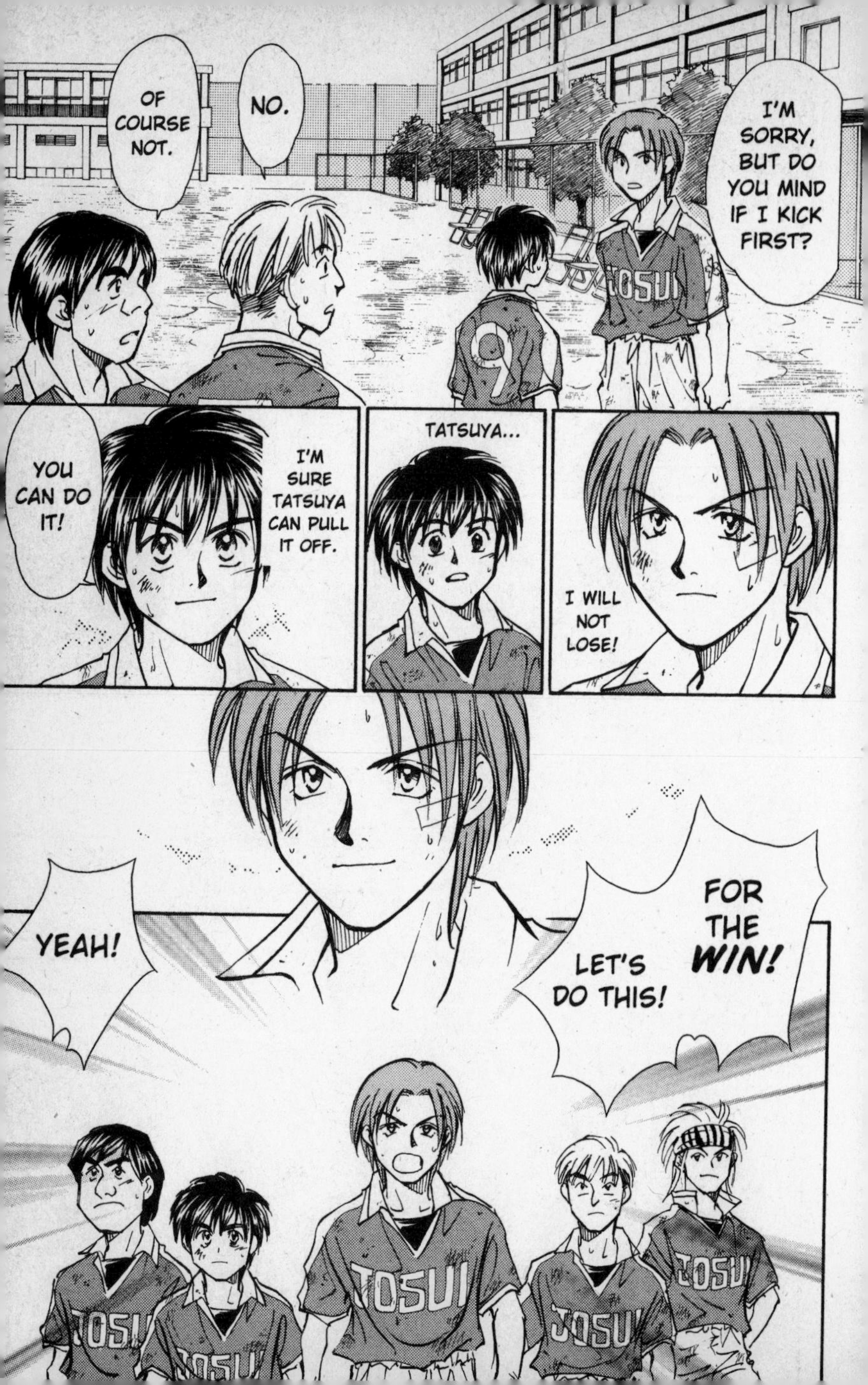
I'M SORRY, BUT DO YOU MIND IF I KICK FIRST?
NO.
OF COURSE NOT.
I WILL NOT LOSE!
TATSUYA...
I'M SURE TATSUYA CAN PULL IT OFF.
YOU CAN DO IT!
FOR THE *WIN!*
LET'S DO THIS!
YEAH!

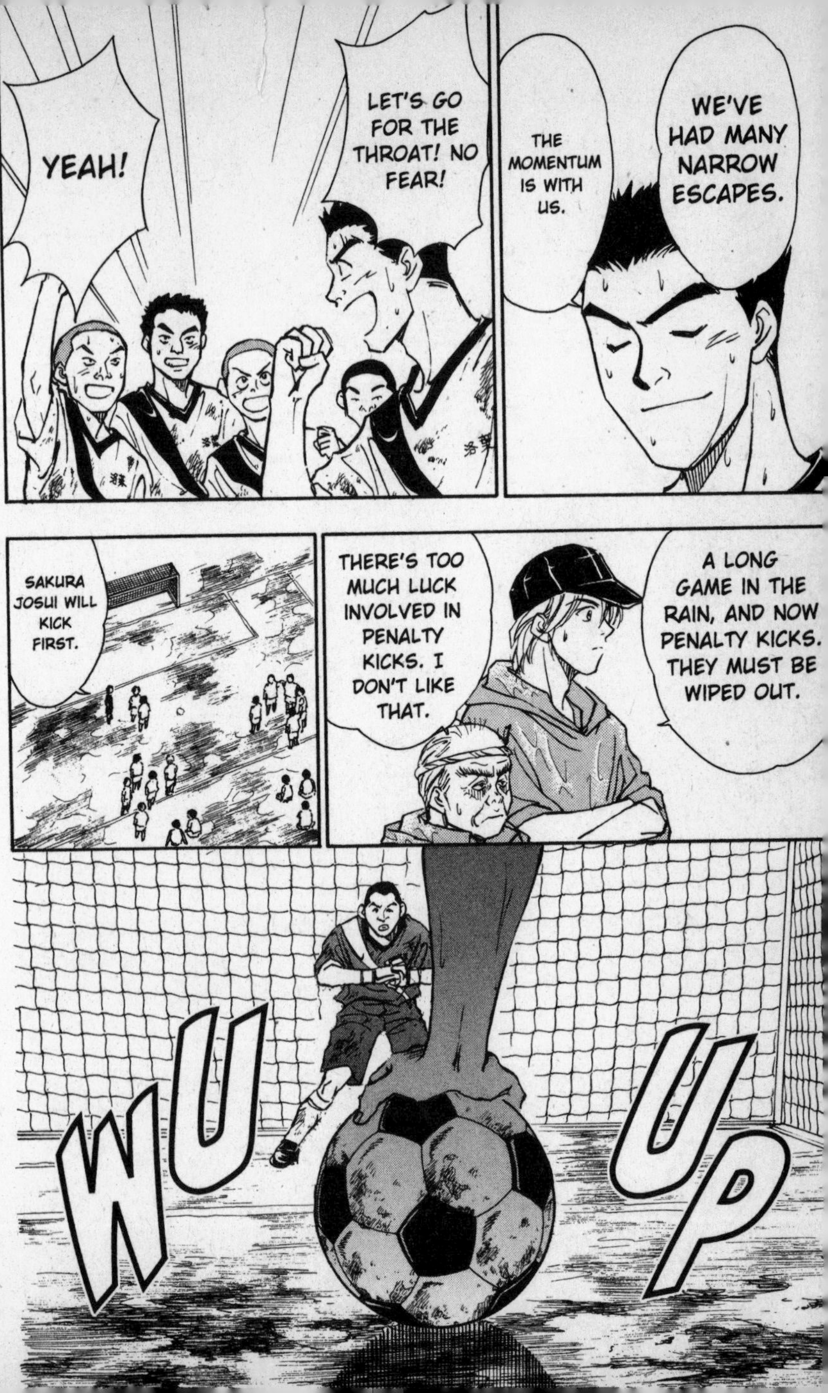

WE'VE HAD MANY NARROW ESCAPES.
THE MOMENTUM IS WITH US.
LET'S GO FOR THE THROAT! NO FEAR!
YEAH!
A LONG GAME IN THE RAIN, AND NOW PENALTY KICKS. THEY MUST BE WIPED OUT.
THERE'S TOO MUCH LUCK INVOLVED IN PENALTY KICKS. I DON'T LIKE THAT.
SAKURA JOSUI WILL KICK FIRST.
WUUP

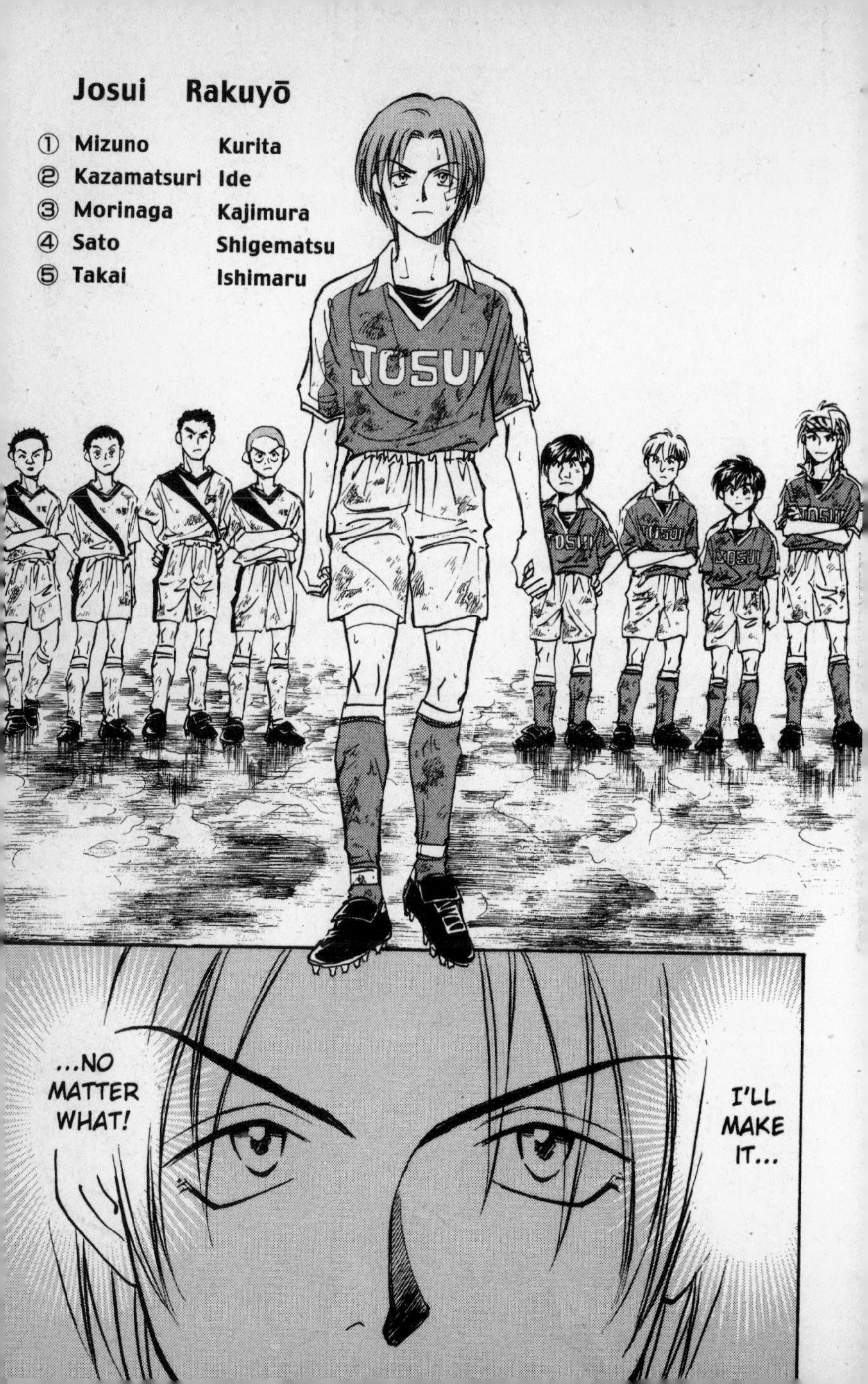
Josui Rakuyō
① Mizuno Kurita
② Kazamatsuri Ide
③ Morinaga Kajimura
④ Sato Shigematsu
⑤ Takai Ishimaru
JOSUI
I'LL MAKE IT...
...NO MATTER WHAT!

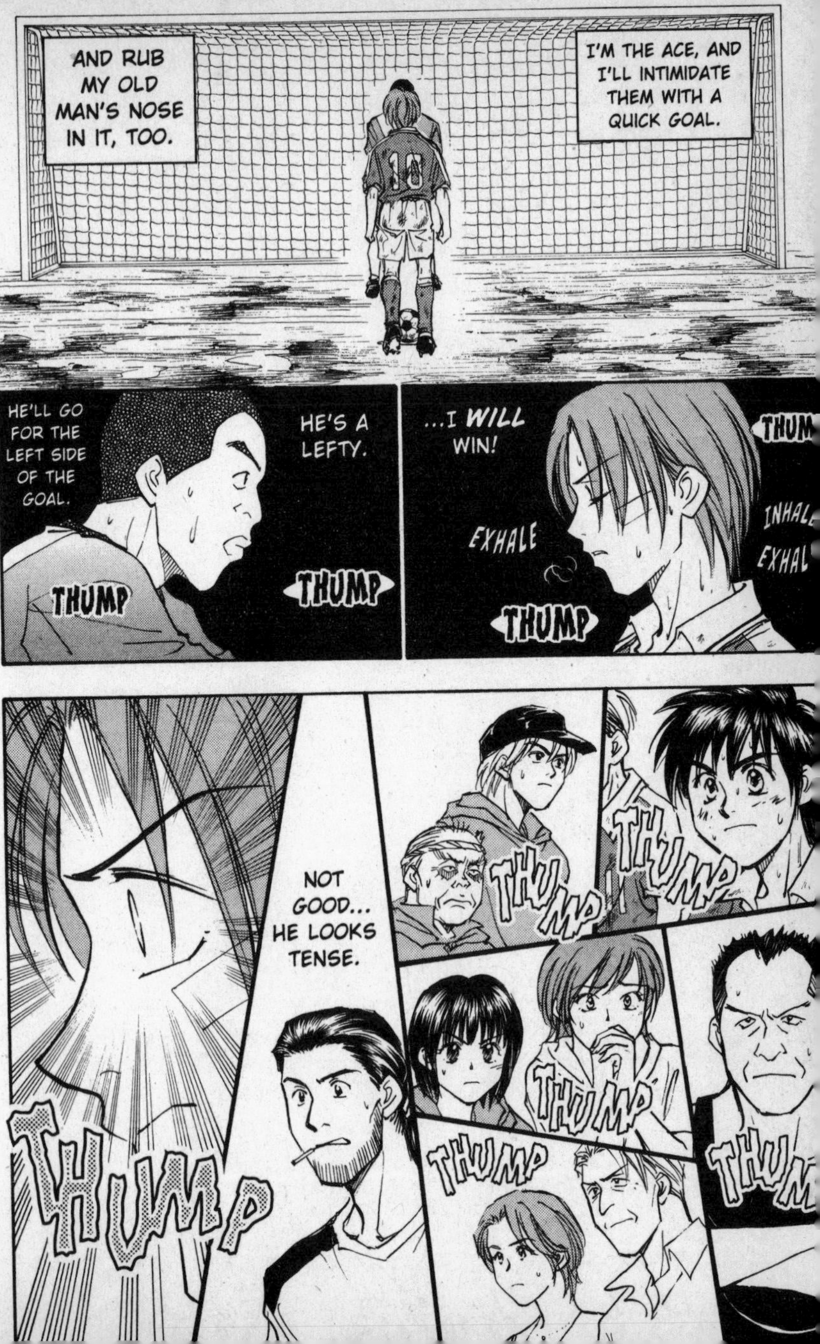
I'M THE ACE, AND I'LL INTIMIDATE THEM WITH A QUICK GOAL.
AND RUB MY OLD MAN'S NOSE IN IT, TOO.
THUM
INHALE
EXHAL
...I WILL WIN!
EXHALE
THUMP
HE'S A LEFTY.
THUMP
HE'LL GO FOR THE LEFT SIDE OF THE GOAL.
THUMP
THUMP
THUMP
THUMP
THUMP
THUMP
NOT GOOD... HE LOOKS TENSE.
THUMP

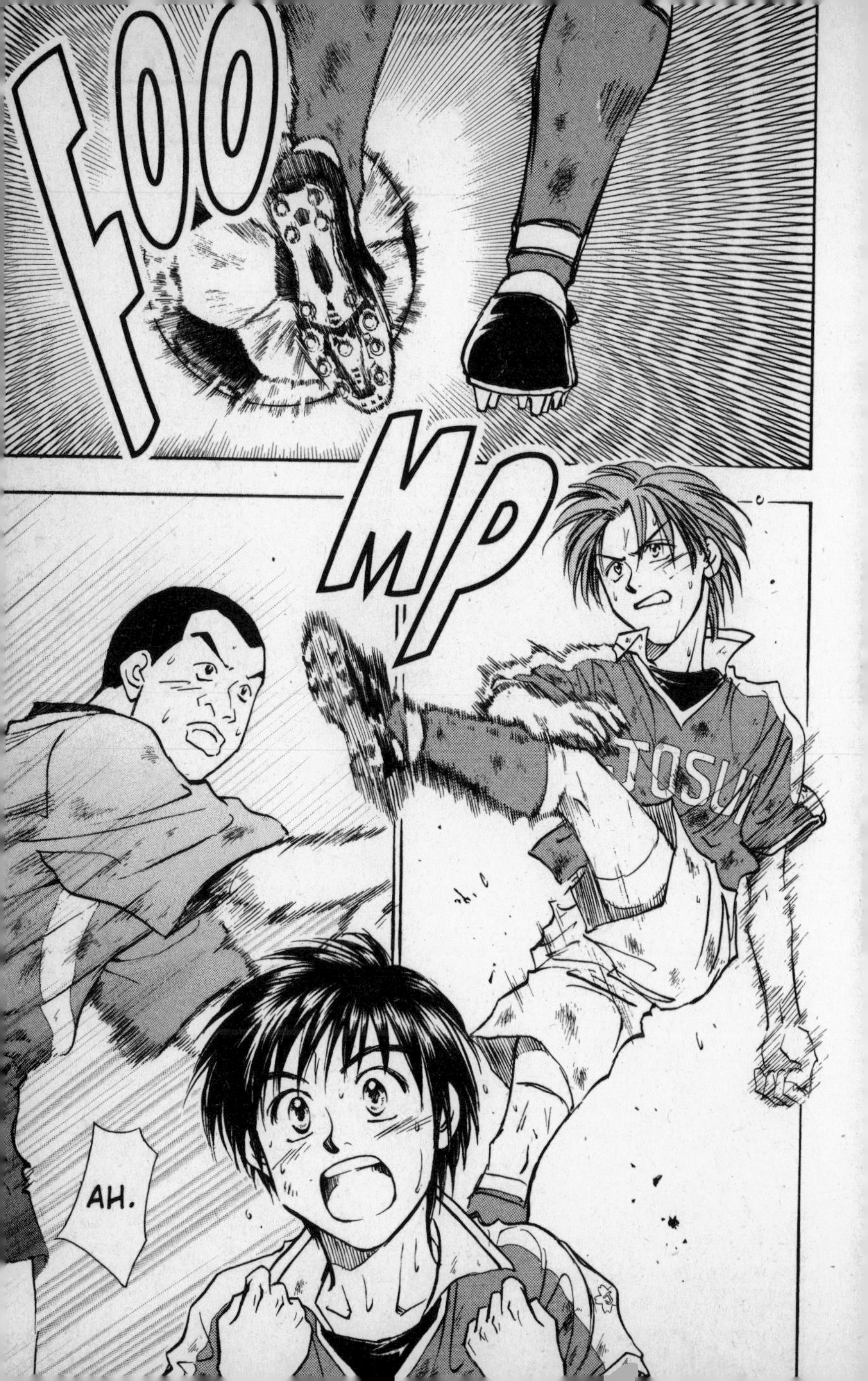
FOOMP
AH.

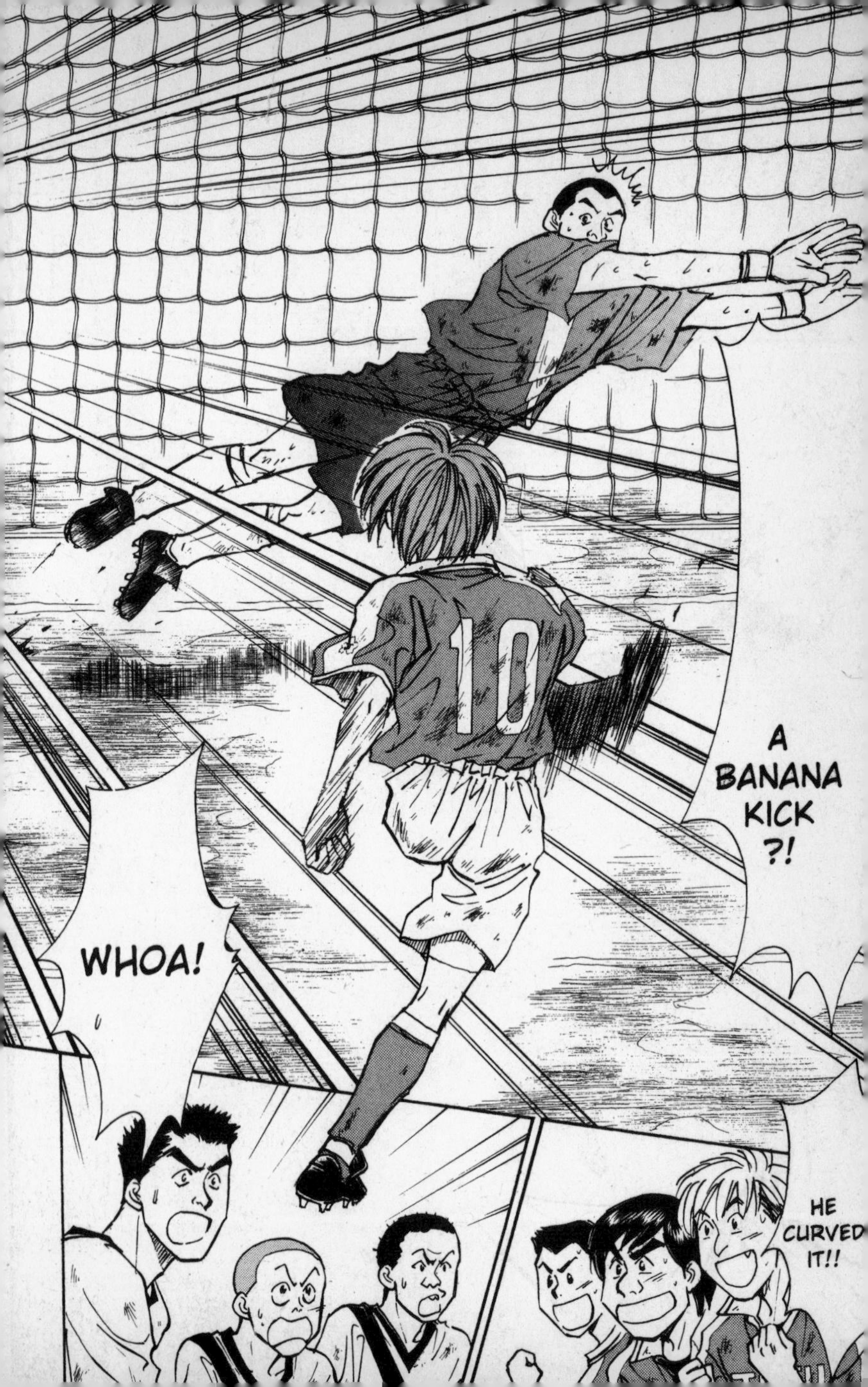
A BANANA KICK ?!
HE CURVED IT!!
WHOA!

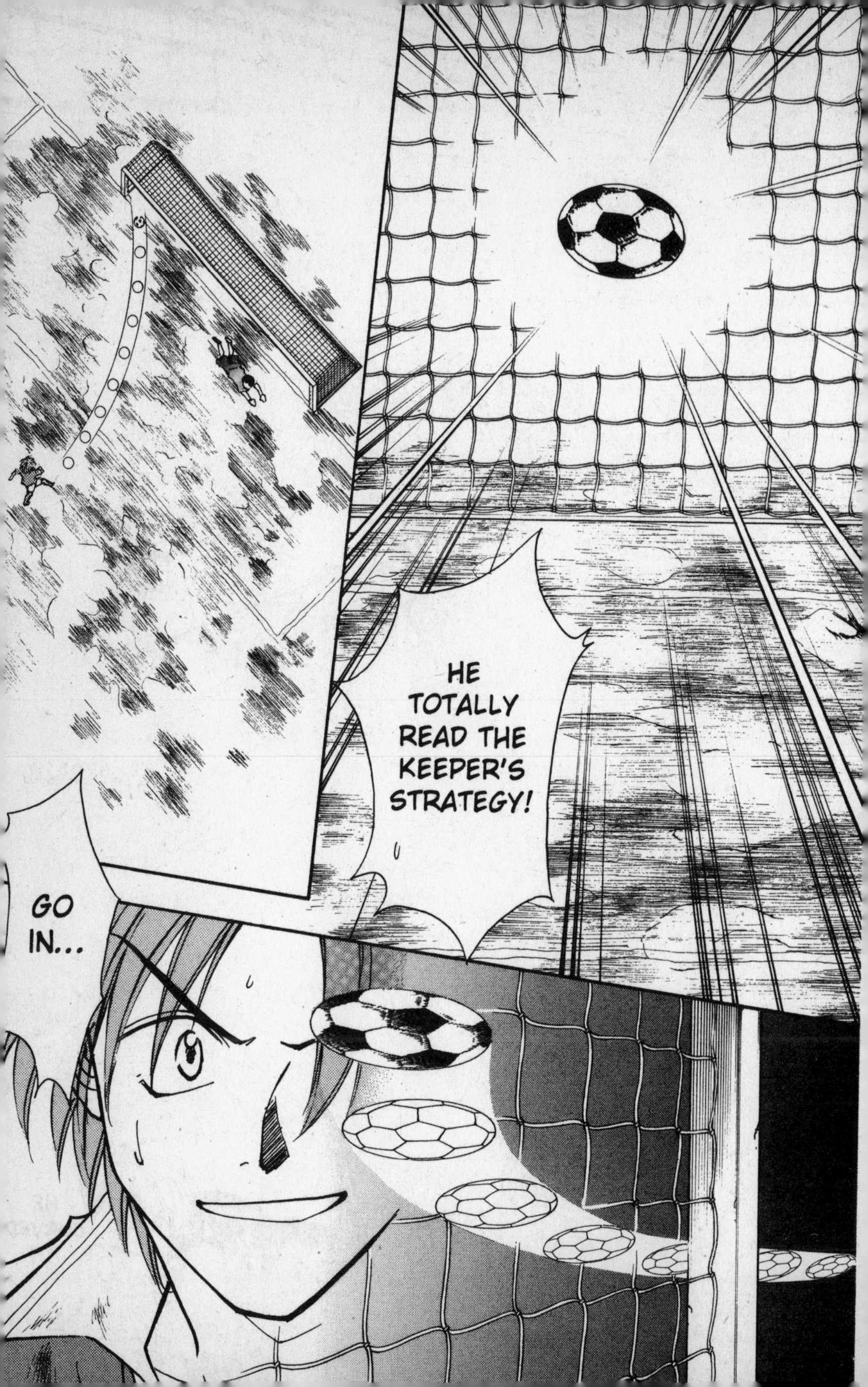
HE TOTALLY READ THE KEEPER'S STRATEGY!
GO IN...

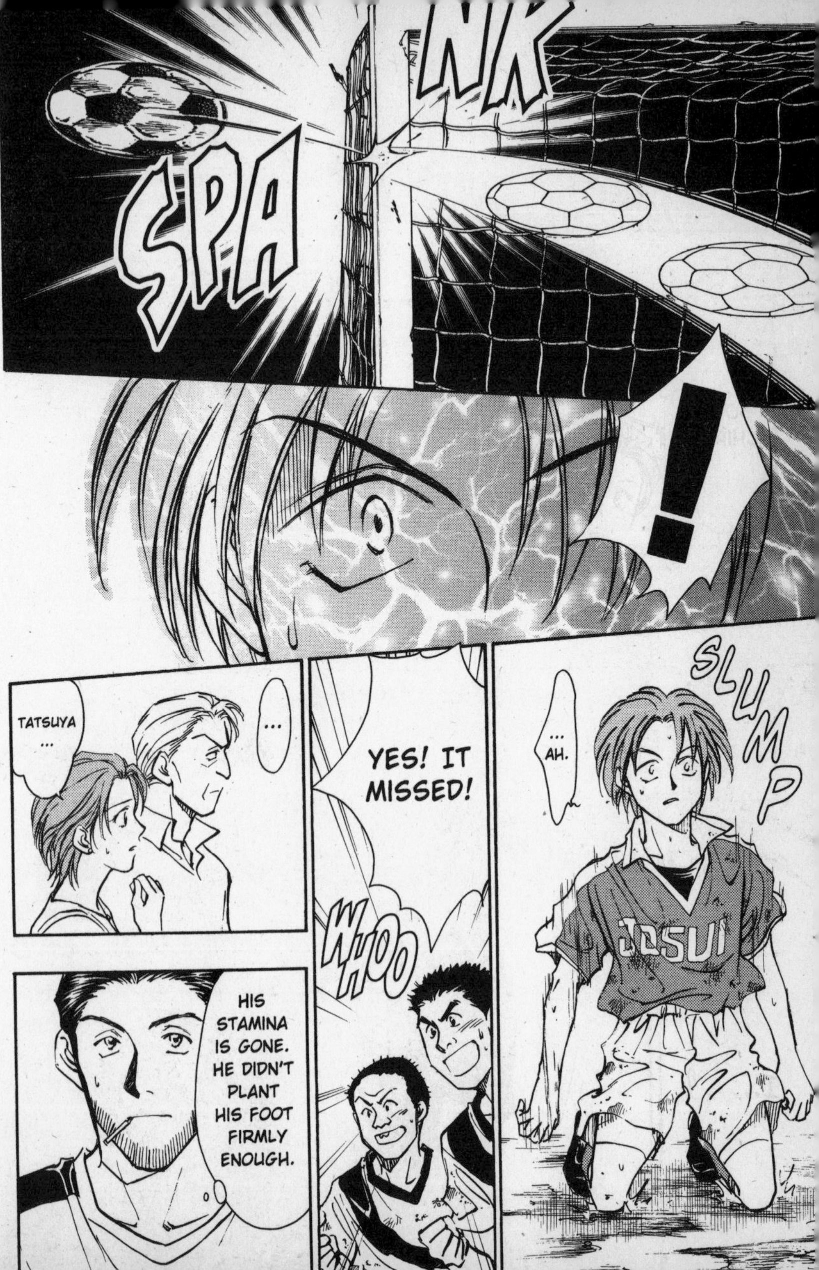

SPA
NK
!
... AH.
SLUMP
YES! IT MISSED!
WHOO
...
TATSUYA ...
HIS STAMINA IS GONE. HE DIDN'T PLANT HIS FOOT FIRMLY ENOUGH.

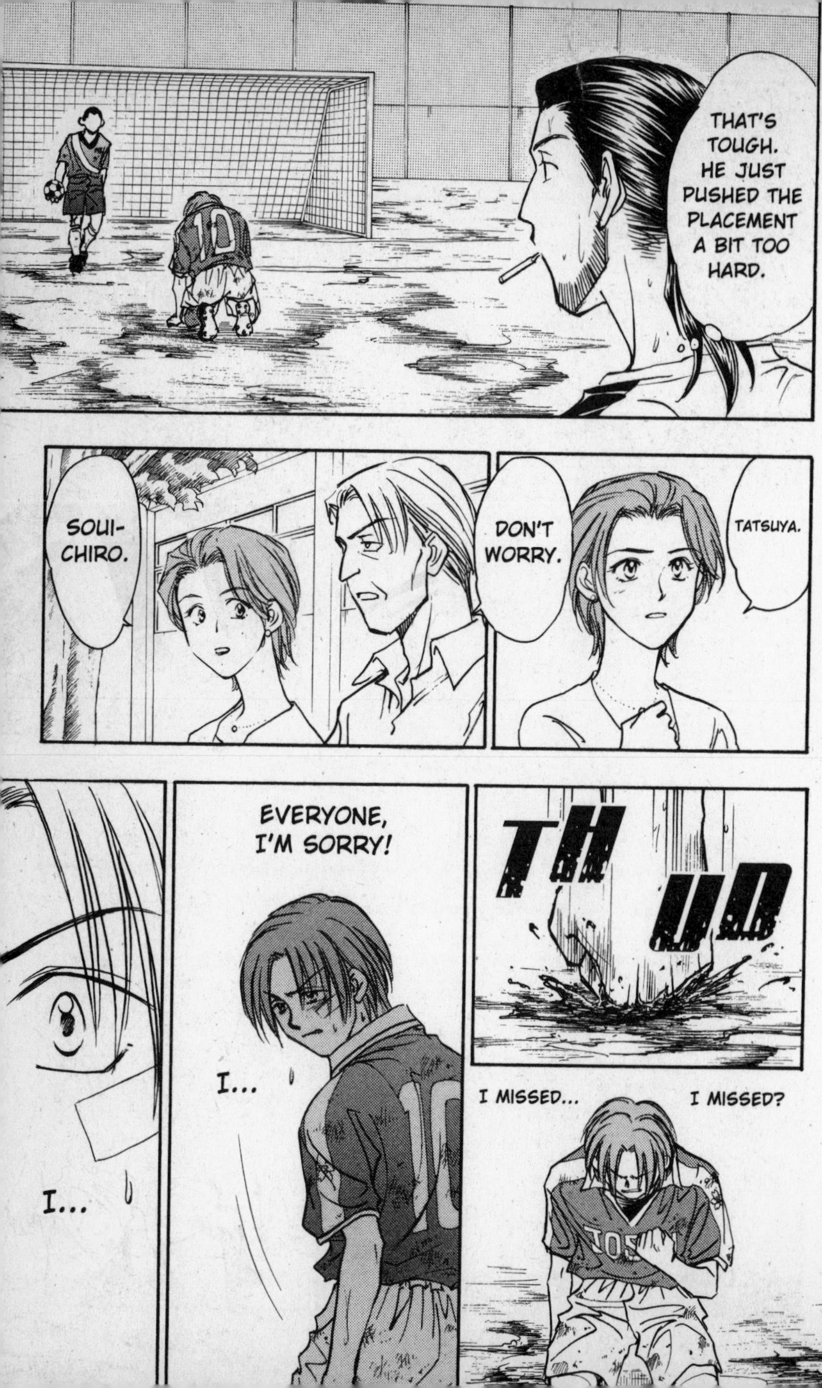
THAT'S TOUGH. HE JUST PUSHED THE PLACEMENT A BIT TOO HARD.
TATSUYA.
DON'T WORRY.
SOUI-CHIRO.
THUD
I MISSED?
I MISSED...
EVERYONE, I'M SORRY!
I...
I...

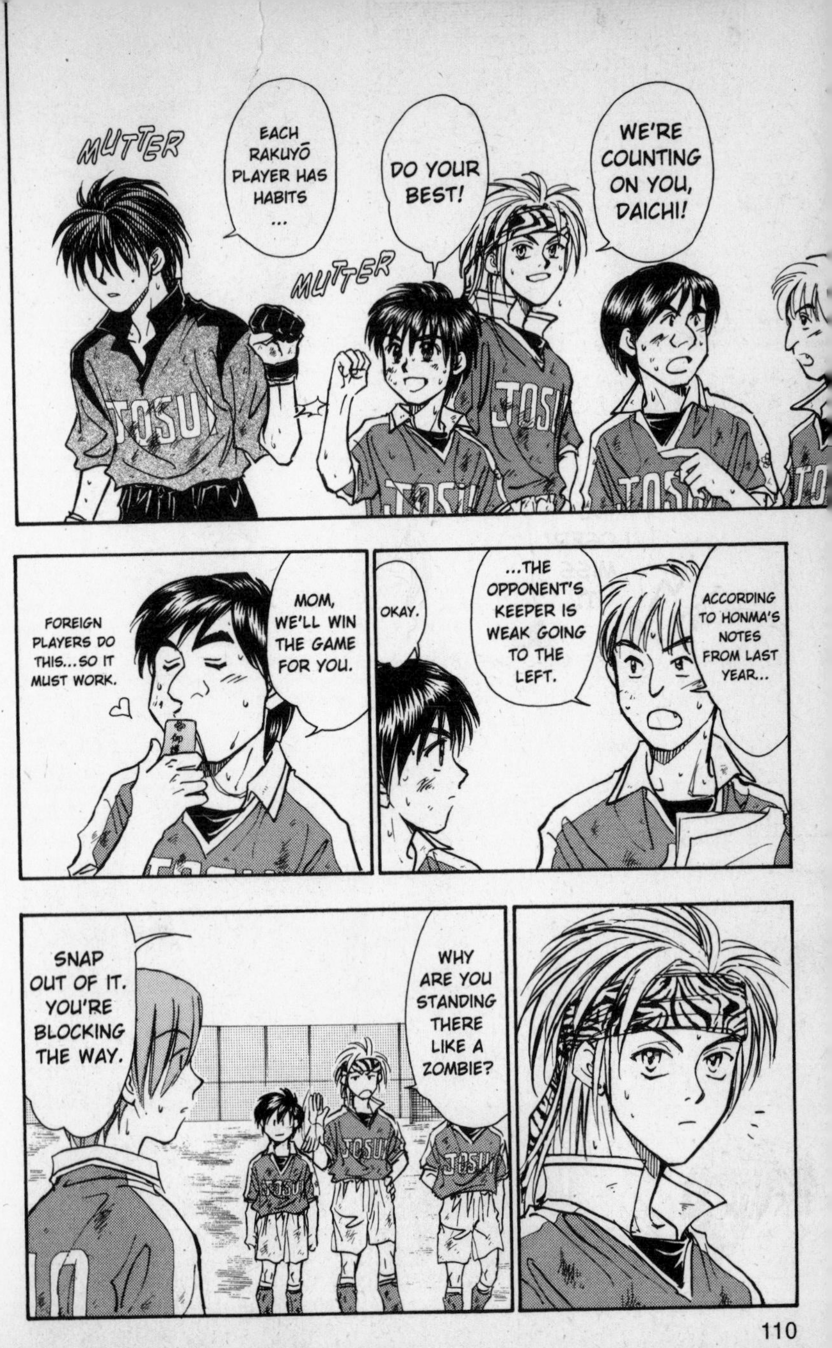
WE'RE COUNTING ON YOU, DAICHI!
DO YOUR BEST!
MUTTER
EACH RAKUYŌ PLAYER HAS HABITS ...
MUTTER
ACCORDING TO HONMA'S NOTES FROM LAST YEAR...
...THE OPPONENT'S KEEPER IS WEAK GOING TO THE LEFT.
OKAY.
MOM, WE'LL WIN THE GAME FOR YOU.
FOREIGN PLAYERS DO THIS...SO IT MUST WORK.
WHY ARE YOU STANDING THERE LIKE A ZOMBIE?
SNAP OUT OF IT. YOU'RE BLOCKING THE WAY.

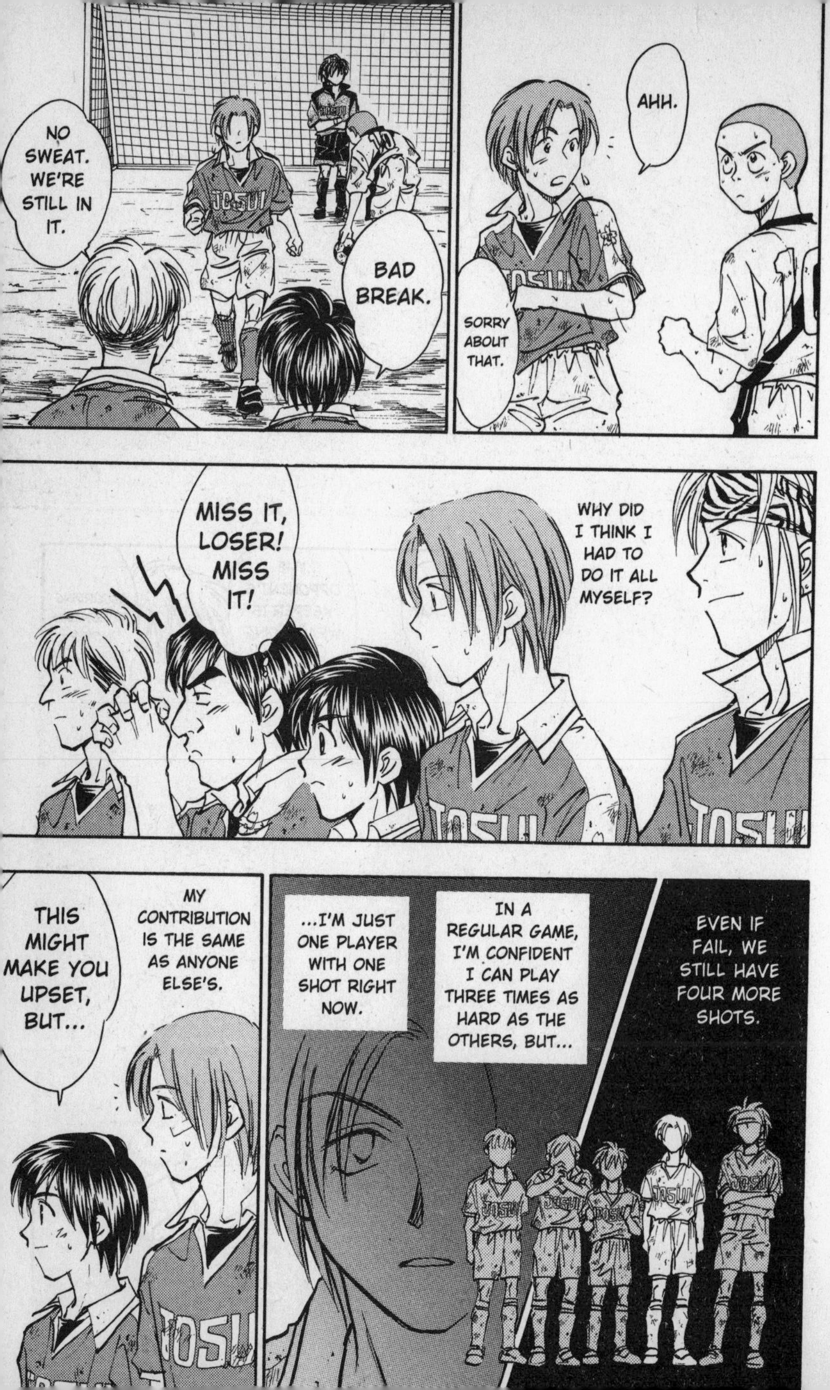
AHH.
SORRY ABOUT THAT.
BAD BREAK.
NO SWEAT. WE'RE STILL IN IT.
WHY DID I THINK I HAD TO DO IT ALL MYSELF?
MISS IT, LOSER! MISS IT!
EVEN IF FAIL, WE STILL HAVE FOUR MORE SHOTS.
IN A REGULAR GAME, I'M CONFIDENT I CAN PLAY THREE TIMES AS HARD AS THE OTHERS, BUT...
...I'M JUST ONE PLAYER WITH ONE SHOT RIGHT NOW.
MY CONTRIBUTION IS THE SAME AS ANYONE ELSE'S.
THIS MIGHT MAKE YOU UPSET, BUT...

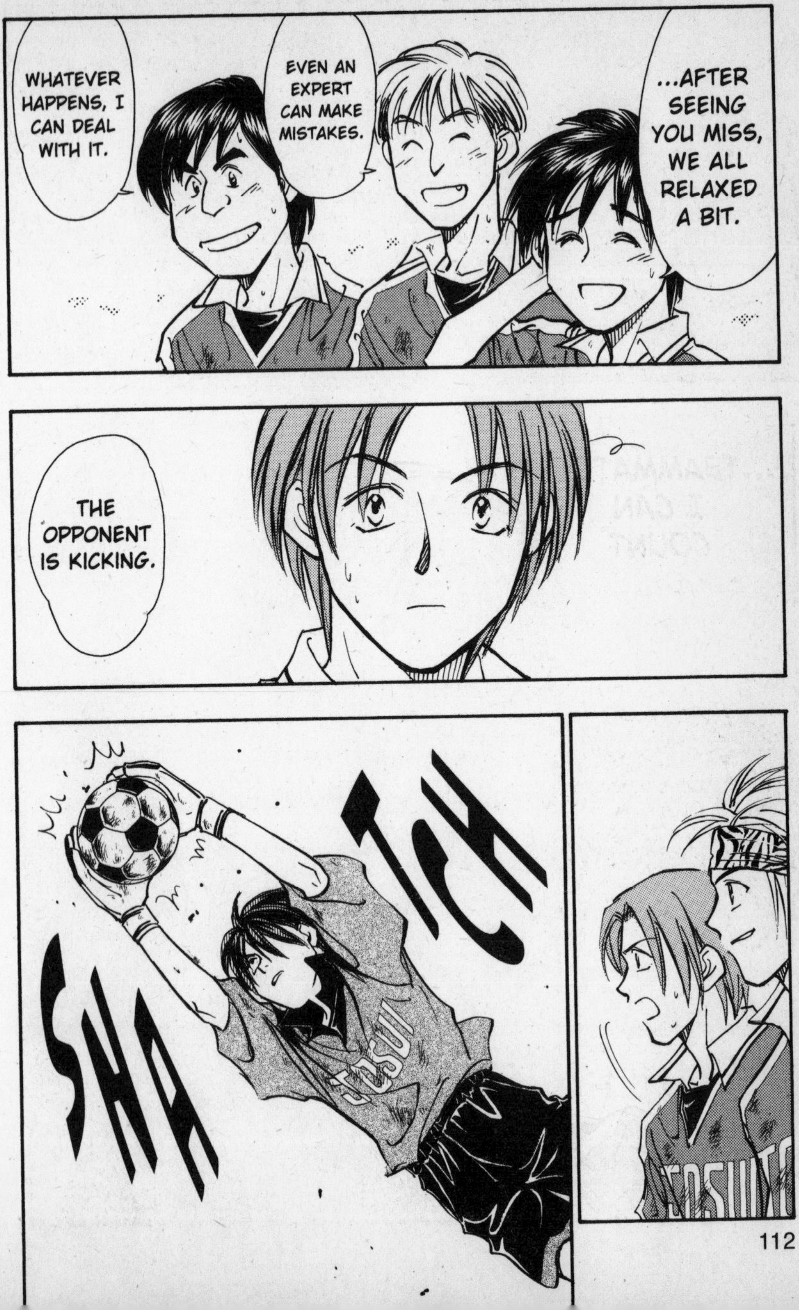
...AFTER SEEING YOU MISS, WE ALL RELAXED A BIT.
EVEN AN EXPERT CAN MAKE MISTAKES.
WHATEVER HAPPENS, I CAN DEAL WITH IT.
THE OPPONENT IS KICKING.
SHA
TCH

READ THIS WAY

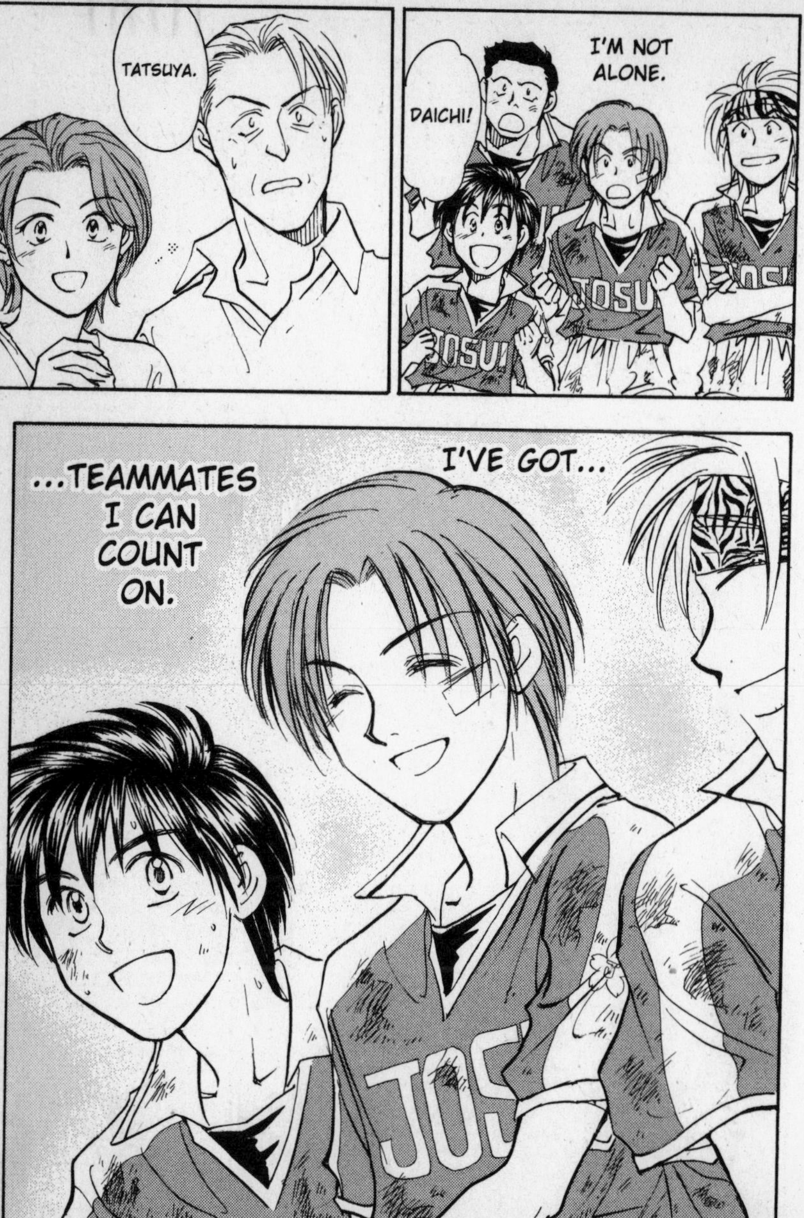
I'M NOT ALONE.
DAICHI!
TATSUYA.
I'VE GOT...
...TEAMMATES I CAN COUNT ON.

WHISTLE!

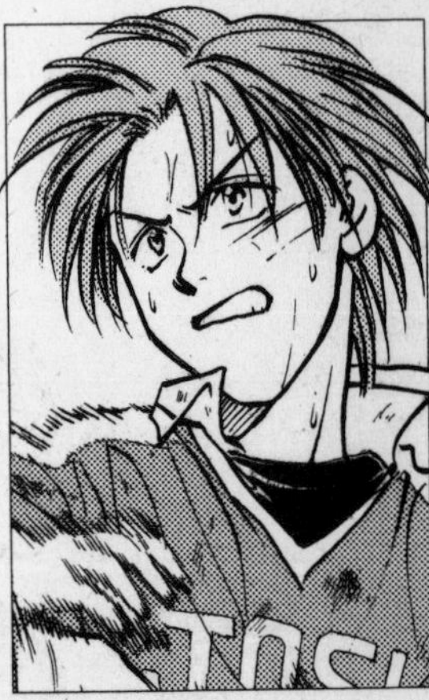

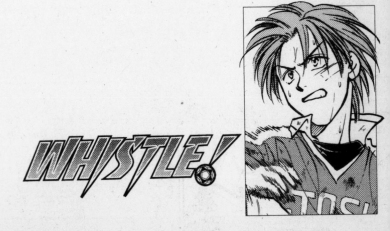

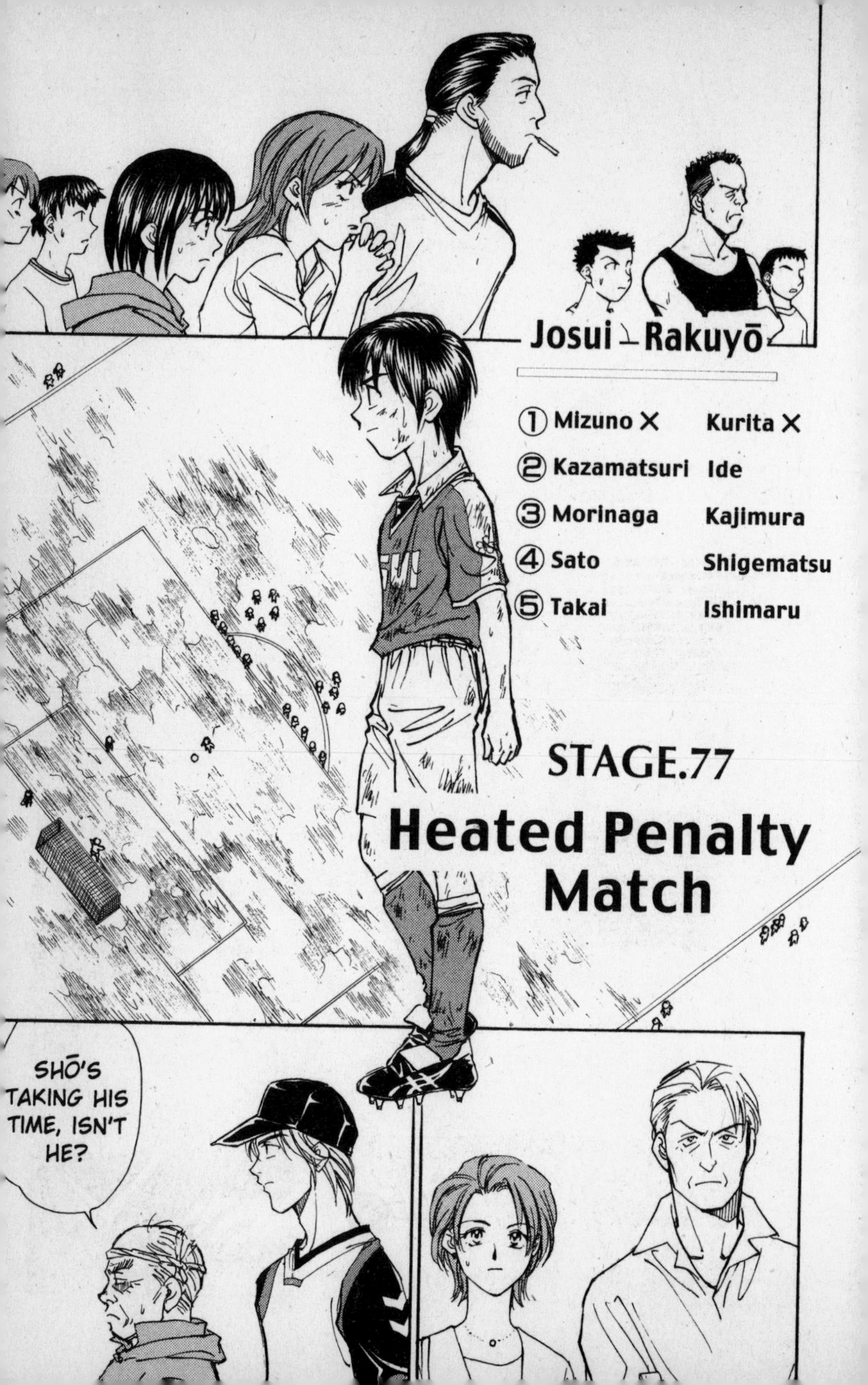
Josui – Rakuyō
① Mizuno ✕ Kurita ✕
② Kazamatsuri Ide
③ Morinaga Kajimura
④ Sato Shigematsu
⑤ Takai Ishimaru
STAGE.77
Heated Penalty Match
SHŌ'S TAKING HIS TIME, ISN'T HE?

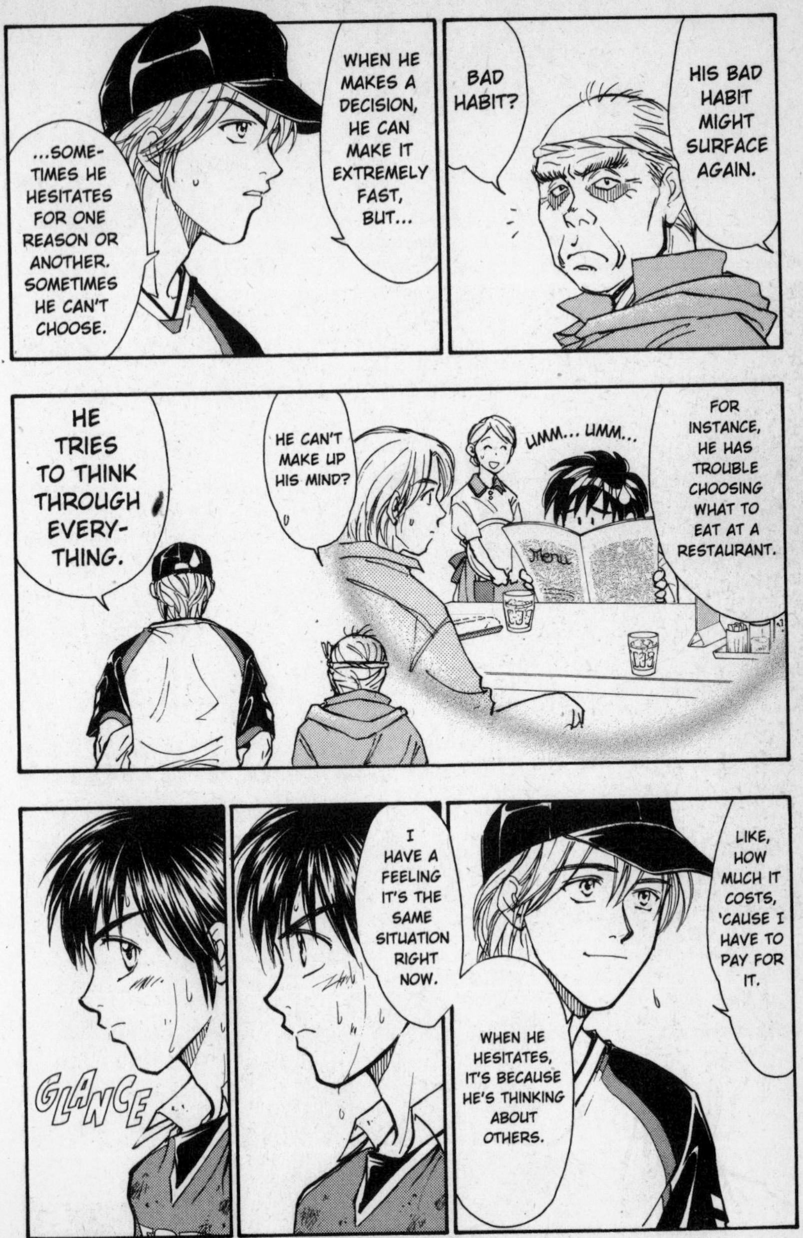
HIS BAD HABIT MIGHT SURFACE AGAIN.
BAD HABIT?
WHEN HE MAKES A DECISION, HE CAN MAKE IT EXTREMELY FAST, BUT...
...SOMETIMES HE HESITATES FOR ONE REASON OR ANOTHER. SOMETIMES HE CAN'T CHOOSE.
FOR INSTANCE, HE HAS TROUBLE CHOOSING WHAT TO EAT AT A RESTAURANT.
UMM... UMM...
HE CAN'T MAKE UP HIS MIND?
HE TRIES TO THINK THROUGH EVERY-THING.
LIKE, HOW MUCH IT COSTS, 'CAUSE I HAVE TO PAY FOR IT.
WHEN HE HESITATES, IT'S BECAUSE HE'S THINKING ABOUT OTHERS.
I HAVE A FEELING IT'S THE SAME SITUATION RIGHT NOW.
GLANCE

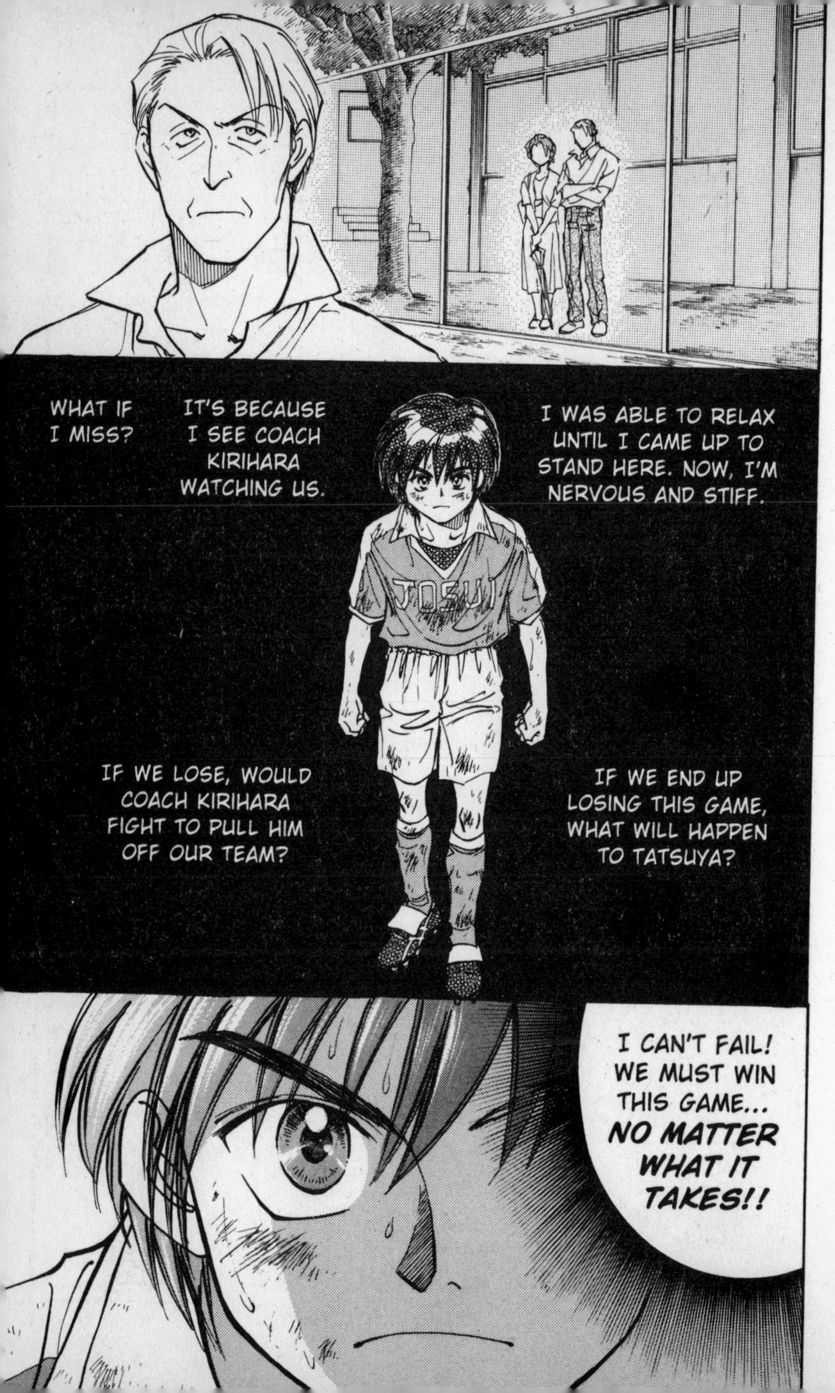
I WAS ABLE TO RELAX UNTIL I CAME UP TO STAND HERE. NOW, I'M NERVOUS AND STIFF.
IT'S BECAUSE I SEE COACH KIRIHARA WATCHING US.
WHAT IF I MISS?
IF WE END UP LOSING THIS GAME, WHAT WILL HAPPEN TO TATSUYA?
IF WE LOSE, WOULD COACH KIRIHARA FIGHT TO PULL HIM OFF OUR TEAM?
JOSUI
I CAN'T FAIL! WE MUST WIN THIS GAME... ***NO MATTER WHAT IT TAKES!!***

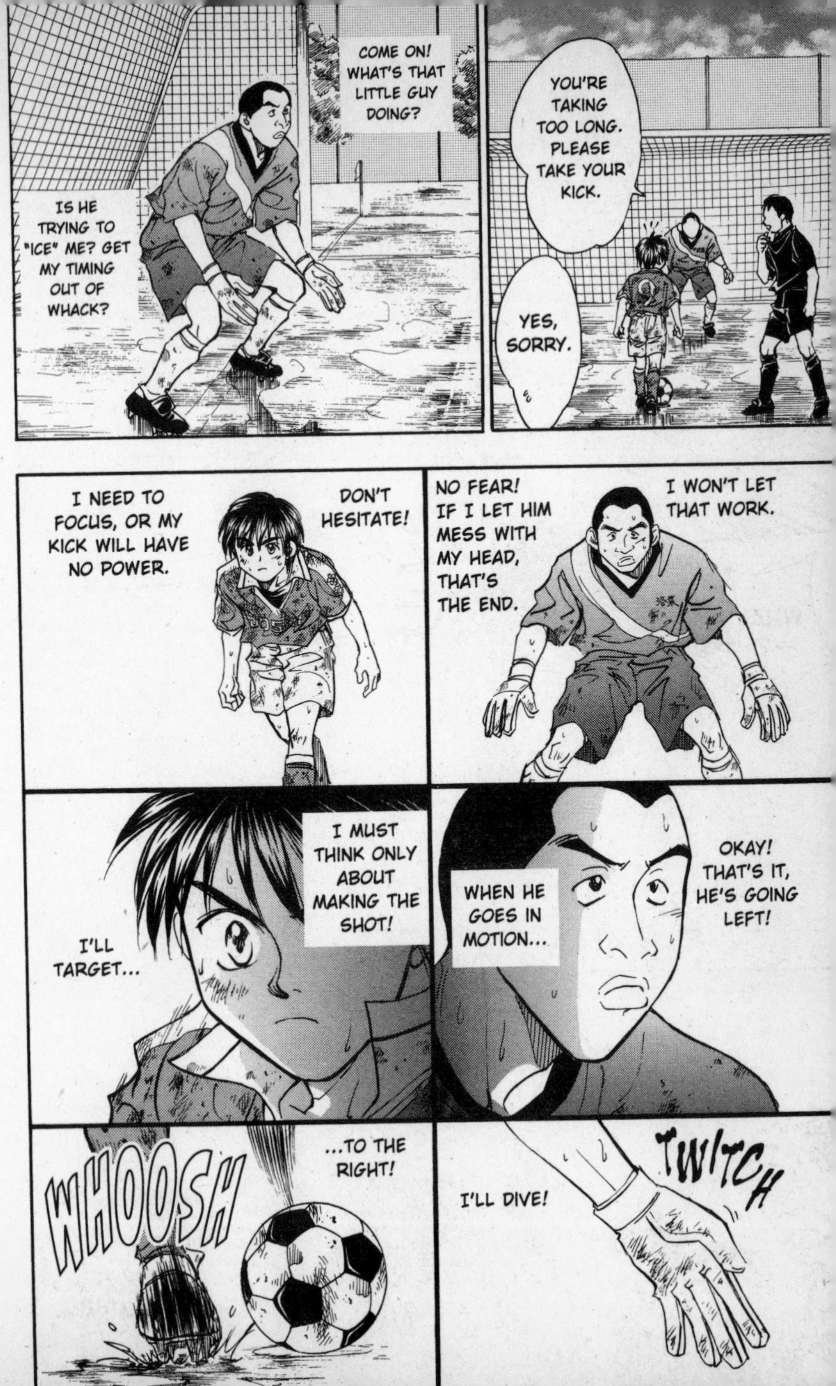
YOU'RE TAKING TOO LONG. PLEASE TAKE YOUR KICK.
YES, SORRY.
COME ON! WHAT'S THAT LITTLE GUY DOING?
IS HE TRYING TO "ICE" ME? GET MY TIMING OUT OF WHACK?
I WON'T LET THAT WORK.
NO FEAR! IF I LET HIM MESS WITH MY HEAD, THAT'S THE END.
DON'T HESITATE!
I NEED TO FOCUS, OR MY KICK WILL HAVE NO POWER.
OKAY! THAT'S IT, HE'S GOING LEFT!
WHEN HE GOES IN MOTION...
I MUST THINK ONLY ABOUT MAKING THE SHOT!
I'LL TARGET...
TWITCH
I'LL DIVE!
...TO THE RIGHT!
WHOOSH

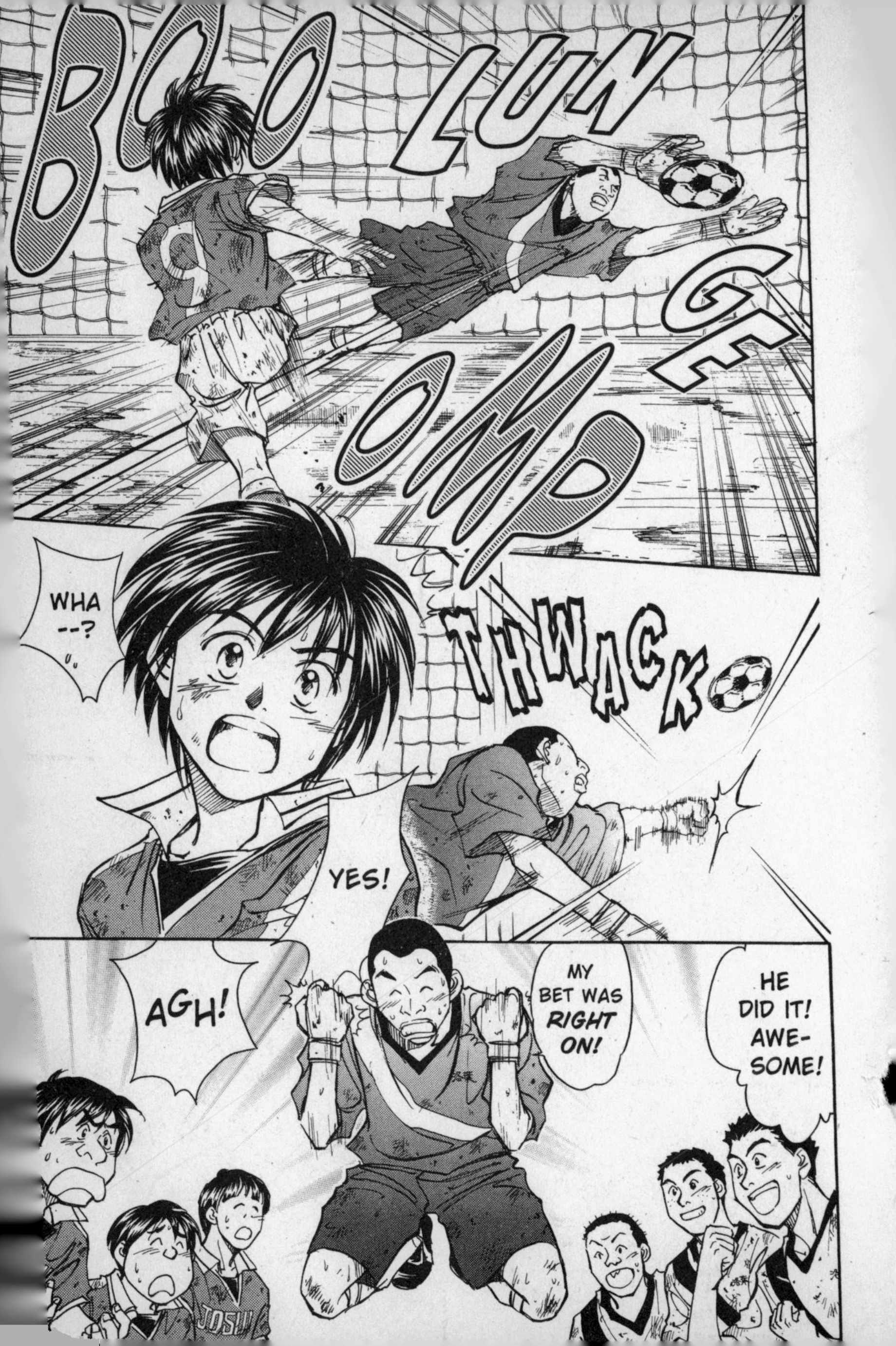
BOOO
LUN
GE
OMP
THWACK
YES!
WHA --?
HE DID IT! AWE-SOME!
MY BET WAS RIGHT ON!
AGH!

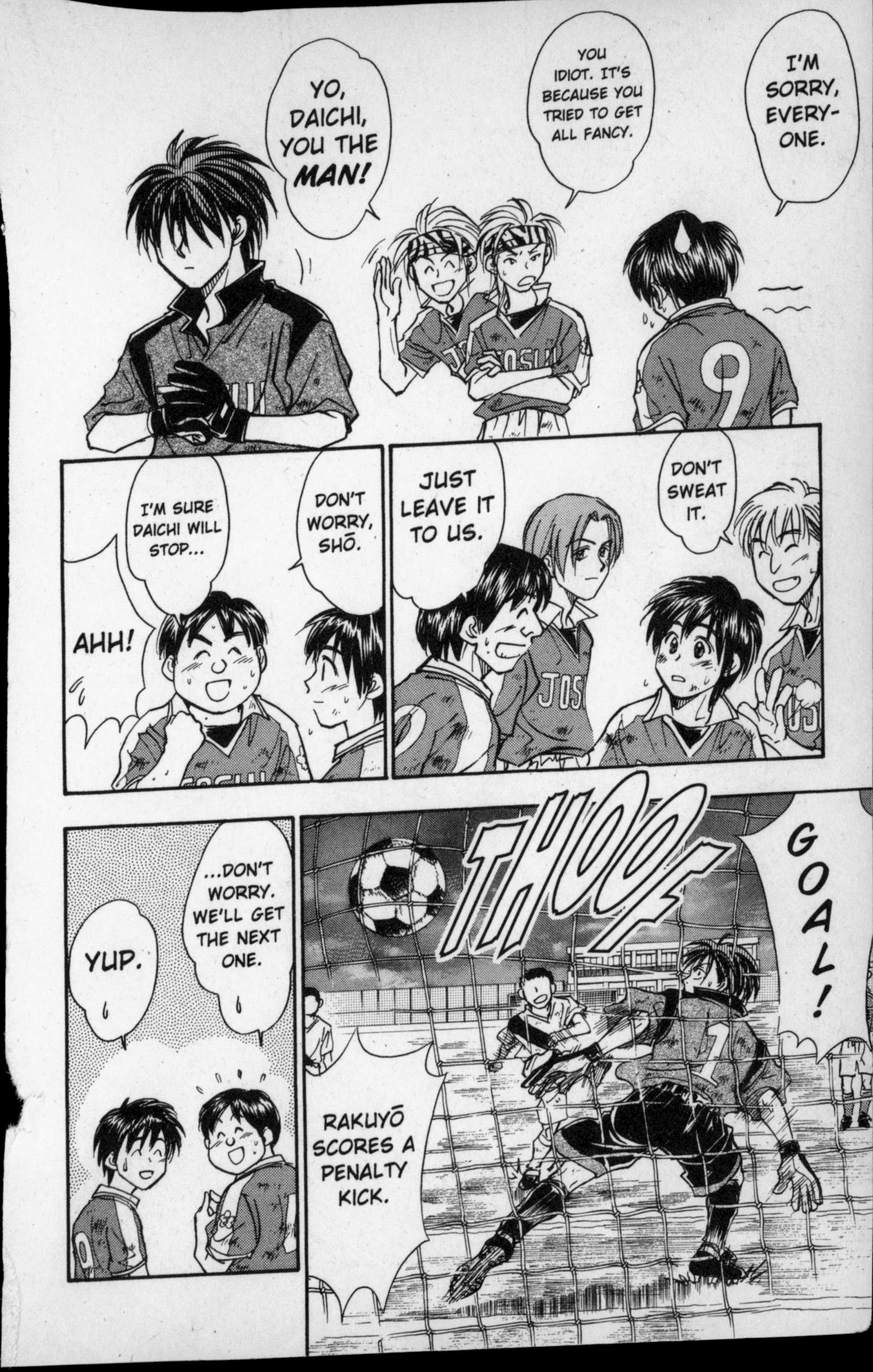
I'M SORRY, EVERY-ONE.
YOU IDIOT. IT'S BECAUSE YOU TRIED TO GET ALL FANCY.
YO, DAICHI, YOU THE *MAN!*
DON'T SWEAT IT.
JUST LEAVE IT TO US.
DON'T WORRY, SHŌ.
I'M SURE DAICHI WILL STOP...
AHH!
GOAL!
THOOF
RAKUYŌ SCORES A PENALTY KICK.
...DON'T WORRY. WE'LL GET THE NEXT ONE.
YUP.

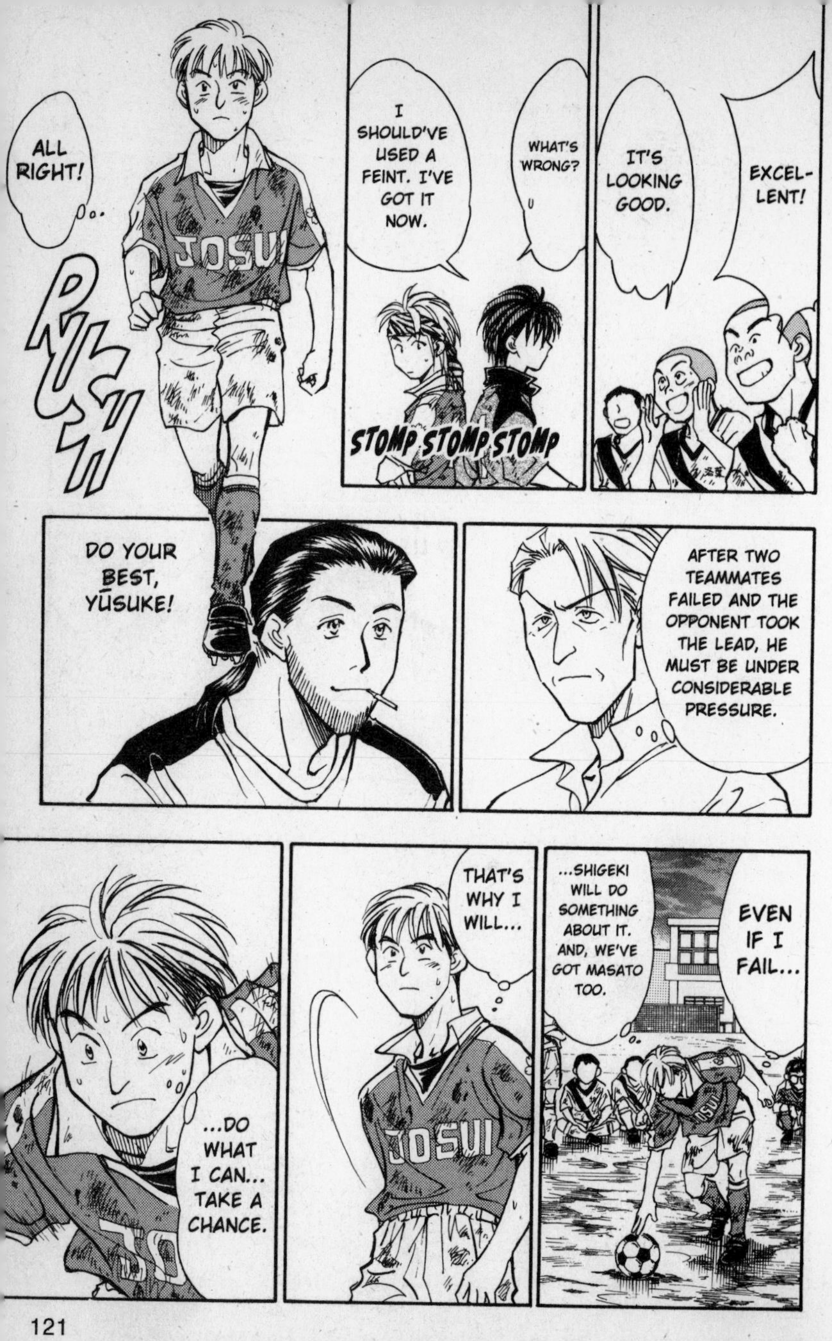
EXCEL-LENT!
IT'S LOOKING GOOD.
WHAT'S WRONG?
I SHOULD'VE USED A FEINT. I'VE GOT IT NOW.
STOMP STOMP STOMP
ALL RIGHT!
RUSH
AFTER TWO TEAMMATES FAILED AND THE OPPONENT TOOK THE LEAD, HE MUST BE UNDER CONSIDERABLE PRESSURE.
DO YOUR BEST, YŪSUKE!
EVEN IF I FAIL...
...SHIGEKI WILL DO SOMETHING ABOUT IT. AND, WE'VE GOT MASATO TOO.
THAT'S WHY I WILL...
...DO WHAT I CAN... TAKE A CHANCE.

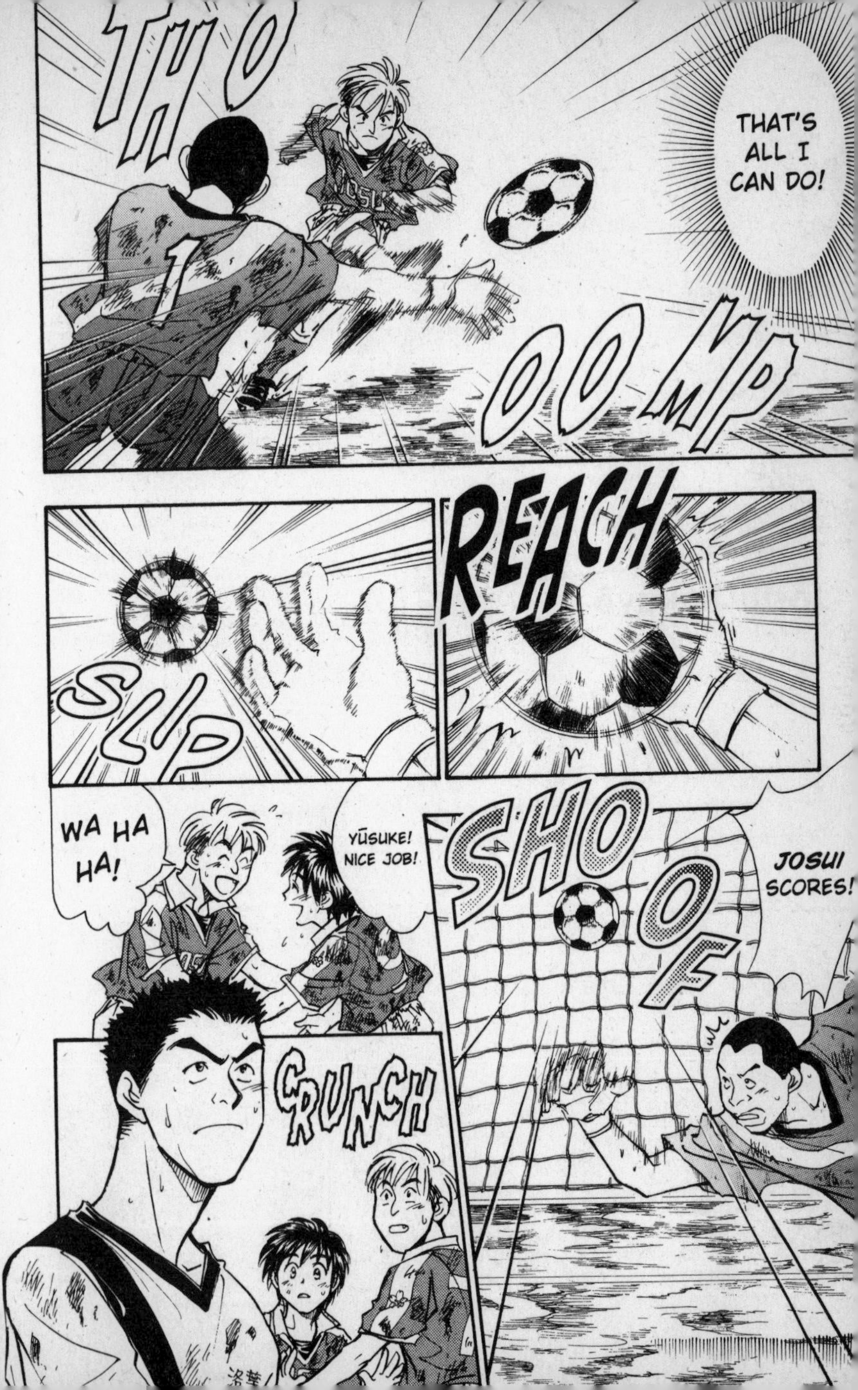
THAT'S ALL I CAN DO!
THOOOMP
REACH
SLIP
JOSUI SCORES!
SHOOOF
YŪSUKE! NICE JOB!
WA HA HA!
CRUNCH

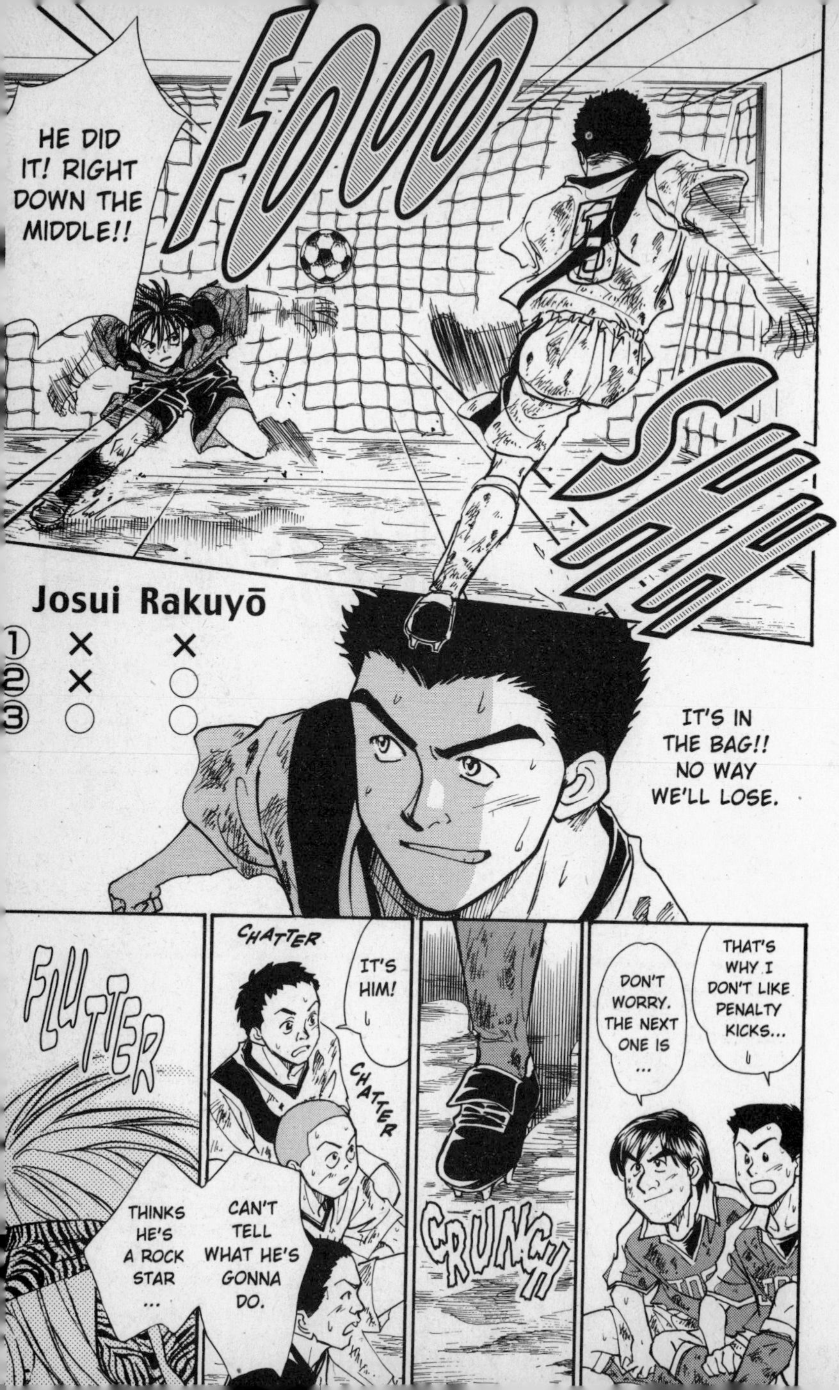
FOOO
HE DID IT! RIGHT DOWN THE MIDDLE!!
SHH
Josui Rakuyō
① × ×
② × ○
③ ○ ○
IT'S IN THE BAG!! NO WAY WE'LL LOSE.
THAT'S WHY I DON'T LIKE PENALTY KICKS...
DON'T WORRY. THE NEXT ONE IS ...
CRUNCH
CHATTER
IT'S HIM!
CHATTER
CAN'T TELL WHAT HE'S GONNA DO.
FLUTTER
THINKS HE'S A ROCK STAR ...

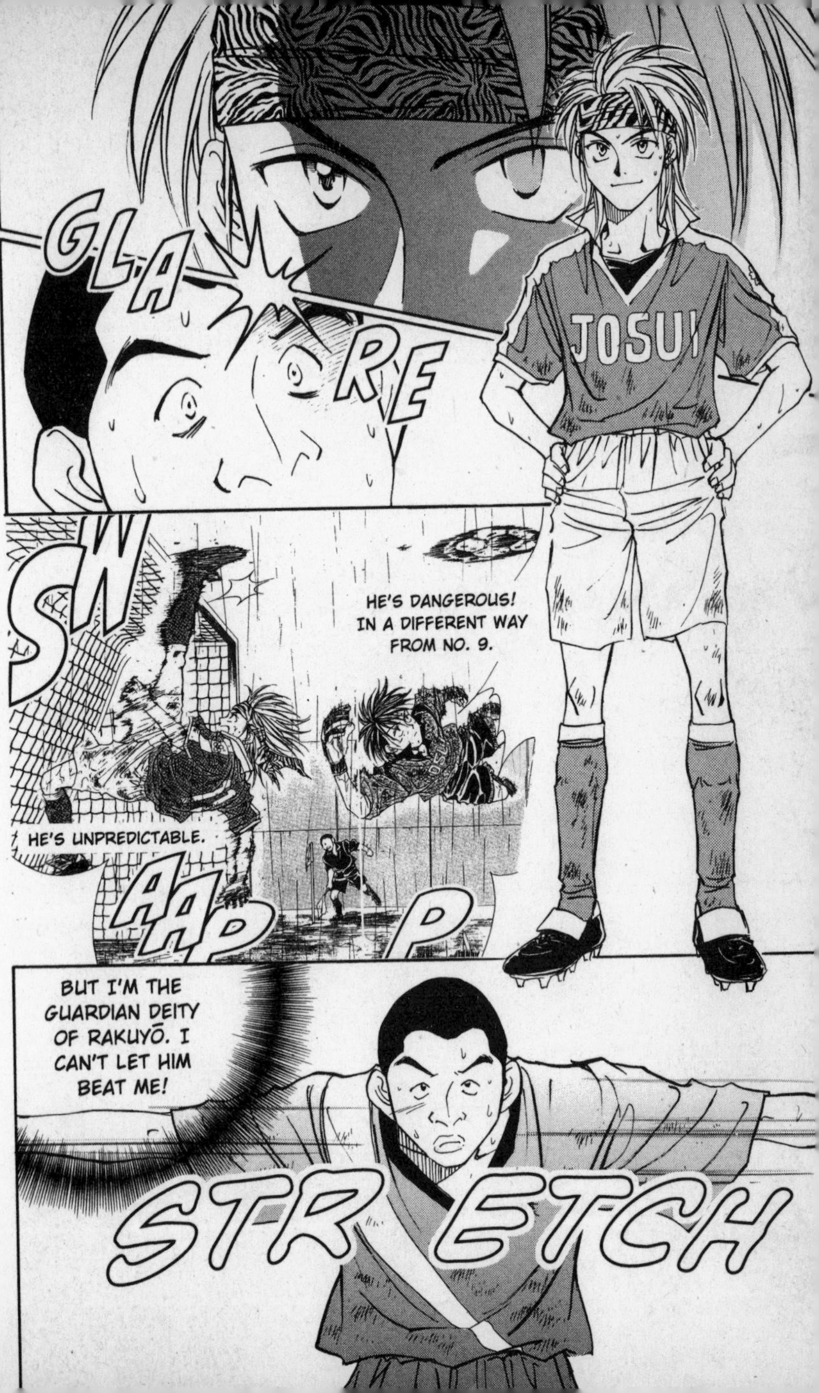
GLARE
HE'S DANGEROUS! IN A DIFFERENT WAY FROM NO. 9.
HE'S UNPREDICTABLE.
BUT I'M THE GUARDIAN DEITY OF RAKUYŌ. I CAN'T LET HIM BEAT ME!
STRETCH

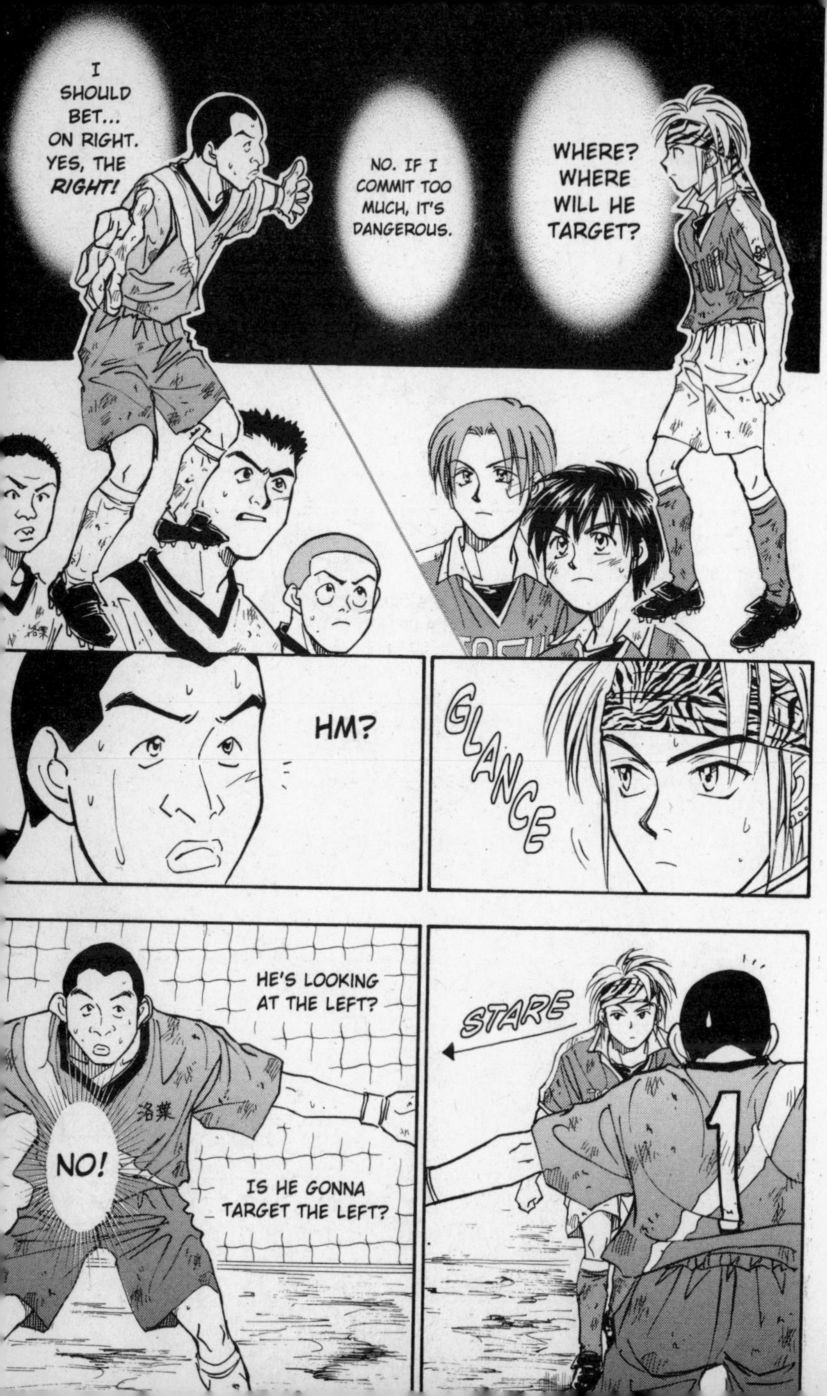
WHERE? WHERE WILL HE TARGET?
NO. IF I COMMIT TOO MUCH, IT'S DANGEROUS.
I SHOULD BET... ON RIGHT. YES, THE RIGHT!
GLANCE
HM?
STARE
HE'S LOOKING AT THE LEFT?
NO!
IS HE GONNA TARGET THE LEFT?

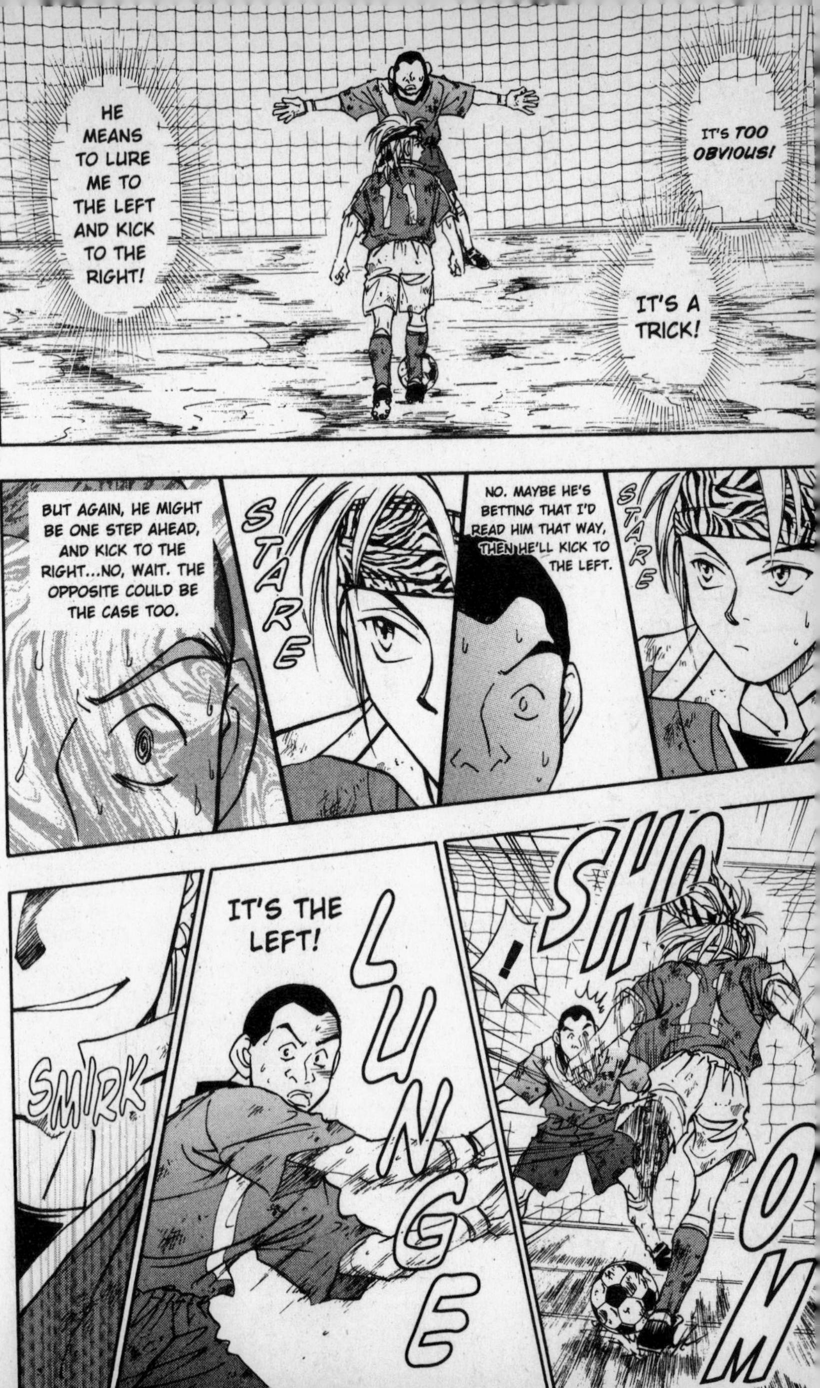
IT'S TOO OBVIOUS!
IT'S A TRICK!
HE MEANS TO LURE ME TO THE LEFT AND KICK TO THE RIGHT!
STARE
NO. MAYBE HE'S BETTING THAT I'D READ HIM THAT WAY, THEN HE'LL KICK TO THE LEFT.
STARE
BUT AGAIN, HE MIGHT BE ONE STEP AHEAD, AND KICK TO THE RIGHT...NO, WAIT. THE OPPOSITE COULD BE THE CASE TOO.
SHOOM
!
IT'S THE LEFT!
LUNGE
SMIRK

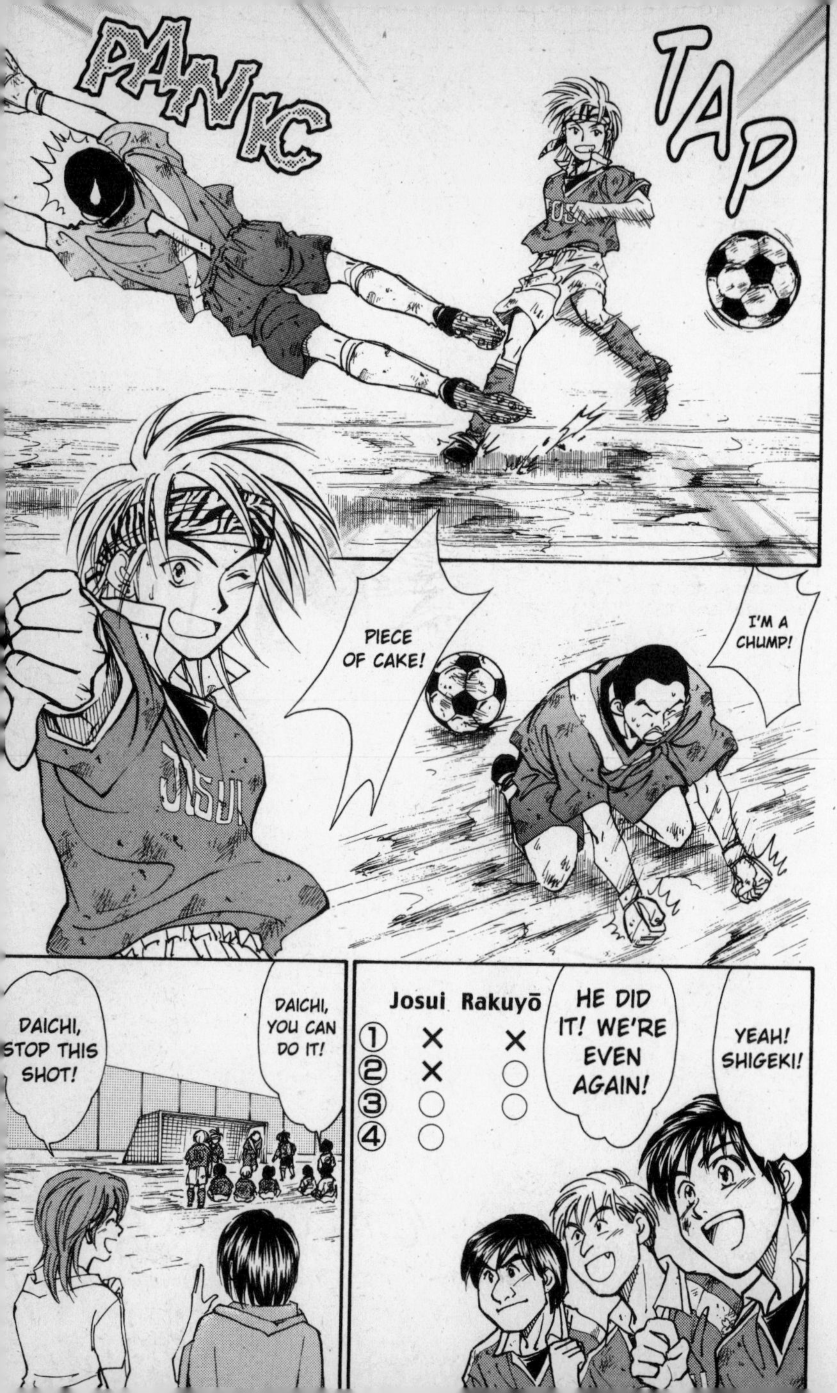
TAP
PANIC
I'M A CHUMP!
PIECE OF CAKE!
YEAH! SHIGEKI!
HE DID IT! WE'RE EVEN AGAIN!
Josui Rakuyō
① × ×
② × ○
③ ○ ○
④ ○
DAICHI, YOU CAN DO IT!
DAICHI, STOP THIS SHOT!

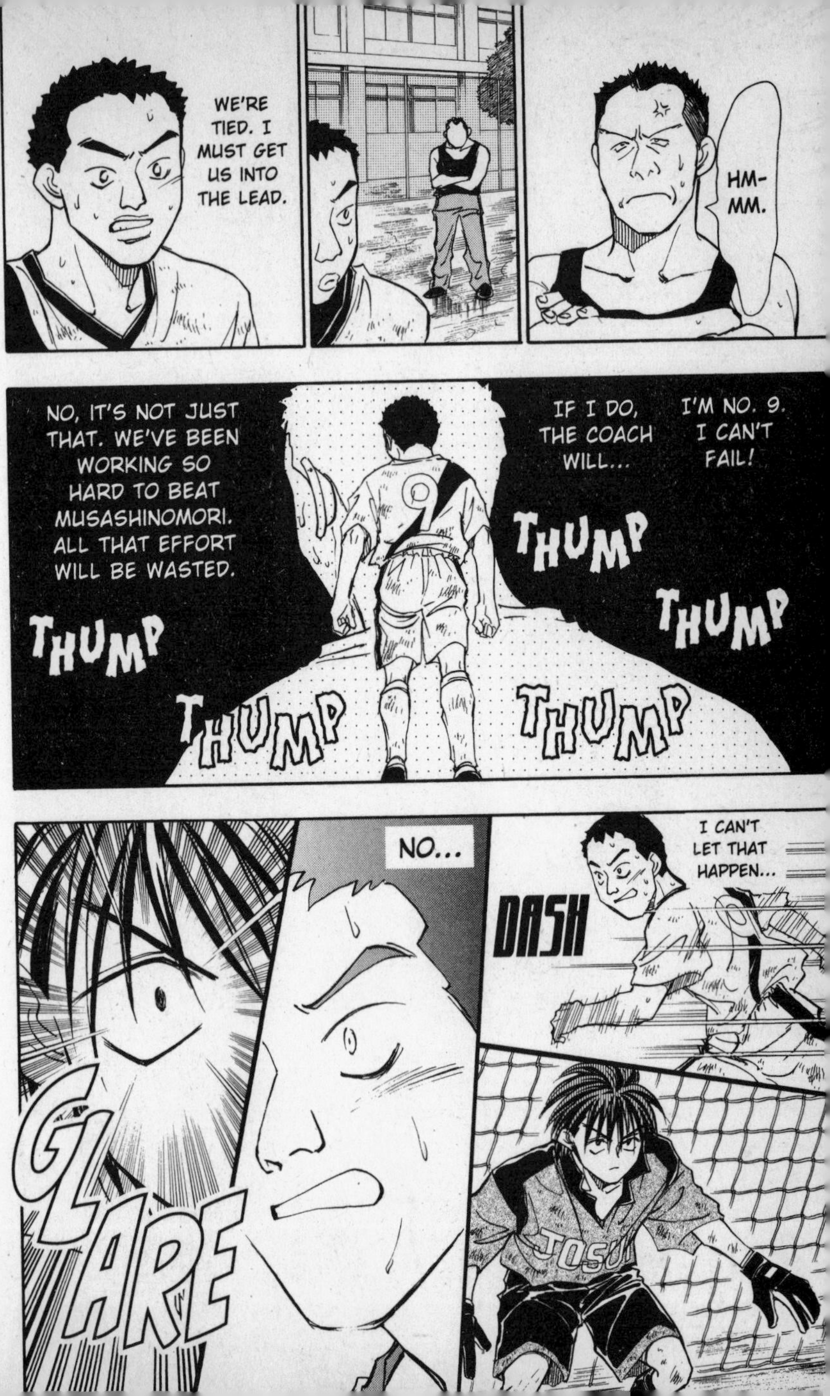
HM-MM.
WE'RE TIED. I MUST GET US INTO THE LEAD.
I'M NO. 9. I CAN'T FAIL!
IF I DO, THE COACH WILL...
NO, IT'S NOT JUST THAT. WE'VE BEEN WORKING SO HARD TO BEAT MUSASHINOMORI. ALL THAT EFFORT WILL BE WASTED.
THUMP
THUMP
THUMP
THUMP
THUMP
I CAN'T LET THAT HAPPEN...
DASH
JOSUI
NO...
GLARE

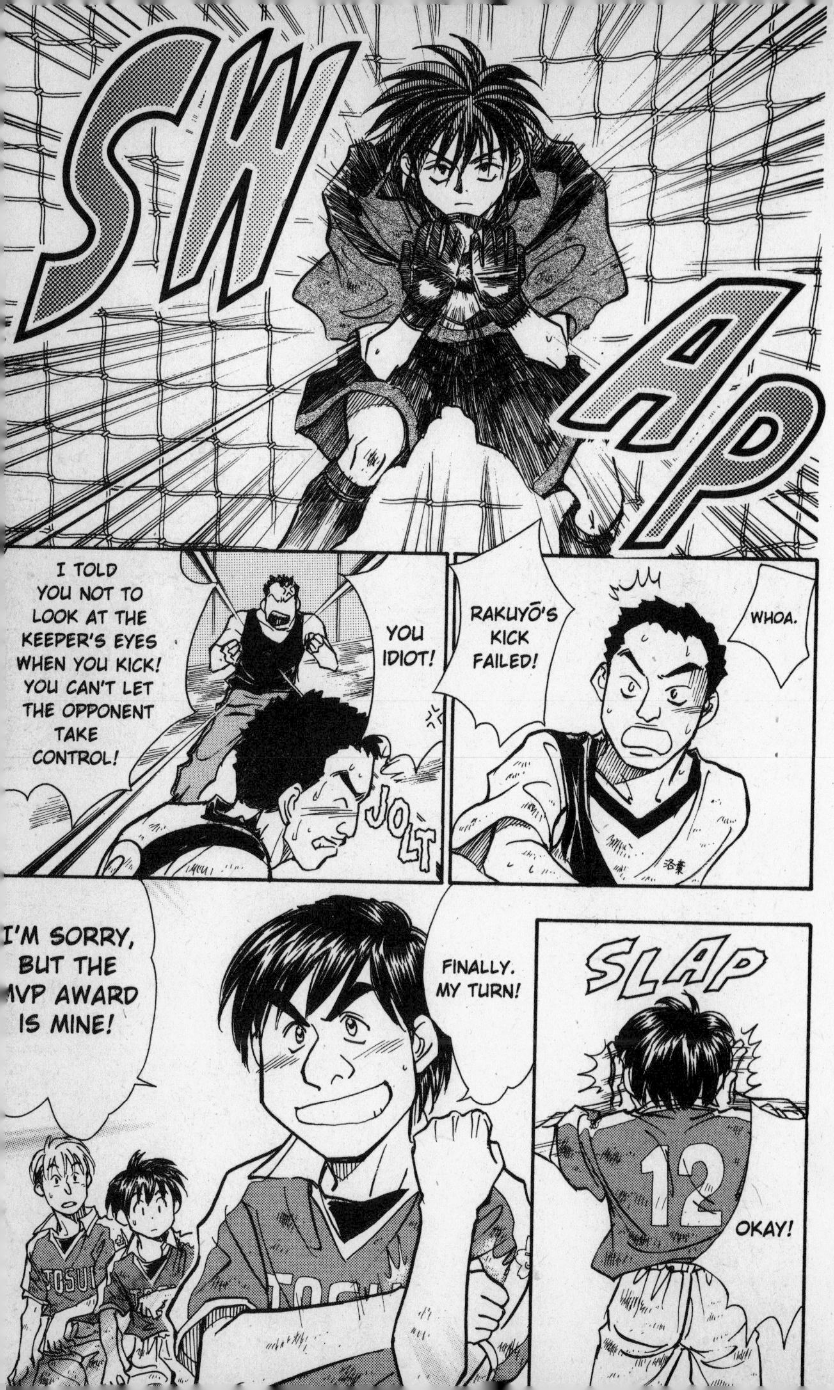
SHAP
WHOA.
RAKUYŌ'S KICK FAILED!
YOU IDIOT!
I TOLD YOU NOT TO LOOK AT THE KEEPER'S EYES WHEN YOU KICK! YOU CAN'T LET THE OPPONENT TAKE CONTROL!
JOLT
SLAP
OKAY!
FINALLY. MY TURN!
I'M SORRY, BUT THE MVP AWARD IS MINE!

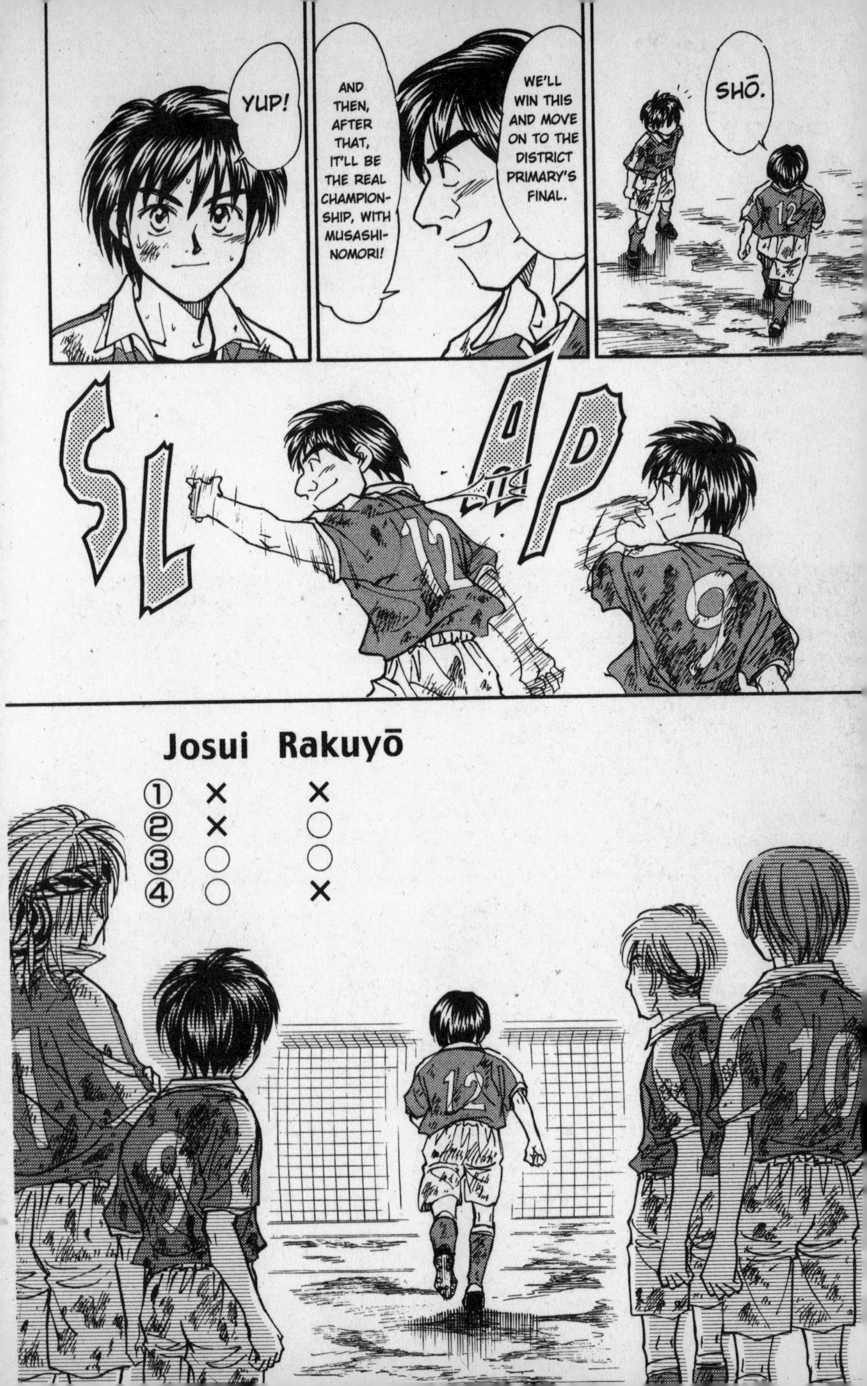
SHŌ.
WE'LL WIN THIS AND MOVE ON TO THE DISTRICT PRIMARY'S FINAL.
AND THEN, AFTER THAT, IT'LL BE THE REAL CHAMPIONSHIP, WITH MUSASHINOMORI!
YUP!
SLAP
Josui Rakuyō
① × ×
② × ○
③ ○ ○
④ ○ ×

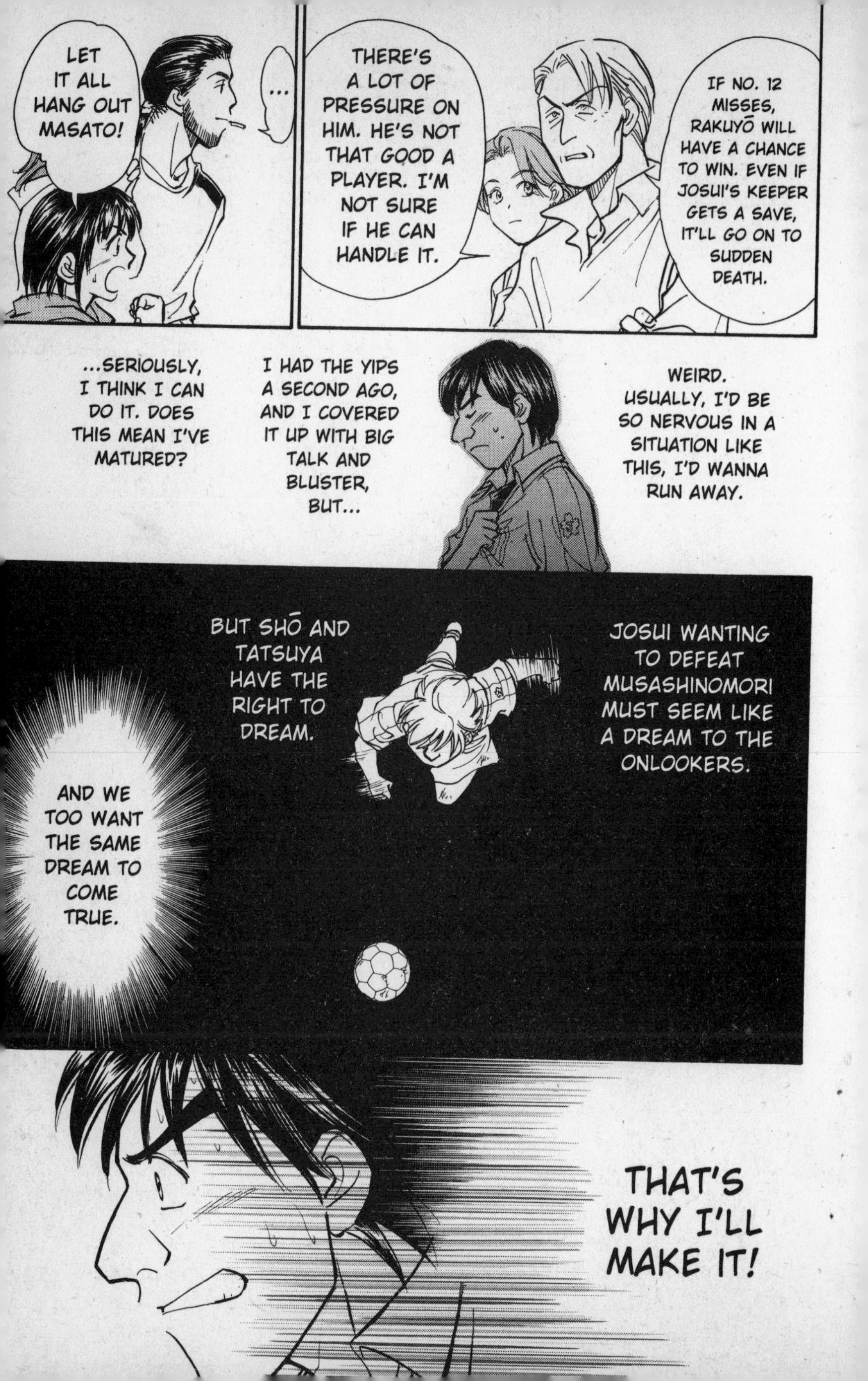
IF NO. 12 MISSES, RAKUYŌ WILL HAVE A CHANCE TO WIN. EVEN IF JOSUI'S KEEPER GETS A SAVE, IT'LL GO ON TO SUDDEN DEATH.
THERE'S A LOT OF PRESSURE ON HIM. HE'S NOT THAT GOOD A PLAYER. I'M NOT SURE IF HE CAN HANDLE IT.
...
LET IT ALL HANG OUT MASATO!
WEIRD. USUALLY, I'D BE SO NERVOUS IN A SITUATION LIKE THIS, I'D WANNA RUN AWAY.
I HAD THE YIPS A SECOND AGO, AND I COVERED IT UP WITH BIG TALK AND BLUSTER, BUT...
...SERIOUSLY, I THINK I CAN DO IT. DOES THIS MEAN I'VE MATURED?
JOSUI WANTING TO DEFEAT MUSASHINOMORI MUST SEEM LIKE A DREAM TO THE ONLOOKERS.
BUT SHŌ AND TATSUYA HAVE THE RIGHT TO DREAM.
AND WE TOO WANT THE SAME DREAM TO COME TRUE.
THAT'S WHY I'LL MAKE IT!

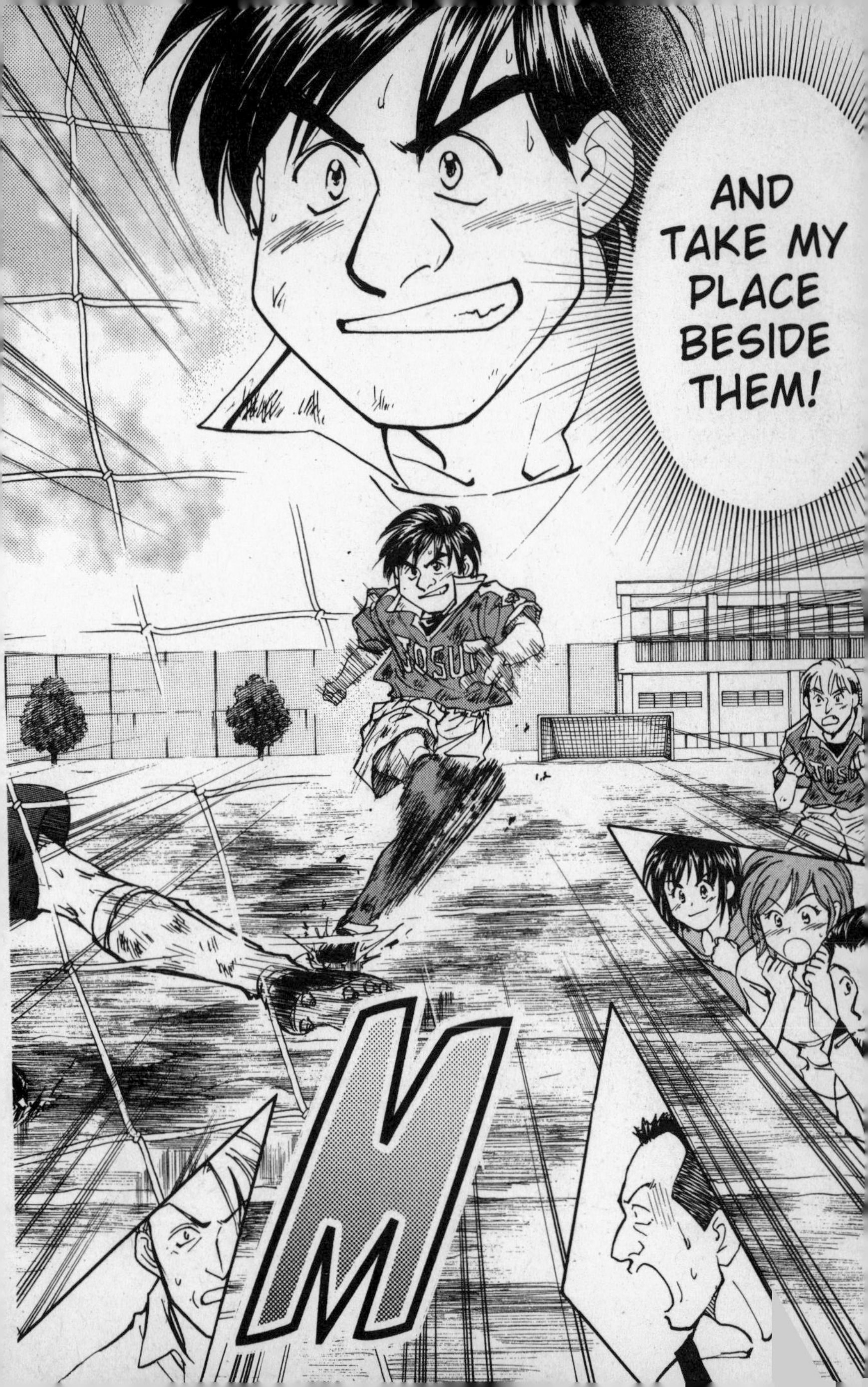
AND TAKE MY PLACE BESIDE THEM!
TOSU
M

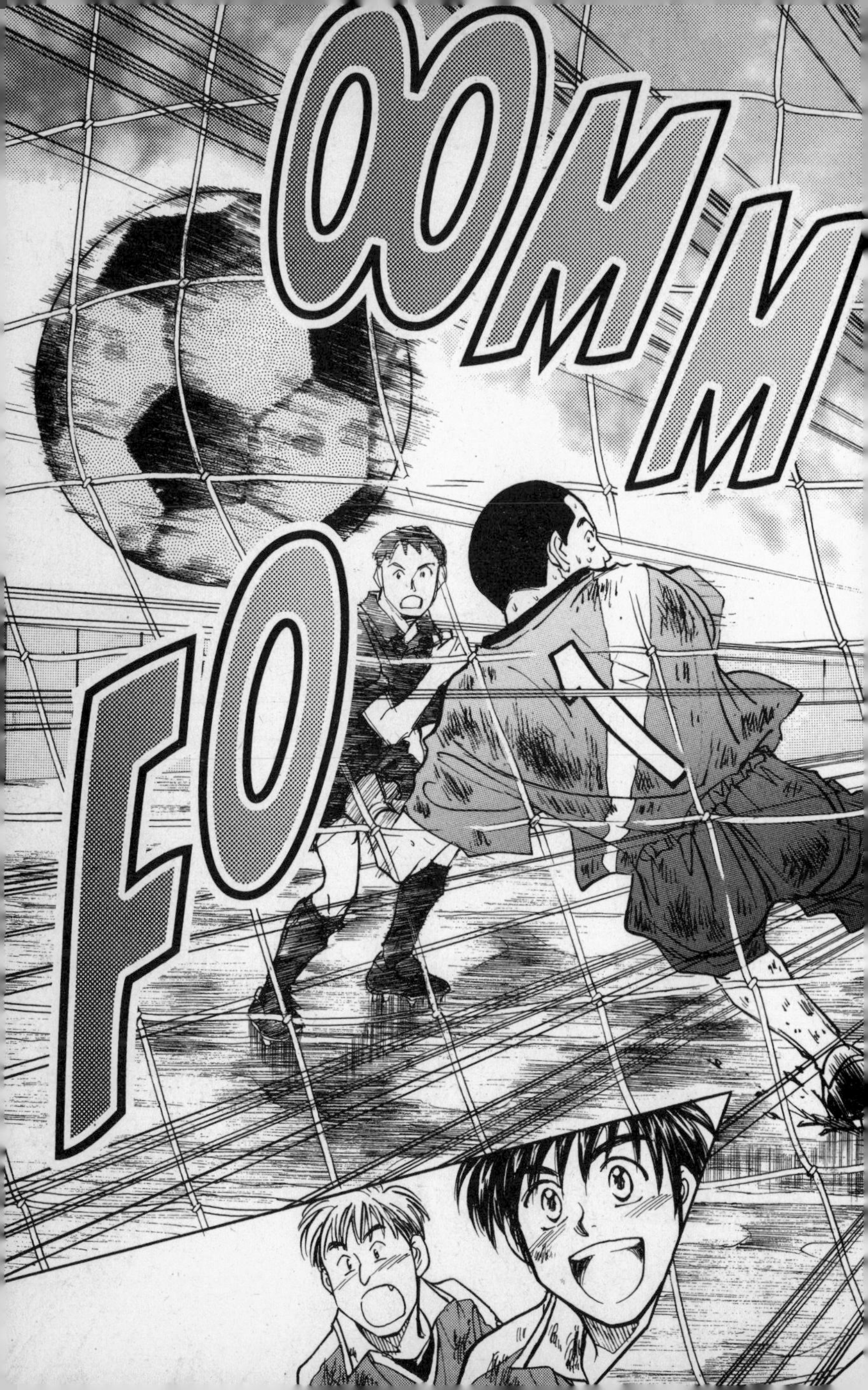
FOOMMM

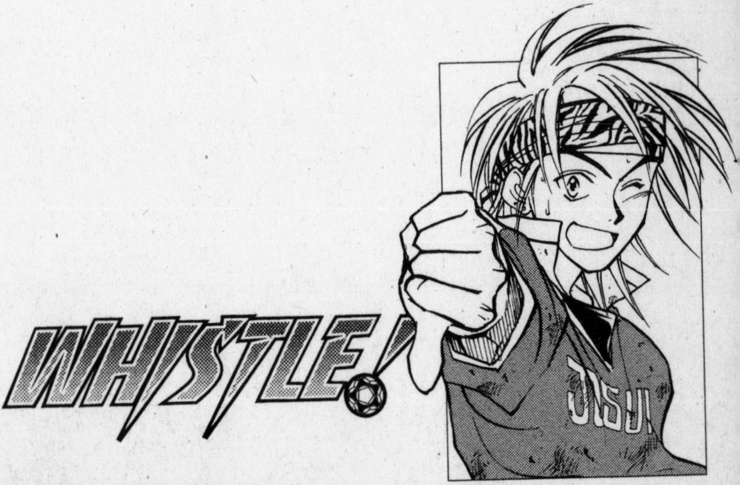
WHISTLE!

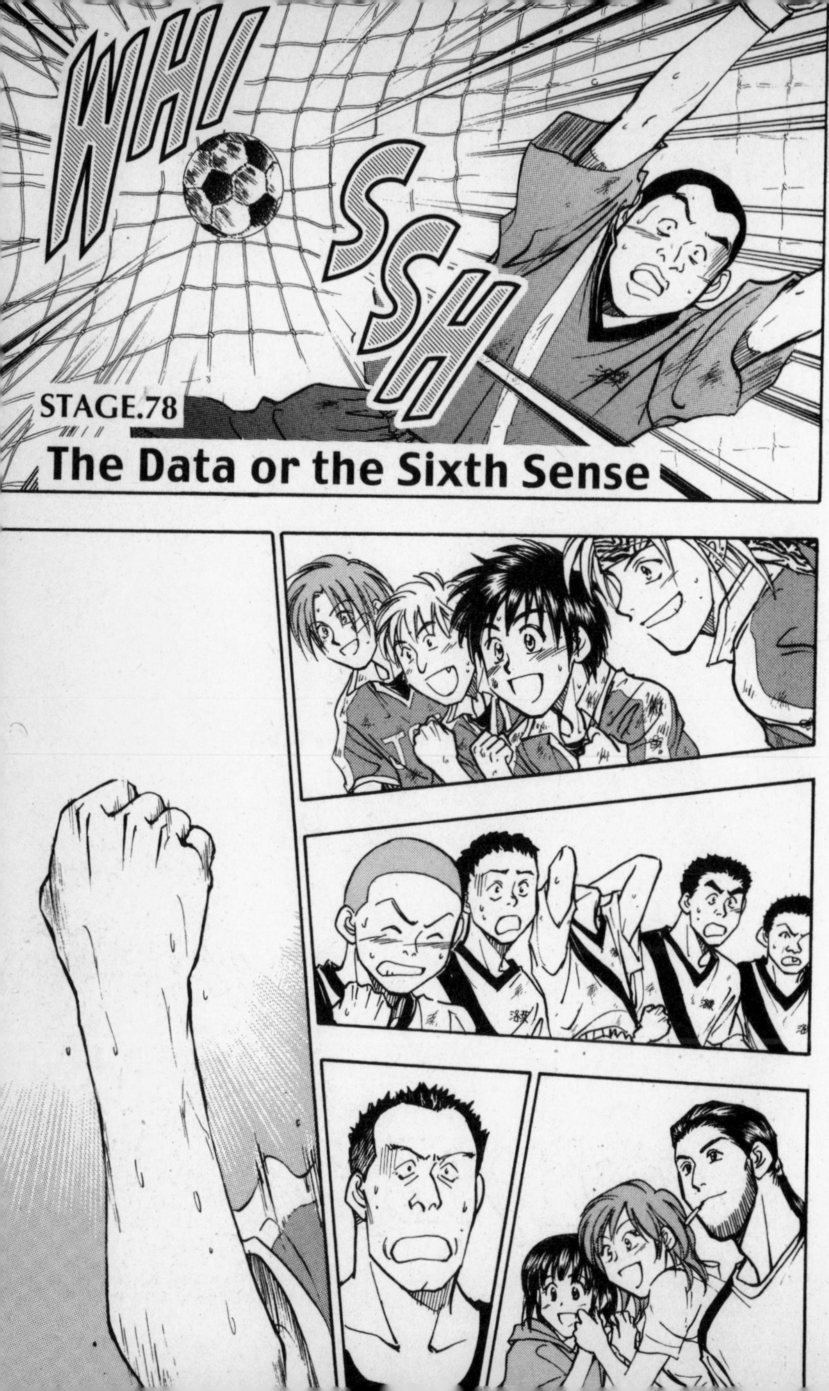
WHISSH
STAGE.78
The Data or the Sixth Sense

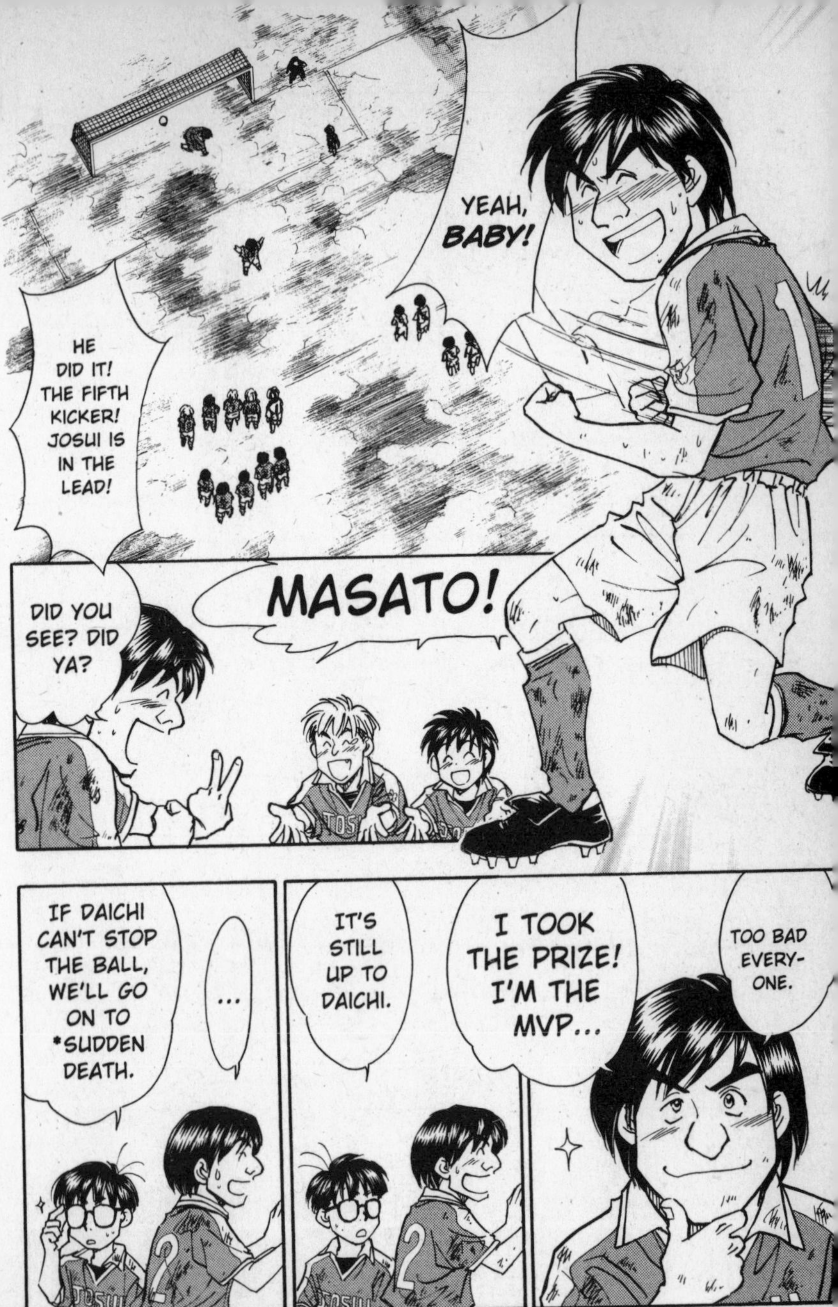
YEAH, BABY!
HE DID IT! THE FIFTH KICKER! JOSUI IS IN THE LEAD!
MASATO!
DID YOU SEE? DID YA?
TOO BAD EVERY-ONE.
I TOOK THE PRIZE! I'M THE MVP...
IT'S STILL UP TO DAICHI.
...
IF DAICHI CAN'T STOP THE BALL, WE'LL GO ON TO *SUDDEN DEATH.

FROM THE SIXTH PENALTY KICK ON, THE WINNER CAN BE DECIDED BY EACH SINGLE TURN.

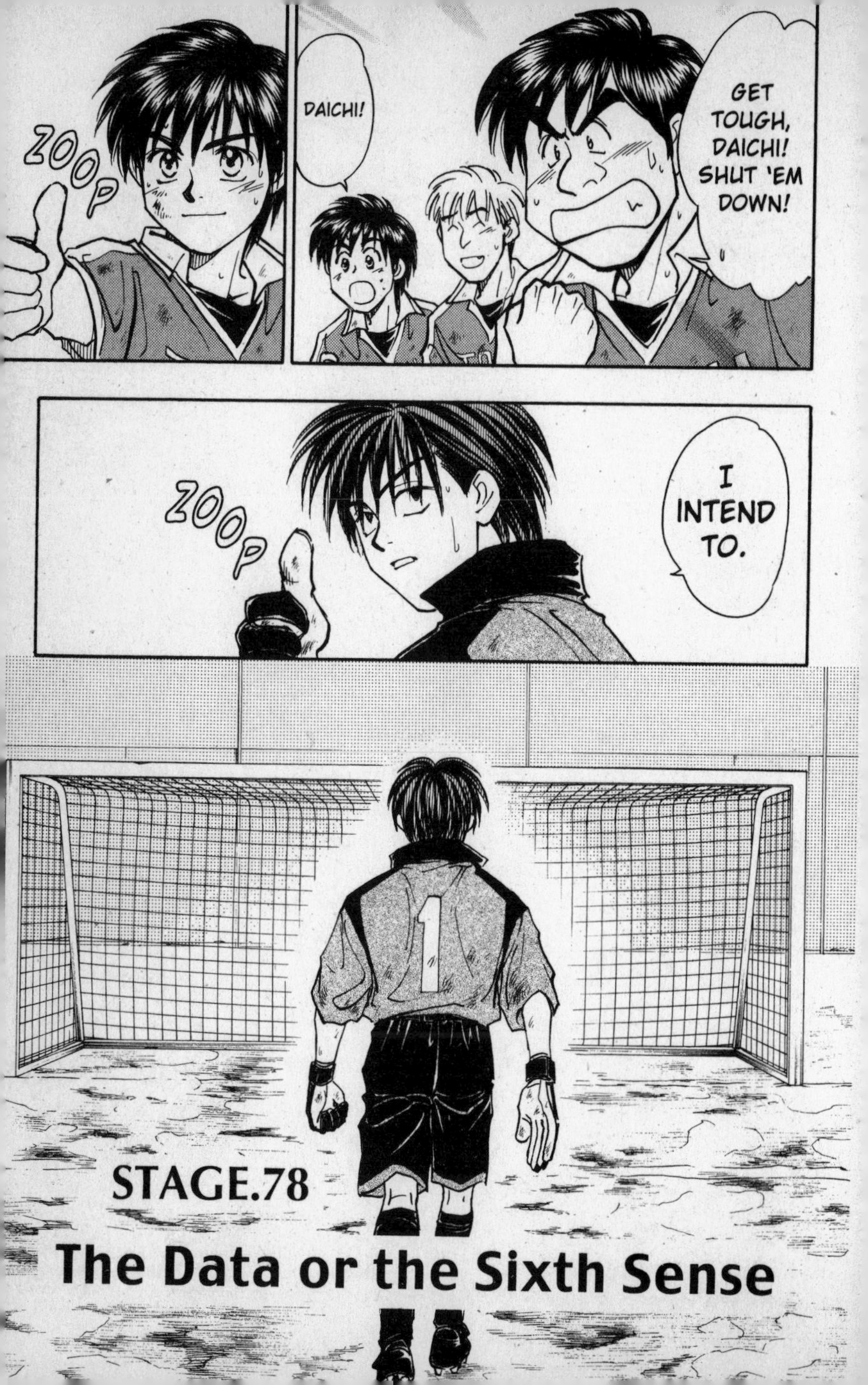
GET TOUGH, DAICHI! SHUT 'EM DOWN!
DAICHI!
ZOOP
ZOOP
I INTEND TO.
STAGE.78
The Data or the Sixth Sense

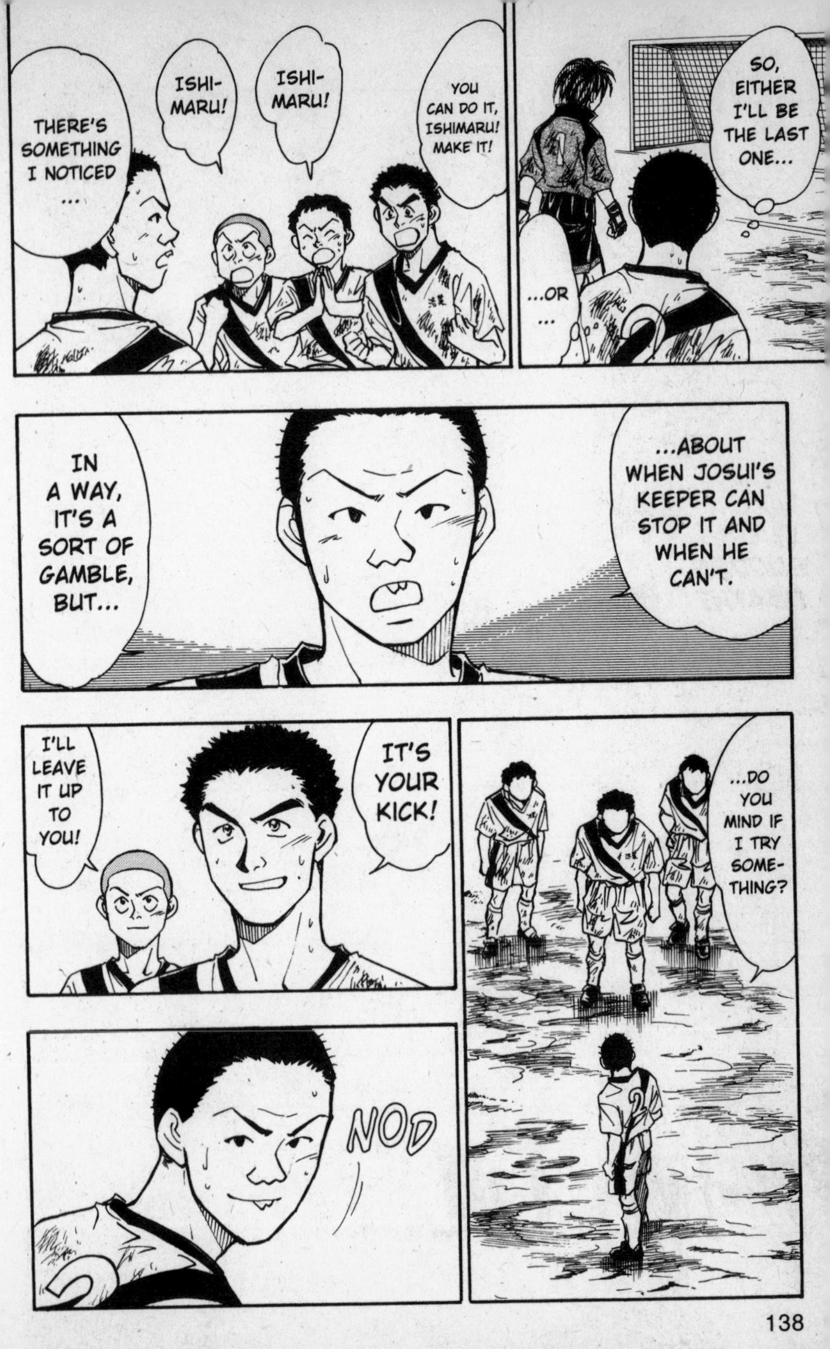
SO, EITHER I'LL BE THE LAST ONE...
...OR ...
YOU CAN DO IT, ISHIMARU! MAKE IT!
ISHI-MARU!
ISHI-MARU!
THERE'S SOMETHING I NOTICED ...
...ABOUT WHEN JOSUI'S KEEPER CAN STOP IT AND WHEN HE CAN'T.
IN A WAY, IT'S A SORT OF GAMBLE, BUT...
...DO YOU MIND IF I TRY SOME-THING?
IT'S YOUR KICK!
I'LL LEAVE IT UP TO YOU!
NOD

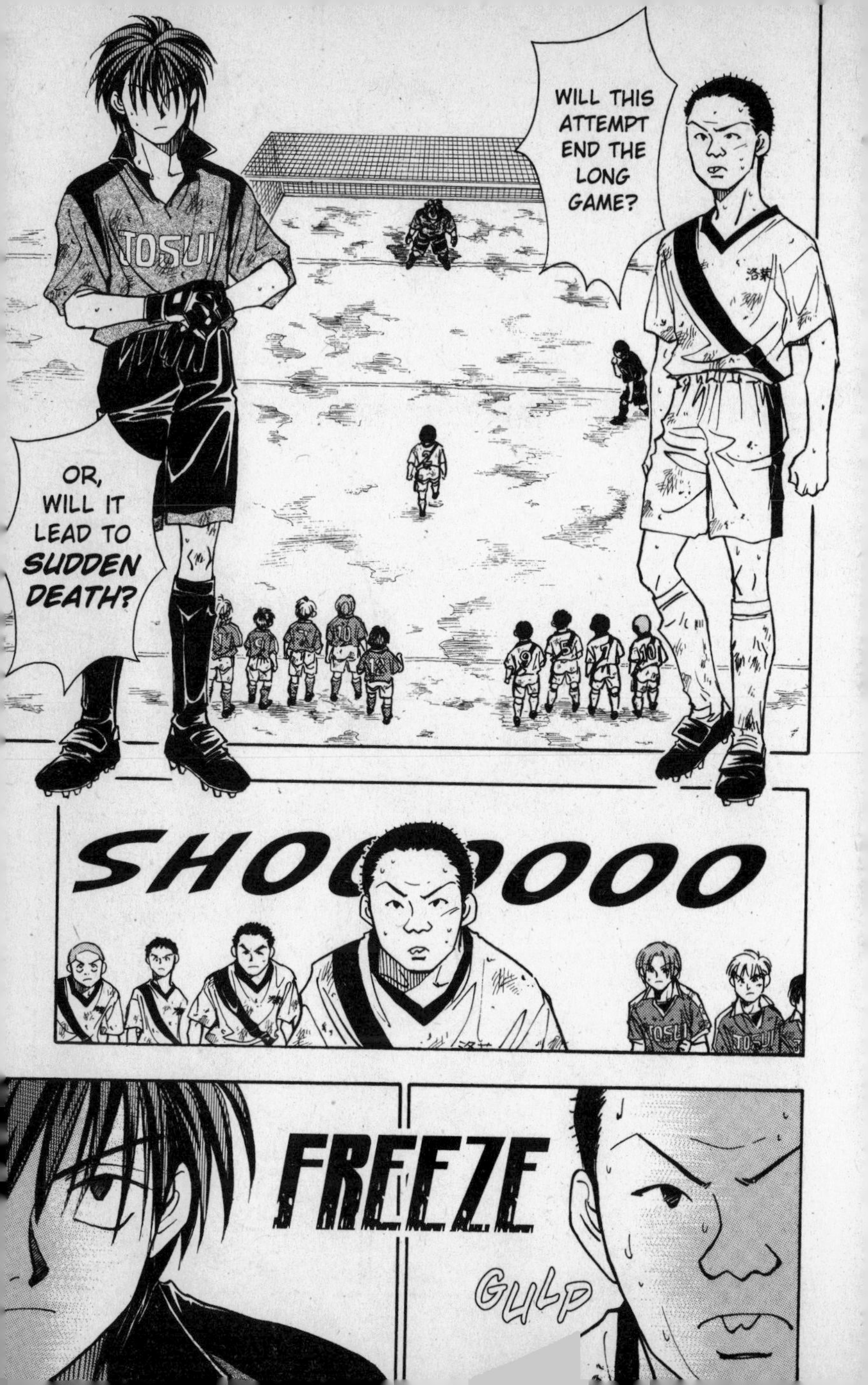
WILL THIS ATTEMPT END THE LONG GAME?
OR, WILL IT LEAD TO SUDDEN DEATH?
SHOOOOOO
FREEZE
GULP

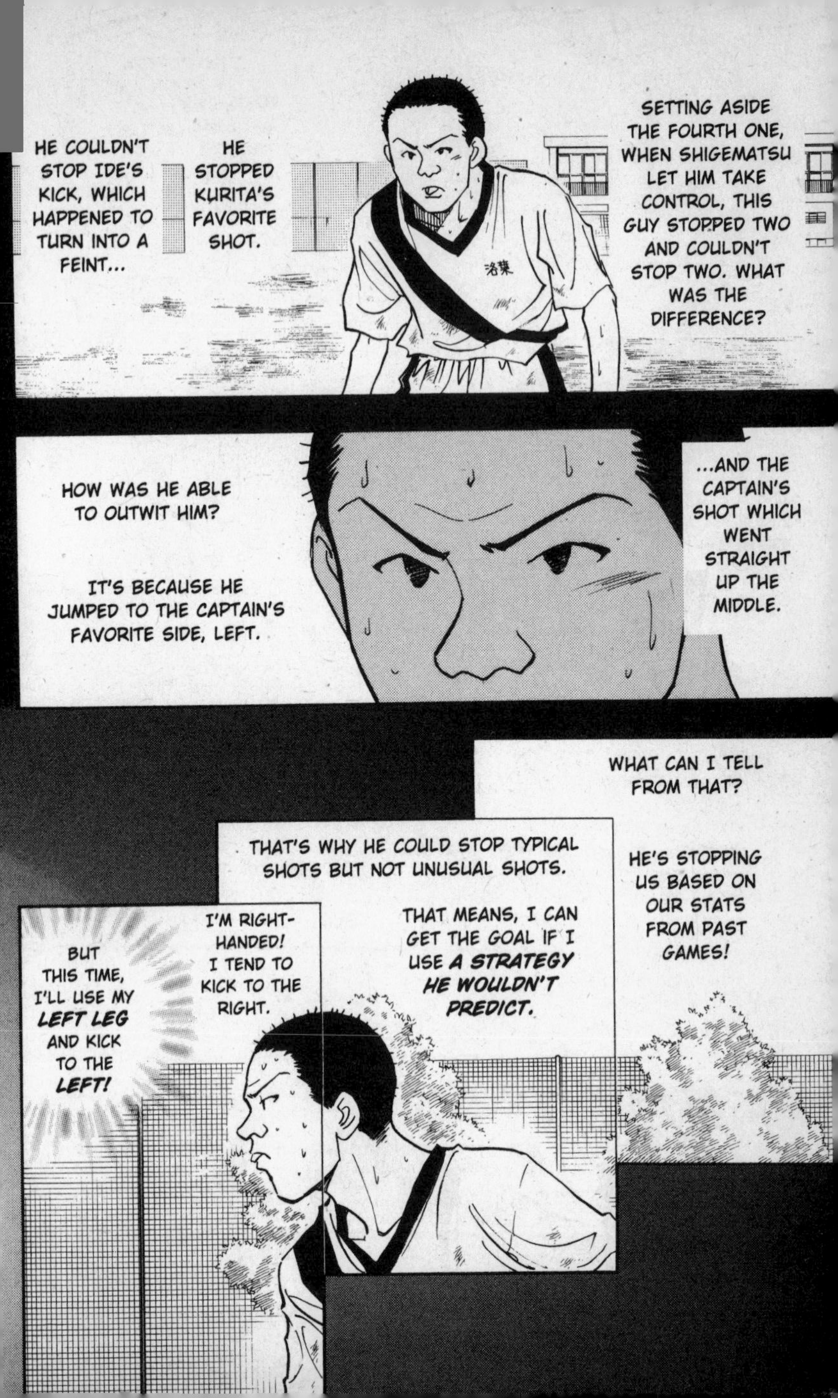
SETTING ASIDE THE FOURTH ONE, WHEN SHIGEMATSU LET HIM TAKE CONTROL, THIS GUY STOPPED TWO AND COULDN'T STOP TWO. WHAT WAS THE DIFFERENCE?
HE STOPPED KURITA'S FAVORITE SHOT.
HE COULDN'T STOP IDE'S KICK, WHICH HAPPENED TO TURN INTO A FEINT...
洛葉
...AND THE CAPTAIN'S SHOT WHICH WENT STRAIGHT UP THE MIDDLE.
HOW WAS HE ABLE TO OUTWIT HIM?
IT'S BECAUSE HE JUMPED TO THE CAPTAIN'S FAVORITE SIDE, LEFT.
WHAT CAN I TELL FROM THAT?
HE'S STOPPING US BASED ON OUR STATS FROM PAST GAMES!
THAT'S WHY HE COULD STOP TYPICAL SHOTS BUT NOT UNUSUAL SHOTS.
THAT MEANS, I CAN GET THE GOAL IF I USE *A STRATEGY HE WOULDN'T PREDICT.*
I'M RIGHT-HANDED! I TEND TO KICK TO THE RIGHT.
BUT THIS TIME, I'LL USE MY *LEFT LEG* AND KICK TO THE *LEFT!*

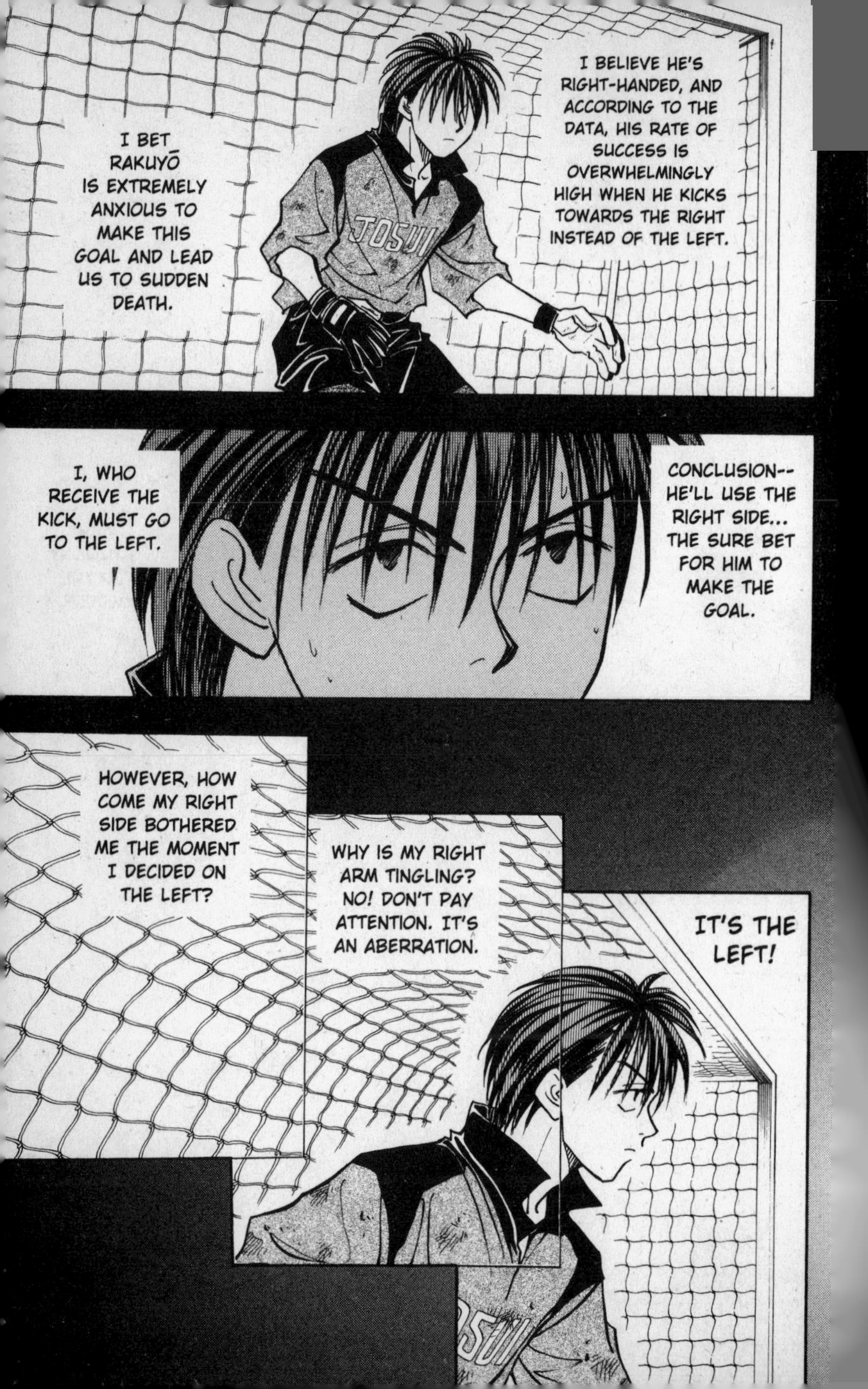
I BELIEVE HE'S RIGHT-HANDED, AND ACCORDING TO THE DATA, HIS RATE OF SUCCESS IS OVERWHELMINGLY HIGH WHEN HE KICKS TOWARDS THE RIGHT INSTEAD OF THE LEFT.
I BET RAKUYŌ IS EXTREMELY ANXIOUS TO MAKE THIS GOAL AND LEAD US TO SUDDEN DEATH.
CONCLUSION-- HE'LL USE THE RIGHT SIDE... THE SURE BET FOR HIM TO MAKE THE GOAL.
I, WHO RECEIVE THE KICK, MUST GO TO THE LEFT.
HOWEVER, HOW COME MY RIGHT SIDE BOTHERED ME THE MOMENT I DECIDED ON THE LEFT?
WHY IS MY RIGHT ARM TINGLING? NO! DON'T PAY ATTENTION. IT'S AN ABERRATION.
IT'S THE LEFT!

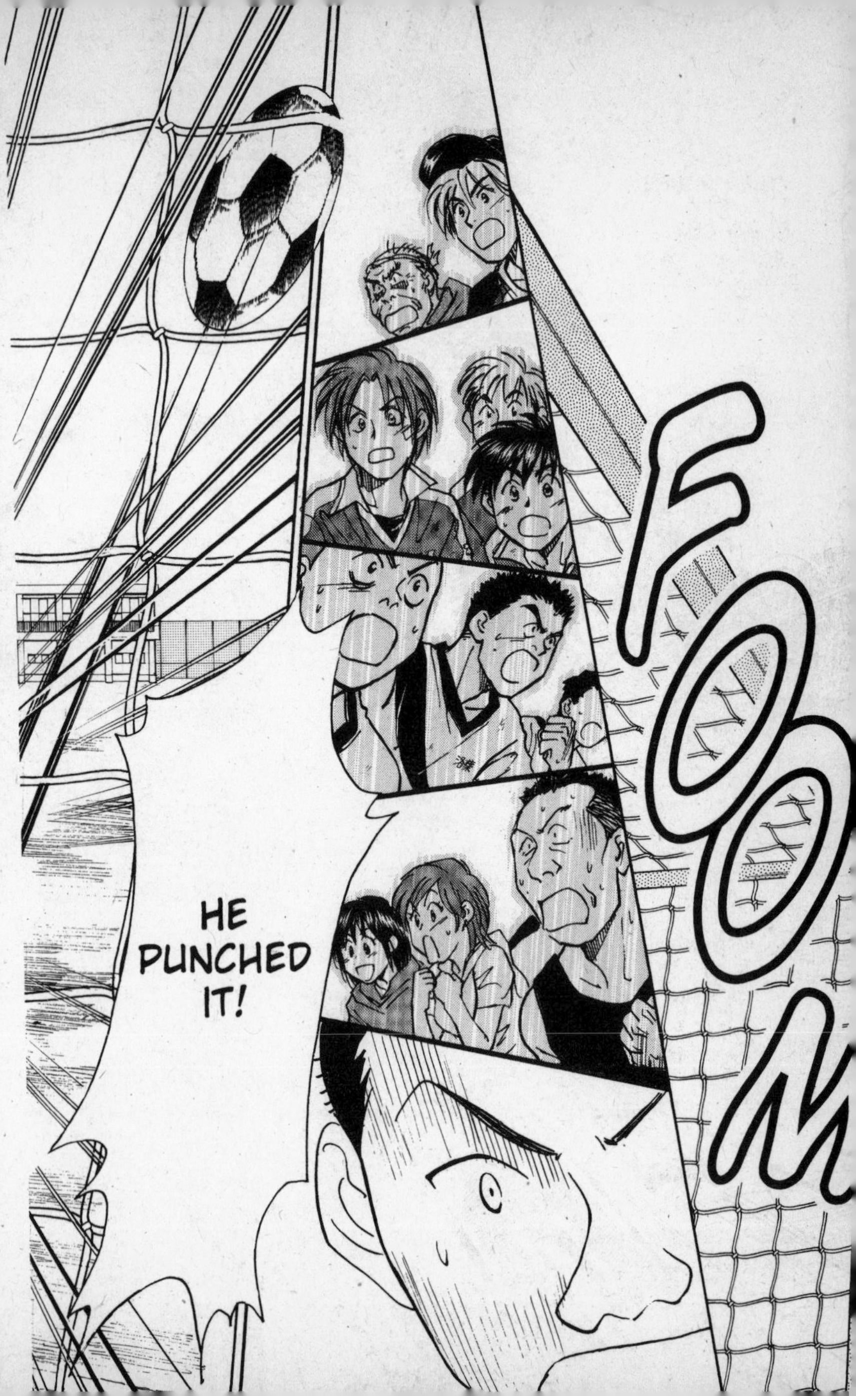
FOOM
HE PUNCHED IT!

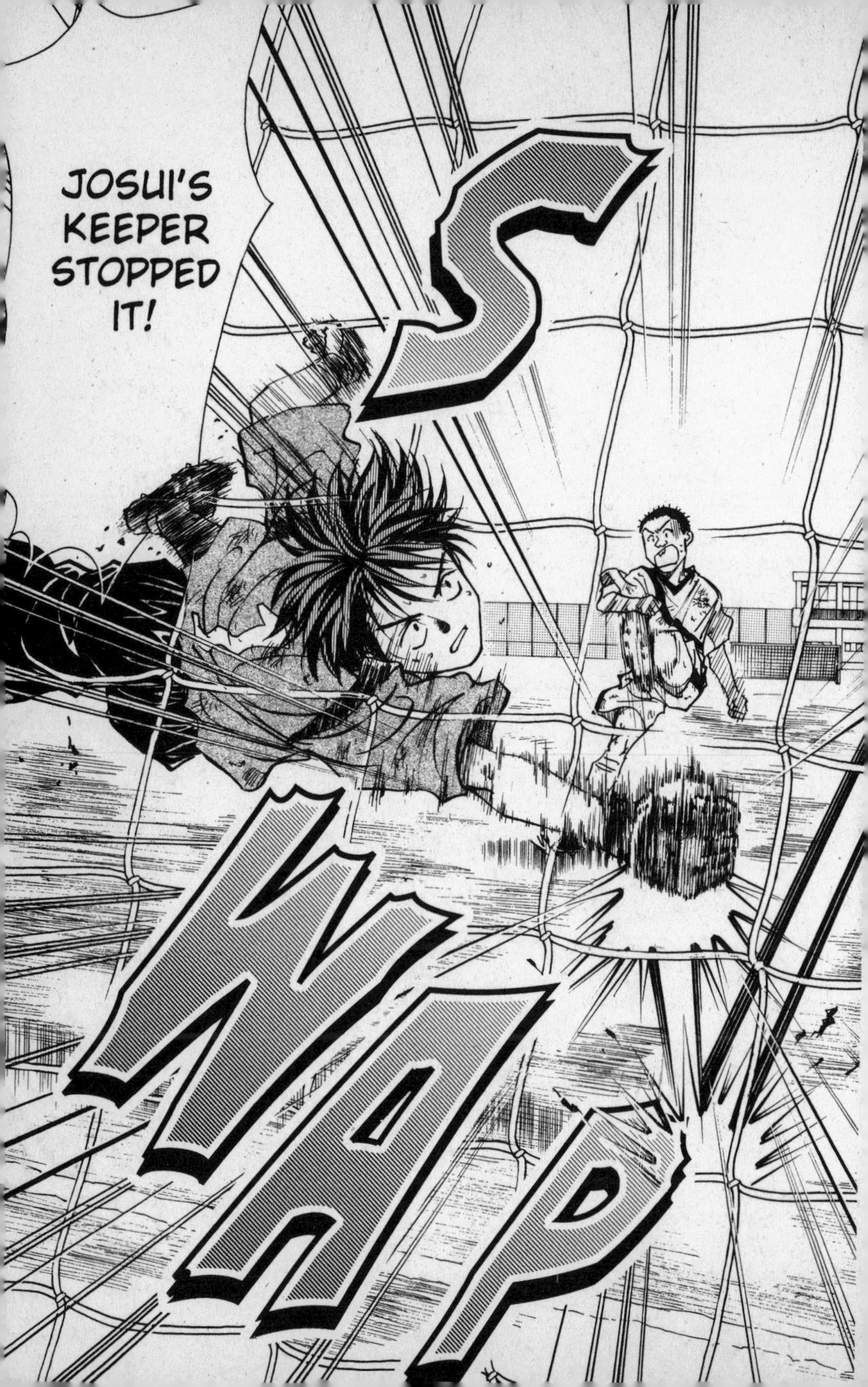
JOSUI'S KEEPER STOPPED IT!
S
WHAP

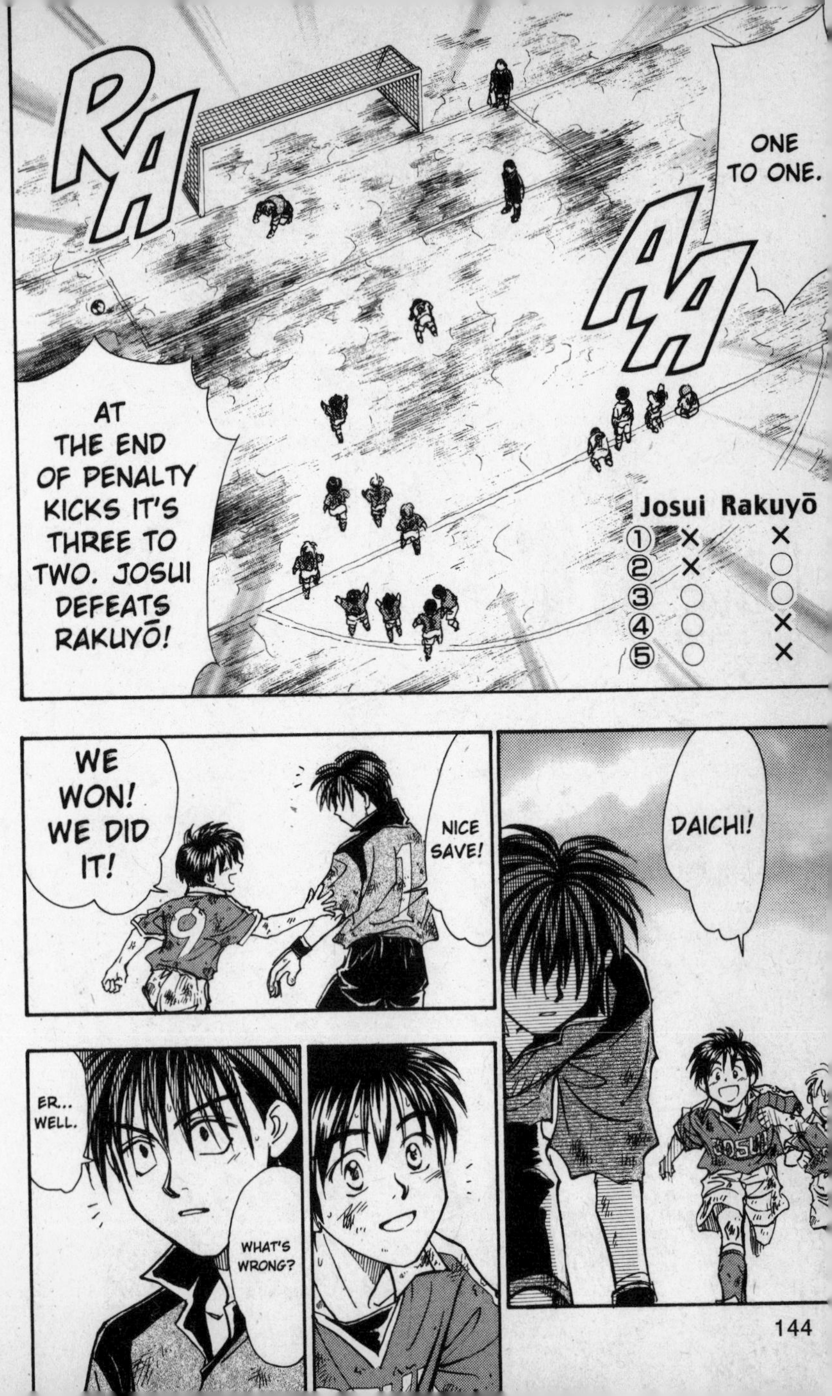
RA
AA
ONE TO ONE.
AT THE END OF PENALTY KICKS IT'S THREE TO TWO. JOSUI DEFEATS RAKUYŌ!
Josui Rakuyō
① × ×
② × ○
③ ○ ○
④ ○ ×
⑤ ○ ×
DAICHI!
NICE SAVE!
WE WON! WE DID IT!
WHAT'S WRONG?
ER... WELL.

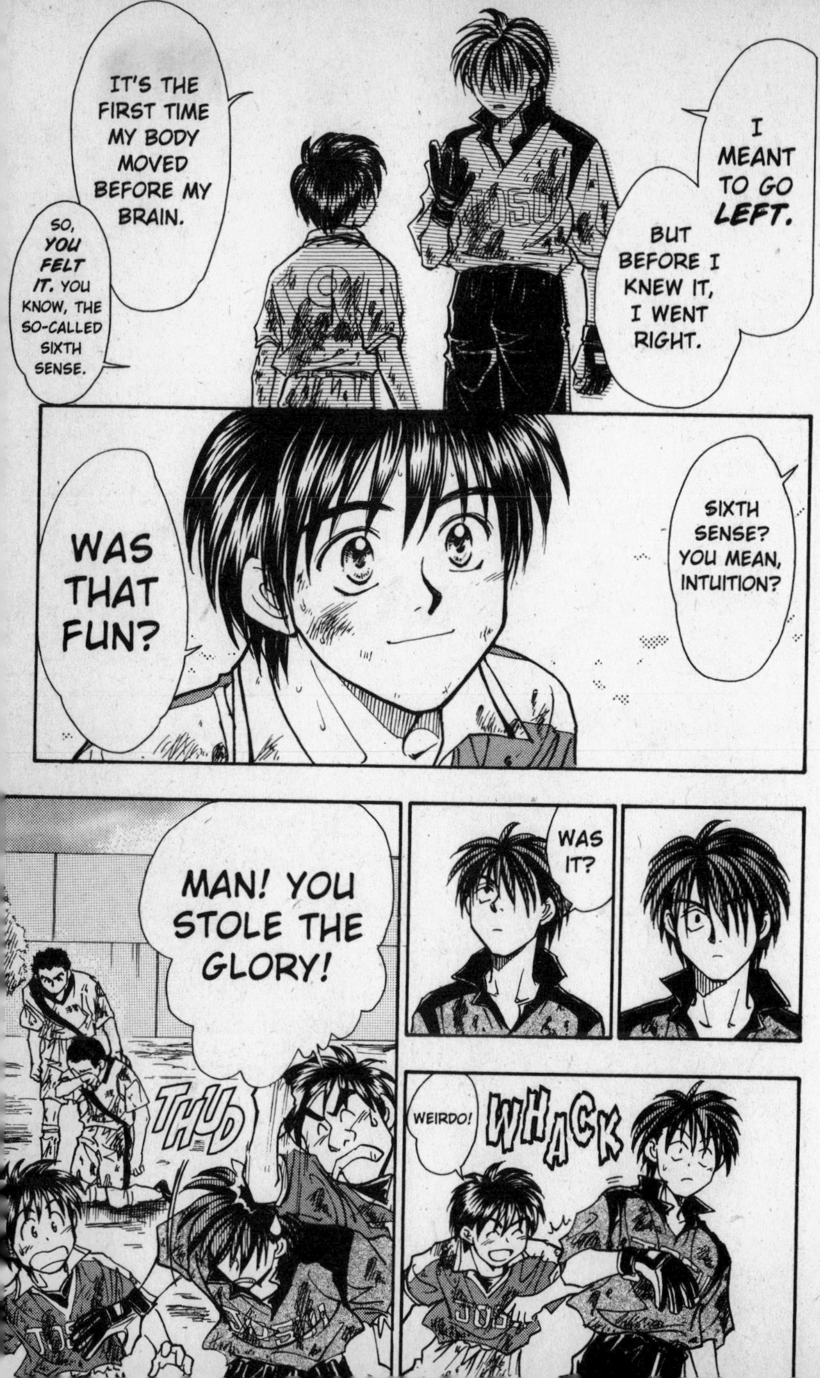
I MEANT TO GO LEFT.
BUT BEFORE I KNEW IT, I WENT RIGHT.
IT'S THE FIRST TIME MY BODY MOVED BEFORE MY BRAIN.
SO, YOU FELT IT. YOU KNOW, THE SO-CALLED SIXTH SENSE.
SIXTH SENSE? YOU MEAN, INTUITION?
WAS THAT FUN?
WAS IT?
WHACK
WEIRDO!
MAN! YOU STOLE THE GLORY!
THUD

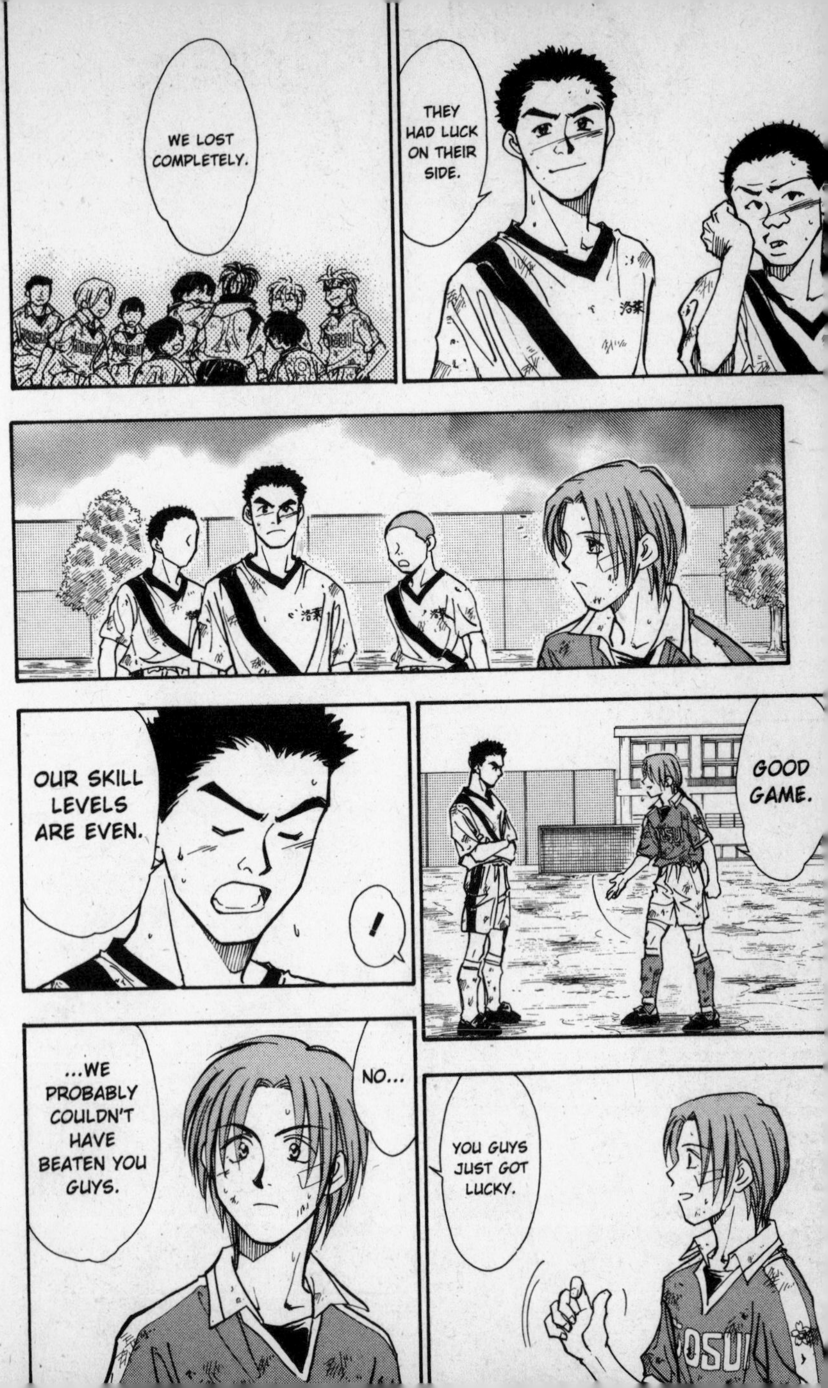
THEY HAD LUCK ON THEIR SIDE.
WE LOST COMPLETELY.
GOOD GAME.
OUR SKILL LEVELS ARE EVEN.
!
YOU GUYS JUST GOT LUCKY.
NO...
...WE PROBABLY COULDN'T HAVE BEATEN YOU GUYS.

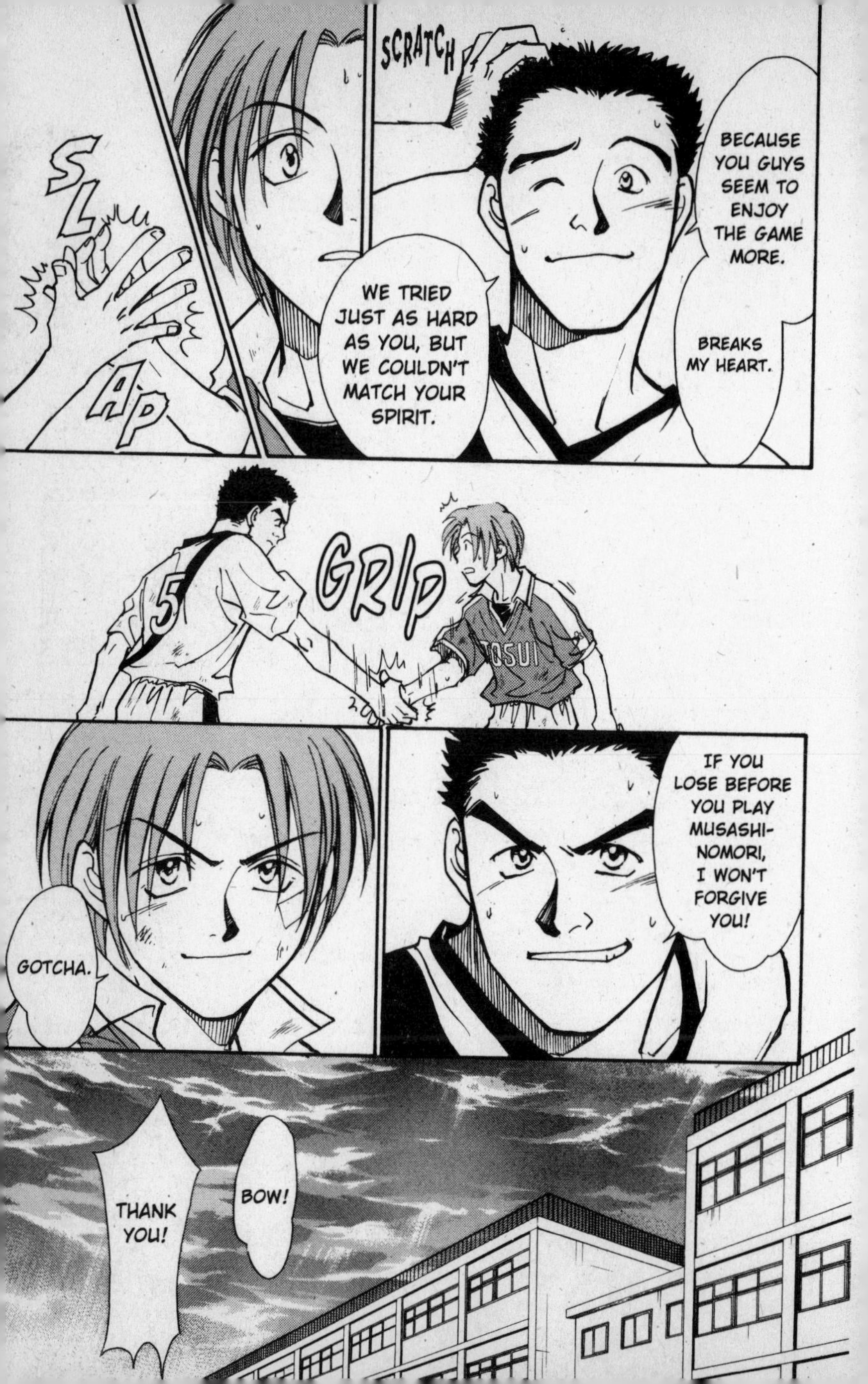
SCRATCH
WE TRIED JUST AS HARD AS YOU, BUT WE COULDN'T MATCH YOUR SPIRIT.
BECAUSE YOU GUYS SEEM TO ENJOY THE GAME MORE.
BREAKS MY HEART.
SLAP
GRIP
TOSUI
IF YOU LOSE BEFORE YOU PLAY MUSASHI-NOMORI, I WON'T FORGIVE YOU!
GOTCHA.
BOW!
THANK YOU!

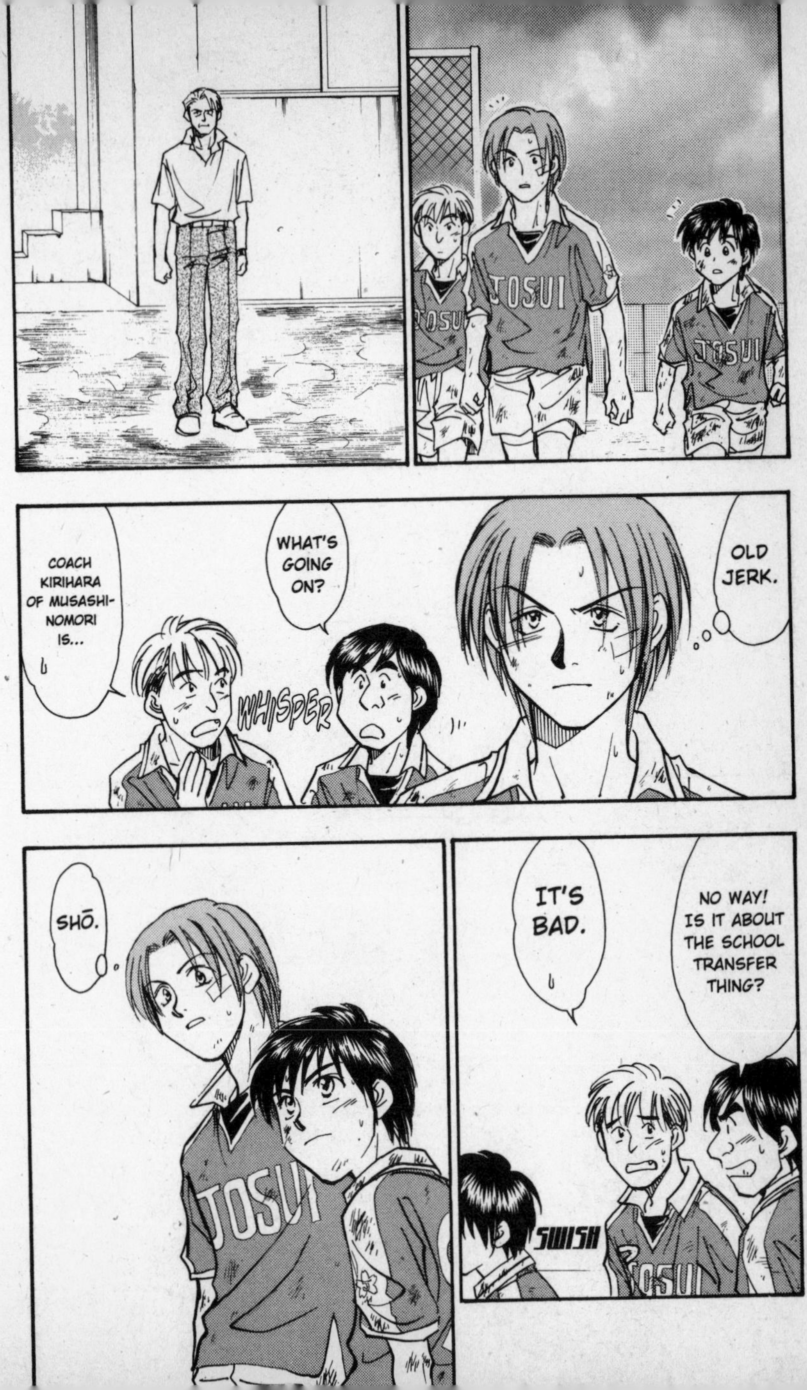
OLD JERK.
WHAT'S GOING ON?
COACH KIRIHARA OF MUSASHI-NOMORI IS...
WHISPER
NO WAY! IS IT ABOUT THE SCHOOL TRANSFER THING?
IT'S BAD.
SWISH
SHŌ.

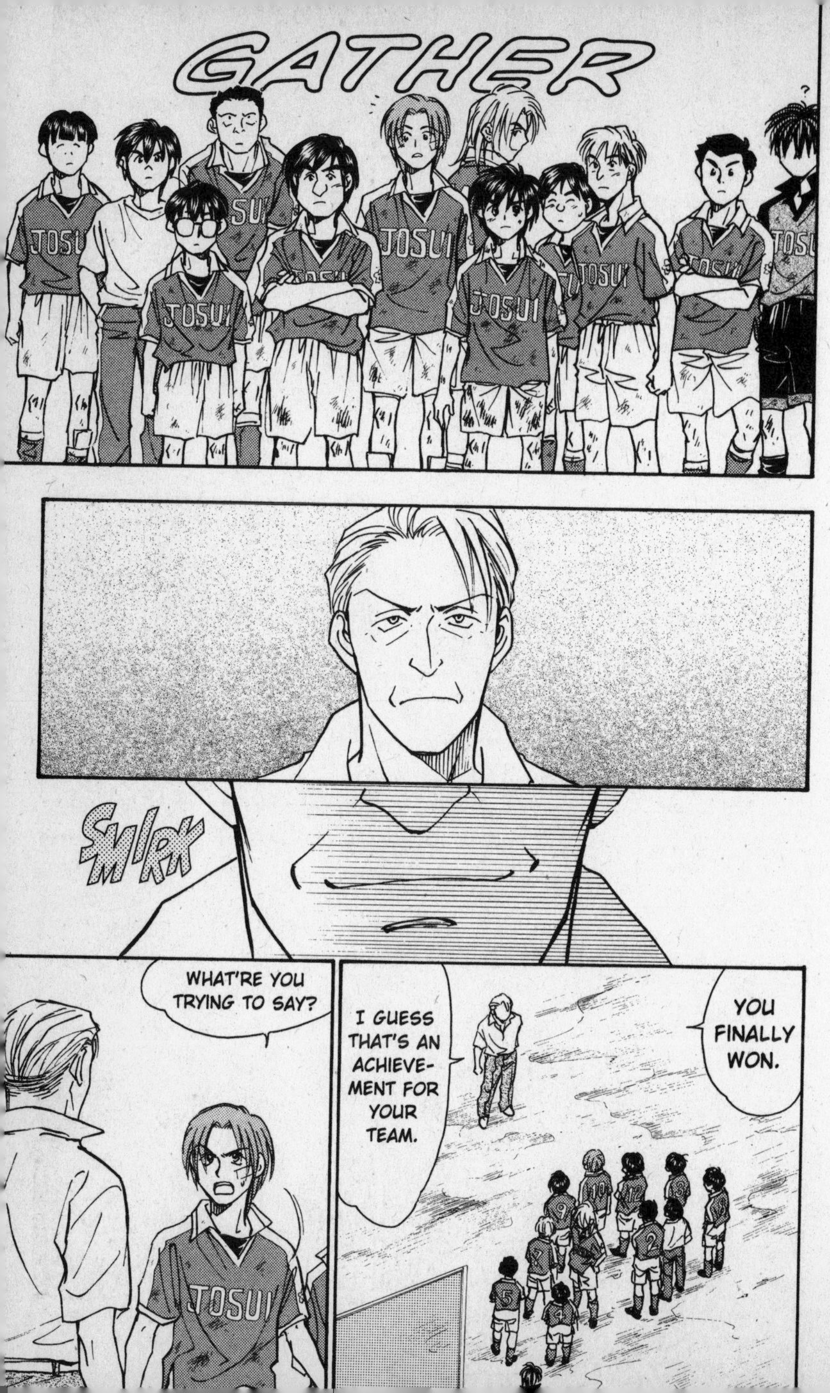
GATHER
SMIRK
YOU FINALLY WON.
I GUESS THAT'S AN ACHIEVEMENT FOR YOUR TEAM.
WHAT'RE YOU TRYING TO SAY?

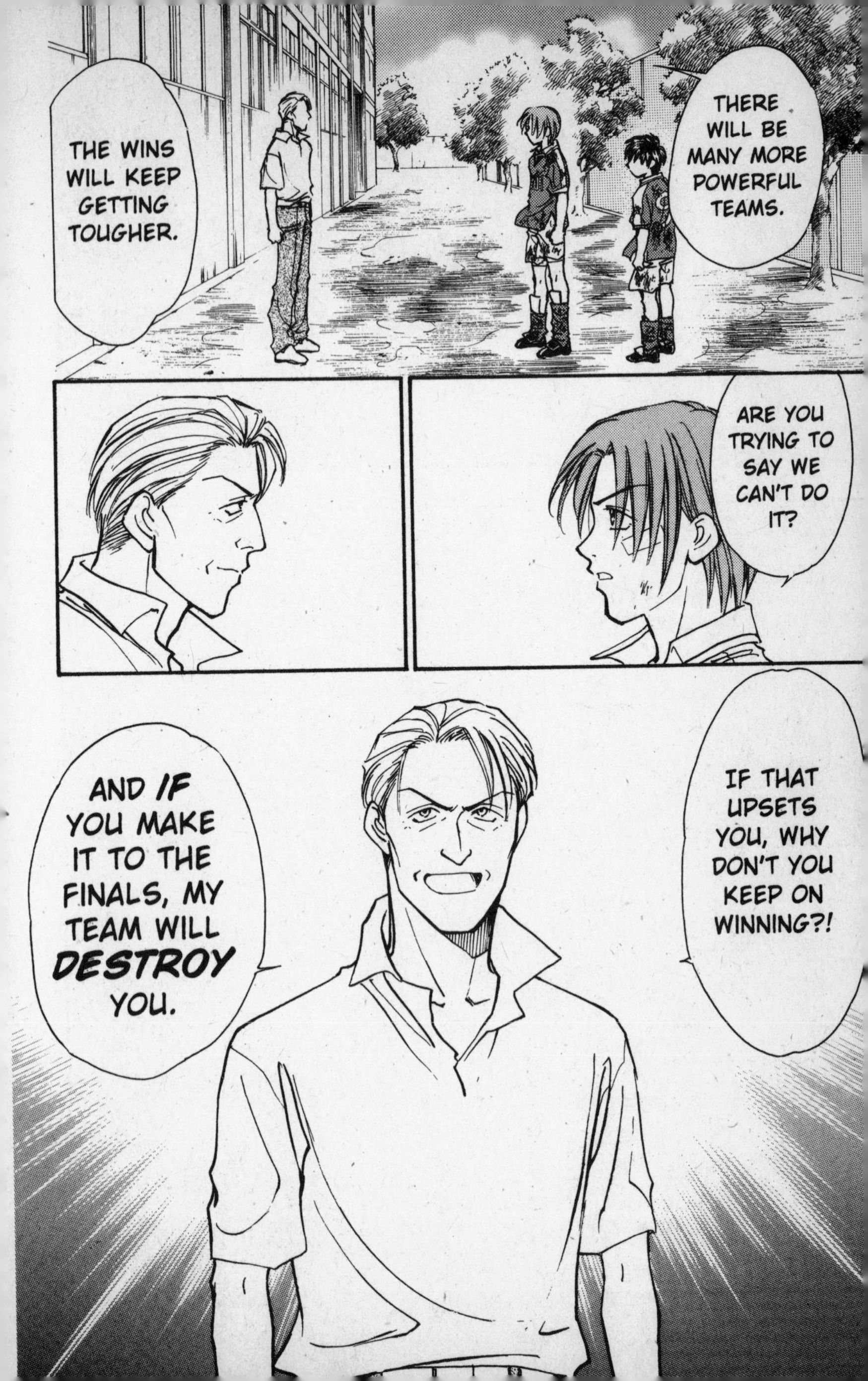
THERE WILL BE MANY MORE POWERFUL TEAMS.
THE WINS WILL KEEP GETTING TOUGHER.
ARE YOU TRYING TO SAY WE CAN'T DO IT?
IF THAT UPSETS YOU, WHY DON'T YOU KEEP ON WINNING?!
AND *IF* YOU MAKE IT TO THE FINALS, MY TEAM WILL **DESTROY** YOU.

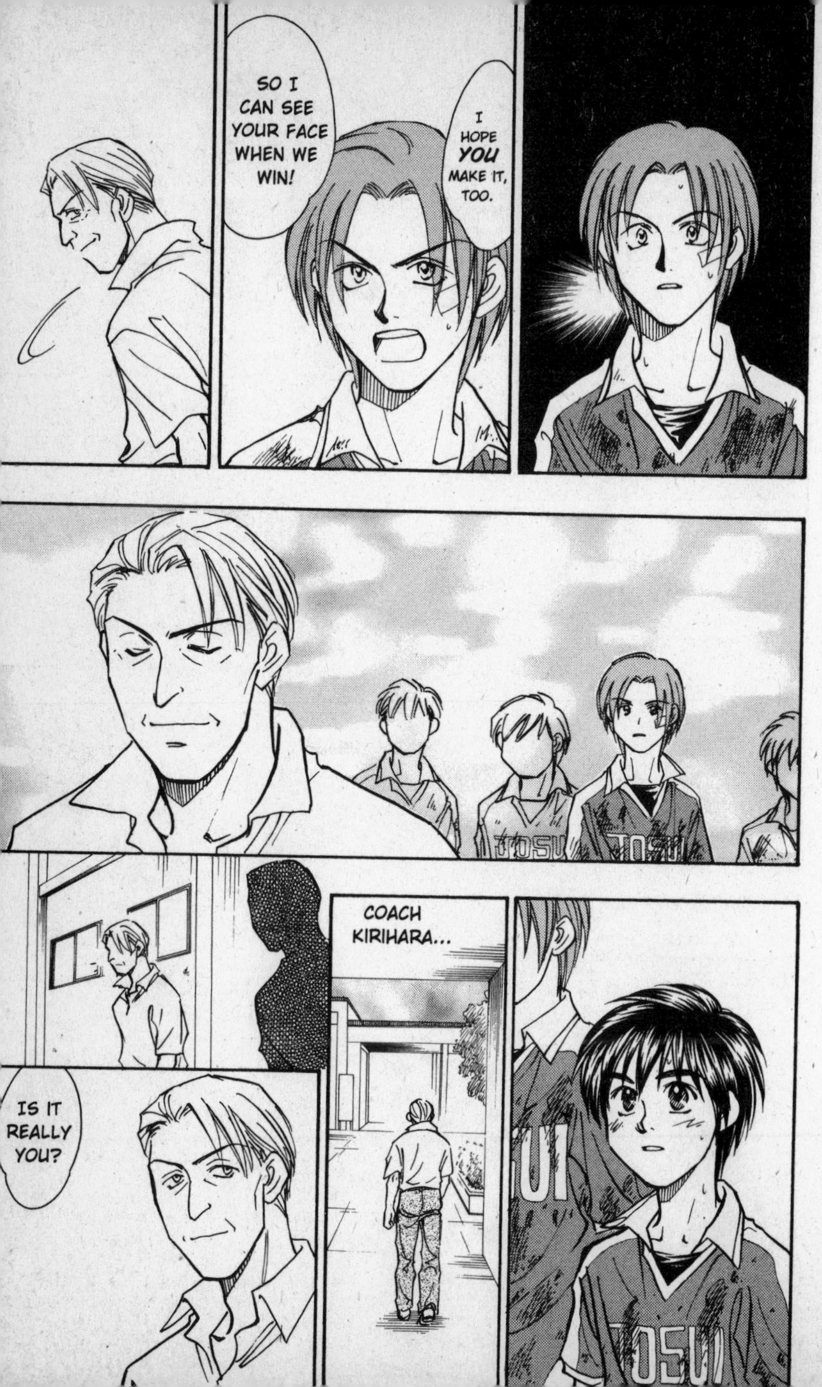
I HOPE YOU MAKE IT, TOO.
SO I CAN SEE YOUR FACE WHEN WE WIN!
COACH KIRIHARA...
IS IT REALLY YOU?

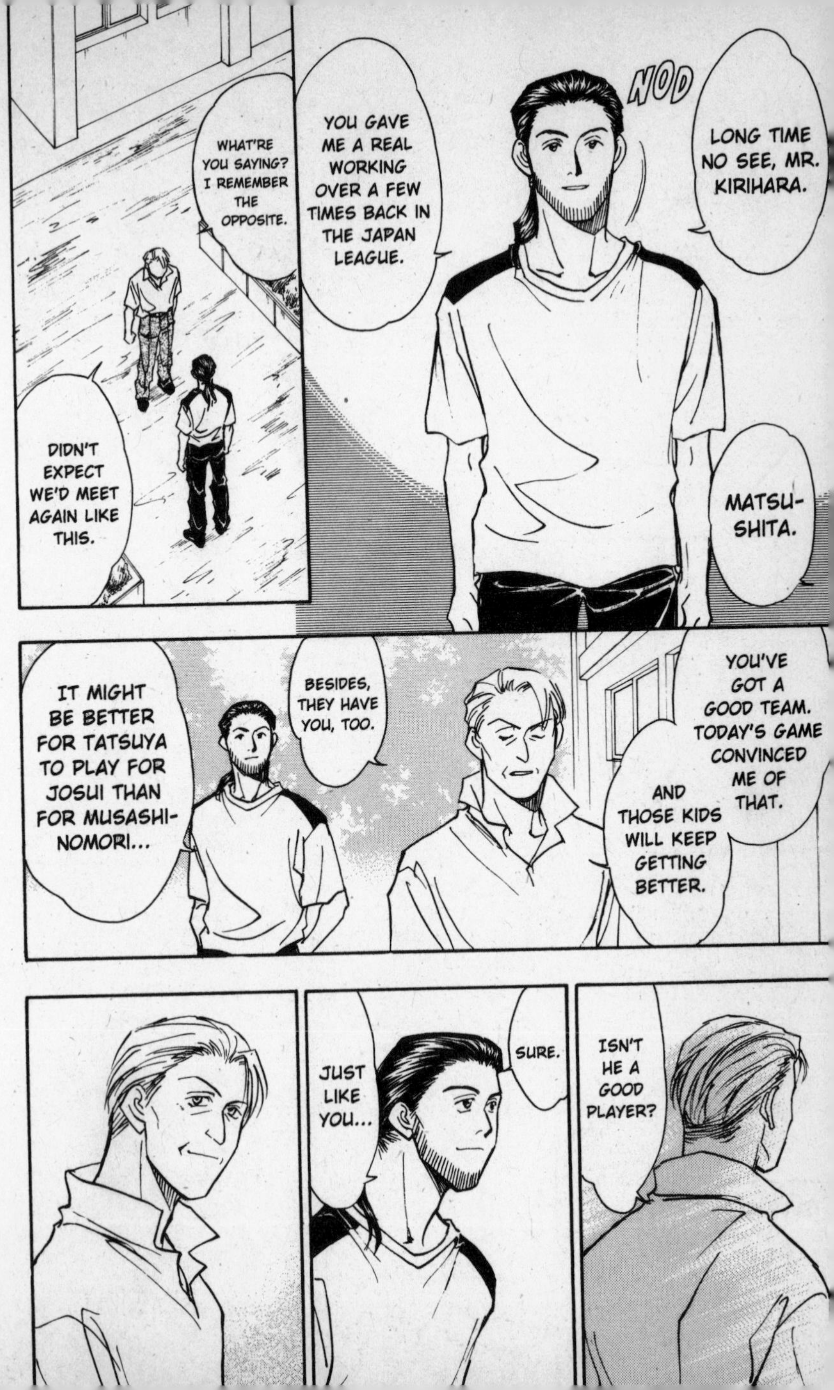
NOD
LONG TIME NO SEE, MR. KIRIHARA.
MATSU-SHITA.
YOU GAVE ME A REAL WORKING OVER A FEW TIMES BACK IN THE JAPAN LEAGUE.
WHAT'RE YOU SAYING? I REMEMBER THE OPPOSITE.
DIDN'T EXPECT WE'D MEET AGAIN LIKE THIS.
YOU'VE GOT A GOOD TEAM. TODAY'S GAME CONVINCED ME OF THAT.
AND THOSE KIDS WILL KEEP GETTING BETTER.
BESIDES, THEY HAVE YOU, TOO.
IT MIGHT BE BETTER FOR TATSUYA TO PLAY FOR JOSUI THAN FOR MUSASHI-NOMORI...
ISN'T HE A GOOD PLAYER?
SURE.
JUST LIKE YOU...

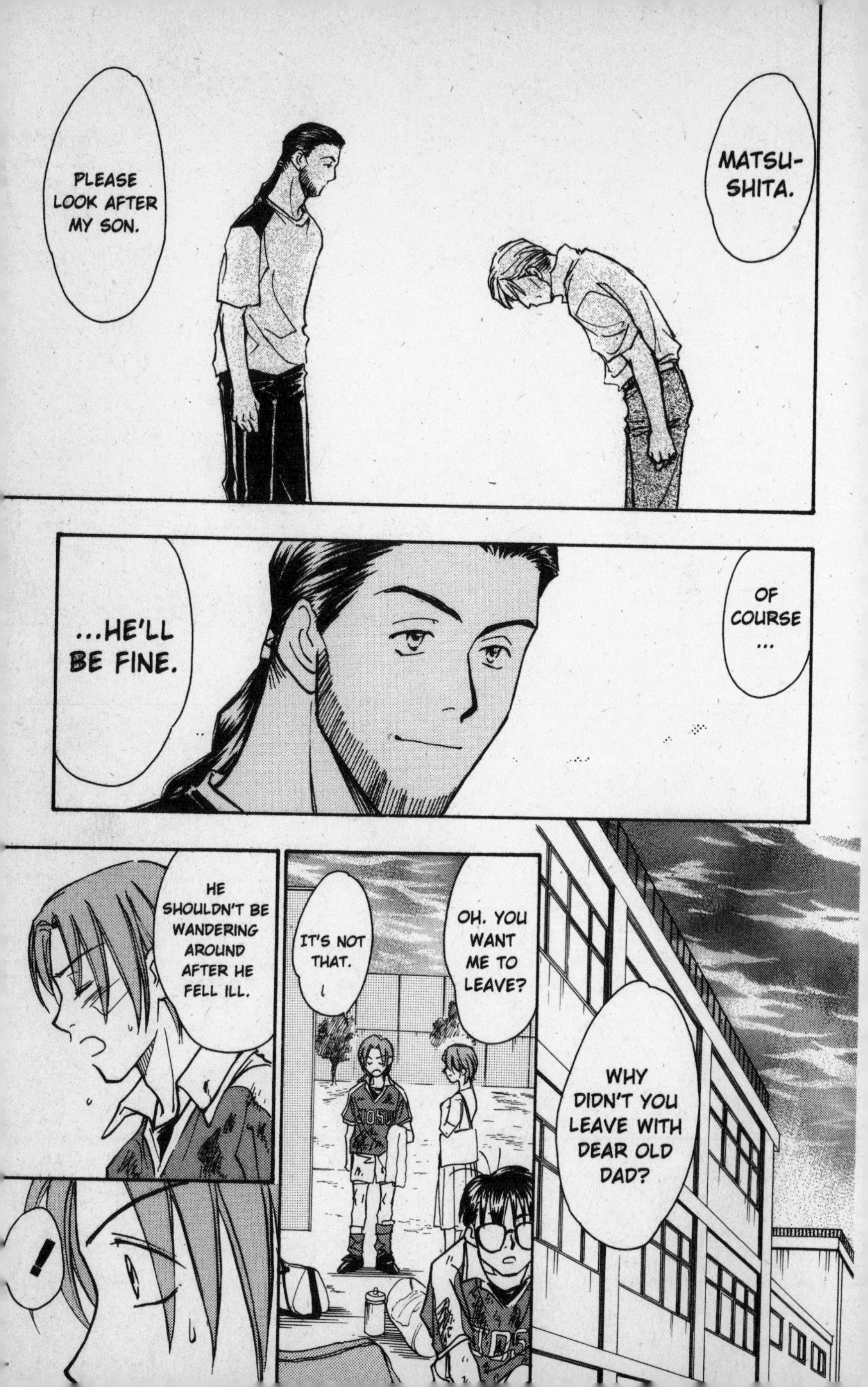
MATSU-SHITA.
PLEASE LOOK AFTER MY SON.
OF COURSE ...
...HE'LL BE FINE.
WHY DIDN'T YOU LEAVE WITH DEAR OLD DAD?
OH. YOU WANT ME TO LEAVE?
IT'S NOT THAT.
HE SHOULDN'T BE WANDERING AROUND AFTER HE FELL ILL.
!

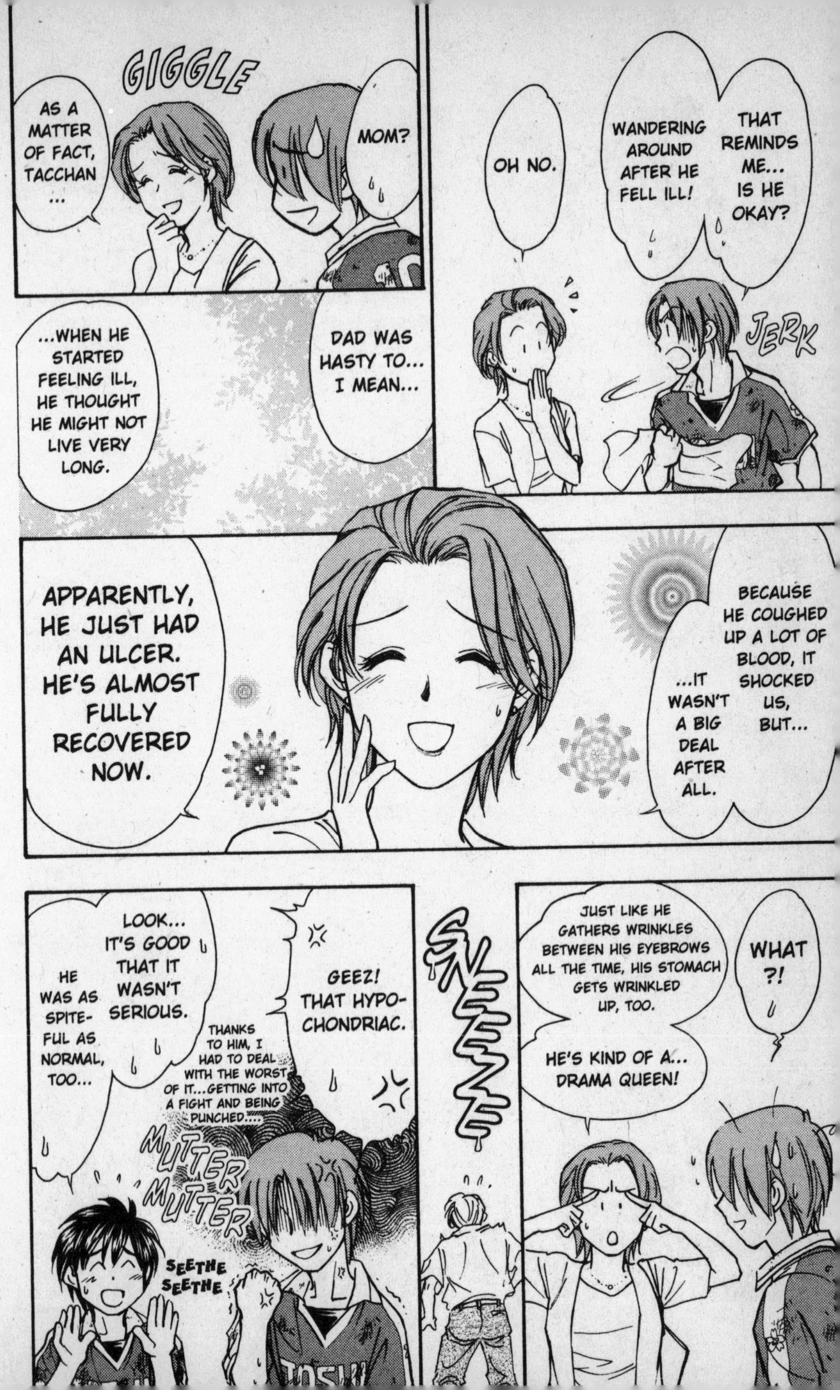
THAT REMINDS ME... IS HE OKAY?
WANDERING AROUND AFTER HE FELL ILL!
OH NO.
JERK
GIGGLE
MOM?
AS A MATTER OF FACT, TACCHAN...
DAD WAS HASTY TO... I MEAN...
...WHEN HE STARTED FEELING ILL, HE THOUGHT HE MIGHT NOT LIVE VERY LONG.
BECAUSE HE COUGHED UP A LOT OF BLOOD, IT SHOCKED US, BUT...
...IT WASN'T A BIG DEAL AFTER ALL.
APPARENTLY, HE JUST HAD AN ULCER. HE'S ALMOST FULLY RECOVERED NOW.
WHAT?!
JUST LIKE HE GATHERS WRINKLES BETWEEN HIS EYEBROWS ALL THE TIME, HIS STOMACH GETS WRINKLED UP, TOO.
HE'S KIND OF A... DRAMA QUEEN!
SNEEZE
GEEZ! THAT HYPO-CHONDRIAC.
LOOK... IT'S GOOD THAT IT WASN'T SERIOUS.
HE WAS AS SPITE-FUL AS NORMAL, TOO...
THANKS TO HIM, I HAD TO DEAL WITH THE WORST OF IT...GETTING INTO A FIGHT AND BEING PUNCHED....
MUTTER MUTTER
SEETHE SEETHE

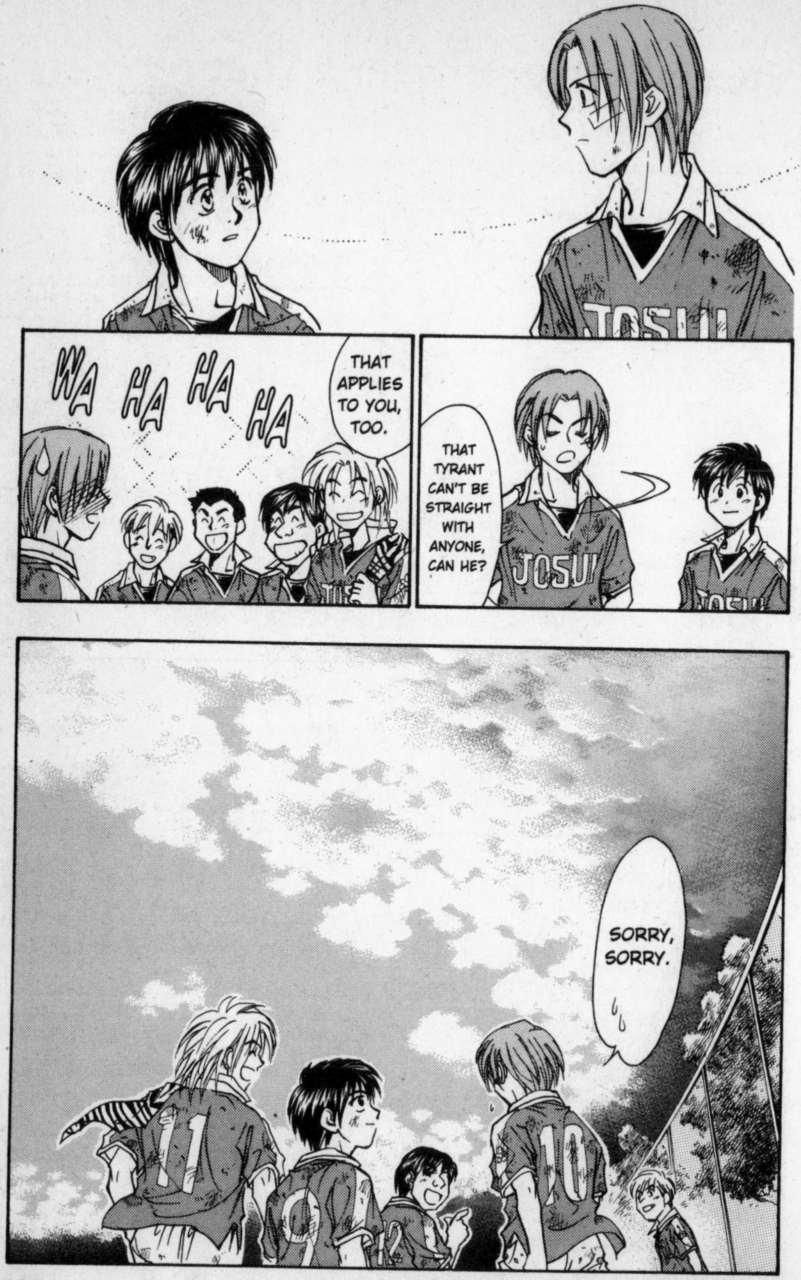
THAT TYRANT CAN'T BE STRAIGHT WITH ANYONE, CAN HE?
THAT APPLIES TO YOU, TOO.
WA HA HA HA
SORRY, SORRY.

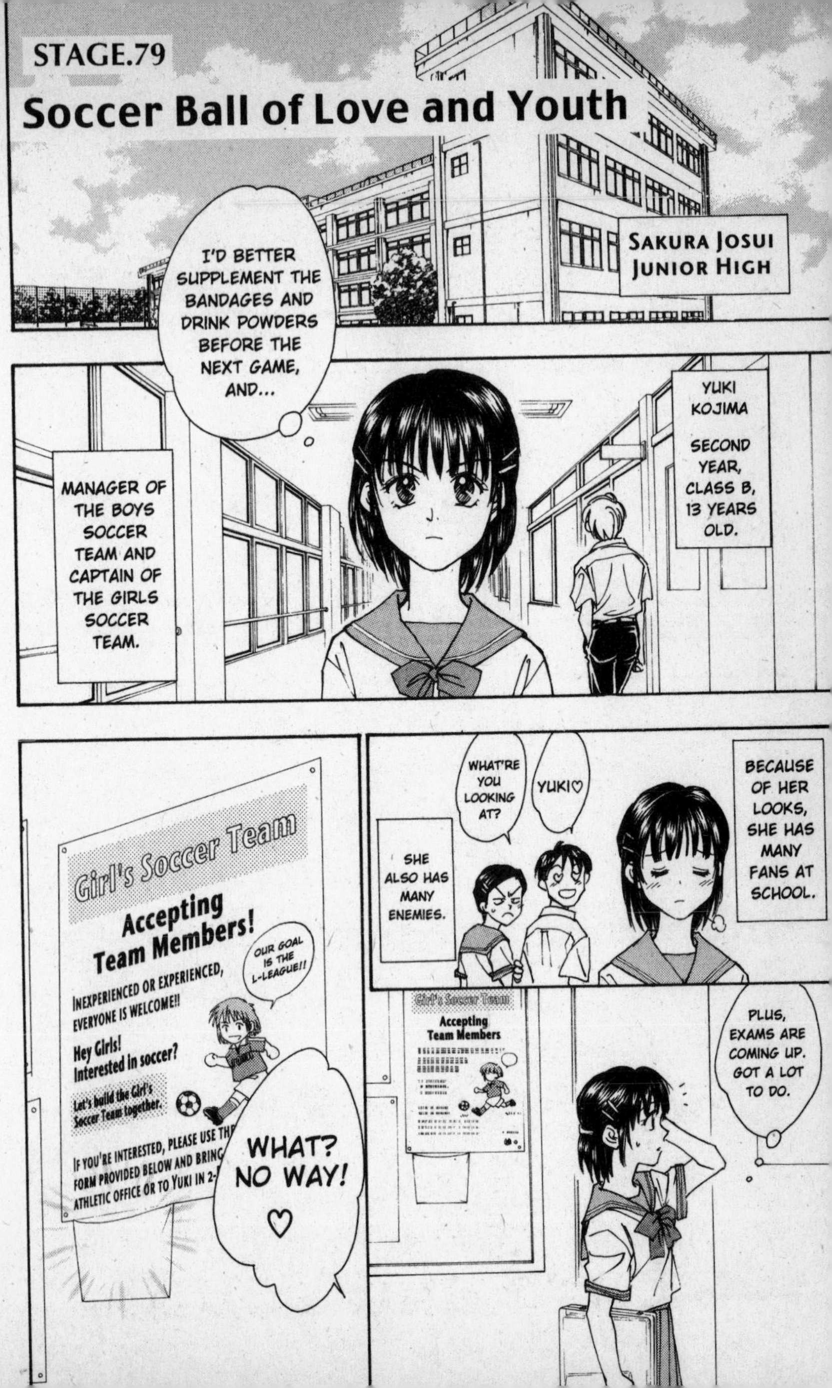
STAGE.79
Soccer Ball of Love and Youth
SAKURA JOSUI JUNIOR HIGH
I'D BETTER SUPPLEMENT THE BANDAGES AND DRINK POWDERS BEFORE THE NEXT GAME, AND...
YUKI KOJIMA
SECOND YEAR, CLASS B, 13 YEARS OLD.
MANAGER OF THE BOYS SOCCER TEAM AND CAPTAIN OF THE GIRLS SOCCER TEAM.
BECAUSE OF HER LOOKS, SHE HAS MANY FANS AT SCHOOL.
YUKI♡
WHAT'RE YOU LOOKING AT?
SHE ALSO HAS MANY ENEMIES.
Girl's Soccer Team
Accepting Team Members
PLUS, EXAMS ARE COMING UP. GOT A LOT TO DO.
Girl's Soccer Team
Accepting Team Members!
INEXPERIENCED OR EXPERIENCED, EVERYONE IS WELCOME!!
OUR GOAL IS THE L-LEAGUE!!
Hey Girls! Interested in soccer?
Let's build the Girl's Soccer Team together.
IF YOU'RE INTERESTED, PLEASE USE THE FORM PROVIDED BELOW AND BRING ATHLETIC OFFICE OR TO YUKI IN 2-
WHAT? NO WAY! ♡

STAGE.79

Soccer Ball of
Love and Youth

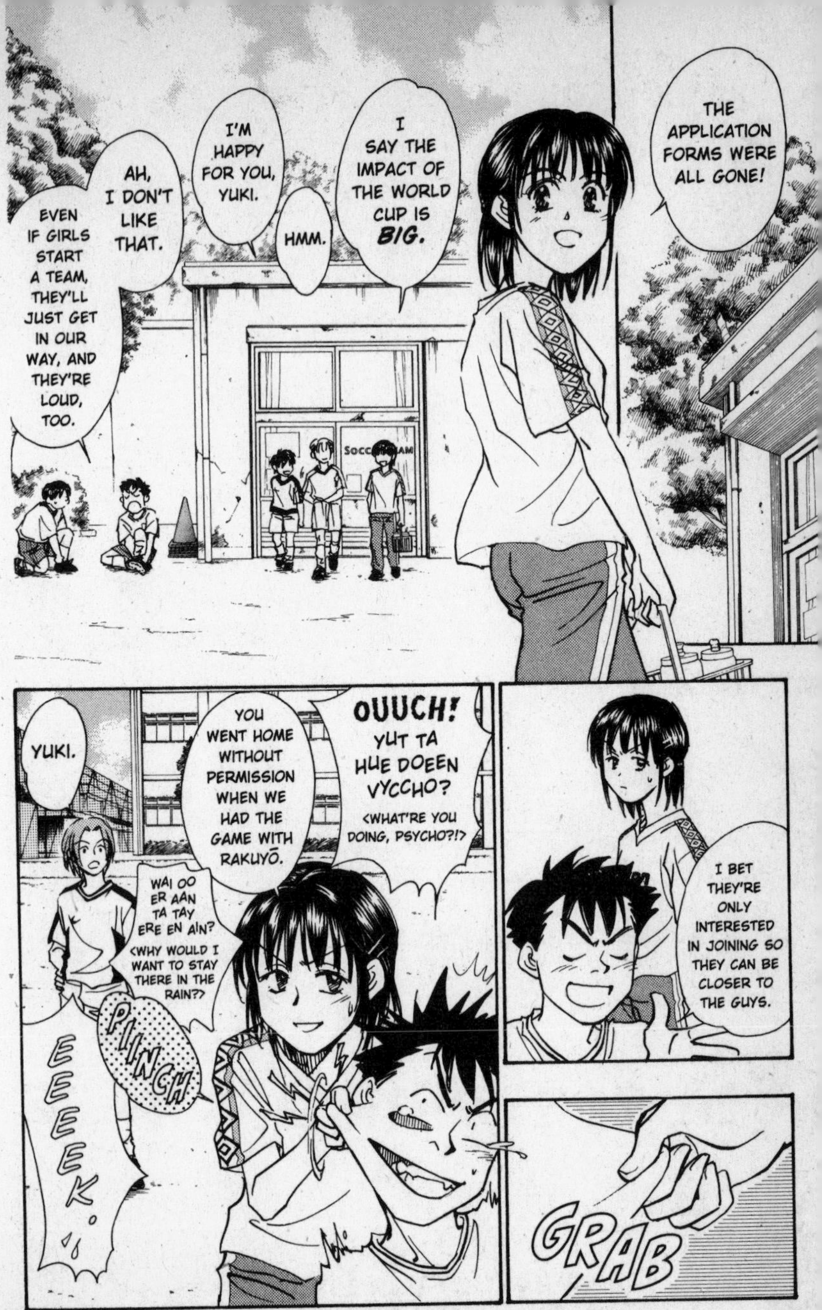
THE APPLICATION FORMS WERE ALL GONE!
I SAY THE IMPACT OF THE WORLD CUP IS BIG.
HMM.
I'M HAPPY FOR YOU, YUKI.
AH, I DON'T LIKE THAT.
EVEN IF GIRLS START A TEAM, THEY'LL JUST GET IN OUR WAY, AND THEY'RE LOUD, TOO.
I BET THEY'RE ONLY INTERESTED IN JOINING SO THEY CAN BE CLOSER TO THE GUYS.
GRAB
OUUCH! YUT TA HUE DOEEN VYCCHO? <WHAT'RE YOU DOING, PSYCHO?!>
YOU WENT HOME WITHOUT PERMISSION WHEN WE HAD THE GAME WITH RAKUYŌ.
YUKI.
WAI OO ER AAN TA TAY ERE EN AIN? <WHY WOULD I WANT TO STAY THERE IN THE RAIN?>
PIINCH
EEEEK.

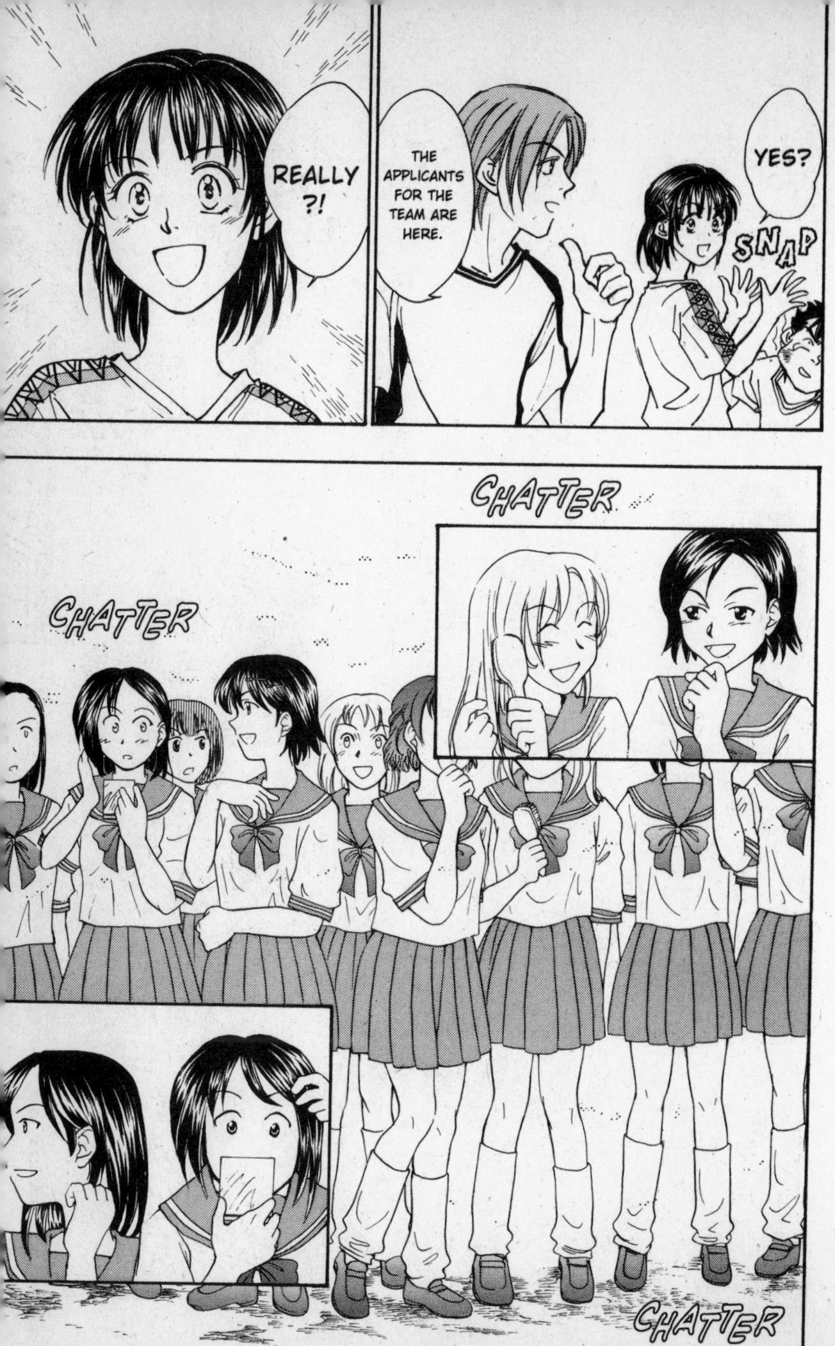
YES?
SNAP
THE APPLICANTS FOR THE TEAM ARE HERE.
REALLY ?!
CHATTER
CHATTER
CHATTER

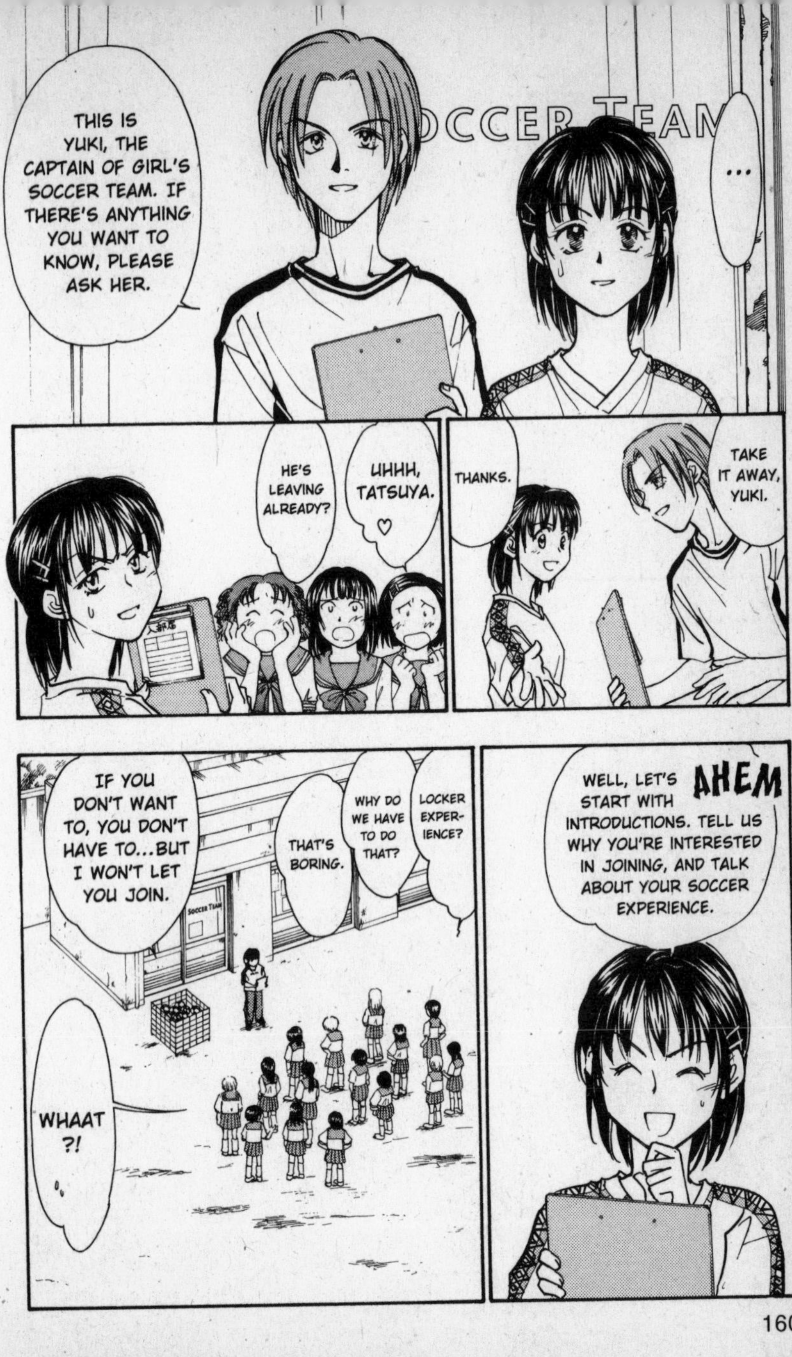
THIS IS YUKI, THE CAPTAIN OF GIRL'S SOCCER TEAM. IF THERE'S ANYTHING YOU WANT TO KNOW, PLEASE ASK HER.
...
TAKE IT AWAY, YUKI.
THANKS.
UHHH, TATSUYA. ♥
HE'S LEAVING ALREADY?
AHEM
WELL, LET'S START WITH INTRODUCTIONS. TELL US WHY YOU'RE INTERESTED IN JOINING, AND TALK ABOUT YOUR SOCCER EXPERIENCE.
LOCKER EXPERIENCE?
WHY DO WE HAVE TO DO THAT?
THAT'S BORING.
IF YOU DON'T WANT TO, YOU DON'T HAVE TO...BUT I WON'T LET YOU JOIN.
SOCCER TEAM
WHAAT ?!

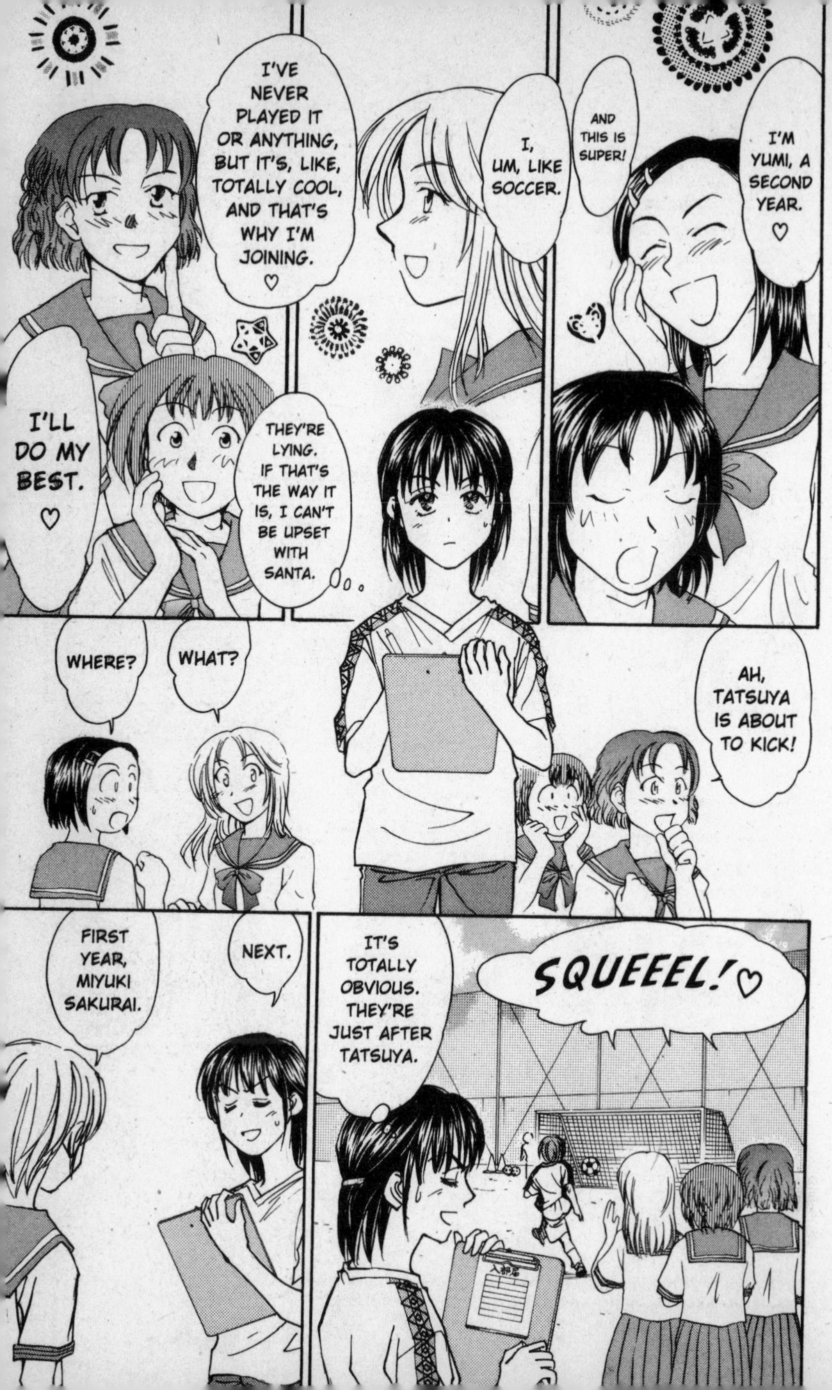
I'M YUMI, A SECOND YEAR. ♡
AND THIS IS SUPER!
I, UM, LIKE SOCCER.
I'VE NEVER PLAYED IT OR ANYTHING, BUT IT'S, LIKE, TOTALLY COOL, AND THAT'S WHY I'M JOINING. ♡
I'LL DO MY BEST. ♡
THEY'RE LYING. IF THAT'S THE WAY IT IS, I CAN'T BE UPSET WITH SANTA.
AH, TATSUYA IS ABOUT TO KICK!
WHAT?
WHERE?
SQUEEEL! ♡
IT'S TOTALLY OBVIOUS. THEY'RE JUST AFTER TATSUYA.
NEXT.
FIRST YEAR, MIYUKI SAKURAI.

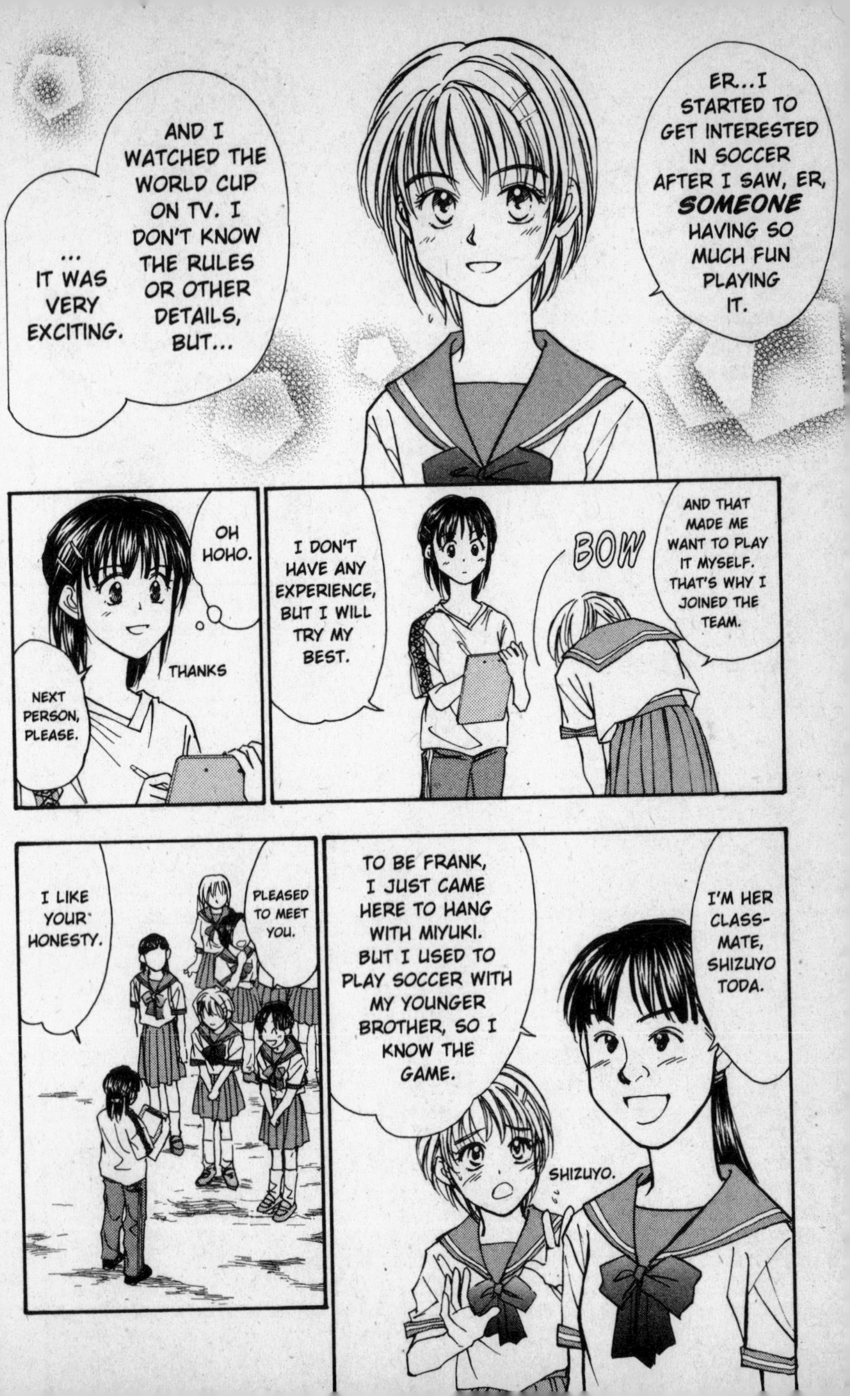
ER...I STARTED TO GET INTERESTED IN SOCCER AFTER I SAW, ER, **SOMEONE** HAVING SO MUCH FUN PLAYING IT.
AND I WATCHED THE WORLD CUP ON TV. I DON'T KNOW THE RULES OR OTHER DETAILS, BUT...
... IT WAS VERY EXCITING.
AND THAT MADE ME WANT TO PLAY IT MYSELF. THAT'S WHY I JOINED THE TEAM.
BOW
I DON'T HAVE ANY EXPERIENCE, BUT I WILL TRY MY BEST.
OH HOHO.
THANKS
NEXT PERSON, PLEASE.
I'M HER CLASS-MATE, SHIZUYO TODA.
TO BE FRANK, I JUST CAME HERE TO HANG WITH MIYUKI. BUT I USED TO PLAY SOCCER WITH MY YOUNGER BROTHER, SO I KNOW THE GAME.
SHIZUYO.
PLEASED TO MEET YOU.
I LIKE YOUR HONESTY.

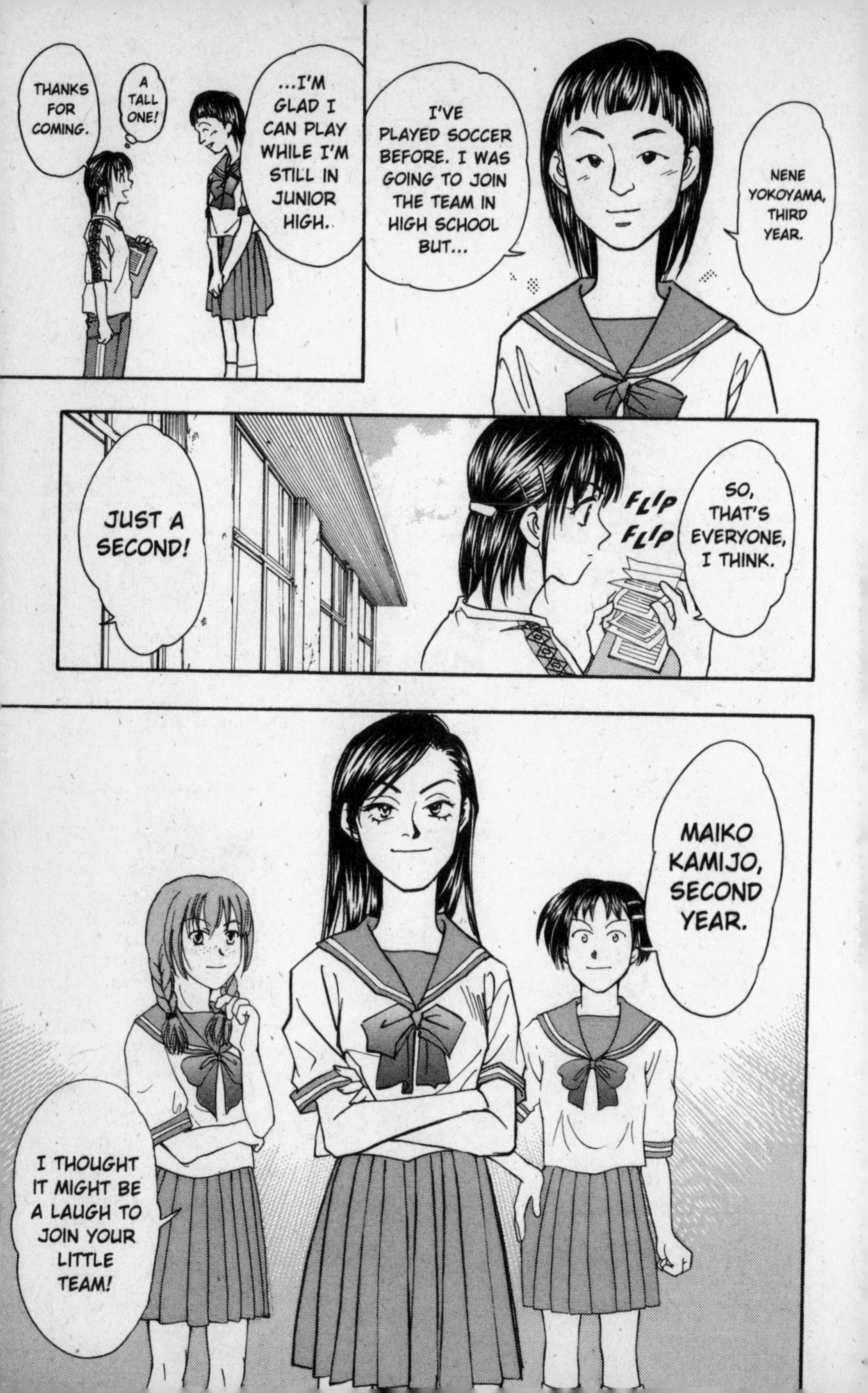
NENE YOKOYAMA, THIRD YEAR.
I'VE PLAYED SOCCER BEFORE. I WAS GOING TO JOIN THE TEAM IN HIGH SCHOOL BUT...
...I'M GLAD I CAN PLAY WHILE I'M STILL IN JUNIOR HIGH.
A TALL ONE!
THANKS FOR COMING.
SO, THAT'S EVERYONE, I THINK.
FLIP FLIP
JUST A SECOND!
MAIKO KAMIJO, SECOND YEAR.
I THOUGHT IT MIGHT BE A LAUGH TO JOIN YOUR LITTLE TEAM!

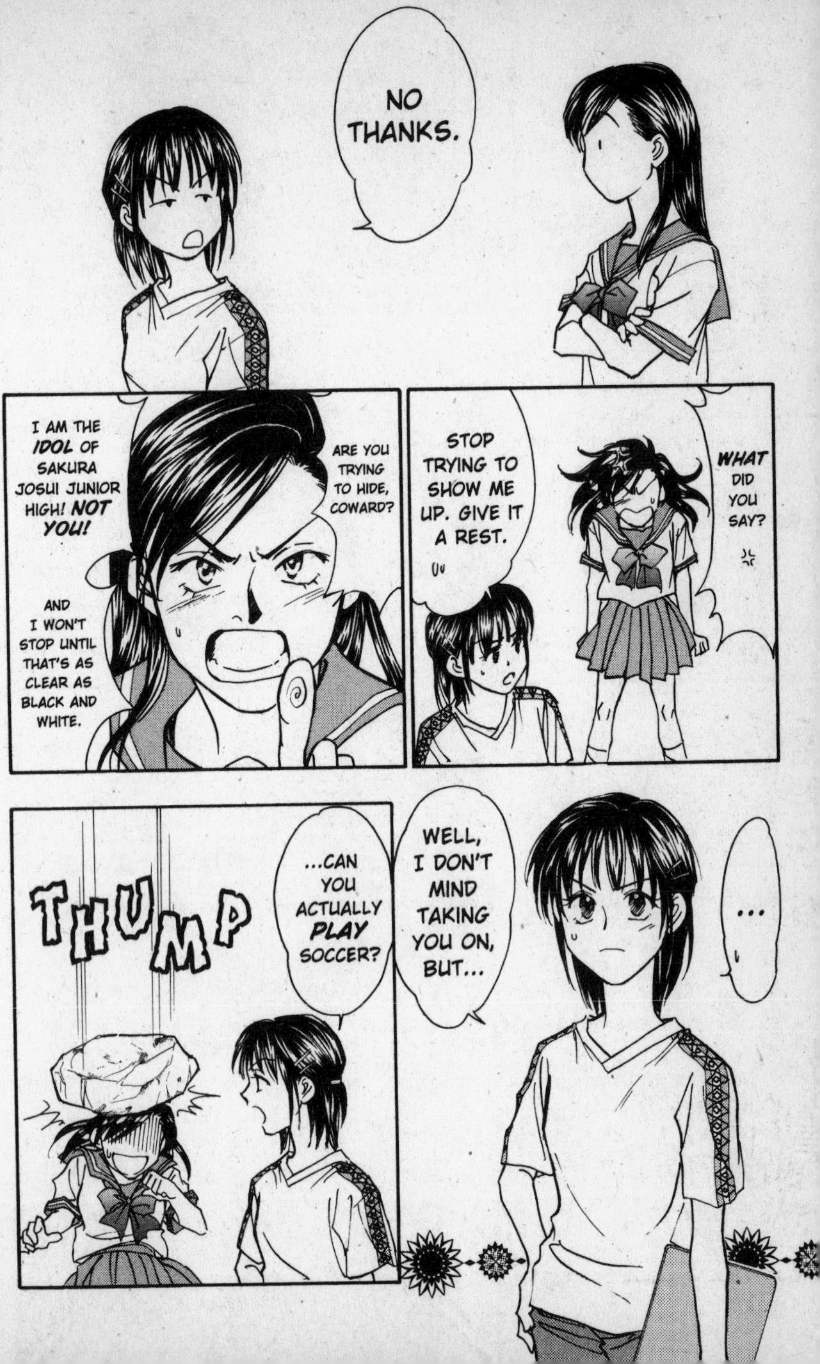
NO THANKS.
WHAT DID YOU SAY?
STOP TRYING TO SHOW ME UP. GIVE IT A REST.
ARE YOU TRYING TO HIDE, COWARD?
I AM THE *IDOL* OF SAKURA JOSUI JUNIOR HIGH! *NOT YOU!*
AND I WON'T STOP UNTIL THAT'S AS CLEAR AS BLACK AND WHITE.
...
WELL, I DON'T MIND TAKING YOU ON, BUT...
...CAN YOU ACTUALLY *PLAY* SOCCER?
THUMP

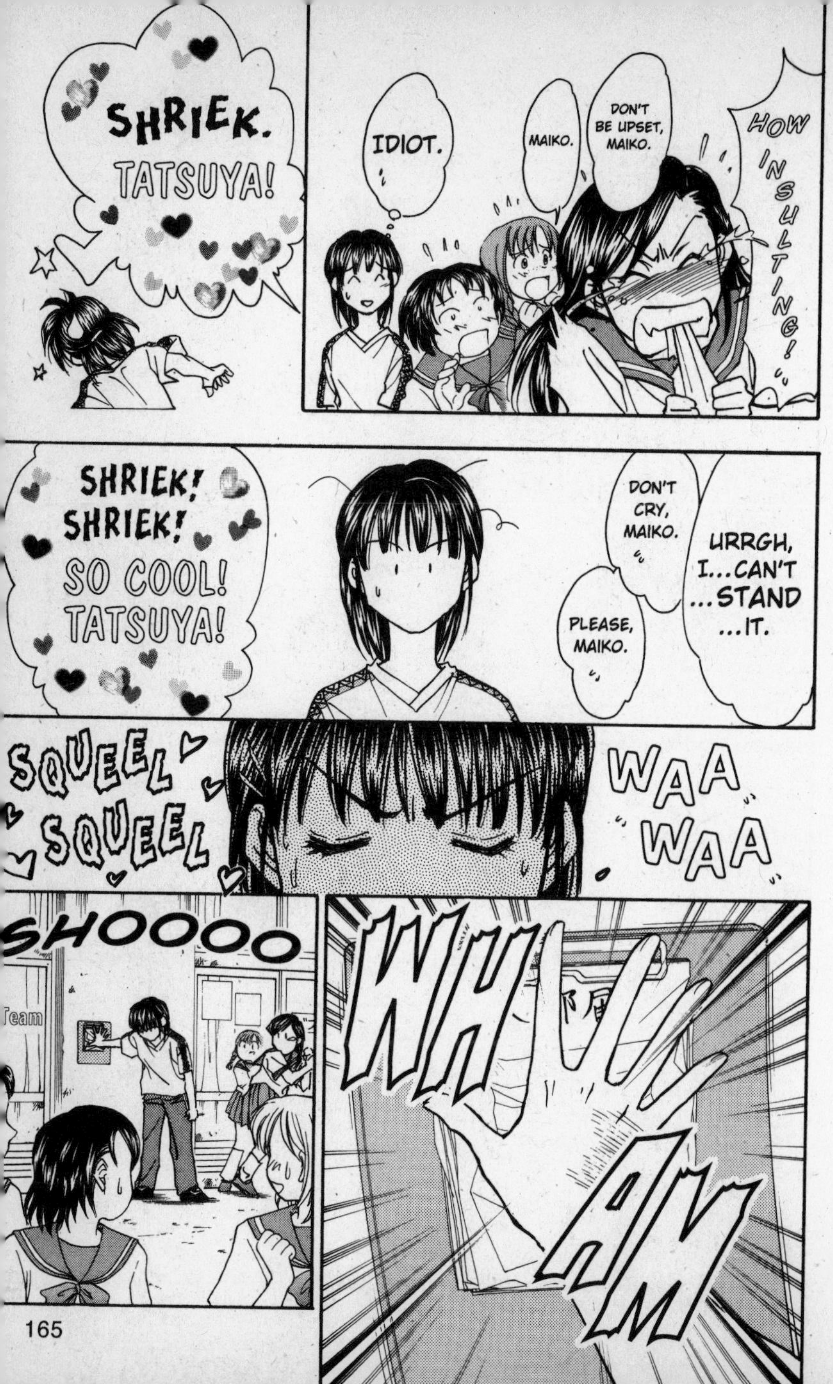
HOW INSULTING!
DON'T BE UPSET, MAIKO.
MAIKO.
IDIOT.
SHRIEK.
TATSUYA!
URRGH, I...CAN'T ...STAND ...IT.
DON'T CRY, MAIKO.
PLEASE, MAIKO.
SHRIEK! SHRIEK!
SO COOL! TATSUYA!
WAA WAA
SQUEEL SQUEEL
WHAM
SHOOOO
Team

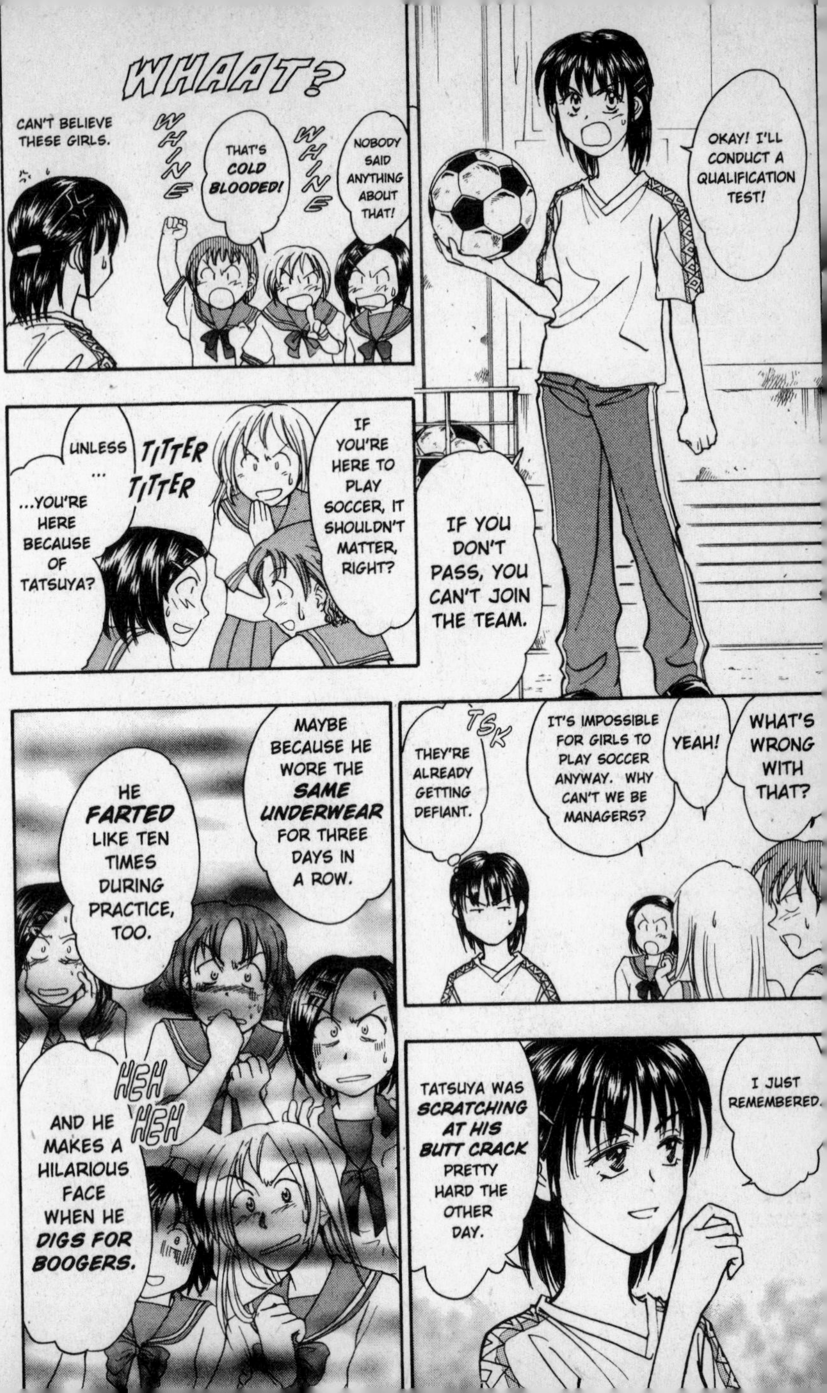
OKAY! I'LL CONDUCT A QUALIFICATION TEST!
IF YOU DON'T PASS, YOU CAN'T JOIN THE TEAM.
WHAAT?
NOBODY SAID ANYTHING ABOUT THAT!
WHINE
THAT'S COLD BLOODED!
WHINE
CAN'T BELIEVE THESE GIRLS.
IF YOU'RE HERE TO PLAY SOCCER, IT SHOULDN'T MATTER, RIGHT?
TITTER TITTER
UNLESS ...
...YOU'RE HERE BECAUSE OF TATSUYA?
WHAT'S WRONG WITH THAT?
YEAH!
IT'S IMPOSSIBLE FOR GIRLS TO PLAY SOCCER ANYWAY. WHY CAN'T WE BE MANAGERS?
TSK
THEY'RE ALREADY GETTING DEFIANT.
I JUST REMEMBERED.
TATSUYA WAS SCRATCHING AT HIS BUTT CRACK PRETTY HARD THE OTHER DAY.
MAYBE BECAUSE HE WORE THE SAME UNDERWEAR FOR THREE DAYS IN A ROW.
HE FARTED LIKE TEN TIMES DURING PRACTICE, TOO.
HEH HEH
AND HE MAKES A HILARIOUS FACE WHEN HE DIGS FOR BOOGERS.

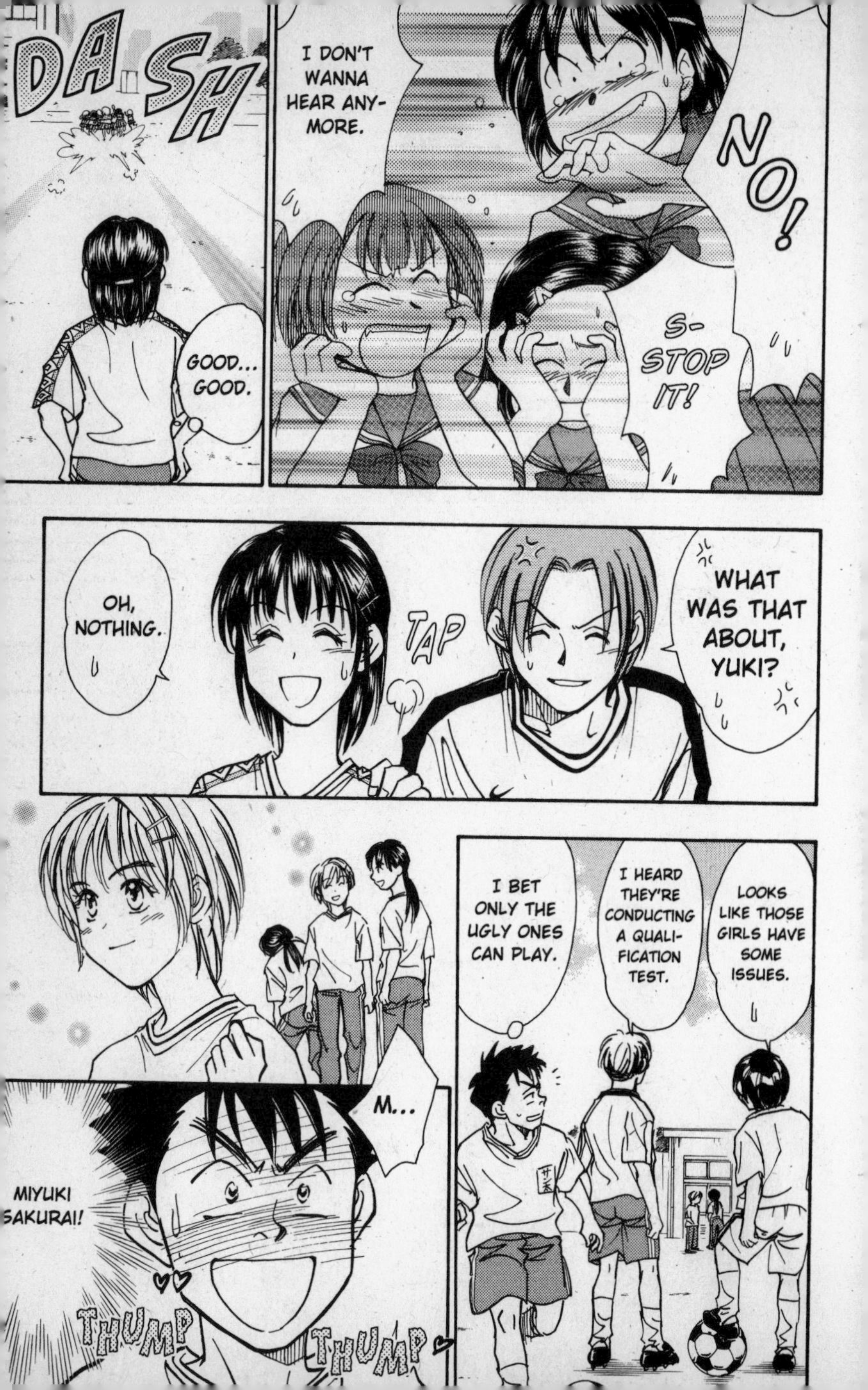
NO!
I DON'T WANNA HEAR ANY-MORE.
S-STOP IT!
DASH
GOOD... GOOD.
WHAT WAS THAT ABOUT, YUKI?
TAP
OH, NOTHING.
LOOKS LIKE THOSE GIRLS HAVE SOME ISSUES.
I HEARD THEY'RE CONDUCTING A QUALI-FICATION TEST.
I BET ONLY THE UGLY ONES CAN PLAY.
M...
MIYUKI SAKURAI!
THUMP
THUMP

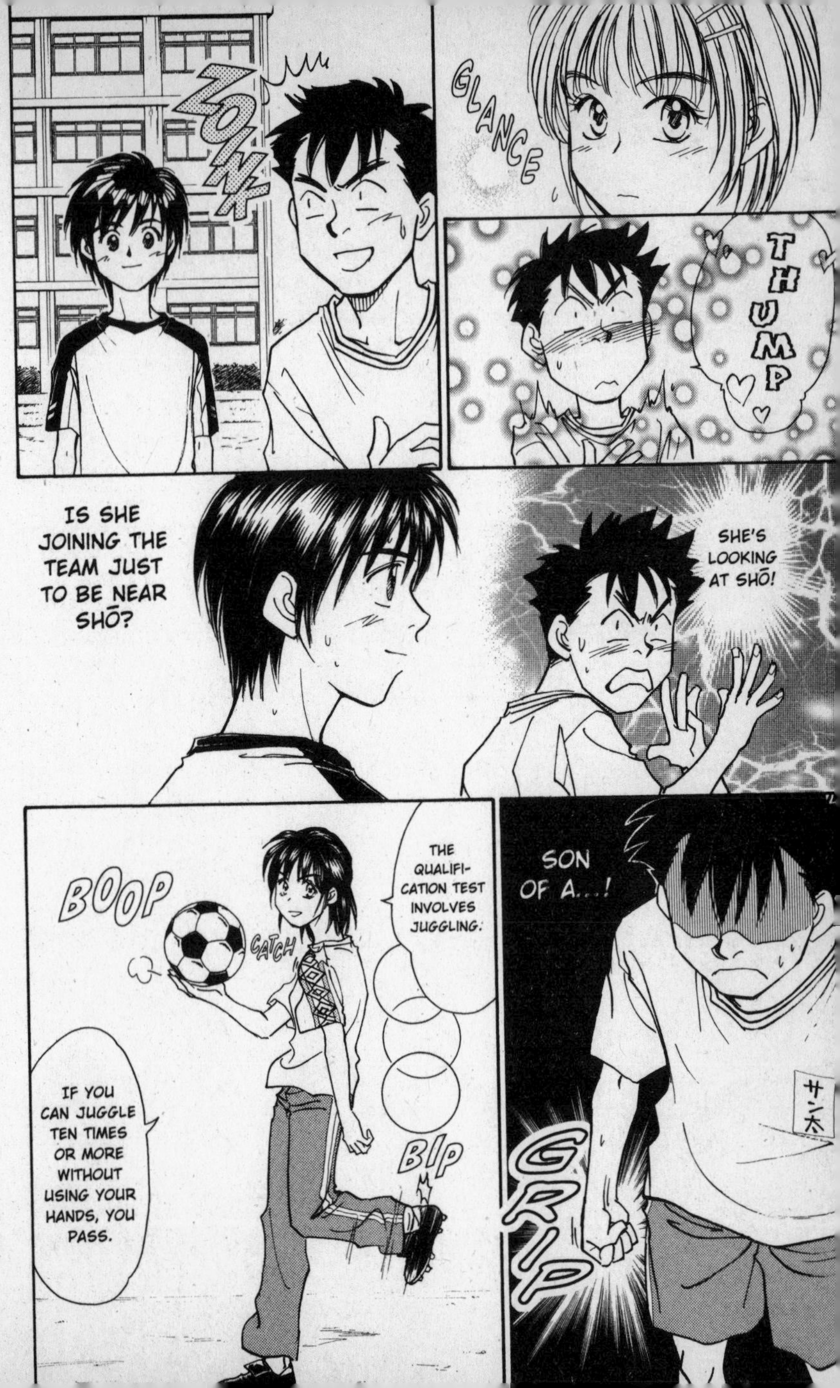
GLANCE
THUMP
ZONK
SHE'S LOOKING AT SHŌ!
IS SHE JOINING THE TEAM JUST TO BE NEAR SHŌ?
SON OF A...!
GRIP
サン太
THE QUALIFI-CATION TEST INVOLVES JUGGLING.
BOOP
CATCH
BIP
IF YOU CAN JUGGLE TEN TIMES OR MORE WITHOUT USING YOUR HANDS, YOU PASS.

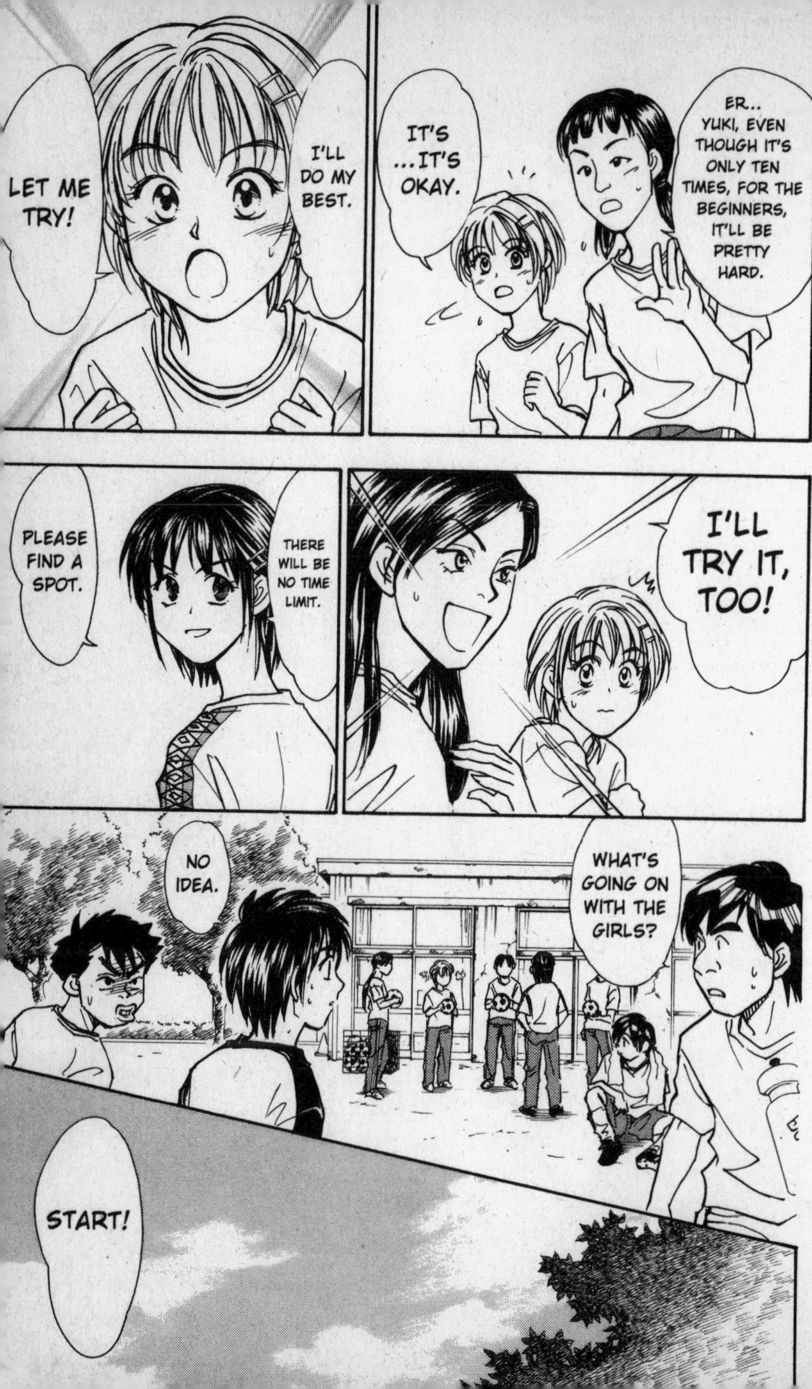
ER.. YUKI, EVEN THOUGH IT'S ONLY TEN TIMES, FOR THE BEGINNERS, IT'LL BE PRETTY HARD.
IT'S ...IT'S OKAY.
I'LL DO MY BEST.
LET ME TRY!
I'LL TRY IT, TOO!
THERE WILL BE NO TIME LIMIT.
PLEASE FIND A SPOT.
WHAT'S GOING ON WITH THE GIRLS?
NO IDEA.
START!

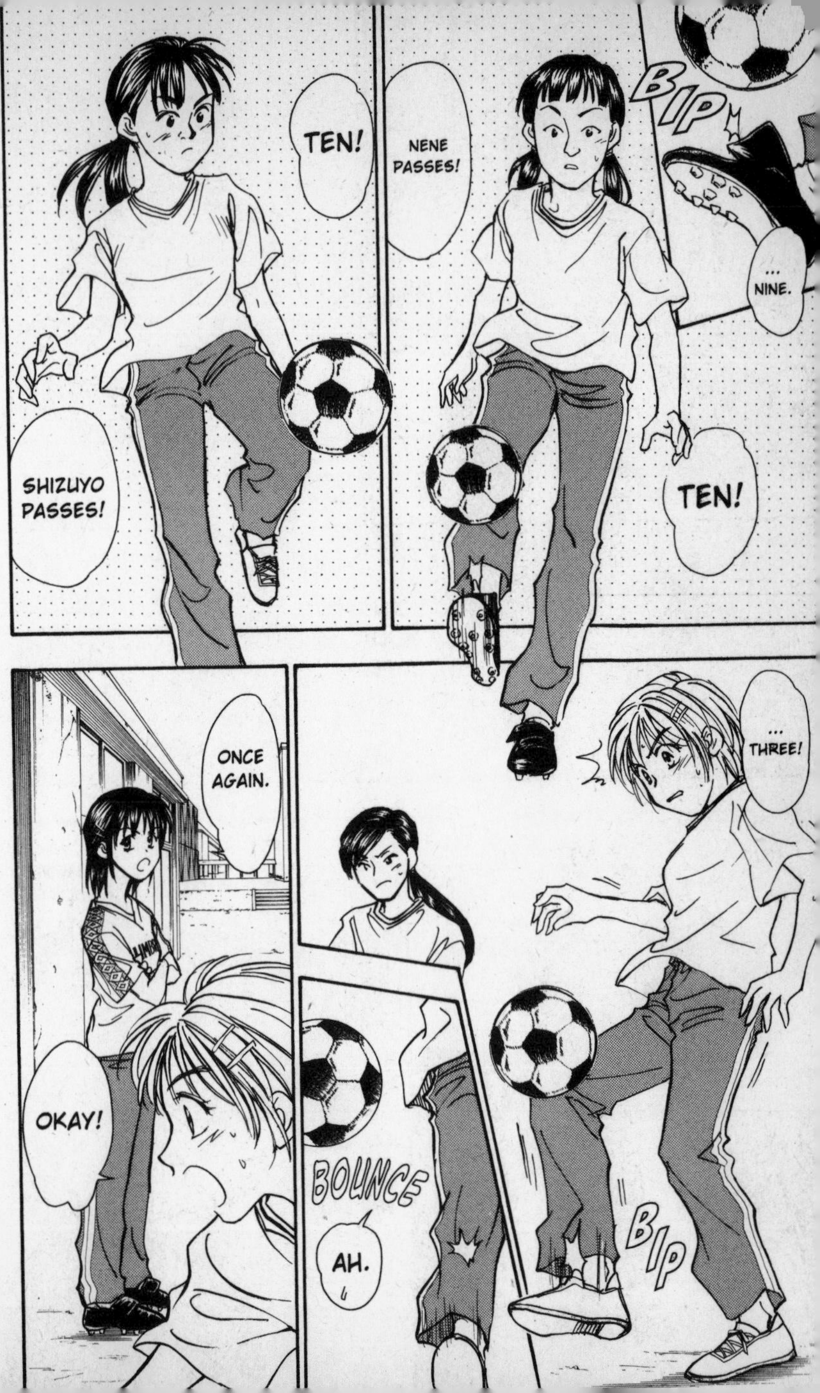
BIP
... NINE.
NENE PASSES!
TEN!
TEN!
SHIZUYO PASSES!
... THREE!
BOUNCE
BIP
AH.
ONCE AGAIN.
OKAY!

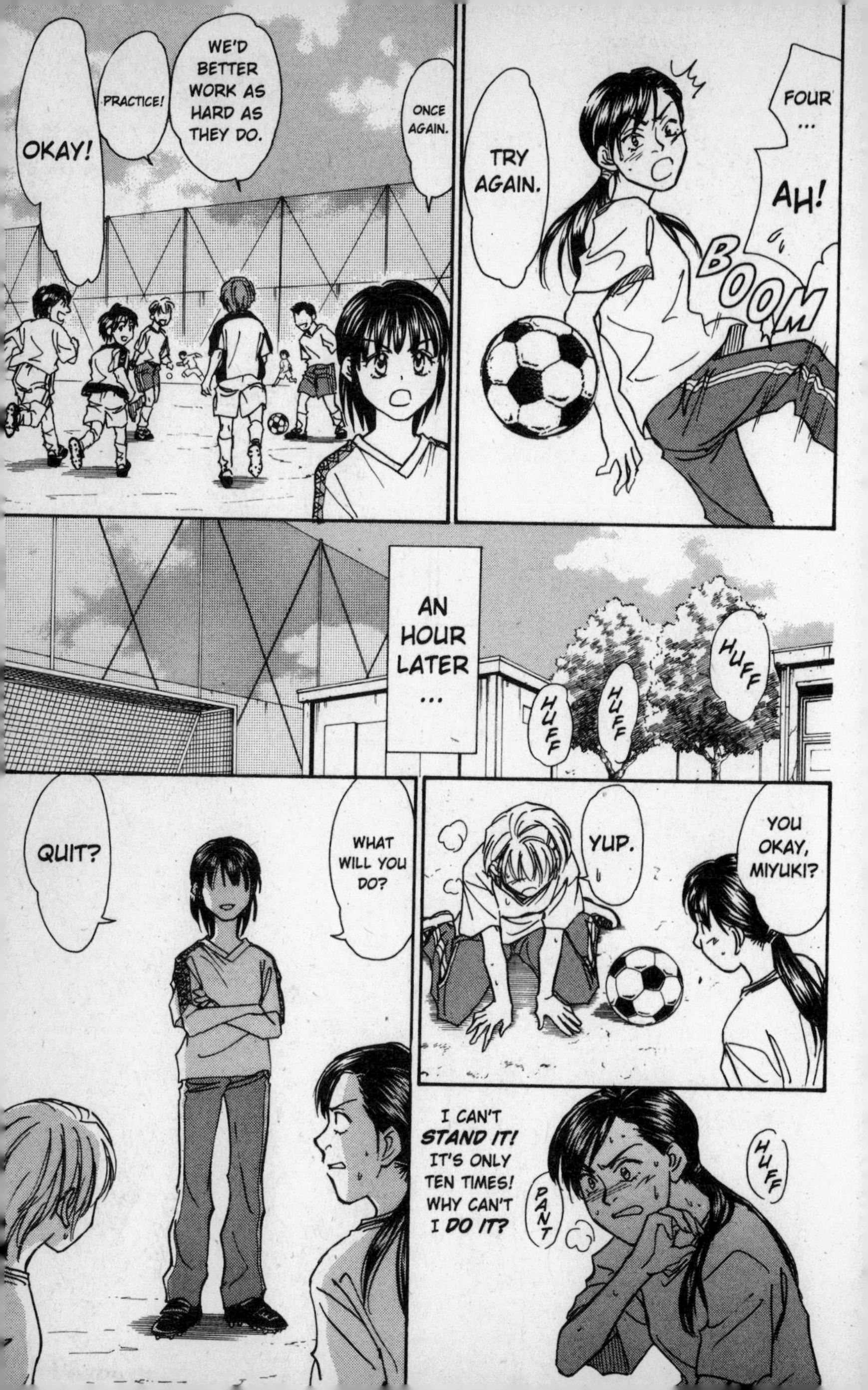
FOUR ...
AH!
BOOM
TRY AGAIN.
ONCE AGAIN.
WE'D BETTER WORK AS HARD AS THEY DO.
PRACTICE!
OKAY!
AN HOUR LATER ...
HUFF
HUFF
HUFF
YOU OKAY, MIYUKI?
YUP.
HUFF
PANT
I CAN'T STAND IT! IT'S ONLY TEN TIMES! WHY CAN'T I DO IT?
WHAT WILL YOU DO?
QUIT?

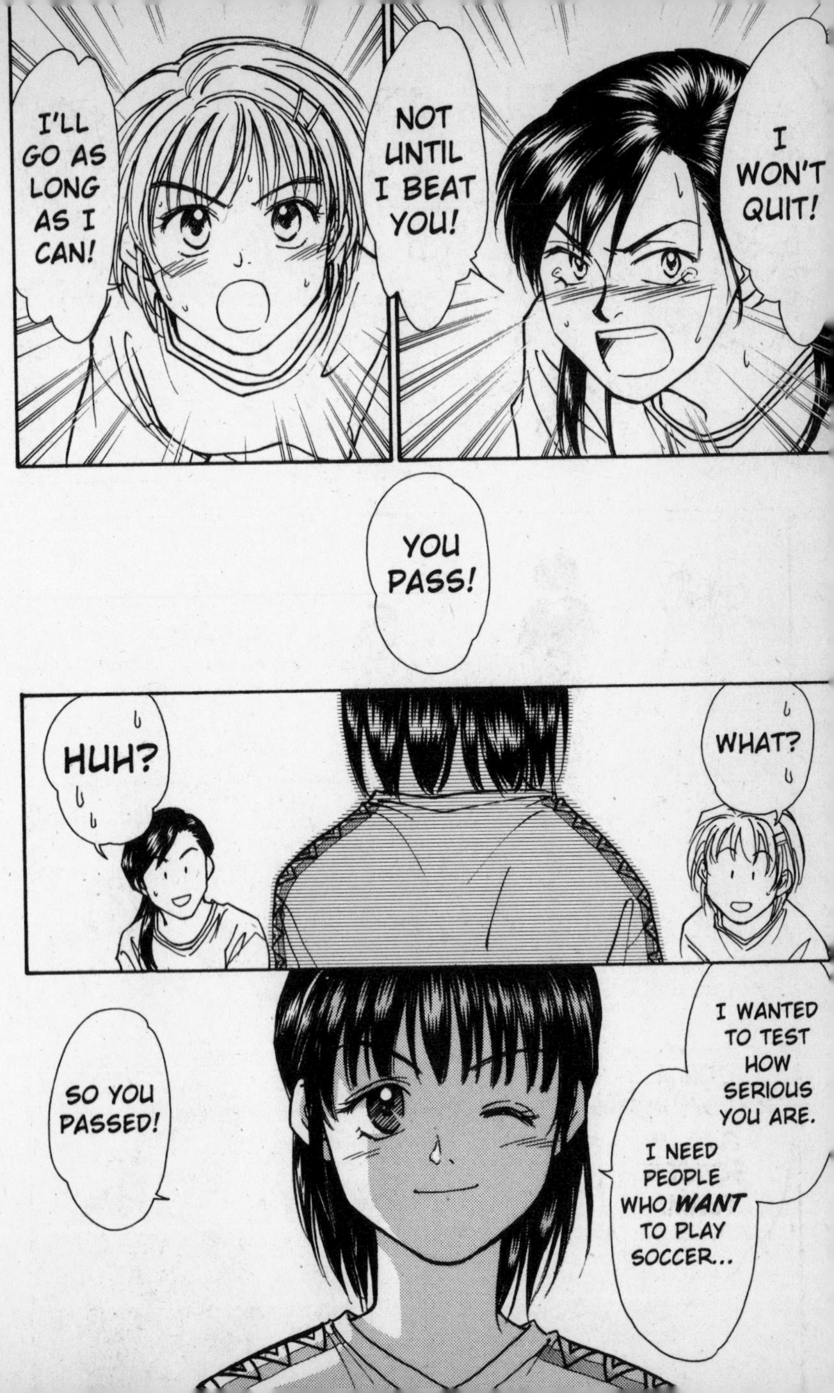
I WON'T QUIT!
NOT UNTIL I BEAT YOU!
I'LL GO AS LONG AS I CAN!
YOU PASS!
WHAT?
HUH?
I WANTED TO TEST HOW SERIOUS YOU ARE.
I NEED PEOPLE WHO *WANT* TO PLAY SOCCER...
SO YOU PASSED!

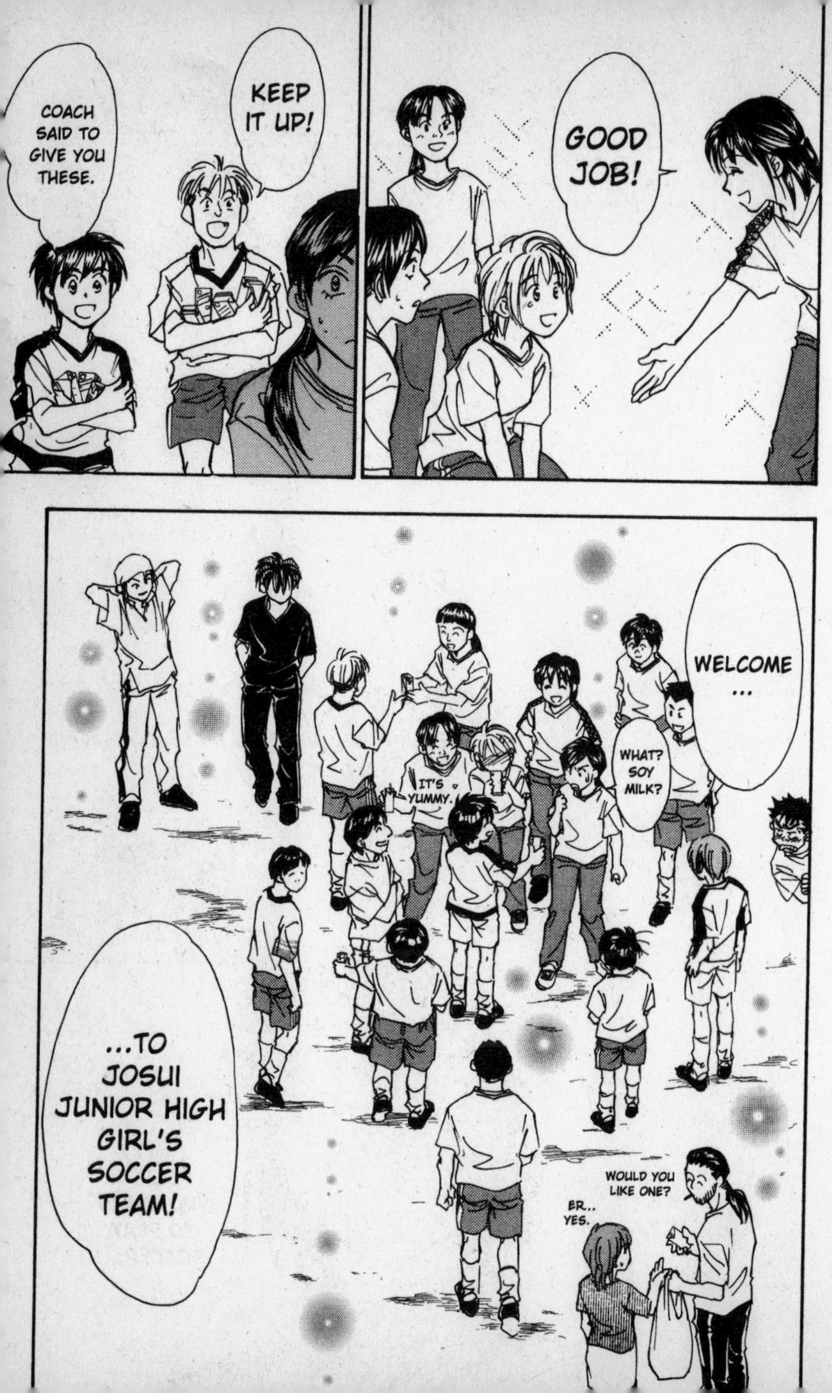
GOOD JOB!
KEEP IT UP!
COACH SAID TO GIVE YOU THESE.
WELCOME ...
WHAT? SOY MILK?
IT'S YUMMY.
WOULD YOU LIKE ONE?
ER.. YES.
...TO JOSUI JUNIOR HIGH GIRL'S SOCCER TEAM!

WHISTLE!

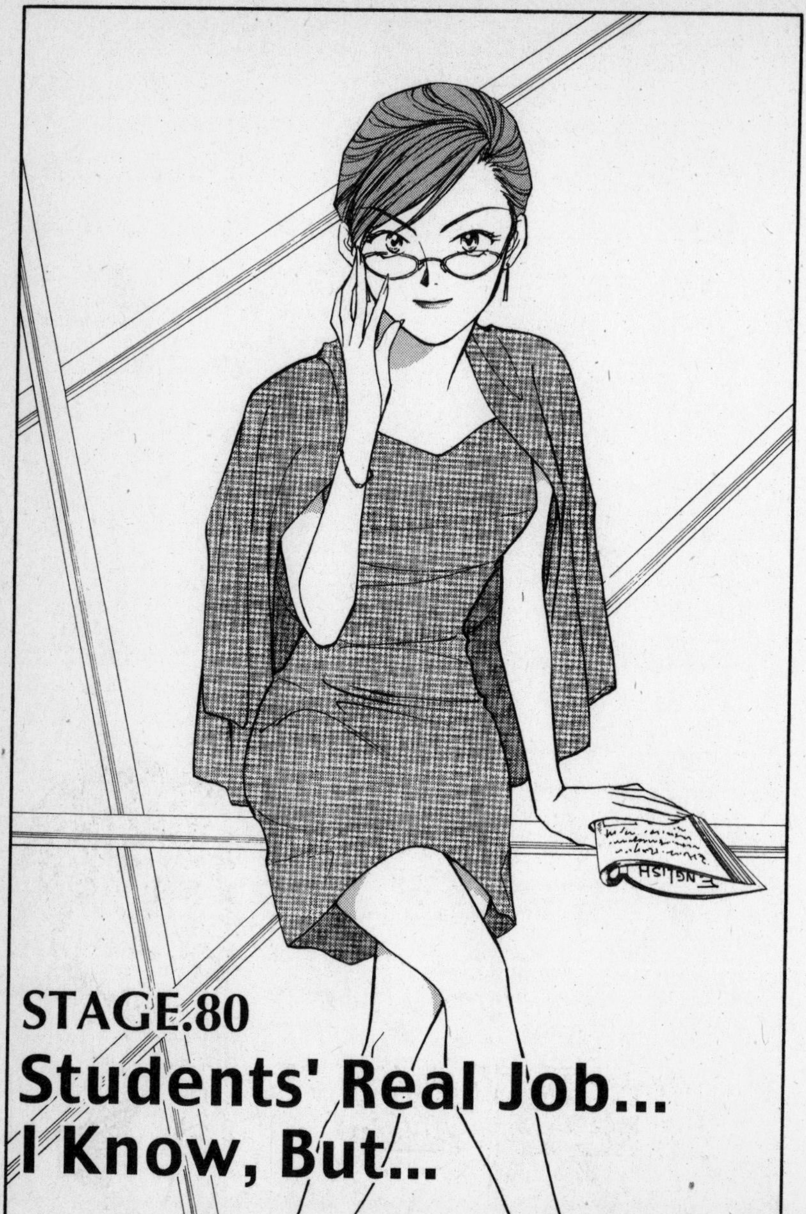

STAGE.80
Students' Real Job... I Know, But...

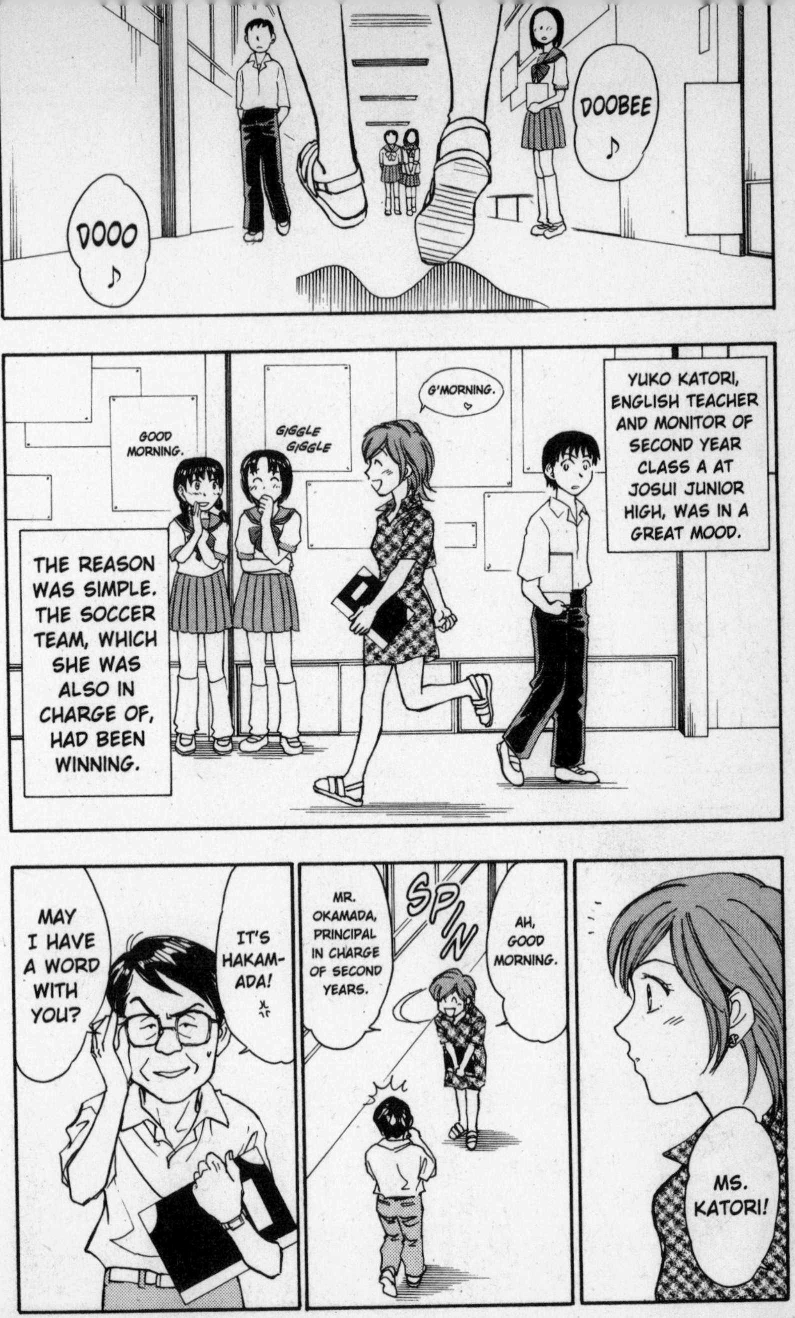
DOOBEE ♪
DOOO ♪
YUKO KATORI, ENGLISH TEACHER AND MONITOR OF SECOND YEAR CLASS A AT JOSUI JUNIOR HIGH, WAS IN A GREAT MOOD.
G'MORNING. ♡
GIGGLE GIGGLE
GOOD MORNING.
THE REASON WAS SIMPLE. THE SOCCER TEAM, WHICH SHE WAS ALSO IN CHARGE OF, HAD BEEN WINNING.
MS. KATORI!
AH, GOOD MORNING.
SPIN
MR. OKAMADA, PRINCIPAL IN CHARGE OF SECOND YEARS.
IT'S HAKAMADA!
MAY I HAVE A WORD WITH YOU?

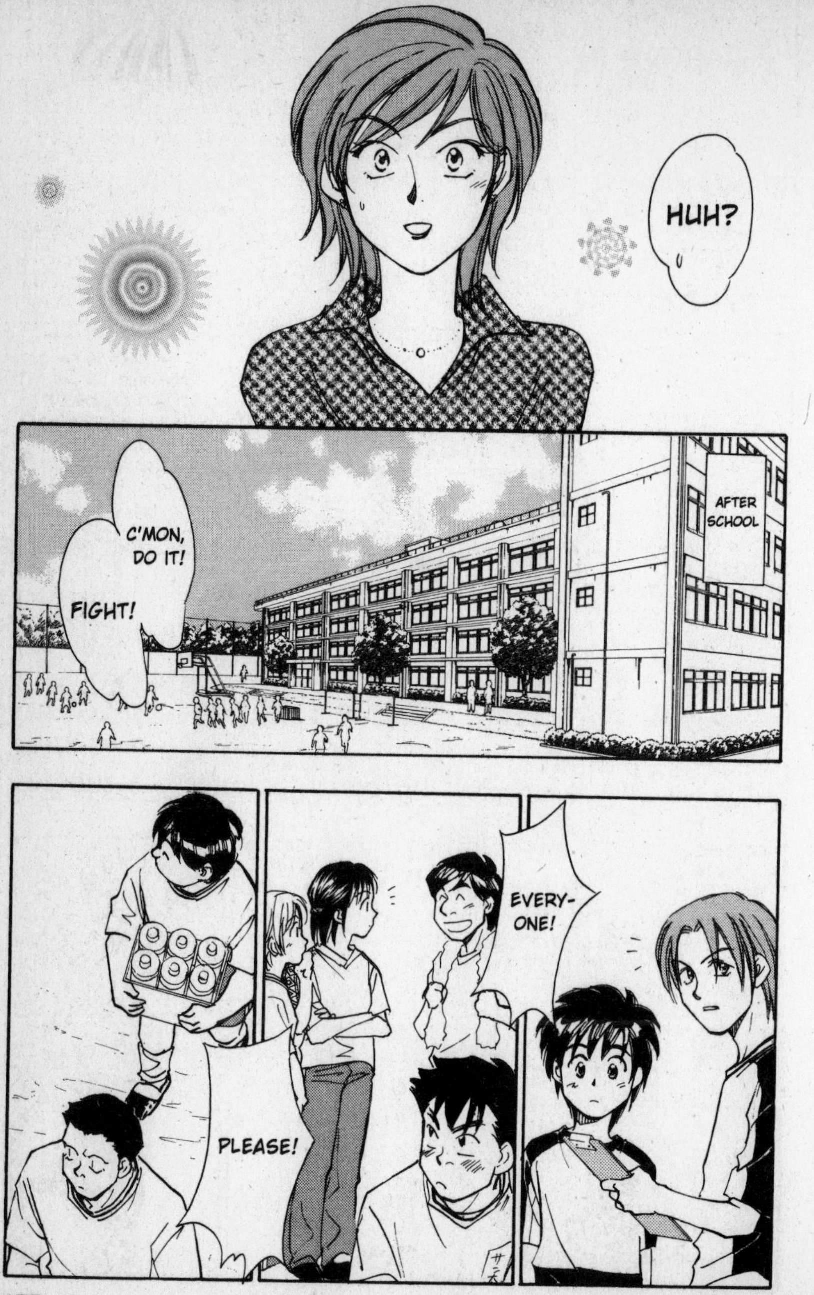
HUH?
AFTER SCHOOL
C'MON, DO IT!
FIGHT!
EVERY-ONE!
PLEASE!

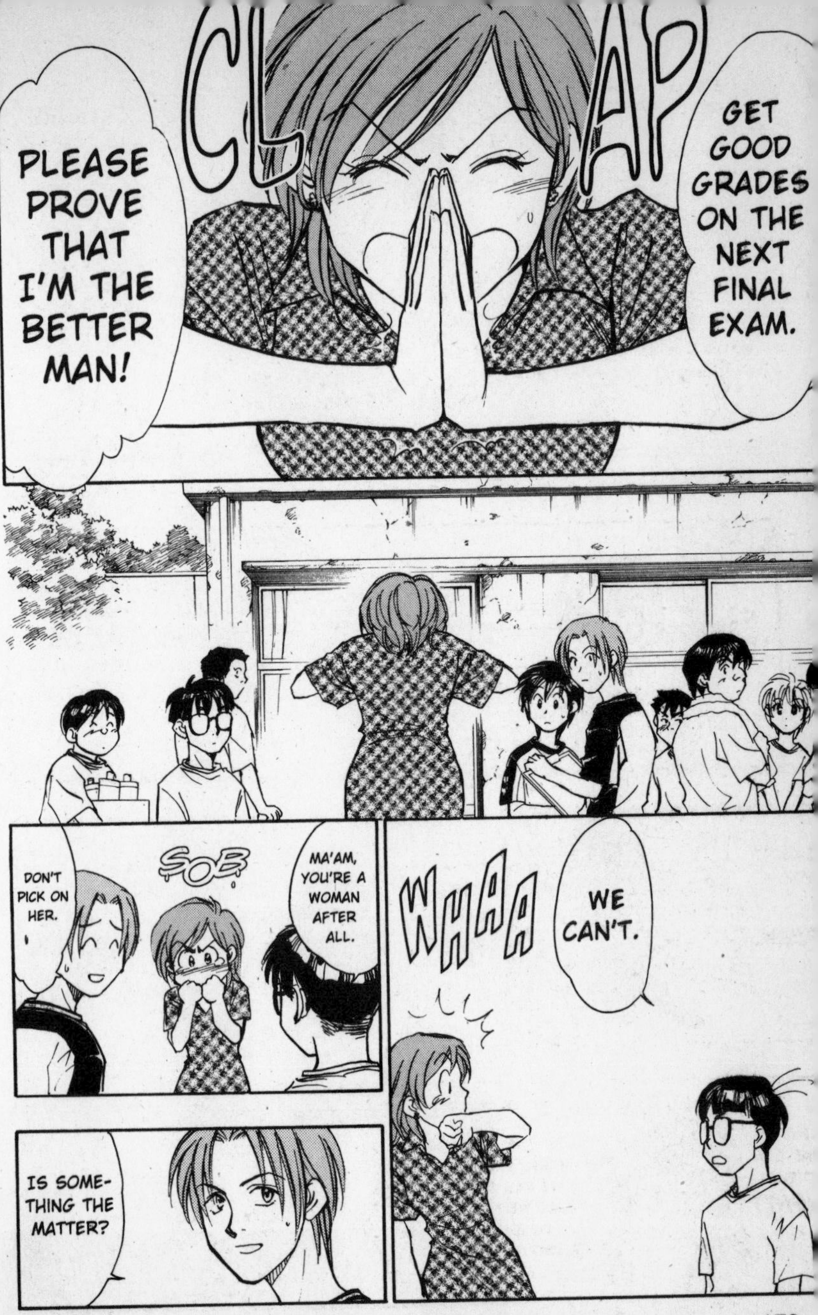
GET GOOD GRADES ON THE NEXT FINAL EXAM.
CLAP
PLEASE PROVE THAT I'M THE BETTER MAN!
WE CAN'T.
WHAA
MA'AM, YOU'RE A WOMAN AFTER ALL.
SOB
DON'T PICK ON HER.
IS SOME-THING THE MATTER?

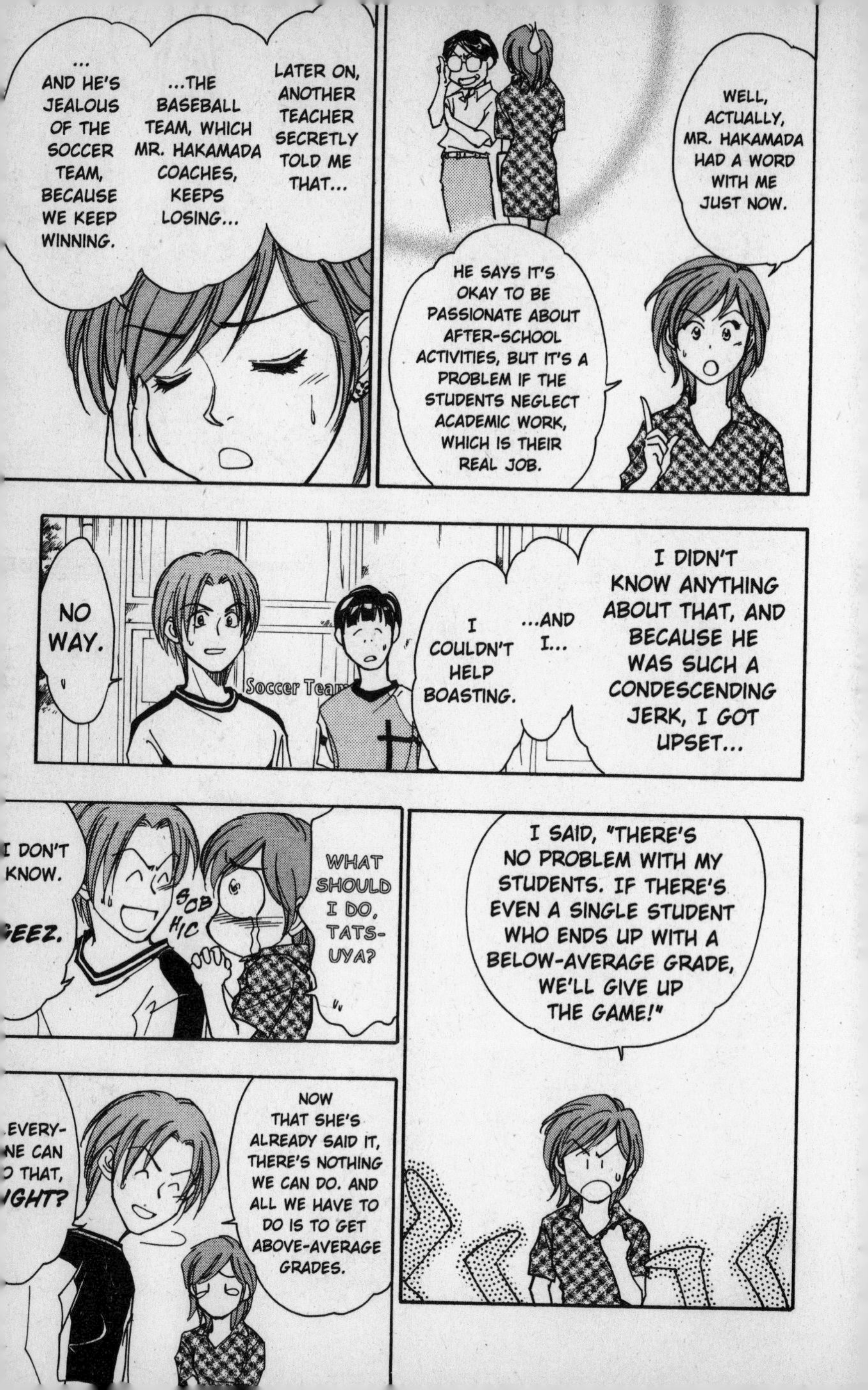
WELL, ACTUALLY, MR. HAKAMADA HAD A WORD WITH ME JUST NOW.
HE SAYS IT'S OKAY TO BE PASSIONATE ABOUT AFTER-SCHOOL ACTIVITIES, BUT IT'S A PROBLEM IF THE STUDENTS NEGLECT ACADEMIC WORK, WHICH IS THEIR REAL JOB.
LATER ON, ANOTHER TEACHER SECRETLY TOLD ME THAT...
...THE BASEBALL TEAM, WHICH MR. HAKAMADA COACHES, KEEPS LOSING...
... AND HE'S JEALOUS OF THE SOCCER TEAM, BECAUSE WE KEEP WINNING.
I DIDN'T KNOW ANYTHING ABOUT THAT, AND BECAUSE HE WAS SUCH A CONDESCENDING JERK, I GOT UPSET...
...AND I...
I COULDN'T HELP BOASTING.
Soccer Team
NO WAY.
I SAID, "THERE'S NO PROBLEM WITH MY STUDENTS. IF THERE'S EVEN A SINGLE STUDENT WHO ENDS UP WITH A BELOW-AVERAGE GRADE, WE'LL GIVE UP THE GAME!"
WHAT SHOULD I DO, TATSUYA?
SOB HIC
I DON'T KNOW.
EEZ.
NOW THAT SHE'S ALREADY SAID IT, THERE'S NOTHING WE CAN DO. AND ALL WE HAVE TO DO IS TO GET ABOVE-AVERAGE GRADES.
EVERY- NE CAN O THAT, IGHT?

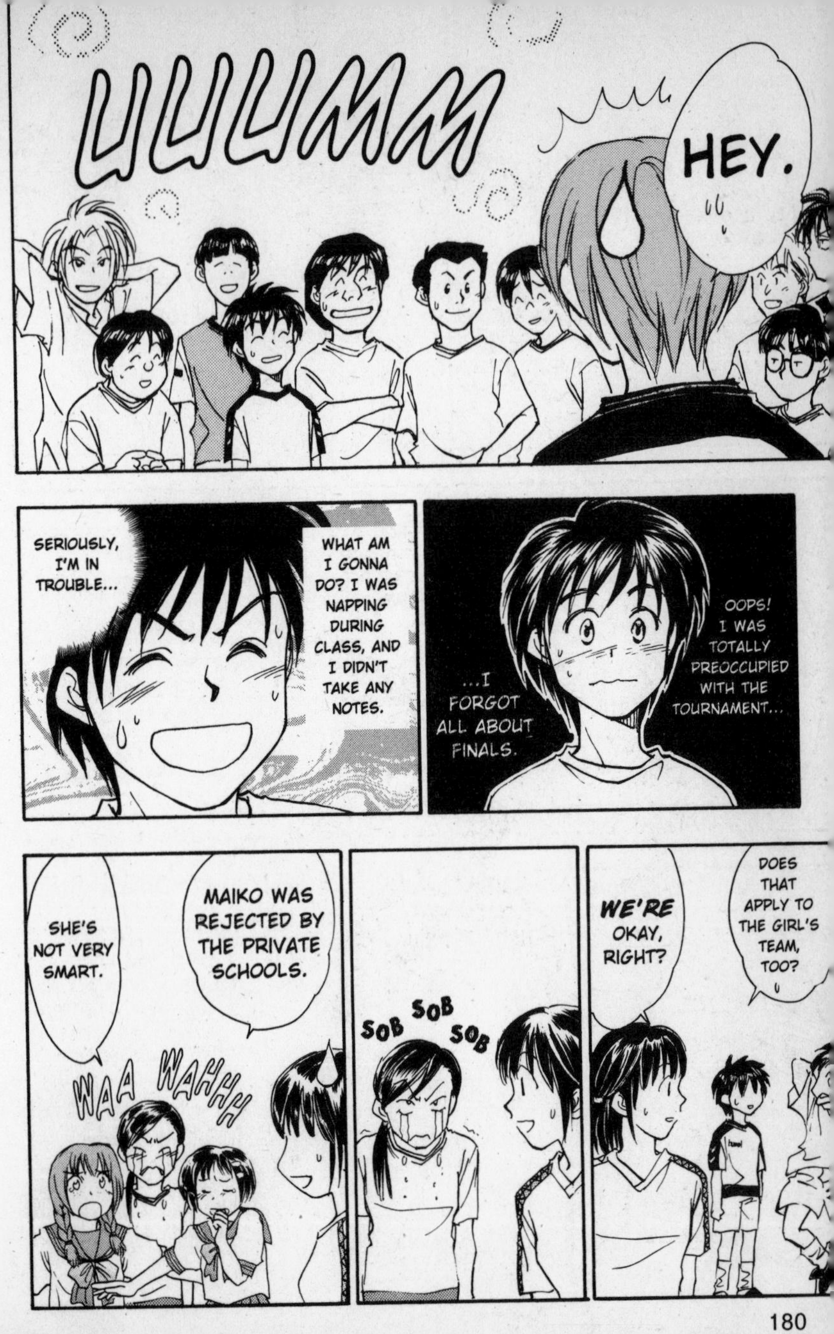
HEY.
UUUMM
OOPS! I WAS TOTALLY PREOCCUPIED WITH THE TOURNAMENT...
...I FORGOT ALL ABOUT FINALS.
WHAT AM I GONNA DO? I WAS NAPPING DURING CLASS, AND I DIDN'T TAKE ANY NOTES.
SERIOUSLY, I'M IN TROUBLE...
DOES THAT APPLY TO THE GIRL'S TEAM, TOO?
WE'RE OKAY, RIGHT?
SOB SOB SOB
MAIKO WAS REJECTED BY THE PRIVATE SCHOOLS.
SHE'S NOT VERY SMART.
WAA WAHHH

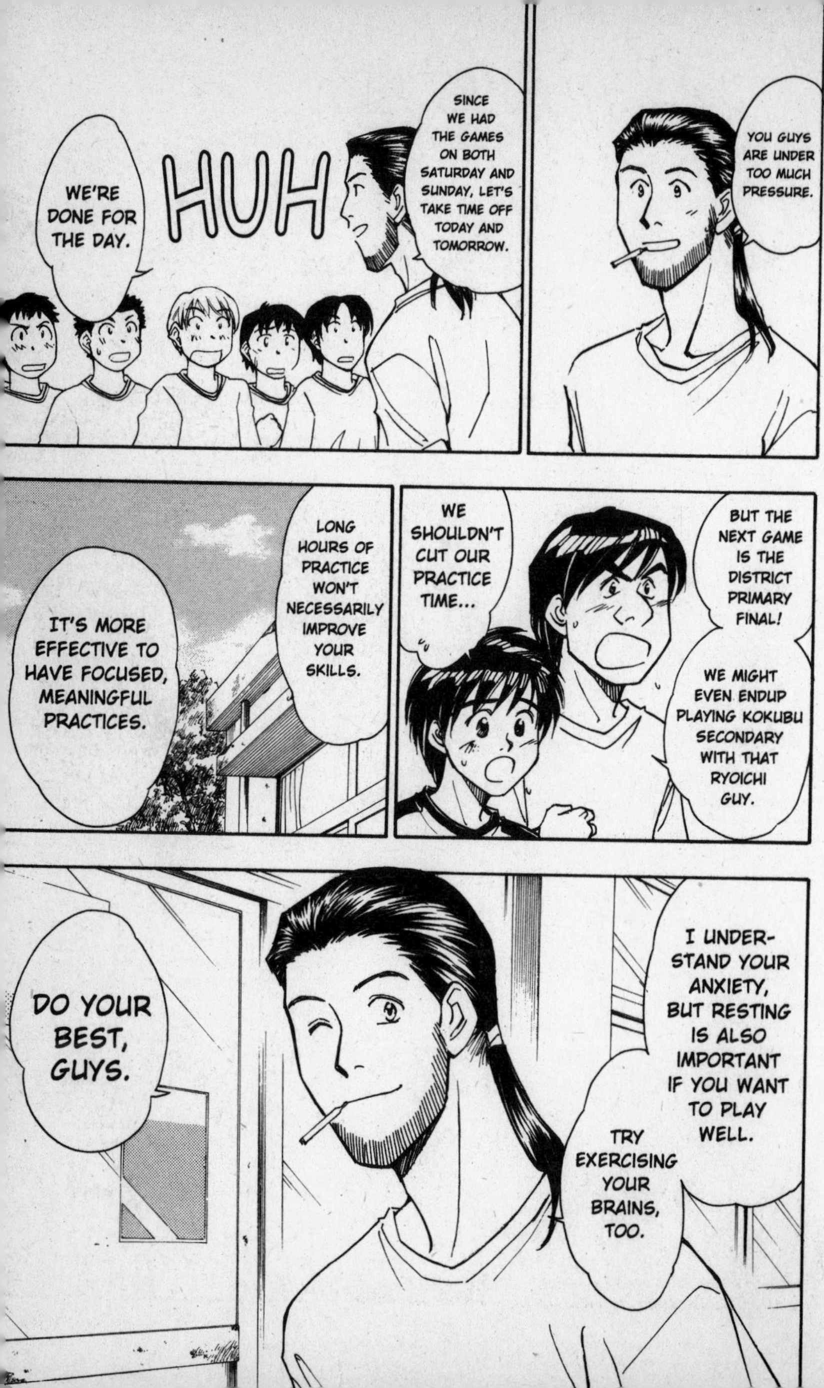
YOU GUYS ARE UNDER TOO MUCH PRESSURE.
SINCE WE HAD THE GAMES ON BOTH SATURDAY AND SUNDAY, LET'S TAKE TIME OFF TODAY AND TOMORROW.
HUH
WE'RE DONE FOR THE DAY.
BUT THE NEXT GAME IS THE DISTRICT PRIMARY FINAL!
WE MIGHT EVEN ENDUP PLAYING KOKUBU SECONDARY WITH THAT RYOICHI GUY.
WE SHOULDN'T CUT OUR PRACTICE TIME...
LONG HOURS OF PRACTICE WON'T NECESSARILY IMPROVE YOUR SKILLS.
IT'S MORE EFFECTIVE TO HAVE FOCUSED, MEANINGFUL PRACTICES.
I UNDERSTAND YOUR ANXIETY, BUT RESTING IS ALSO IMPORTANT IF YOU WANT TO PLAY WELL.
TRY EXERCISING YOUR BRAINS, TOO.
DO YOUR BEST, GUYS.

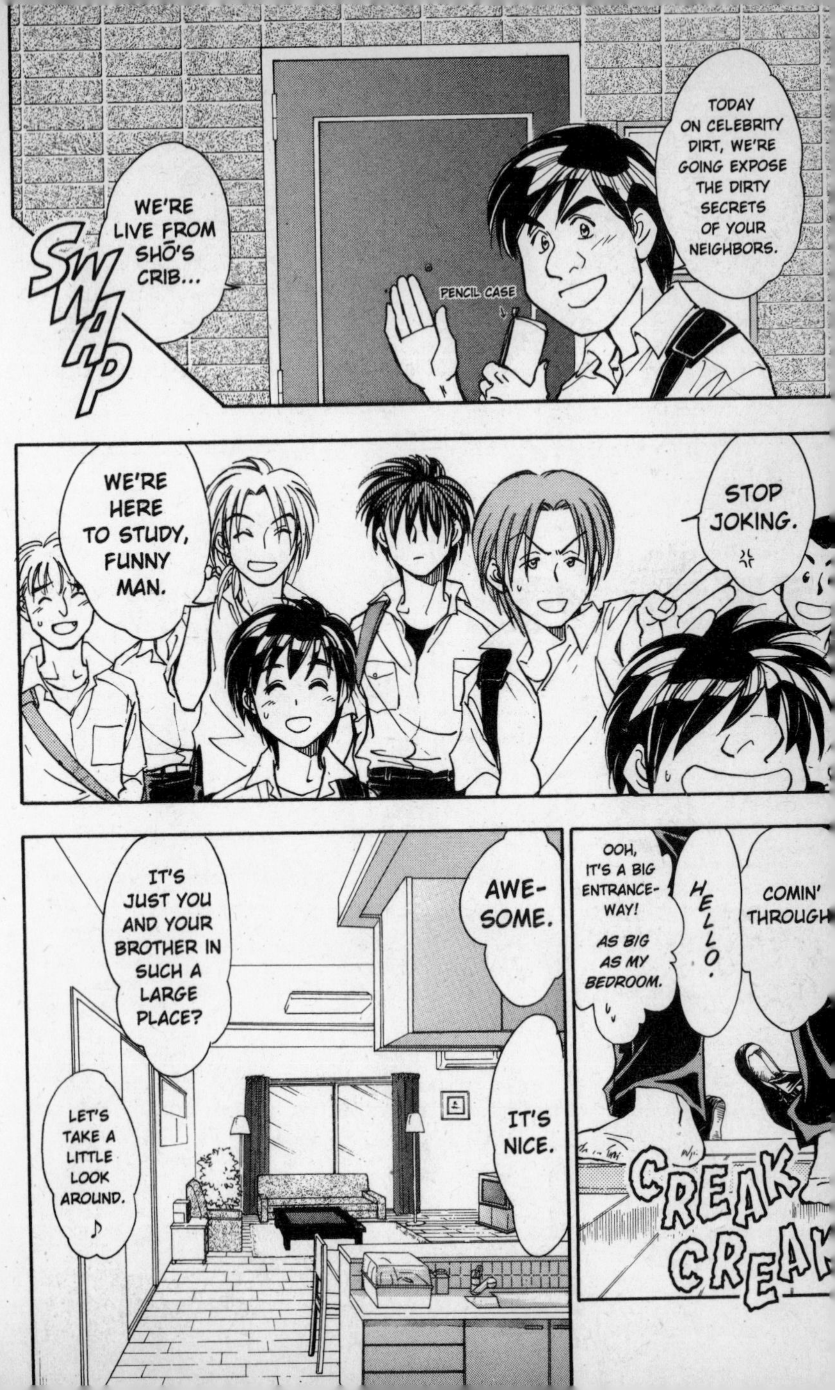
TODAY ON CELEBRITY DIRT, WE'RE GOING EXPOSE THE DIRTY SECRETS OF YOUR NEIGHBORS.
PENCIL CASE
WE'RE LIVE FROM SHŌ'S CRIB...
SWAP
STOP JOKING.
WE'RE HERE TO STUDY, FUNNY MAN.
COMIN' THROUGH
HELLO.
OOH, IT'S A BIG ENTRANCE-WAY!
AS BIG AS MY BEDROOM.
CREAK CREAK
AWE-SOME.
IT'S JUST YOU AND YOUR BROTHER IN SUCH A LARGE PLACE?
IT'S NICE.
LET'S TAKE A LITTLE LOOK AROUND. ♪

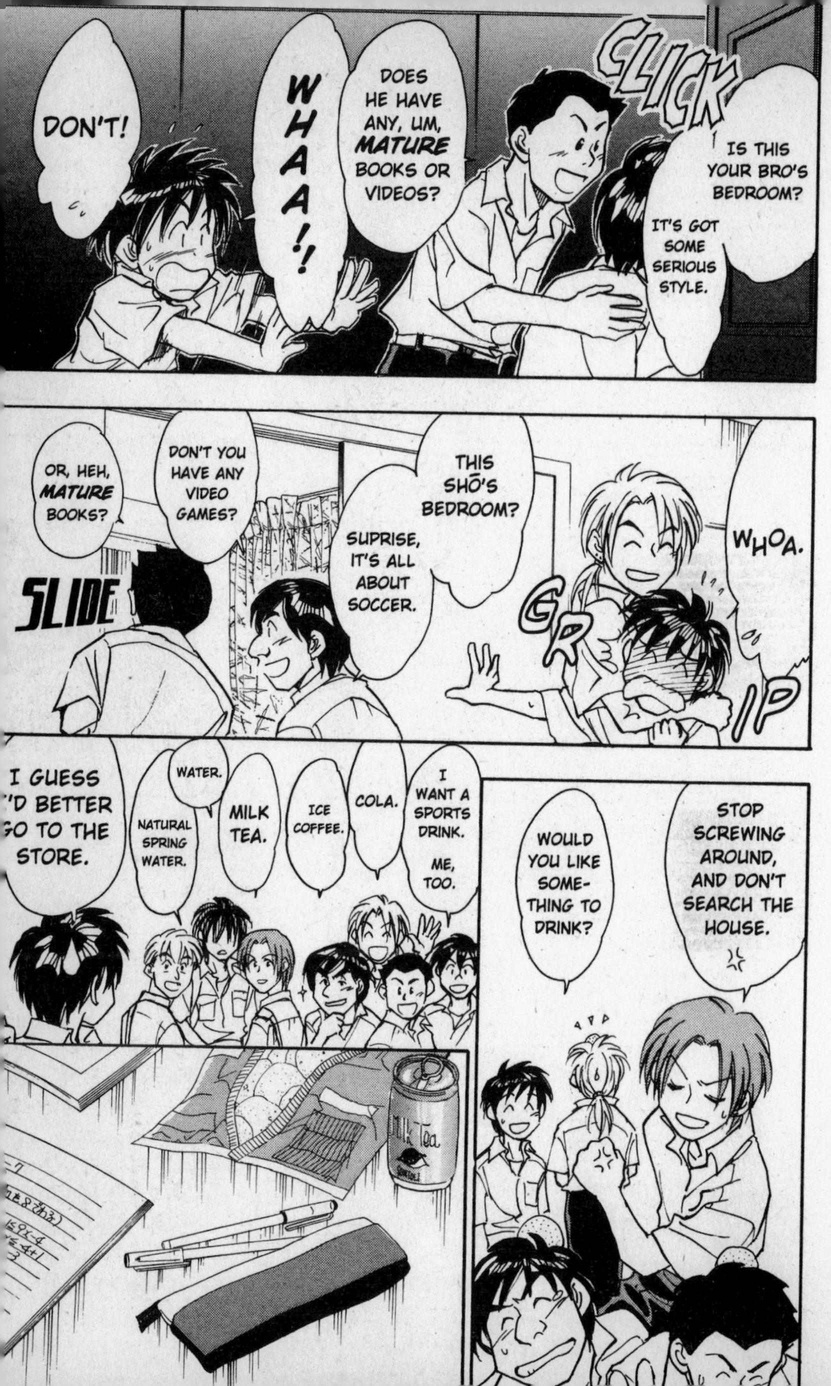
CLICK
IS THIS YOUR BRO'S BEDROOM?
IT'S GOT SOME SERIOUS STYLE.
DOES HE HAVE ANY, UM, **MATURE** BOOKS OR VIDEOS?
WHAAA!!
DON'T!
WHOA.
GRIP
THIS SHŌ'S BEDROOM?
SUPRISE, IT'S ALL ABOUT SOCCER.
DON'T YOU HAVE ANY VIDEO GAMES?
OR, HEH, **MATURE** BOOKS?
SLIDE
STOP SCREWING AROUND, AND DON'T SEARCH THE HOUSE.
WOULD YOU LIKE SOME-THING TO DRINK?
I WANT A SPORTS DRINK.
ME, TOO.
COLA.
ICE COFFEE.
MILK TEA.
WATER.
NATURAL SPRING WATER.
I GUESS 'D BETTER GO TO THE STORE.
Milk Tea

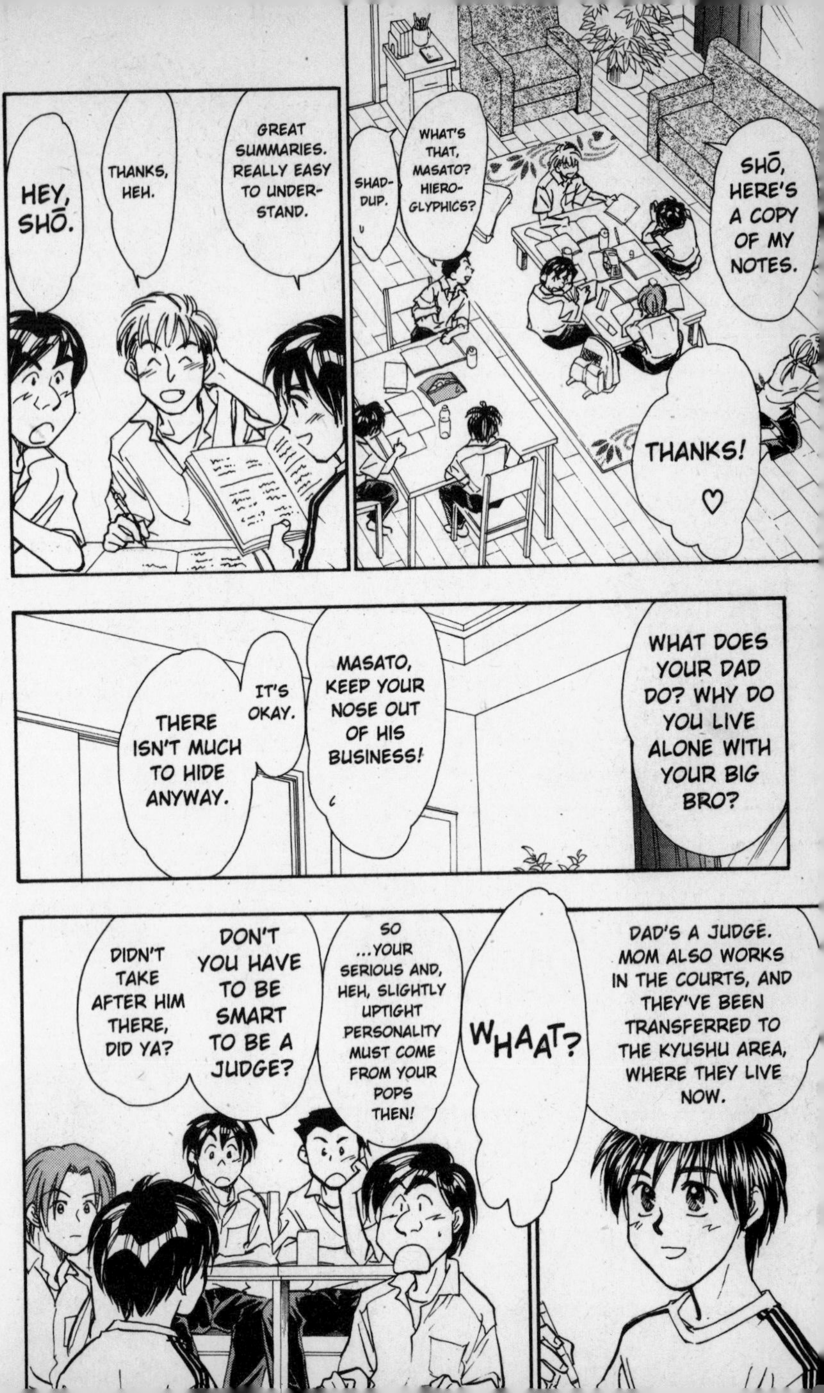
SHŌ, HERE'S A COPY OF MY NOTES.
THANKS! ♡
WHAT'S THAT, MASATO? HIEROGLYPHICS?
SHAD-DUP.
GREAT SUMMARIES. REALLY EASY TO UNDER-STAND.
THANKS, HEH.
HEY, SHŌ.
WHAT DOES YOUR DAD DO? WHY DO YOU LIVE ALONE WITH YOUR BIG BRO?
MASATO, KEEP YOUR NOSE OUT OF HIS BUSINESS!
IT'S OKAY.
THERE ISN'T MUCH TO HIDE ANYWAY.
DAD'S A JUDGE. MOM ALSO WORKS IN THE COURTS, AND THEY'VE BEEN TRANSFERRED TO THE KYUSHU AREA, WHERE THEY LIVE NOW.
WHAAT?
SO ...YOUR SERIOUS AND, HEH, SLIGHTLY UPTIGHT PERSONALITY MUST COME FROM YOUR POPS THEN!
DON'T YOU HAVE TO BE SMART TO BE A JUDGE?
DIDN'T TAKE AFTER HIM THERE, DID YA?

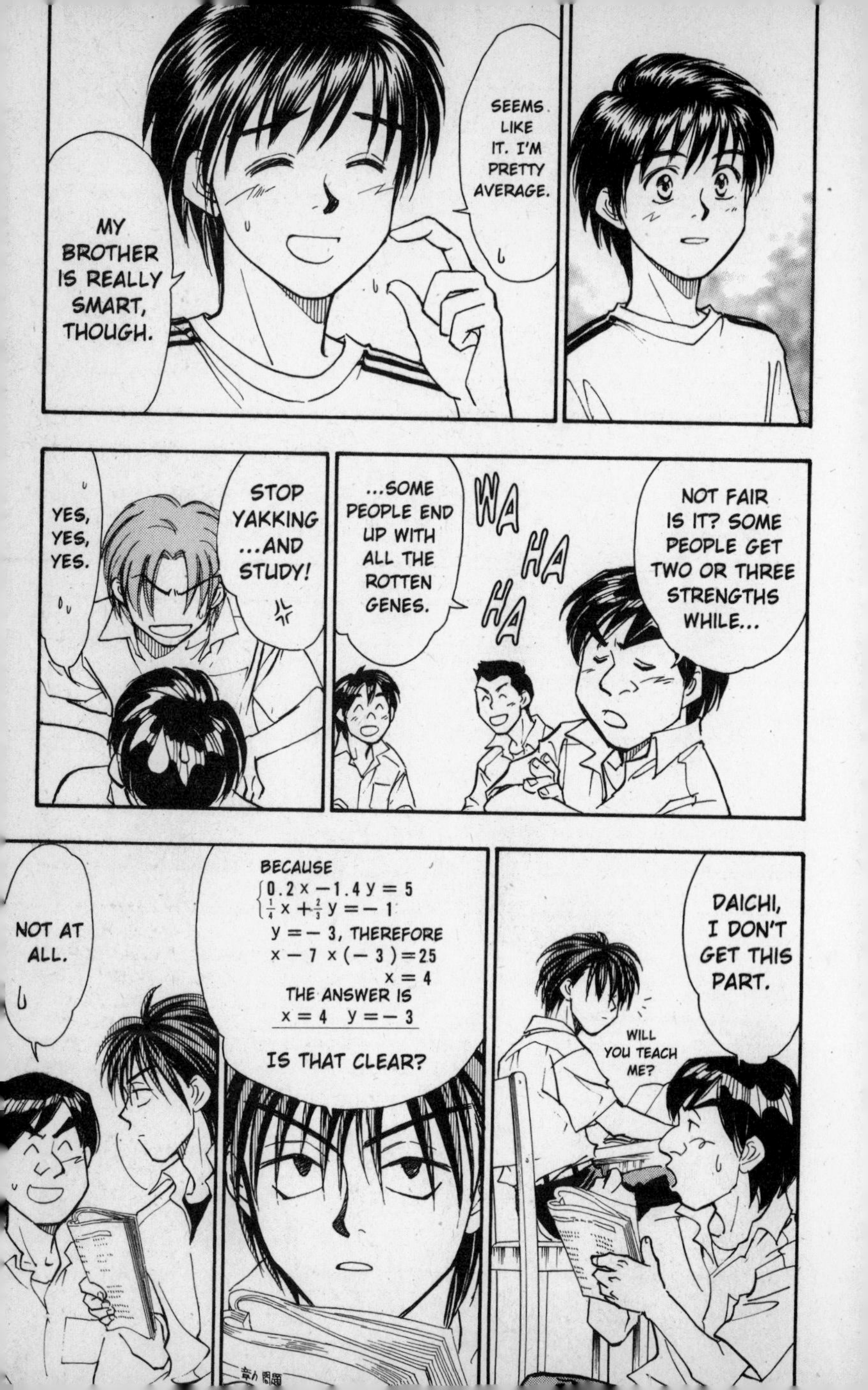
SEEMS LIKE IT. I'M PRETTY AVERAGE.
MY BROTHER IS REALLY SMART, THOUGH.
NOT FAIR IS IT? SOME PEOPLE GET TWO OR THREE STRENGTHS WHILE...
WA HA HA HA
...SOME PEOPLE END UP WITH ALL THE ROTTEN GENES.
STOP YAKKING ...AND STUDY!
YES, YES, YES.
DAICHI, I DON'T GET THIS PART.
WILL YOU TEACH ME?
BECAUSE
0.2 x − 1.4 y = 5
1/4 x + 2/3 y = − 1
y = − 3, THEREFORE
x − 7 × (− 3) = 25
x = 4
THE ANSWER IS
x = 4 y = − 3
IS THAT CLEAR?
NOT AT ALL.

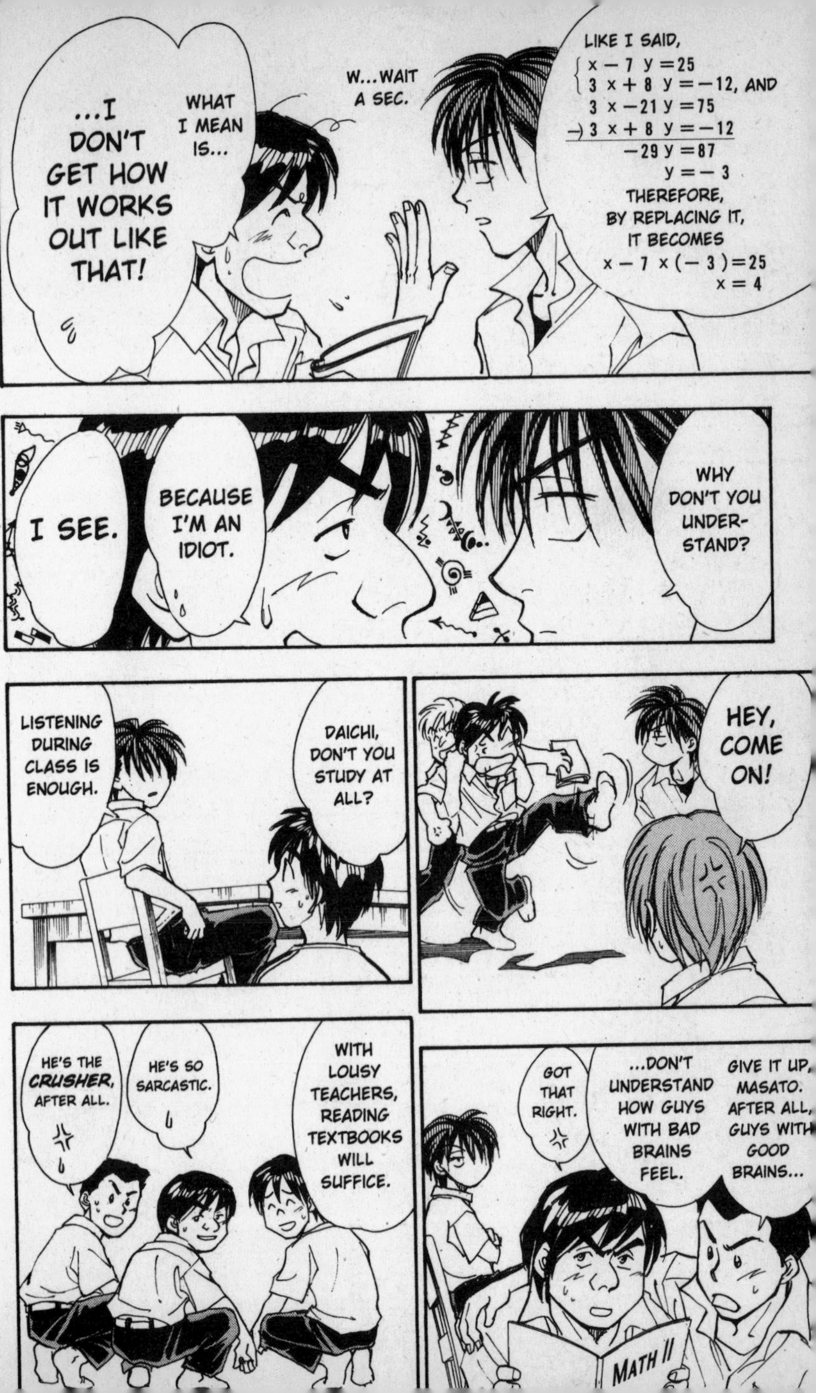
LIKE I SAID,
x − 7 y = 25
3 x + 8 y = −12, AND
3 x − 21 y = 75
−) 3 x + 8 y = −12
−29 y = 87
y = − 3
THEREFORE, BY REPLACING IT, IT BECOMES
x − 7 x (− 3) = 25
x = 4
W...WAIT A SEC.
WHAT I MEAN IS...
...I DON'T GET HOW IT WORKS OUT LIKE THAT!
WHY DON'T YOU UNDERSTAND?
BECAUSE I'M AN IDIOT.
I SEE.
HEY, COME ON!
DAICHI, DON'T YOU STUDY AT ALL?
LISTENING DURING CLASS IS ENOUGH.
GIVE IT UP, MASATO. AFTER ALL, GUYS WITH GOOD BRAINS...
...DON'T UNDERSTAND HOW GUYS WITH BAD BRAINS FEEL.
GOT THAT RIGHT.
MATH II
WITH LOUSY TEACHERS, READING TEXTBOOKS WILL SUFFICE.
HE'S SO SARCASTIC.
HE'S THE CRUSHER, AFTER ALL.

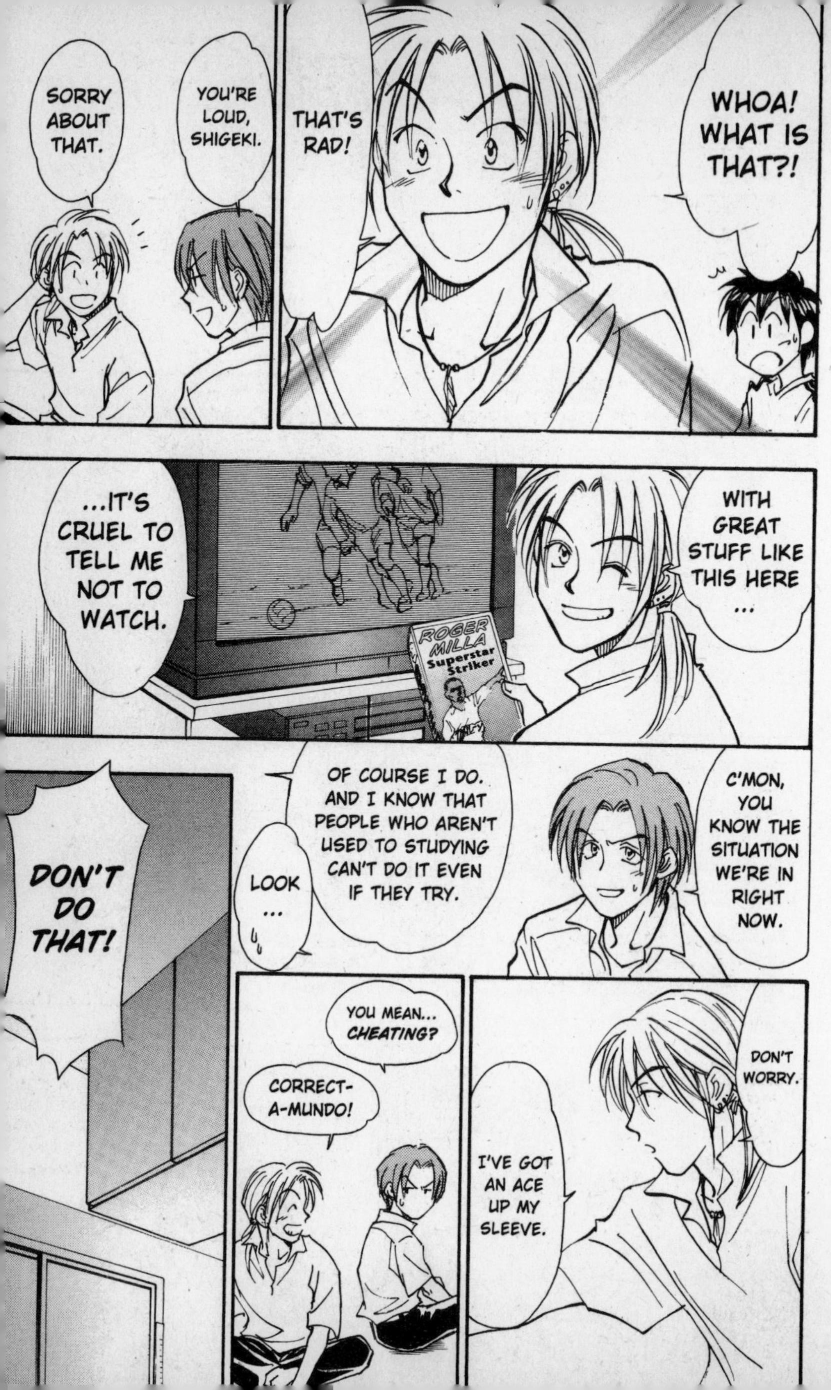

WHOA! WHAT IS THAT?!
THAT'S RAD!
YOU'RE LOUD, SHIGEKI.
SORRY ABOUT THAT.
WITH GREAT STUFF LIKE THIS HERE ...
ROGER MILLA Superstar Striker
...IT'S CRUEL TO TELL ME NOT TO WATCH.
C'MON, YOU KNOW THE SITUATION WE'RE IN RIGHT NOW.
OF COURSE I DO. AND I KNOW THAT PEOPLE WHO AREN'T USED TO STUDYING CAN'T DO IT EVEN IF THEY TRY.
LOOK ...
DON'T WORRY.
I'VE GOT AN ACE UP MY SLEEVE.
YOU MEAN... CHEATING?
CORRECT-A-MUNDO!
DON'T DO THAT!

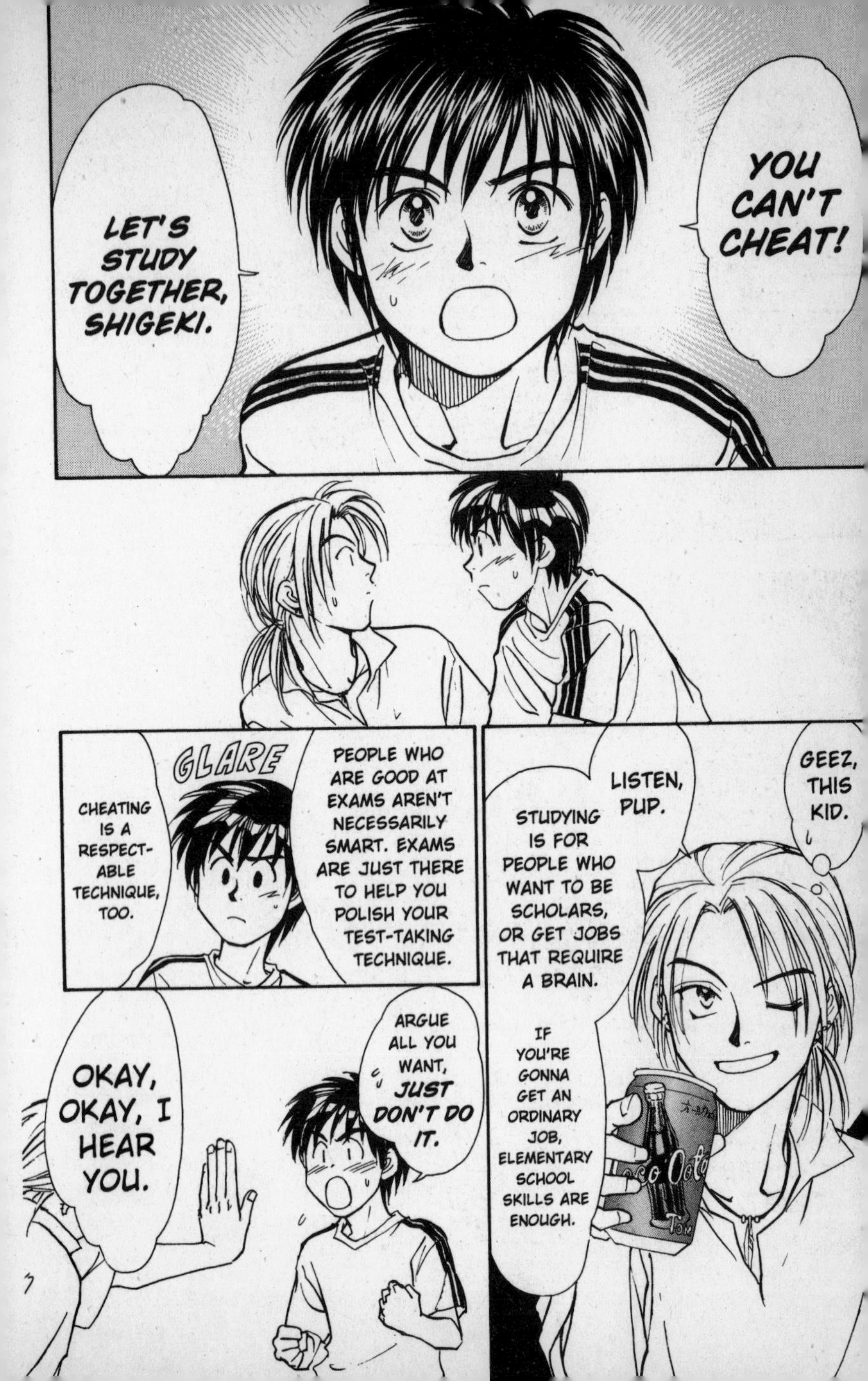
YOU CAN'T CHEAT!
LET'S STUDY TOGETHER, SHIGEKI.
GEEZ, THIS KID.
LISTEN, PUP.
STUDYING IS FOR PEOPLE WHO WANT TO BE SCHOLARS, OR GET JOBS THAT REQUIRE A BRAIN.
IF YOU'RE GONNA GET AN ORDINARY JOB, ELEMENTARY SCHOOL SKILLS ARE ENOUGH.
PEOPLE WHO ARE GOOD AT EXAMS AREN'T NECESSARILY SMART. EXAMS ARE JUST THERE TO HELP YOU POLISH YOUR TEST-TAKING TECHNIQUE.
GLARE
CHEATING IS A RESPECTABLE TECHNIQUE, TOO.
ARGUE ALL YOU WANT, JUST DON'T DO IT.
OKAY, OKAY, I HEAR YOU.

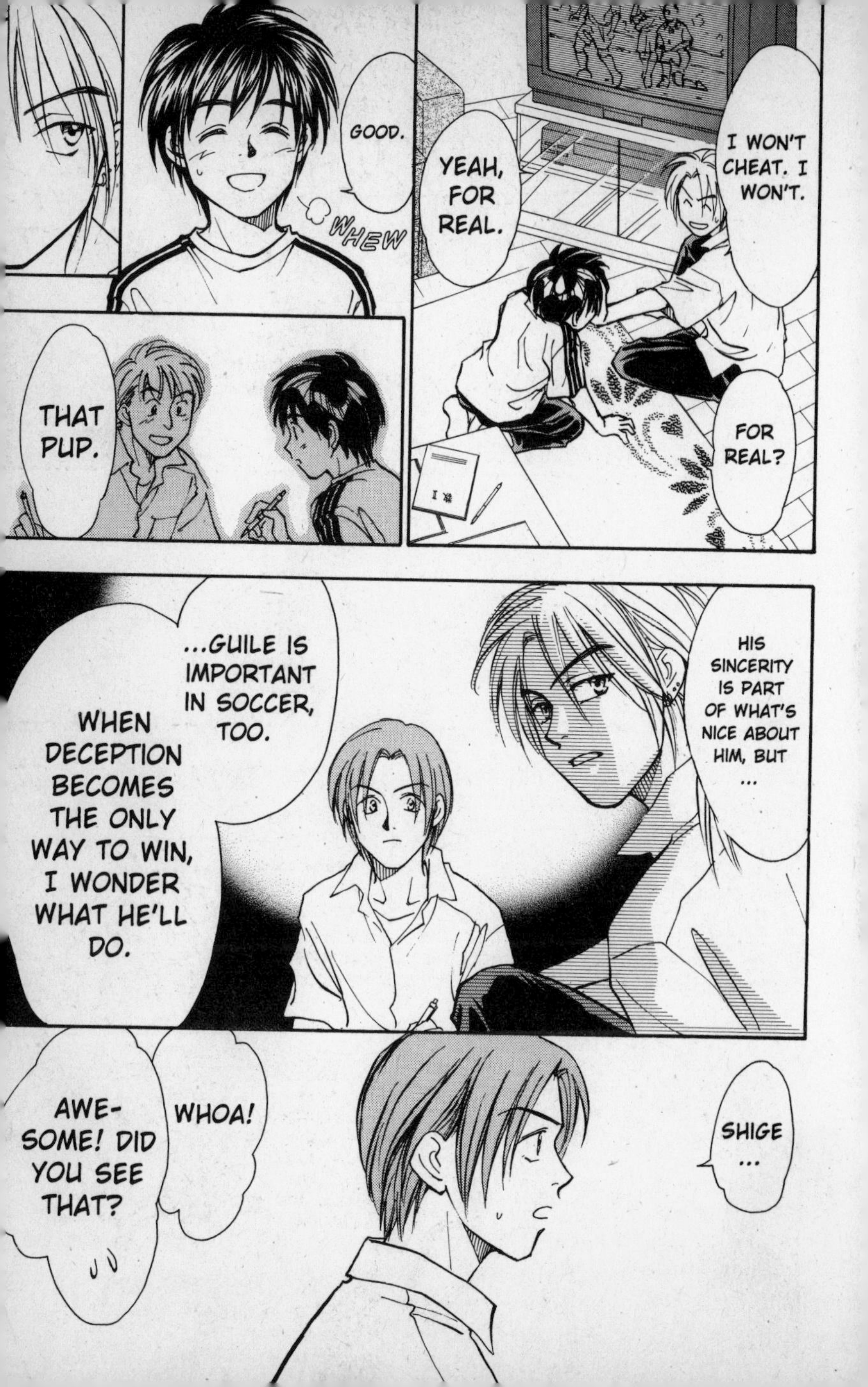

I WON'T CHEAT. I WON'T.
YEAH, FOR REAL.
FOR REAL?
GOOD.
WHEW
THAT PUP.
HIS SINCERITY IS PART OF WHAT'S NICE ABOUT HIM, BUT ...
...GUILE IS IMPORTANT IN SOCCER, TOO.
WHEN DECEPTION BECOMES THE ONLY WAY TO WIN, I WONDER WHAT HE'LL DO.
SHIGE ...
WHOA!
AWE-SOME! DID YOU SEE THAT?

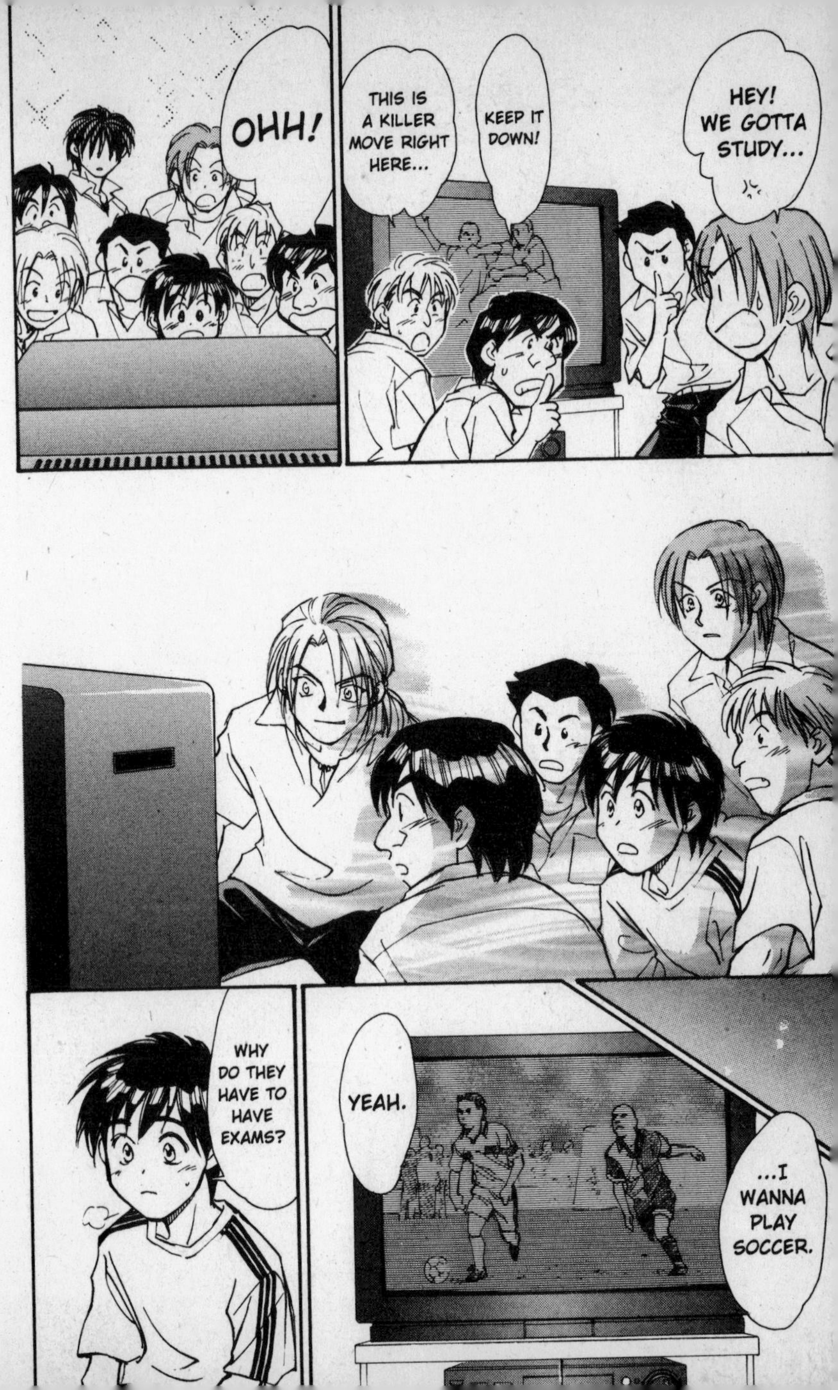
HEY! WE GOTTA STUDY...
KEEP IT DOWN!
THIS IS A KILLER MOVE RIGHT HERE...
OHH!
YEAH.
...I WANNA PLAY SOCCER.
WHY DO THEY HAVE TO HAVE EXAMS?

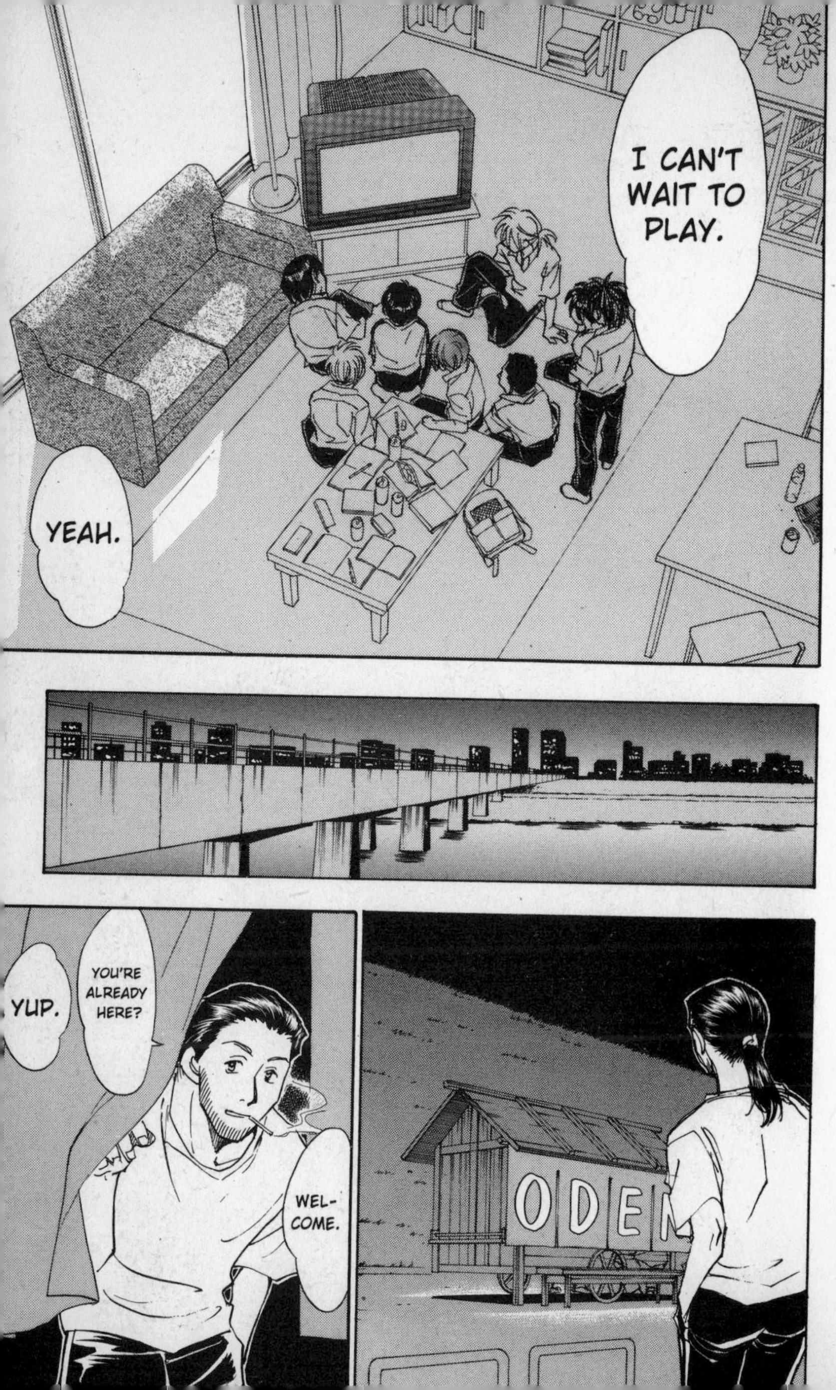
I CAN'T WAIT TO PLAY.
YEAH.
ODE
YOU'RE ALREADY HERE?
YUP.
WEL-COME.

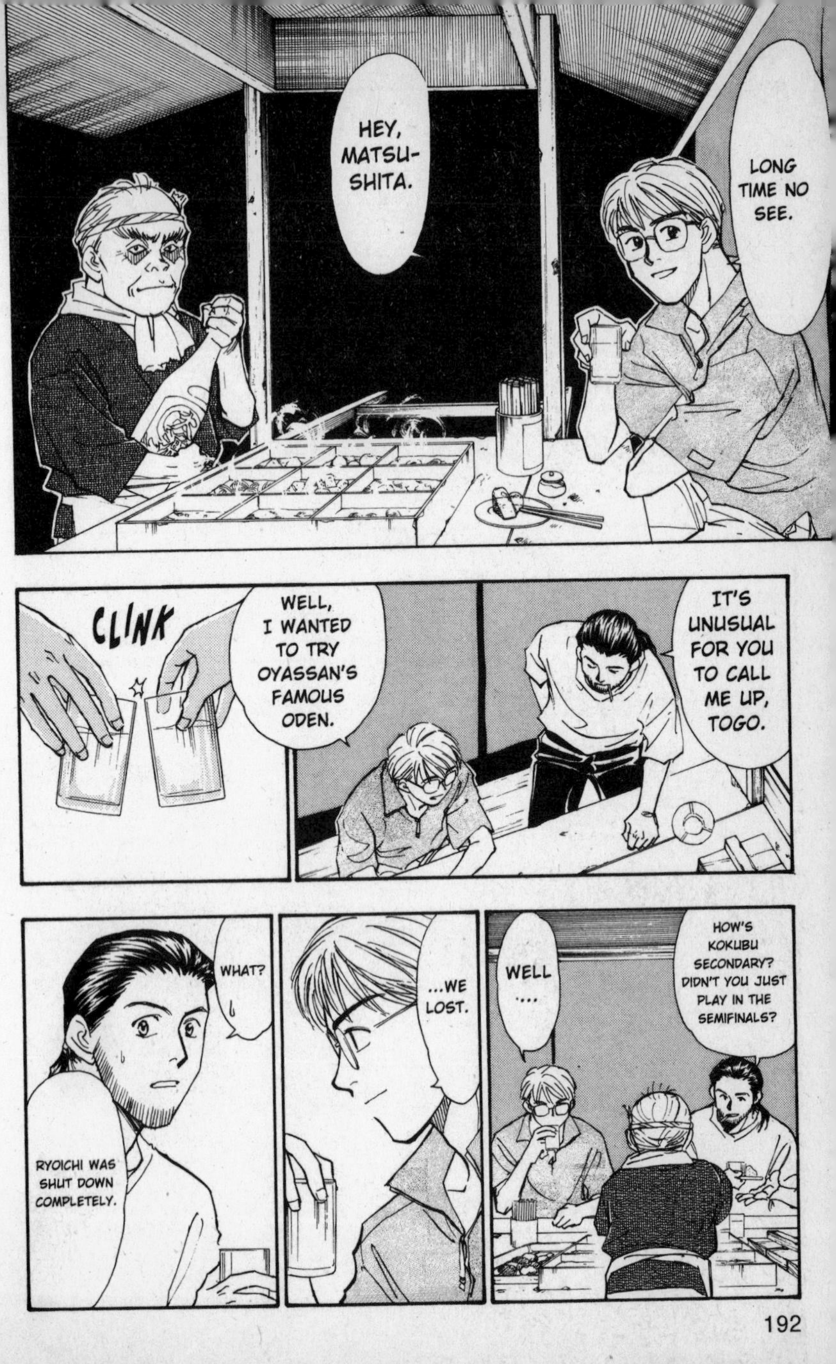
LONG TIME NO SEE.
HEY, MATSU-SHITA.
IT'S UNUSUAL FOR YOU TO CALL ME UP, TOGO.
WELL, I WANTED TO TRY OYASSAN'S FAMOUS ODEN.
CLINK
HOW'S KOKUBU SECONDARY? DIDN'T YOU JUST PLAY IN THE SEMIFINALS?
WELL ....
...WE LOST.
WHAT?
RYOICHI WAS SHUT DOWN COMPLETELY.

READ THIS WAY

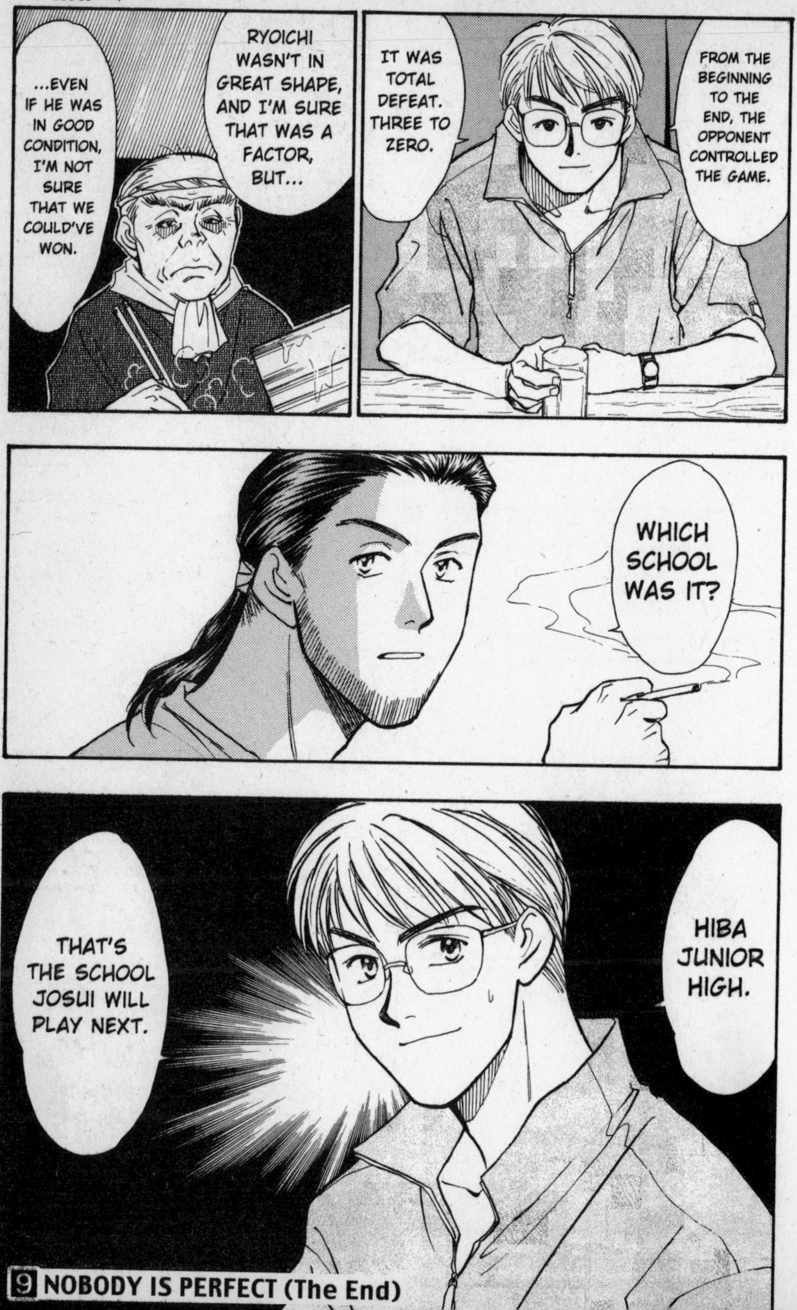
FROM THE BEGINNING TO THE END, THE OPPONENT CONTROLLED THE GAME.
IT WAS TOTAL DEFEAT. THREE TO ZERO.
RYOICHI WASN'T IN GREAT SHAPE, AND I'M SURE THAT WAS A FACTOR, BUT...
...EVEN IF HE WAS IN GOOD CONDITION, I'M NOT SURE THAT WE COULD'VE WON.
WHICH SCHOOL WAS IT?
HIBA JUNIOR HIGH.
THAT'S THE SCHOOL JOSUI WILL PLAY NEXT.

9 NOBODY IS PERFECT (The End)

WHISTLE! THEATRE !!

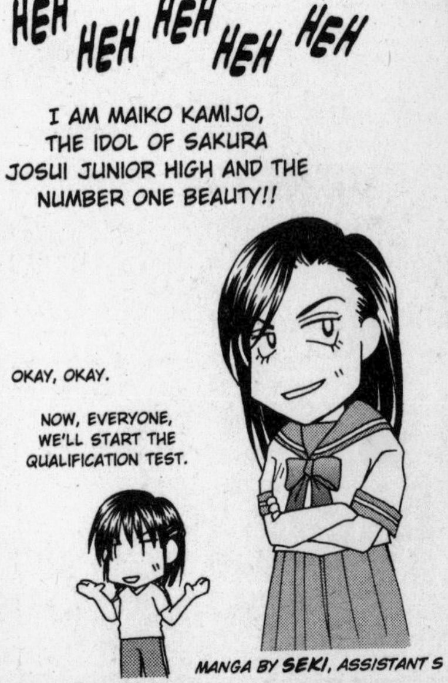
HEH HEH HEH HEH HEH
I AM MAIKO KAMIJO, THE IDOL OF SAKURA JOSUI JUNIOR HIGH AND THE NUMBER ONE BEAUTY!!
OKAY, OKAY.
NOW, EVERYONE, WE'LL START THE QUALIFICATION TEST.

MANGA BY SEKI, ASSISTANT S

Even at a Time Like This

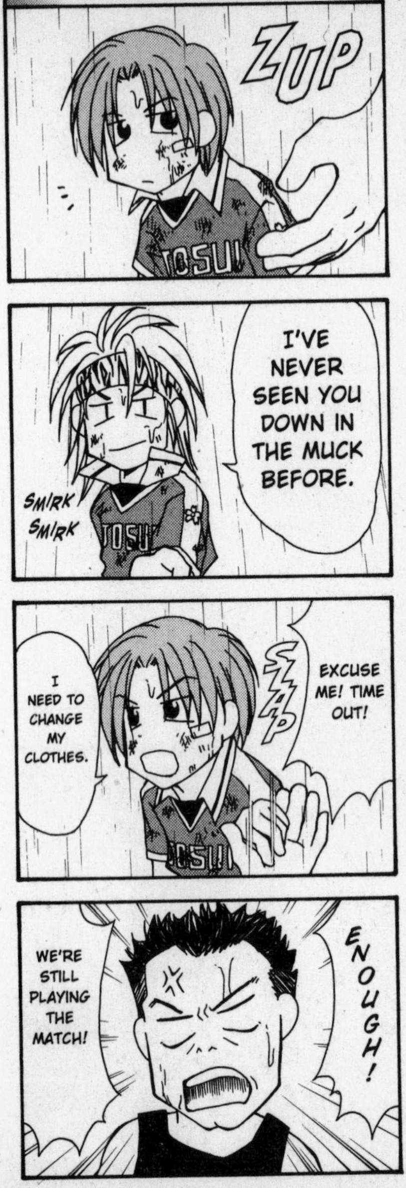
ZUP
JOSUI
I'VE NEVER SEEN YOU DOWN IN THE MUCK BEFORE.
SMIRK SMIRK
JOSUI
SLAP
EXCUSE ME! TIME OUT!
I NEED TO CHANGE MY CLOTHES.
JOSUI
ENOUGH!
WE'RE STILL PLAYING THE MATCH!

Just as Expected

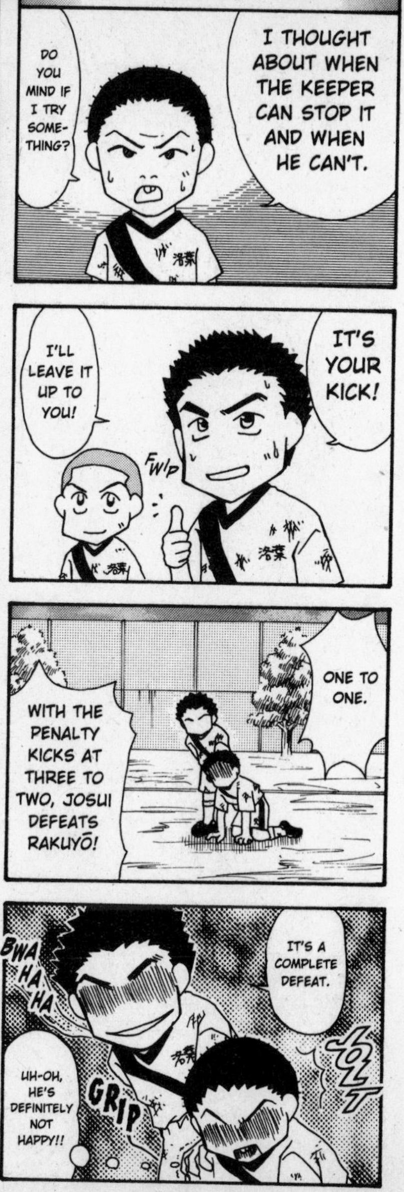
I THOUGHT ABOUT WHEN THE KEEPER CAN STOP IT AND WHEN HE CAN'T.
DO YOU MIND IF I TRY SOMETHING?
IT'S YOUR KICK!
FWIP
I'LL LEAVE IT UP TO YOU!
ONE TO ONE.
WITH THE PENALTY KICKS AT THREE TO TWO, JOSUI DEFEATS RAKUYŌ!
IT'S A COMPLETE DEFEAT.
JOLT
BWA HA HA
GRIP
UH-OH, HE'S DEFINITELY NOT HAPPY!!

Peaceful Moment

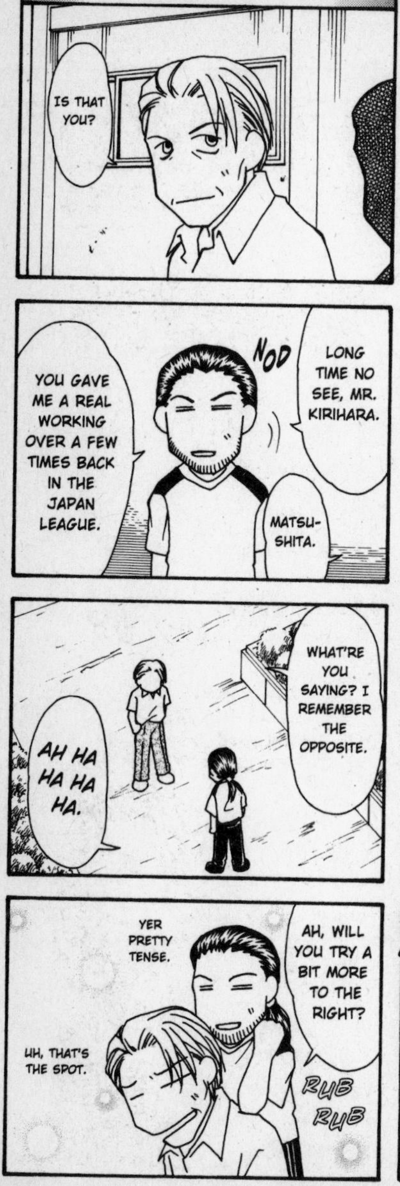
IS THAT YOU?
NOD
LONG TIME NO SEE, MR. KIRIHARA.
MATSUSHITA.
YOU GAVE ME A REAL WORKING OVER A FEW TIMES BACK IN THE JAPAN LEAGUE.
WHAT'RE YOU SAYING? I REMEMBER THE OPPOSITE.
AH HA HA HA HA.
AH, WILL YOU TRY A BIT MORE TO THE RIGHT?
YER PRETTY TENSE.
RUB RUB
UH, THAT'S THE SPOT.

DOODLES

THESE ARE EARLY CHARACTER DESIGNS FOR SEIYA AND KATSURŌ THAT WERE ABANDONED. (*WHISTLE!* WAS ORIGINALLY TO BE ABOUT PROFESSIONAL SOCCER). THIS KATSURŌ LOOKS LIKE A GROWN-UP VERSION OF KATSURŌ OF *WHISTLE!*, BUT THE SEIYA OF *WHISTLE!* DOESN'T LOOK AS GREAT AS THIS ONE (HA HA!). AND ACTUALLY, KATSURŌ IS MODELED AFTER THE ACTOR TADANOBU ASANO.

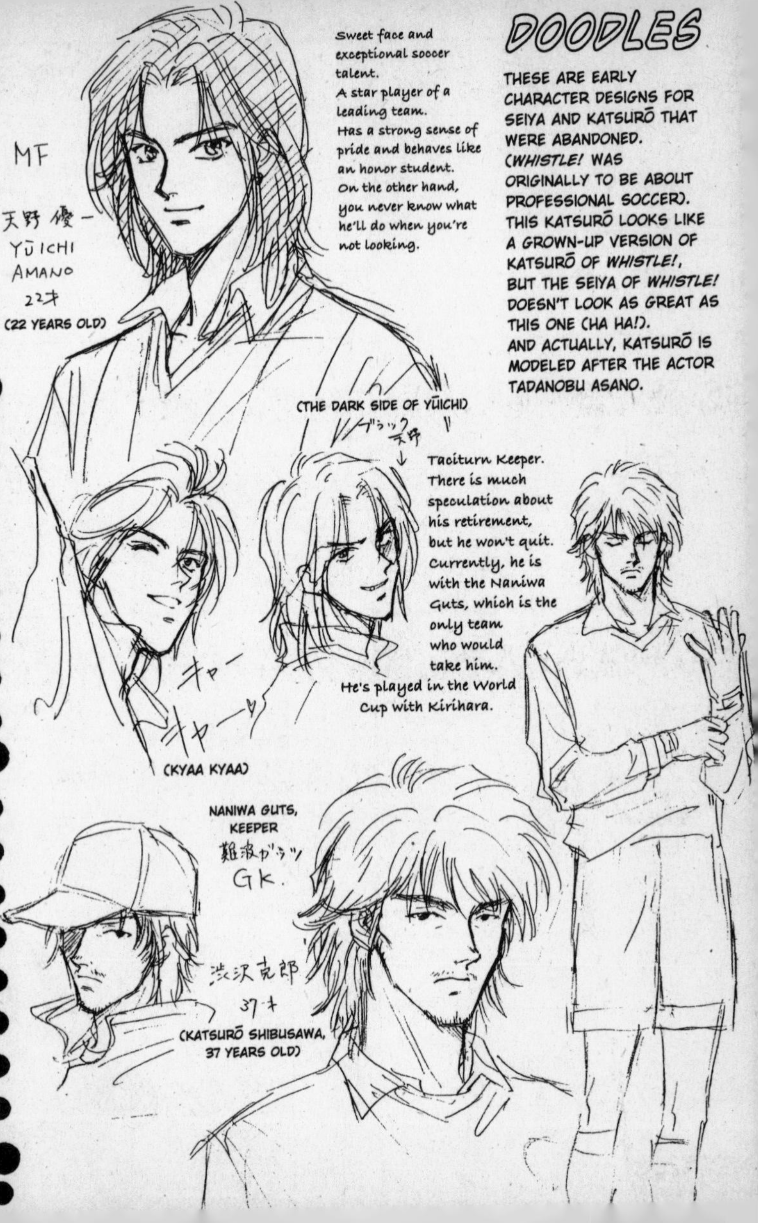
MF
天野優一
YŪICHI AMANO
22才
(22 YEARS OLD)
Sweet face and exceptional soccer talent. A star player of a leading team. Has a strong sense of pride and behaves like an honor student. On the other hand, you never know what he'll do when you're not looking.
(THE DARK SIDE OF YŪICHI)
ブラック天野
キャー キャー♡
(KYAA KYAA)
Taciturn Keeper. There is much speculation about his retirement, but he won't quit. Currently, he is with the Naniwa Guts, which is the only team who would take him. He's played in the World Cup with Kirihara.
NANIWA GUTS, KEEPER
難波ガッツ
GK.
渋沢克郎
37才
(KATSURŌ SHIBUSAWA, 37 YEARS OLD)

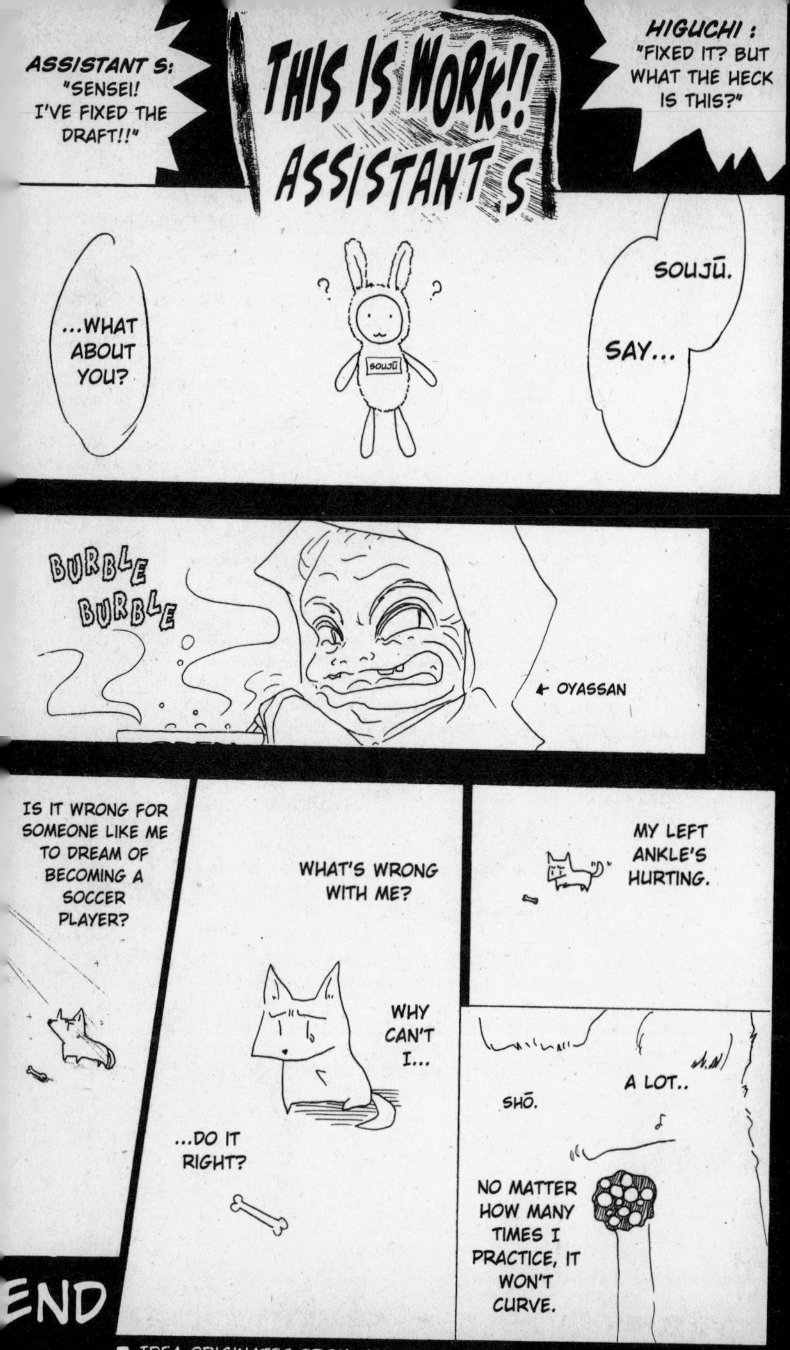
HIGUCHI : "FIXED IT? BUT WHAT THE HECK IS THIS?"
THIS IS WORK!! ASSISTANT S
ASSISTANT S: "SENSEI! I'VE FIXED THE DRAFT!!"
SOUJŪ.
SAY...
SOUJŪ
...WHAT ABOUT YOU?
BURBLE BURBLE
← OYASSAN
MY LEFT ANKLE'S HURTING.
A LOT..
SHŌ.
NO MATTER HOW MANY TIMES I PRACTICE, IT WON'T CURVE.
WHAT'S WRONG WITH ME?
WHY CAN'T I...
...DO IT RIGHT?
IS IT WRONG FOR SOMEONE LIKE ME TO DREAM OF BECOMING A SOCCER PLAYER?
END

■ IDEA ORIGINATES FROM VOLUME 4, STAGE.29, PAGE 10.
CO-PRODUCED BY ASSISTANT T AND ASSISTANT S.

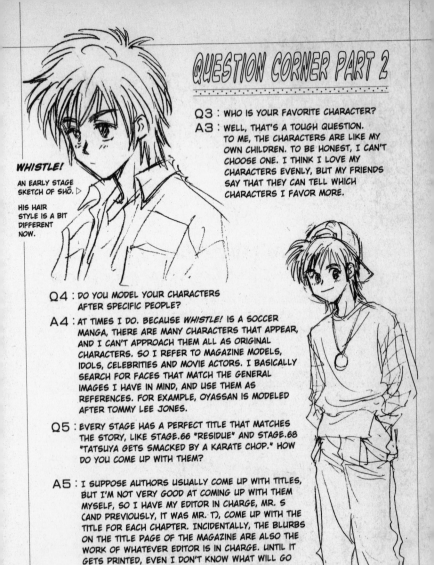

QUESTION CORNER PART 2

WHISTLE!

AN EARLY STAGE SKETCH OF SHŌ. ▷

HIS HAIR STYLE IS A BIT DIFFERENT NOW.

Q3 : WHO IS YOUR FAVORITE CHARACTER?

A3 : WELL, THAT'S A TOUGH QUESTION. TO ME, THE CHARACTERS ARE LIKE MY OWN CHILDREN. TO BE HONEST, I CAN'T CHOOSE ONE. I THINK I LOVE MY CHARACTERS EVENLY, BUT MY FRIENDS SAY THAT THEY CAN TELL WHICH CHARACTERS I FAVOR MORE.

Q4 : DO YOU MODEL YOUR CHARACTERS AFTER SPECIFIC PEOPLE?

A4 : AT TIMES I DO. BECAUSE *WHISTLE!* IS A SOCCER MANGA, THERE ARE MANY CHARACTERS THAT APPEAR, AND I CAN'T APPROACH THEM ALL AS ORIGINAL CHARACTERS. SO I REFER TO MAGAZINE MODELS, IDOLS, CELEBRITIES AND MOVIE ACTORS. I BASICALLY SEARCH FOR FACES THAT MATCH THE GENERAL IMAGES I HAVE IN MIND, AND USE THEM AS REFERENCES. FOR EXAMPLE, OYASSAN IS MODELED AFTER TOMMY LEE JONES.

Q5 : EVERY STAGE HAS A PERFECT TITLE THAT MATCHES THE STORY, LIKE STAGE.66 "RESIDUE" AND STAGE.68 "TATSUYA GETS SMACKED BY A KARATE CHOP." HOW DO YOU COME UP WITH THEM?

A5 : I SUPPOSE AUTHORS USUALLY COME UP WITH TITLES, BUT I'M NOT VERY GOOD AT COMING UP WITH THEM MYSELF, SO I HAVE MY EDITOR IN CHARGE, MR. S (AND PREVIOUSLY, IT WAS MR. T), COME UP WITH THE TITLE FOR EACH CHAPTER. INCIDENTALLY, THE BLURBS ON THE TITLE PAGE OF THE MAGAZINE ARE ALSO THE WORK OF WHATEVER EDITOR IS IN CHARGE. UNTIL IT GETS PRINTED, EVEN I DON'T KNOW WHAT WILL GO THERE. BUT TO BE HONEST, I ACTUALLY LOOK FORWARD TO FINDING OUT WHAT ENDS UP THERE. SOMETIMES IT MAKES ME LAUGH, AND SOMETIMES I THINK IT IS REALLY EXCELLENT. IT'S UNFORTUNATE THAT THEY ARE NOT INCLUDED IN THE BOOK. I WISH I COULD SHOW THEM TO YOU.

ANOTHER EARLY SKETCH. HE LOOKS PRETTY MUCH THE SAME AS HE DOES △ NOW. HE LOOKS LIKE HE'S FROM A JOHNNY'S JUNIOR BOY BAND (HA HA).

THE REAL WHISTLE!

Director's Cut
The Rakuyō Game Complete Edition

NOW IT CAN BE TOLD: THE TRUE STORY OF HOW THE RAKUYŌ MATCH ACTUALLY ENDED. CAN YOU EVER READ VOL. 9 AGAIN AFTER WITNESSING THE HORRIFYING ***TRUE*** STORY?

OH NO!! THE GROUND HAS BECOME A DEADLY MUD PIT BECAUSE OF THE RAIN...!
"YEAH! I FOUND IT...!"
FINALLY, RAKUYŌ'S CAPTAIN PULLED THE BALL FROM THE MUDDY GROUND.
BUT AT THE TIME, NO ONE REALIZED HE USED HIS HANDS.

BY ASSISTANT **AIKO MESO.**

Nex... ...stle!